FIRST FIRE

DR. HUGH FOX is a Professor in the Department of American Thought and Language at Michigan State University. He holds a doctorate in American Literature from the University of Illinois, and twice was Fulbright Professor of American Studies in Latin America. A member of the board of directors of the Committee of Small Magazine Editors and Presses (COSMEP), he has published critical essays, poems, and stories in various magazines, journals, and quarterlies. He has also published fourteen volumes of poetry with small presses, and is the author of *Gods of the Cataclysm.*

FIRST FIRE

Central and South American Indian Poetry

EDITED WITH AN INTRODUCTION BY *Hugh Fox*

ANCHOR BOOKS
Anchor Press / Doubleday   Garden City, New York   1978

gain.

First fire

The Anchor Press edition is the first publication of
First Fire: Central and South American Indian Poetry

Anchor Press edition: 1978
Library of Congress Cataloging in Publication Data
Main entry under title:

First fire.

Includes bibliographical references.
1. Indian literature—Translations into English.
2. American literature—Translations from Indian
languages. 3. Indians—Religion and mythology.
I. Fox, Hugh, 1932–
PM198.E3F5 897
ISBN: *0-385-03815-1*
Library of Congress Catalog Card Number 77–11528
Copyright © 1978 by Hugh Fox

Grateful acknowledgment is made for the inclusion of the following material in First Fire:

"The Creation of the World," "Solstices and Eclipses," and "The Old Religion and the Old Times" from *The Book of Chilam Balam of Chumayel,* translated by Ralph L. Roys (1967). Reprinted by permission of the University of Oklahoma Press. New edition copyright © 1967 by University of Oklahoma Press.

CONTENTS

xi

INTRODUCTION

SOURCES

It is almost a rule—the "easier" any given text is, the more logical, coherent and familiar, the less authentic it is. Conversely, if a given text seems illogical, confused, completely "foreign," incomprehensible, practically "insane," you can begin to suspect that it is highly authentic, because the Amerindian mind has very little to do with the empirical, secularized, symbol-stripped mind of twentieth-century America.

When the Spaniards conquered Central and South America in the sixteenth and seventeenth centuries, they did whatever they could to wipe out pre-Columbian religion. They destroyed the written books of the Aztecs and Mayas, destroyed the hieratic priesthood that had grown up to preserve the hieroglyphic writing, leveled temples, destroyed idols, set up their own churches, brought in their own priests, made Catholicism mandatory and any "reversion" back to the old gods punishable by death, so that within two generations the ancient, isolated orthodoxy of the pre-Columbian world was, where not completely wiped out, transformed into a syncretic and confused blend of pre- and post-Columbian.

What I always want to do is get back to the *pre*-Columbian— get inside the Amerindian mind the way it was before the Spaniards. For me the most "authentic" (and hence the most "difficult") sources in this volume are those works that survive from the very earliest post-Conquest times, works like the Maya *Popul Vuh* and the books of *Chilam Balam* (essentially "Jaguar Priest Books"). Both these books are post-Conquest, but written by Amerindian priest-scholars whose minds survived intact from the pre-Conquest world. In a sense, they are laments for a lost/destroyed way of life, and at the same time attempt to capture as faithfully as possible pre-Conquest history/myth/vision.

One of the great ironies of the Conquest is that the same priests who were instrumental in replacing pre-Columbian religions with Catholicism were also often "collectors" of pre-Columbian materials. In 1540 the Franciscan Andrés de Olmos gathered together a large bundle of Aztec materials, and from the Olmos manuscript in the Library of Congress come "The Way: Father to Son" and "The Way: King to His Sons." The sacred Aztec poems in the section thereafter come from another very interesting sixteenth-century manuscript preserved in the library of the national university in Mexico: *Cantares de los Mexicanos y Otros Opusculos.* From internal evidence you can more or less prove that these songs are "relics" of the pre-Conquest world preserved by converts to Catholicism. The "Song of Quetzalcoatl" is taken from Fray Bernardino de Sahagún's magnificent sixteenth-century gathering of original Aztec materials, the *General History of the Things of New Spain* (*Historia de las Cosas de la Nueva España*). Although this work (especially the "poetry" that Sahagún collected) was on the Inquisition's to-be-burned list, a complete manuscript has survived in the Biblioteca Laurentio-Mediceana in Florence—the original source for the "Song of Quetzalcoatl."

One great lack in the books of *Chilam Balam*, the *Popul Vuh*, and even in Sahagún, however, is the concentration on history/myth rather than on ritual. The material is very general: we're told about the gods and multiple creations, about huge periods of time, migrations . . . yet we're not given specific texts pertaining to specific rituals. In a sense, there aren't any of what would be the pre-Columbian equivalents of hymnbooks and missals. In addition, as far as we know, there wasn't any Amazonian Sahagún, nor any Amazonian *Chilam Balam* or *Popul Vuh*, so we're forced to rely on post-Columbian sources, with this wry twist: because the Amazon has been isolated for so long, oftentimes fairly contemporary collecting *does* reach back to a purer form of the pre-Columbian than even the already "polluted" *Chilam Balam* and *Popul Vuh*. Of course sometimes you can find fairly isolated tribes even in places like Guatemala. Witness the *Chorti (Maya) Texts*, which are literal transcriptions of the myths of a contemporary Maya—which have an authentic though somewhat truncated and condensed ring about them. They're "real," but you can feel the distance from the consolidated, unified religiosity of the great Maya past.

Sometimes a contemporary ethnologist can find a tribe practically untouched by outside influences and then takes the *next* step of thoroughly getting inside the tribal mentality so that: (1) He understands it like a tribesman; and (2) the tribe will open up to him and actually allow him to partake of the full authenticity of their complex world vision. This is certainly the case with the work of the Villas Boas brothers in their *Xingu: The Indians, Their Myths*. The Villas Boas brothers actually live with the Xingus, have set up a kind of hospital/help-center right in the middle of the jungle. I'm reminded of Schweitzer in Africa.

Two other collectors who have really gotten inside the skins of the tribes they're collecting from are the priest Basilio M. de Barral, who lived with and worked with the Guarao Indians of Venezuela, and Leon Cadogan, who specialized in the Guarani (Paí-Kaiová).

Some ethnologists, although not quite as thoroughly capable of "going native" as Basilio M. de Barral, Cadogan, or the Boas brothers, compensate by approaching their particular myth-collection territory with a fund of comparative Amerindian mythology so that they immediately see any one myth that they collect from a particular tribe in the context of other myths from other tribes. They find patterns, then move toward the creation of myth-territory *maps*. This is certainly true of Alfred Métraux (*Myths of the Toba and Pilagá Indians of the Gran Chaco*).

At times the actual collection of myths is a minor by-product of a larger ethnological attempt to encompass the world view, the entire sociocosmological vision of a given tribe. G. Reichel-Dolmatoff's *Amazonian Cosmos: The Sexual and Religious Symbolism of the Tukano Indians*, L. C. Faron's *Hawks of the Sun* (centering on the Mapuches of Chile), and Otero's *La Piedra Mágica* (dealing with the Bolivian Aymaras) are such books. The anthologizer has to look in all the anthropological corners and closets. Sometimes the most authentic, revealing myths come from a study that just incidentally concerned itself about myth.

The most challenging texts, though, are those that are taken down literally from the most isolated tribes and are *not* run through the occidental Indo-European word- and psychology-conversion units, but retained just as they were gathered, with *no* quarter given to our modes of logic, our conventions of narration. Such is the work of Henry Osborn (Warao text "The Great Dark") and Anton Lukesch (Kayapo text "The Man Who Became a Snake"). The anthologist then becomes an interpreter trying to bend the "alien" syntaxes and world views of the collected material at least enough so that the occidental reader can understand it. It's all very well to try to capture the flavor of the original world views of the Indians studied, but one has always to be aware that the contemporary occidental mind doesn't really work the same way as that of the pre-Columbian. The closer you move toward authenticity the more opaque the material becomes.

Perhaps the least "authentic" material comes from those areas which were first and most thoroughly colonized by Spain—namely, Peru and Bolivia. I certainly don't mean to disparage the work of collectors such as Lara (whose *Literatura de los Quechuas,* is the source for "Mother Moon" and "Hymn to the World Tree"), but there are inherent difficulties in trying to get back to the *pre*-Columbian in tribes whose pre-Columbian beliefs have been persecuted for *five hundred years.* Still, even in these "occidentalized" tribes, more original beliefs are retained—in the World Tree, for example—than one might ever expect.

The reader should keep in mind, however, that reading this anthology is a kind of initiation process. As much as I've tried to "tame" and "digest" the materials, I haven't wanted to remove their original vigor and fiber, and besides, I see the process of getting inside the pre-Columbian mind as requiring a change in the very structuring of the occidental reader's mind. The point is to get inside the pre-Columbian so you feel comfortable with it. It's an exercise not merely in comparative mythology, but in comparative ontology, cosmology, linguistics, and psychology. You move from a familiar, empirical, secularized world view devoid of spiritual "presences" and sacred symbolism, into a world view where everything is *symbolic presence* and history (being oral) necessarily becomes "myth." Certainly my main purpose in editing this anthology in the first place was to enable an occidental reader to slowly enter into the Amerindian yogic mind, and, once inside, find himself looking back at the world view he left behind as something oddly flat and estranged. In order to fulfill this purpose I've largely limited the texts either to materials that come from the period directly after the Conquest or from tribes far enough removed from missionary zeal to have retained most of their original *esprit* intact.

2.

AMERINDIAN CULTURAL UNITY

In Peru a *huaco* is a "sacred object." Some ten years ago my Peruvian uncle gave me some *huacos* that he'd dug out of a pre-

Columbian cemetery at Chancay, north of Lima: a pot with two monkeys for handles, and a figure with a triangular-shaped head and outstretched arms reminiscent of Christ crucified. The cemetery he'd dug them out of he called a *huaca;* in Peru when you dig *huacos* in a *huaca* you're *huaqueroing,* and the person who's doing the digging is called a *huaquero.* It isn't coincidence that the Sioux called their gods *wakanda.* Though the spelling's different—in Spanish the "wa" sound is written "hua"—the same word means essentially the same thing on the Great Plains in North America and on the Peruvian Coast. After coming across similar instances a few dozen times, one begins to formulate a theory that, underneath all the diversity of Amerindian languages, there was some kind of fundamental unity. One even hypothesizes that at one time all Amerindian languages may have been the same; that in ancient times they may have formed a single linguistic group.

Another example? There's a Cherokee myth (from what is now North Carolina) about Kanati and Selu; Kanati is Father Snake. In Maya, *Kan* means both snake and sky. The ruins of a pre-Inca culture on the Peruvian Coast: Chan Chan. Kanata, Kan, Chan. This kind of linguistic game becomes a little mind-boggling when you move across the Pacific to India and find that in a contemporary Dravidian language in southern India a certain kind of green snake is also called *kan.*

The unity extends beyond the Americas and, as I show in my book *The Gods of the Cataclysm,* you can take lists of words in Quechua (one of the Peruvian Indian languages), put them side by side with Sanskrit and demonstrate that Sanskrit and Quechua are very close linguistic relatives—which implies that ancient India and ancient America are somehow linked together. Of course the links aren't just linguistic, they extend to every facet of cultural life: costumes, customs, religion, art, and myth. This anthology is to a large extent an anthology of myths, so it's important to realize that practically all Amerindian myths have counterparts in Hindu myth.

The Hopis have an elaborate, symbolic "emergence myth" that —if you take it literally—accounts for the ancient link between India and the New World. Here's the way Frank Waters sums it up in *The Book of the Hopi:*

> . . . the Hopis came to America from the west, crossing the sea on boats or rafts from one "stepping stone" or island to the next.

And then Waters notes: "A similar interpretation can be made of the myth of the ancient Quiché Maya, which relates that the waters parted and the tribes crossed on stepping stones in a row over the sand—'Stones in a Row, Sand under the Sea.' "[1]

So the Indians themselves seem to be saying that they came across the Pacific, and, as I point out in *Gods of the Cataclysm*, there are ruins throughout the South Pacific filled with temples, stone gates, and walls that match up very nicely with the earliest known stonework in South America. I also point out how Easter Island script matches up exactly with the script from the Indus Valley in what is today Pakistan—the voyages left a record in both stone and script.

It's a very complex story, and only recently have scholars begun to notice that the North American Trickster Cycles sound very much like Greek legends about Hermes; that the North American Orpheus stories sound just like the Greek legend of Orpheus and Persephone; that there are Mandan-Hidatsa myths about a Wind King who sounds just like Aeolus in Homer's *Odyssey;* that the stories about Coyote (or Raven or Hare), the Fire-Bringer, sound just like the Prometheus legend; in fact that, one for one, right down the line, all the characters in Greek myth are the same characters in Amerindian myth, and that these same characters reappear again in Hindu myth. It's a very complex story, but any attempt to simplify it diminishes its essential truth. What I've tried to do in this anthology is show Amerindian myth for what it is—a variation of ancient Indo-Mediterranean myth.

MYTH AS HISTORY

The Argonautica is an ancient Greek poem that in many episodes parallels *The Odyssey* and is about a voyage across Ocean to the land of the Colchians where one of the crew steals the Golden Fleece from the King of the Colchians, King Aeëtes—the grandson of Hyperion, the Sun-King Titan. Pure Greek myth. But the legendary founder of the Inca Sun Empire was named Viracocha, and hero in Sanskrit is *vir* and sea in Quechua is *cocha*, and the ancient Colchians were the Sea People; and you wonder if there is any possibility that the *Argonautica* is about a voyage to Lake Titicaca in Bolivia, the legendary place of origin of the Incas. There is a ruin on the shores of Titicaca called Tiahuanaco, which translates in Mycenaean Greek as "Home of the Young God."

[1](New York: Ballantine Books, 1971), p. 31.

And who is the young God? The Sun, Aeëtes, the King of Tiahuanaco.

Viracocha, King of the Cochians. The Cochians are the Colchians, and the Colchians are the people visited by the Argonautica. The Colchians in the ancient Mediterranean were The Sea People, and word *colcha* still means river in Peru and Ecuador.

THE DIVINE "BEING-FLOW"

To the Amerindian-Dravidian mind, everything is "divine." There isn't any real dualism in Amerindia. The core of reality is spirit. God is in everything, we are surrounded by a spirit world, we are spirit. Matter isn't really in conflict with spirit but is seen as the fringes, the tail-ends of spirit.

We live, die, and are reincarnated, always spiraling up out of the world of Maya (illusion), out of Sansara (the phenomenal world) into Nirvana. The core of Amerindian-Dravidian spirituality is the Vision Quest; the Vision Quest isn't something incidental in a person's life, but all of life. You can find out a lot about New World spirituality by studying Indian Yoga; conversely, you can find out a lot about Yoga by studying Sioux or Maya or Quechua or Pawnee spirituality. They are slightly variant forms of the same basic world view: THE CENTER OF EXISTENCE IS SPIRIT, THE PURPOSE OF LIFE IS ENLIGHTENMENT.[2]

As you'll see in the myths in this volume, the most important dramas in human life take place in the invisible spirit world that surrounds us. Everything that happens in the physical world is caused, determined by happenings in the spiritual world. Hardly anything has a physical cause. Death, life, disease, fortune and misfortune are all determined by spirit dynamics. The dead come back, some people can change themselves into animals (*naguales*), the world around us is peopled with voices, influences, spirits; the main purpose of living is to learn how to tune in to this invisible world. Becoming a guru means becoming an inhabitant of the invisible Power World.

Yoga, meditation, fasting, going out on the mountain like Christ going into the desert, even the ritual taking of drugs, all point to the moment of vision, the merging with the spirit world.

As you read through this anthology, it is important to keep in

[2] In *The Book of the Hopi* Frank Waters notes (p. 222) the sameness of Hopi, northern Indian and Tibetan spiritual theory.

mind the importance of the spirit world to the Indian, because many of the myths, although they take place in the here-and-now world, really aren't about the here-and-now world at all, but about how the Power World influences, shapes, controls the here and now. Good spirits, bad spirits, good and evil *Karma*, they all precede and dominate the everyday.

THE MANDALA SHAPE OF THE COSMOS

Before all ceremonies/spiritual exercises, the Amerindian priest pays homage to the four quarters. In classical Hinduism the four quarters are dominated by the Regents of the Four Quarters, and I suspect that the original idea of shaping the world into four quarters originated from the actual configuration of the Dravidian-Amerindian empire. I suspect that originally there *was* a King of the North, a King of the South, a King of the West, and a King of the East. As I point out in *Sun-World Across Ocean*, the second volume of my Amerindian trilogy, there are easily identifiable temples in Peru (Chavin) devoted to the bull-headed, trident-carrying Regent of the South (Yama), and the images of Kubera (the Regent of the North) and Indra (the Regent of the East) appear prominently in Maya art.

But whatever the origin of the four-quarter structure, it is important to realize that Amerindian sacred geography has a structure, a shape. The hoop—the "circle of the nation," as the Sioux put it—is divided like a mandala into quarters.

The year also has its structure, hinging on solstices and equinoxes, the coming and going of the sun to and from the earth. The ruins at Tiahuanaco are, like all the Maya cities, calendrical New World Stonehenges that divide and give order to the four seasons.

After twenty years of studying the structures of the Amerindian year (and sacred geography), I suspect that the almost obsessive attention paid to the equinoxes, solstices, and "circularity" is ultimately connected to a spheroid world view needed for sea peoples (Colchians) who were part of what amounted to a worldwide maritime empire. I suspect that there was a regular "route" of voyages to the New World across both the Pacific and Atlantic, and that the voyagers had to know the seasons with precision in order to catch the right winds, sail at the best moments. The equinoctial-solstice structure is also agricultural—it is a sowing and harvesting rhythm—but more than that, it is a sailor's calendar, scheduled so as to find optimum order in the midst of meteorological caprice.

THE MASTER MYTH

The fundamental myth structure that you'll see repeated over and over again in this anthology is essentially the Genesis myth of Adam, Eve, the Serpent, the Fall, the war between good and evil angels. Time after time in Amerindian myth you come across this war of the gods and the anti-gods. Transculturally, the characters in the Genesis story may be equated as follows:

Eve=Lakshmi (Hindu)=Pandora-Circe-Aphrodite (Greek)= Selu (Cherokee)=Coatlicue (Aztec), etc.

Serpent=Siva (Hindu)=Prometheus-Hermes (Greek)=Kanati (Cherokee)=Quetzalcoatl (Aztec).

God the Father=Vishnu (Hindu)=Zeus-Hyperion (Greek)= Huizilpochtli (Aztec)=Sun (Hopi), etc.

Perhaps the clearest Amerindian version of this myth in the anthology is the Aymara story of the condor whose daughter elopes with the son of a rival condor. When the father finds out about the daughter's "betrayal," he condemns her and the young condor to live "underground" for the rest of their lives. The daughter is Eve, the young condor is Satan, the condor father is God the Father.

"Historically" the condor often appears in the myths as the Vulture-King, and the myth takes place on the Bolivian *altiplano* next to a gate on the bank of a lake, a setting which is recognizable as Lake Titicaca and the ruins of Tiahuanaco with its monolithic sun gate. At times it seems that the Eve figure in the myths is married to someone else (an Adam), then a "seducer" comes along, she is seduced, and she and the seducer are "exiled" from heaven.

In Greek myth the story appears in the *Argonautica* as the story of Jason and Medea. Jason comes to the land of the Colchians, Medea helps him steal the Golden Fleece, then leaves with him and returns to Greece. Medea seems to be an Eve figure; Jason, a Serpent figure; and Aeëtes (Medea's father), God the Father. Elsewhere the Genesis story is approximated even more closely. Hephaistos is married to Aphrodite, but she has an affair with Ares, the God of War. Another story containing the same characters is that of Epimetheus, who marries Pandora, the source of all evil in the world.

There are a number of Greek myths that have the same essential structure: a coquette, a seducer, an angry father and/or husband. And the more you study Greek myth the more you realize that behind the vast cast of mythical characters there are what might be called prototypical or ur-characters, primitive emblematic models from which a vast repertory of tales are derived.

The war of the Titans and the Olympians in Greek myth appears in Hindu myth as the war of the gods and anti-gods, the Asuras, Nagas, Rakshasas, and a whole list of characters who collectively are thought to represent the Dravidians at war with the Aryans (the gods). The condor story in Hindu myth appears in the *Siva-Purana* in which Siva (the young condor) marries the daughter of King Himalaya (the old condor). In the *Siva-Purana*, Siva and his bride (Parvati) are not exiled from heaven—but after their marriage the by-now-familiar war of the gods and anti-gods begins. One suspects that in an earlier version Siva was at the head of the anti-god forces.

The Hindu version is especially revealing because in Hindu myth Siva is known as Lord Naga. The Dravidians were the "Naga people," the snake people, and Siva was the chief lord of the Dravidian clans.

I suspect that, underlying the story of the revolt of the Titans in Greek myth; the story of the *Argonautica;* Hephaistos and Epimetheus; the stories about Siva, Parvati, Vishnu (the Sun God), and Lakshmi; the Amerindian stories of Trickster as adulterer; and the young condor seducer—there is, in the dim, dim past, the historical reality of a Naga chief who seduced the Sun King's daughter and initiated the war between the gods (the Sun Tribes) and the anti-gods (the Snake Tribes). I also suspect that this drama of the Twilight of the Gods was acted out on the Bolivian *altiplano* when the Americas were still a known part of the very ancient world.

3 ·

STRUCTURE

A word about the structure of this anthology.

In the first eight sections I've tried to present the mythohistorical events (Creation, the Great Flood, the Great Dark, Emergence, the "Twilight of the Gods") that the Amerindians themselves saw as *the* major events in their past. For all peoples there's always a "mythic" time when "The Sacred" was alive; then, in the majority of cases, The Sacred in a sense "dies," and their "mythic" time becomes enclosed in amber. These first eight sections are the mythic, sacred events of the pre-Columbian mind. Even when you go through the myths of the Cherokees, Hopi, or Pimas thousands of years after these events happened (in places removed by thousands of miles), these are *still* the major events that constantly recur.

In Sections IX through XV I move from this rather large mythohistorical circle into the circle of a particular life, beginning with a general statement on the "taming of the sacred" into birth and name ceremonies, curing ceremonies, exorcism, vision quest, and death. Section XVI, along with Section IX, forms a "frame" for the life cycle.

Section XVII illustrates the importance of the year in Amerindian thought. The individual exists not merely within his own personal or tribal-mythic time, but also within the time framework of the mythic year, dominated by/contained within the cycles of solstices and equinoxes.

In Sections XVIII through XXVII I try to "particularize," in a sense "orchestrate," the general mythic history of the first nine sections. Certain characters totally dominate pre-Columbian mythic history: the Snake People (Nagas/Nabas/Nahuas), the Trickster (Fox/Coyote/Hermes/Siva), Amazons (Cannibal Women), the Sky King (Sun). I see these *dramatis personae* as mythologized real persons who lived out their reality within the parameters of the mythic/sacred time. Here I try to flesh them out.

Sections XXVIII–XXX touch on the Amerindian "Tao," or Way —not just in terms of formal moral codes (Section XXVIII) but also in a "sacred way of 'seeing'" (Section XXIX), even providing two yogic heros (The Twins of Section XXX) as martial-mystical examples of perfection.

The very last section is an attempt to illustrate (via what purports to be a relic of pre-Columbian drama) Inca life *in action*.

What I've tried to do, then, is work from a very general overview of Amerindian mythic history to specific life events within that mythic frame, then flesh out the major characters that occupy the vast archives of Amerindian myth cycles/histories, touch on the yogic flavor of Amerindian moral codes, and end with an example of The Everyday seen in dramatic form. Notes on all the selections (which include sources, discussion of transcultural analogues, definitions, etc.) are at the end of the book.

To really *read* this book *is* an initiation. I don't see it as an "end," but merely a beginning, the first door into an almost lost world that we desperately need—in mid-twentieth-century-empirical America as the empiricism runs down and corrodes—to refind.

One last note. I translated all the sections that were originally in Spanish, but I couldn't have translated the German without the help of Chris Bushell and Gene DeBenko of the Michigan State University library.

I. IN THE BEGINNING

The Creation of the World (Maya)

It is most necessary to believe this. These are the precious stones which our Lord, the Father, has abandoned. This was his first repast, this balché, with which we, the ruling men revere him here. Very rightly they worshiped as true gods these precious stones, when the true God was established, our Lord God, the Lord of heaven and earth, the true God. Nevertheless, the first gods were perishable gods. Their worship came to its inevitable end. They lost their efficacy by the benediction of the Lord of heaven, after the redemption of the world was accomplished, after the resurrection of the true God, the true Dios, when he blessed heaven and earth. Then was your worship abolished, Maya men. Turn away your hearts from your old religion.

This is the history of the world in those times, because it has been written down, because the time has not yet ended for making these books, these many explanations, so that Maya men may be asked if they know how they were born here in this country, when the land was founded.

It was Katun 11 Ahau when the Ah Mucencab came forth to blindfold the faces of the Oxlahun-ti-ku; but they did not know his name, except for his older sister and his sons. They said his face had not yet been shown to them also. This was after the creation of the world had been completed, but they did not know it was about to occur. Then Oxlahun-ti-ku was seized by Bolon-ti-ku. Then it was that fire descended, then the rope descended, then rocks and trees descended. Then came the beating of things with wood and stone. Then Oxlahun-ti-ku was seized, his head was wounded, his face was buffeted, he was spit upon, and he was thrown on his back as well. After that, he was despoiled of his scepter and cloud-making black powder. Then shoots of the yaxum tree were taken. Also lima beans were taken with crumbled tubercles, hearts of small squash seeds, large squash seeds and beans, all crushed. He wrapped up the seeds composing this first Bolon Dz'acab, and went to the thirteenth heaven. Then a mass of maize dough with the tips of corncobs remained here on earth. Then its heart departed because of Oxlahun-ti-ku, but they did not know the heart of the tubercle was gone. After that, the fatherless ones, the miserable ones, and those without husbands all fell apart; they were alive though they had no hearts. Then they were buried in the sands, in the sea.

There would be a sudden rush of water when the theft of Oxlahun-ti-ku's scepter occurred. Then the sky would fall, it would fall down upon the earth, when the four Bacabs were set up, who brought about the destruction of the world. Then, after the destruction of the world was completed, they placed a tree to set up in its order the yellow cock oriole. Then the white tree of abundance was set up. A pillar of the sky was set up, a sign of the destruction of the world; that was the white tree of abundance in the north. Then the black tree of abundance was set up in the west for the black-breasted Pidz'oy bird to sit upon. Then the yellow tree of abundance was set up in the south as a symbol of the destruction of the world, for the yellow-breasted Pidz'oy bird to sit upon, for the yellow cock oriole to sit upon, the yellow timid bird. Then the green tree of abundance was set up in the center of the world as a record of the destruction of the world.

The plate of another katun was set up and fixed in its place by the messengers of their lord. The red Piltec was set at the east of the world to conduct people to his lord. The white Piltec was set at the north of the world to conduct people to his lord. Lahun Chaan was set at the west to bring things to his lord. The yellow Piltec was set at the south to bring things to his lord. But it was over the whole world that Ah Uuc Cheknal was set up. He came from the seventh stratum of the earth, when he came to fecundate Itzam-kab-ain when he came with the vitality of the angle between earth and heaven. They moved among the four lights, among the four layers of the stars. The world was not lighted; there was neither day nor night nor moon. Then they perceived that the world was being created. Then creation dawned upon the world.

DESANA CREATION MYTH (*Tukano*)

I

In the beginning there were the Sun and the Moon. They were twin brothers. At first they lived alone, but then the Sun had a daughter, and he lived with her as if she were his wife. The Moon brother did not have a wife and became jealous. He tried to make love to the wife of the Sun, but the Sun heard about it. There was a dance up in the sky, in the house of the Sun, and when the Moon brother came to dance, the Sun took from him, as a punishment, the large feather crown he wore that was like the crown of the Sun. He left the Moon brother with a small feather crown and with a pair of copper earrings. From that time on, the Sun and the Moon have been separate, and they are always far apart in the sky as a result of the punishment that the Moon brother received for his wrongdoing.

The Sun created the Universe, and for this reason he is called Sun Father (pagë abé). He is the father of all the Desana. The Sun created the Universe with the power of his yellow light and gave it life and stability. From his dwelling-place, bathed in yellow reflections, the Sun made the earth, with its forests and rivers, with its animals and plants. The Sun planned his creation very well, and it was perfect.

The world we live in has the shape of a large disc, an immense round plate. It is the world of men and animals, the world of life. While the dwelling-place of the Sun has a yellow color, the color of the power of the Sun, the dwelling-place of men and animals is of a red color, the color of fecundity and of the blood of living beings. Our earth is mari turí (mari/our, turí/level), and is called "the upper level" (vehká-maha turí) because below is another world, the "lower level" (dohkamaha turí). This world below is called Ahpikondiá, Paradise. Its color is green, and the souls of those who were

3

good Desana throughout their lifetime go there. On the side where the Sun rises, in Ahpikondiá, there is a large lake, and the rivers of the earth pour into it because all flow toward the east. Thus, Ahpikondiá is connected to our earth by the water of the rivers. On the side where the Sun sets, in Ahpikondiá, lies the Dark Region. This is the region of night and is an evil place.

Seen from below, from Ahpikondiá, our earth looks like a large cobweb. It is transparent, and the Sun shines through it. The threads of this web are like the rules that men should live by, and they are guided by these threads, seeking to live well, and the Sun sees them.

Above our earth, the Sun created the Milky Way. The Milky Way emerges as a large, foaming current from Ahpikondiá and runs from east to west. Strong winds rush through the Milky Way, and it is blue in color. It is the intermediate region between the yellow power of the Sun and the red color of the earth. For this reason, it is a dangerous region because it is there people establish contact with the invisible world and with the spirits.

The Sun created the animals and the plants. To each one he assigned the place he should live. He made all of the animals at once, except the fish and the snakes; these he made afterward. Also, together with the animals, the Sun made the spirits and demons of the forest and the waters.

The Sun created all of this when he had the yellow intention—when he caused the power of his yellow light to penetrate, in order to form the world from it.

II

The Sun had created the earth with its animals and plants, but there were still no people. Now he decided to people the earth, and for this he made a man of each tribe of the Vaupés; he made a Desana and a Pira-Tapuya, a Uanano, a Tuyuka, and others, one from each tribe. Then, to send the people to the earth, the Sun made use of a being called Pamurí-mahsë. He was a man, a creator of people, whom the Sun sent to people the earth. Pamurí-mahsë was in Ahpikondiá, and he set forth from there in a large canoe. It was a live canoe, in reality a large snake that swam on the bottom of the river. This Snake Canoe was called Pamurí-gahsíru, and its skin was painted yellow and had stripes with black diamonds. On the inside, which was red, sat the people: a Desana, a Pira-Tapuya, a Uanano, one from each tribe. Together with the Snake Canoe came the fish; but they were not in the inside but outside, in the gills; the crabs also came, attached to the rear. It was a very long journey, and the Snake Canoe was going up the river because Pamurí-mahsë was going to establish mankind at the headwaters. Whenever they arrived at a large rapids, the Snake Canoe made the waters rise in order to pass by and caused the torrent to be calm. Thus they went on for a long time, and the people became very tired.

At that time night did not yet exist, and so they traveled in the light, always under the yellow light of the Sun. When the first men set forth, the Sun had given each one something, some object, for him to carry carefully. To one of them he had given a small black purse, closed tightly, and now, as the journey was so long, the man looked inside the purse. He did not know what was inside. He opened it, and suddenly a multitude of black ants came out of the purse, so many that they covered the light, making everything dark. This was the First Night. Pamurí-mahsë gave to each man a firefly in order to light his way, but the light was very weak. The ants multiplied, and the men tried to invoke them to return to the purse, but at that time they did not know about invocations. Then the Sun Father himself descended and with a stick beat the purse and made the ants enter it again. But those which did not obey remained in the forest and made their anthills. From that time on, there have been ants. Once the ants were inside the purse, the light returned; but since then night has come into existence. This was the First Night, nyamí mengá, the Night of the Ant, and the man who had opened the purse was called nyamíri mahsë, Man of Night.

So they continued on in the Snake Canoe, but when they arrived at Ipanoré, on the Vaupés River, they struck against a large rock near the bank. The people went ashore because they were tired of the long journey and thought that they had already reached their destination. They left by way of an opening at the prow of the canoe. Pamurí-mahsë did not want them to disembark there because he was thinking of taking them to the headwaters of the rivers, and therefore he stopped up the opening with his foot. But the people had already got out, having rushed from the Snake Canoe; they were dispersing throughout the rivers and the forests. But before they got away, Pamurí-mahsë gave each one of them the objects they had brought from Ahpikondiá and that, from then on, were going to indicate the future activities of each tribe. He gave a bow and arrow to the Desana; to the Tukano, the Pira-Tapuya, Vaiyára, and the Neéroa he gave a fishing rod; to the Kuripáko he gave the manioc grater; he gave a blowgun and a basket to the Makú, and a mask of barkcloth to the Cubeo. He gave a loincloth to each one, but to the Desana he gave only a piece of string. He pointed out the places where each tribe should live, but when he was about to indicate the future home of the Desana, this one had fled to seek refuge at the headwaters. The Uanano had also gone and went up to the clouds in the sky. Then Pamurí-mahsë entered the Snake Canoe again and returned to Ahpikondiá.

III

The Sun created the various beings so that they would represent him and serve as intermediaries between him and the earth. To these beings he gave the duty of caring for and protecting his Creation and of promoting the fertility of life.

First the Sun created Emëkóri-mahsë and Diroá-mahsë and put them in the sky and in the rivers so that, from there, they could protect the world. Emëkóri-mahsë is the Being of Day, and his job is to set down all the norms, the rules, and the laws according to which the spiritual life of human beings should develop. Diroá-mahsë, who is the Being of Blood, is in charge of all that is corporeal, all that is connected with health and the good life. Then he created Vihó-mahsë, the Being of Vihó, the hallucinogenic powder, and ordered him to serve as an intermediary so that through hallucinations people could put them-

6

selves in contact with all the other supernatural beings. The powder of vihó itself had belonged to the Sun, who had kept it hidden in his navel, but the Daughter of the Sun had scratched his navel and had found the powder. While Emëkóri-mahsë and Diroá-mahsë always represent the principle of good, the Sun gave Vihó-mahsë the power of being good and evil and put him in the Milky Way as the owner of sickness and witchcraft.

Then the Sun created Vaí-mahsë, the Master of Animals. There are two beings called Vaí-mahsë—one for the animals of the forest, and the other for the fish. The Sun assigned to each one the places where he ought to live; one was given a large maloca inside the rocky hills of the forest, and the other a large maloca at the bottom of the waters of the rapids. He put them there so that they could watch over the animals and their multiplication. Together with the Vaí-mahsë of the waters, the Sun put Vaí-bogó, the Mother of Fish. The Sun also created Wuá, the Owner of Thatch, the owner of the palm leaves that are used to make the roofs of the malocas.

Then the Sun created Nyamikëri-mahsë, the Night People, and put them in the Dark Region to the west of Ahpikondiá. To them he gave the job of serving as intermediaries for witchcraft and sorcery, because the Sun did not create only the principle of good but also of evil, to punish mankind when it did not follow the customs of tradition.

Then the Sun created the jaguar so that he would represent him in this world. He gave him the color of his power and gave him the voice of thunder that is the voice of the Sun; he entrusted him to watch over his Creation and to protect it and take care of it, especially of the malocas. The Sun created all these beings so that there would be life in this world.

IV

The Daughter of the Sun had not yet reached puberty when her father made love to her. The Sun committed incest with her at Wainambí Rapids, and her blood flowed forth; since then, women must lose blood every month in remembrance of the incest of the Sun and so that this great wickedness will not

7

be forgotten. But his daughter liked it and so she lived with her father as if she were his wife. She thought about sex so much that she became thin and ugly and lifeless. Newly married couples become pale and thin because they only think of the sexual act, and this is called gamúri. But when the Daughter of the Sun had her second menstruation, the sex act did harm to her and she did not want to eat anymore. She lay down on a rock, dying; her imprint there can still be seen on a large boulder at Wainambí Rapids. When the Sun saw this, he decided to make gamú bayári, the invocation that is made when the girls reach puberty. The Sun smoked tobacco and revived her. Thus, the Sun established customs and invocations that are still performed when young girls have their first menstruation.

V

The Sun had the first maloca built. This was in gahpí-bu ("place of the yajé plant") on the Macú-paraná River, in the place that is now called Wainambí. He ordered Emëkóri-mahsë, Diroá-mahsë, Vihó-mahsë, and Vaí-mahsë to teach the first Desana how to make their homes. When they had built the first maloca, Vihó-mahsë, and with him, sickness and sorcery, hid in the cracks and crannies of the houseposts to do evil to the people. Vihó-mahsë made use of the "ancient eagles" (ga'a mëera) which were sitting in the trees near the house. The eagles were chewing coca, and their beaks were flecked with white. The eagles brought nets in the shape of funnels; they were like the nets that are now used for fishing, and they put them on the doors of the maloca to trap the people. But Diroá-mahsë saw this and came to defend the people. Then the evilness hid again in the cracks of the houseposts, and the eagles put up other nets until there were two at each door. But Diroá-mahsë trapped the eagles and wrapped them up in the nets and threw them into the Milky Way. There the eagles took on bodily form again; since then they have been beneficent and take care of the malocas. All of this happened because there were no invocations and the people did not know how to protect themselves, but now they began to learn to make invisible and impenetrable enclosures around the malocas; they also learned to put invisible nets on the doors to trap all the evil that might penetrate the maloca from the outside.

At that time there were only men, the first men having come with Pamurí-mahsë in the Snake Canoe. The animals of the forest already had their mates, and the fish too. Vaí-mahsë, the Master of Fish, had his wives, the Vaí-nomé, and with them he had a daughter, Vaí-mangó. The daughter was an aracú fish, and the aracú were, as they are now, the main fish of the rivers and lived in their malocas under the water.

One night the men had a feast and danced. The Daughter of Aracú (boréka-mangó) saw the light, the yellow light of the men's fire, and came out of the water. She approached the maloca and saw the Desana; she fell in love with him. The man gave her honey, and she tried it and liked it. So she stayed with him on land. The first Desana was called gahkí. This happened at Wainambí Rapids where the first maloca stood, and one can still see there on the rocks the imprint of the buttocks of the woman when she lay with the man. From the union between the first Desana and the Daughter of Aracú, sons and daughters were born. The first sib of the Desana was born, and then all of the Desana tribe.

When the first Desana cohabited with the Daughter of Aracú, there were several animals who were witnesses to the act. The water turtle saw it, and from that time on it has had the color of the vagina; when one eats the meat of this turtle, welts break out on the skin. The curassow saw the penis of the man, and since that time it has had a red neck and always lives on the riverbank. The sloth was also watching, but the Daughter of Aracú saw it and changed it into a slow animal; before this it had been a very nimble climber.

When she was pregnant, the Daughter of Aracú ate a uarí fish and threw the leftovers of her meal into the river. The bones were changed into fish, and since that time these fish are

9

so slow that they can be caught by hand; it is the laziness of the pregnant woman that made them be like this.

When the Daughter of Aracú gave birth to her child, there were also some animals watching. The bat was a bird then and was watching and singing. Then the Daughter of Aracú said to it: "I at least have my offspring where I should give birth, but you will defecate by mouth from now on." The centipede and a large, black, poisonous spider came to lick the blood of the childbirth, and from that time on the centipede looks like an unbilical cord and the spider like a vagina. Also the scorpion and a large black ant licked the blood, and from that time on the bite of these two makes one vomit and produces great pains similar to those of childbirth. The stingray is the placenta of the Daughter of Aracú, and its poisonous sting produces the same pains.

When all of this happened, the invocations that should be said when a woman gives birth were not yet known. The Daughter of Aracú was not able to bathe herself because she was afraid of going to the landing place because there were so many animals there: so she became covered with lice.

A small bird that sang at dawn and saw her was singing: "This lazy woman! Maybe she doesn't know about invocations?" Then the Daughter of Aracú thought this over and invented the first incantations for the bath following childbirth. In a trough she prepared herbs and tobacco and went to the river to wash. Her husband was very frightened, but she said the incantations and thus the animals could do no harm to her.

When her first son was born, the mother of the Daughter of Aracú took the child to the river to bathe it. Then the aracú fish from all parts gathered and rubbed themselves against the child and recognized it as one of their kin. As soon as the father of the child saw that there were so many aracú fish in the river he took his bow and arrow and killed them. The Daughter of Aracú did not know about this because she was in the chagra, but when she returned to the maloca and saw the dead aracú, all her kin, she began to cry and carried them back to the river to set them loose. Then she herself also went into the river to her large house under the water.

Thus, mankind was born and the tribe was formed. The second Desana also married a woman from the river, and when she became pregnant for the first time she asked her husband to bring her some fish because she was tired of the other food. The man went to the forest and cut a heart of palmito (mihí); he took it to the landing place where the woman was and put small pieces of palmito into the water, reciting at the same time incantations to the fish. Then bubbles began to rise, and suddenly a large wooden drum came out of the water. It had the same shape as the Snake Canoe, pamurí-gahsíru, and in its gills the fish were held fast. The man took hold of the fish and gave them to his wife, but he put the drum again in the river where it submerged. Since then, the large drums are kept at times under the water so that they may have a new life.

The Daughter of Aracú made the first field, the first chagra. She had brought manioc with her which had been in the malocas of the Aracú people under the water, and she planted it so that the Desana people could have it to eat. Once the Daughter of Aracú was going to wash manioc tubes in the brook. Then the Aracú people saw this and tried to carry the manioc off again to their malocas; but they failed to do so. Then the Aracú people made a pact with the paca to steal the manioc and return it to them. The paca found the manioc and began to eat it, and when he remembered that he was supposed to carry it to the Aracú people there was none left. Then the Aracú people ordered that, from then on, the paca should destroy the manioc of the Desana. The peccary came, the paca, the deer, and others, and the snakes came, too. Then the Daughter of Aracú asked the eagles for help, especially the eagle of the chagra (po'é ga'a) and the brown eagle (pun ga'a). The eagles killed the snakes and put them into the guarumo trees that stood around the field. They also scattered the birds that had come to eat the seeds of chili and tobacco. When the Daughter of Aracú washed manioc roots in the river, the Aracú people came to visit her. She also invented the woven tube used to squeeze the manioc.

VII

Below Wainambí Rapids the Sun had made a large snake that was the mother of all snakes. The traces of that snake are still

seen on the rocks along the riverbanks. When the first son of
the Desana was born, the snake devoured the child. The
Desana complained to the Sun, and the Sun put a trap in the
river to catch the snake. The trap can still be seen in the rocks
above Ipanoré; there the Sun trapped the snake and bit off its
head. The snake was called pirú se'e ("gull snake") because it
was the same color as this bird, white and black and dark gray
on top. These birds, the gulls, come flying down to dive into
the river and lagoons, and then they fly upward again after
having bathed themselves. They are the representatives of this
snake.

The large river that was to be the place for the Desana to es-
tablish themselves was the Papurí. Near Piramirí there is a hill,
and one day the Sun met Pamurí-mahsë with the first Desana
on top of it. They met there in order to bring the fish because
there were still very few of them. Then the Sun told Pamurí-
mahsë to make a sign on the water so that the fish would go
up the Vaupés and enter the Papurí River. Pamurí-mahsë told
the Desana not to urinate. Then the water came like a torrent,
and the fish came with it; the river began to rise. The Desana
looked and suddenly saw coming a gigantic centipede. It had
huge fangs and was grabbing at trees and was coming closer
with the huge oncoming wave. The Desana became frightened
and urinated. Then the water became salty, and only a few
fish came up the Papurí River. On the rocks one can still see
today where the first wave came, and one can see the fish en-
graved in the stone. The centipede, nyangí, was the repre-
sentation of the seas, not of the rivers. The monsters of the sea
are just like the centipede. It is not the progenitor of the fish
in the sea; there are huge monsters. The centipede is a monster
that eats the fish. But then it only came to bring the fish, but
because the Desana became frightened and urinated, only a
small part of the water came through the Papurí River. But
much water came up the Vaupés River, and many fish too,
and the force of the water came as far as the upper Vaupés, at
the rapids of Yurapurí.

When everything had already been created, the world began to be filled with plagues and monsters. No one knows why. There were many monsters and demons everywhere: the boráro, the uahtí, and others. Then there were some very bad people called vearí-mahsá, the cheaters or kidnapers. They carried off people by stealth. They appeared on the trails and near the malocas in the guise of friends or relatives and violated women. They invited them to follow them, and then they arranged it so that they were lost in the forest. The vihó-mahsá also appeared, and when the women had their menstruation they rushed the malocas to violate them. All of these monsters wanted to have sexual relations with the people, and they tried to violate them. They were always near the malocas, listening to what was said. The monsters took the form of a brother, of an uncle, or of some relative, and thus cheated the people. They said, "Let's go fishing," but it was to violate them that they accompanied them.

The Kusíro also came. They were like huge horseflies that attack people and sting them. There was a great humming noise when these horseflies flew in circles around people, attacking them with their stingers. Then the men decided to kill the horseflies. They killed them with tobacco, blowing the smoke over their bodies and thereby killing them. They ate the dead horseflies, and they tasted like honey.

When the Sun saw that his Creation was suffering and that there were many evil things, he decided to go down to the earth to take charge and to get rid of the monsters. First he ordered a great flood, and all the monsters were drowned. Then he sent a great drought, and everything caught fire and was burned. The only ones saved were those who lived in the direction of the eastern Llanos. Only the armadillo was saved because he dug a hole and hid, but his tail was burned; it had been big and fluffy before. Of the birds, only the boru was saved, this being a little white bird that sings in the afternoon and is a good omen, and the tinamou was saved, too. Then life returned again. That was two hundred fifty years ago.

13

The Sun had a daughter who was called Abé mangó. He sent his daughter to the earth to teach the people how to live well. The Daughter of the Sun went to a place called abé góro; it means uninhabited place that is good for living. She came to teach the people. She taught them to make pottery and to use baskets. She taught them to eat fish, but only certain fish. She also taught them to eat wild fruit of sëmé, nyumú, and më'ë. Because the Sun was in love with her, she taught people to put on loincloths so that they would know shame.

The Daughter of the Sun invented fire and taught the people to make it with two little sticks of wood. She also invented the stone ax, but did not give it to all the men but only to those who rose early to bathe in the river and who took the juice from emetic plants to cleanse their bodies; only to these did she give the stone ax.

When everything had been created, and the Daughter of the Sun was thus teaching the people, Vihó-mahsë came to get acquainted with the Creation. The Daughter of the Sun showed him everything; she showed him how the plants were cared for, how they were eaten, and how they were used. She had been cooking, and suddenly the contents of the vessel boiled over, almost putting out the fire. The Daughter of the Sun became angry and cried, "Well, then, go out!" and she urinated on the embers. Then they burned her pubic hairs and the odor spread out everywhere. Vihó-mahsë was looking and became distracted. Then, instead of observing the world from the Milky Way, he began to think of the vagina of the Daughter of the Sun.

XI

The first death was that of a son of the Daughter of the Sun. She had two sons and both were apprentices to become payés. One was doing well, but the other was not because he was always thinking about women. He was wilting away until he almost died. The Daughter of the Sun tried to cure him with invocations, but it was too late; his ornaments were no longer becoming to him. His copper earrings, which were like grooves, like halves of a tube, turned so that the concave parts were toward his face, indicating that life was not with him and that it was floating away. When he died, the Daughter of the Sun taught the people the proper burial rites and fixed the places where they were to celebrate them.

When she had taught them all of this, the Daughter of the Sun went away again and returned to Ahpikondiá. From there on, the old people of each tribe taught what she had said and thus the traditions were established.

XII

The one who first drank chicha was Pamurí-mahsë. This happened at Wainambí where the first maloca stood. He was there with the Desana. Above Wainambí was a large rock that was called dihtiró, and there one can see, engraved in the rock, what happened then. There is in the rock a large vessel like those that are now used to make chicha, and there is also the circle marking the spot where Pamurí-mahsë put down his blowgun with the mouthpiece downward. One can also see where he put his stick rattle down. When they were there, a purple-colored bird flew by, and a Desana shot it, and the dart fell upon the rock; one can still see the imprint. They were cohabiting, and one can even see the imprints of the buttocks of the women and the spot where they urinated. All of this can be seen on the rocks of Wainambí and dihtiró.

XIII

The same Sun Father was a payé, and Pamurí-mahsë was also a payé. The Sun established the functions of the payé, the invocations he should use, and the uses that tobacco was to have and also the hallucinogenic plants. The Sun already had his bench, his shield, and his stick rattle. He had his gourd rattle, and over his left shoulder he carried his hoe. The Sun had everything that the payés have now, and he established the custom of using them. The Sun showed how the dances should be done and how people ought to talk when they got together for feasts.

The Sun had the vihó powder in his navel, but a daughter of Vaí-mahsé owned the yajé plant. She was pregnant and with the pain of childbirth she went to the beach and, lying down, twisted in pain. An old Desana woman wanted to help her and took hold of her hand, but the daughter of Vaí-mahsé twisted so hard that she broke her finger, and the old woman kept it. She kept the finger in her maloca, but a young man stole it and planted it. The yajé plant originated from this finger. The same thing happened with another daughter of Vaí-mahsé. When she had the pains of childbirth, she was lying twisting on the beach, and an old woman came to help her. She seized hold of her hand and broke off one of the girl's fingers and buried it. The coca plant originated from this finger.

Curare poison was invented by the Sun Father himself. The Daughter of the Sun was in love with a man, and the Sun became jealous and wanted to kill him. Then he invented the poison and shot the man with a dart from his blowgun.

Thus it was that the earth was created. It was the Sun, the Daughter of the Sun, and the Daughter of Aracú who created things and taught people how to live well. There were Emëkóri-mahsá and Diroá-mahsá; they were the Beings of Day and of Night who are now in charge of the world. But the Sun is above all these, with his yellow power, the yellow power of the Sun Father who takes care of his Creation and covers it with his yellow light.

THE ORIGIN OF THE YAGUA

A very long time ago the Yagua lived in a place high up in the sky. The part of the sky where they lived was far away from this site and was above a great river. The place where they lived was full of game. The animals had no forest to hide in and lived in the open. Tapirs, wild pigs, and forest chickens lived so close to the people that it was not necessary to hunt them by stalking, as we do now, for one could catch them with his hands. People, therefore, were all very fat and ate too much. As hunting was so easy, many of the animals were killed. Finally, the game became scarce because all the men killed much game, ate only the best part, and threw the rest away. The people grew very hungry.

Noreho, a wise hunter, then decided to go with his wife, Sohya, and search for another place where game was plentiful. They wandered with their children and were hungry for many, many days. Finally they arrived at a place from which they saw below them a very big mountain. This mountain was so high that it almost reached the sky. They could see many animals below eating the leaves. As they were very hungry, Noreho decided to go down and kill some of the animals to feed his children who were crying from hunger.

Sohya, the wife, then rolled many chambira strings on her thigh, and spun them together to make a long rope strong enough to hold Noreho. Then Noreho saw that the forest below them had many chambira trees. He therefore asked his son, Moto, to climb down and cut him some chambira. Kovante, the little sister of Moto, cried terribly because she wanted to go with Moto down where the animals grazed, because she was hungry and in a hurry to eat. So Noreho tied the chambira rope around the waist of Kovante, and lowered her to the ground below. Moto followed his sister by climbing down the rope, but it was not strong enough to hold him, and just as he was above the ground the rope broke. Moto fell to the ground but was unhurt.

Noreho and Sohya then went to search for chambira to make a new rope to reach their children. They could not find any, and returned to their people, where they died of hunger with all the rest of them.

Moto and Kovante cried a long time for their parents. As they were very hungry, Moto killed a pigeon with a stick, and they ate. Then they slept for a long time.

Afterwards Moto and Kovante wandered in the forest and ate much meat. They grew up and got fat. Moto was a very good hunter, and he had many children by Kovante. These children are the Yagua.

GUARANI CREATION MYTH

PART ONE

1. The Primitive Ways of Hummingbird.

I.

Our First Father, the Absolute,
arose in the middle of the primal mists.

II.

The divine soles of his feet
his small round seat,
in the middle of the primal mists he created them,
in the course of his evolution.

III.

The reflection of the divine eye/wisdom
the divine all-hearing ear,
the divine palms of his hands inscribed with the divine rod,
the divine palms and the flowering twigs of his fingers and
    fingernails,
Namandu created them all in the course of his evolution,
in the middle of the primal mists.

IV.

The flowers at the tips of the feathers atop the divine head
    were drops of dew.
Out of the midst of the divine flower-plume headdress
the primal bird, the Hummingbird, flew fluttering.

V.

While our First Father created his divine body in the course
    of his evolution,
he dwelt in the middle of the primal winds;
before having conceived his future earthly home,
before having conceived the future firmament,
he was fed by the Hummingbird;
the Hummingbird sustained Namandu with
the food of paradise.

Our Father Namandu, the First, before having created
his future paradise,
in the course of his evolution,
saw no mists:
although the Sun still did not exist,
he existed illuminated by the reflection of his own heart;
before the sun existed he was illuminated by the light con-
    tained
within his own divinity.

VII.

Our true Father, Namandu, the First,
existed in middle of the first winds;
where the Owl stopped to rest there
the mists began;
before the bed of night-mists
existed.

VIII.

Before our true, first father, Namandu,
in the course of his evolution had created his
future paradise,
before having created the first earth,
he lived in the midst of the first winds,
the first wind that brings back
the first time again every winter.
When the First Age ended, the Age of Lapacho
began, the winds moved Space-Time;
the winds move again and
Space-Time resurrects in
Spring.

2. *The Beginning of Human Language.*

I.

Our true father, Namandu, the First,
out of a small portion of his own divinity,

out of the wisdom contained in his own divinity,
and because of the inevitability of his own creative wisdom,
caused flames to break out and a soft fog.

II.

Having assumed human form,
and because of the wisdom contained in his own divinity,
and in virtue of his creative/creating knowledge,
he brought forth human language.
From the wisdom contained in his own divinity,
and because of his creative intelligence,
our Father created the beginnings of human language
and made it part of his own divinity.
Before the earth existed,
in the middle of the primal mists,
before he even had thought of "things,"
he created that which would serve as the foundation of
human language
and our true First Father Namandu
made it part of his own divinity.

III.

Having conceived the origin of future human language,
from the wisdom contained in his own divinity,
and in virtue of his creative intelligence,
he conceived the idea of LOVE,
before the earth existed,
in the midst of the primal mists,
before he had even thought of "things,"
and in virtue of his creative intelligence,
he conceived the idea of LOVE.

IV.

Having created the beginnings of human language,
having created a small parcel of LOVE,
from the wisdom contained in his own divinity,

and in virtue of his creative wisdom,
he next created one sacred hymn in his solitude.
Before the earth existed,
in the midst of the mists from which all things originated,
before he had even thought of "things,"
he created for himself in his solitude the idea
of one sacred hymn.

V.

In his solitude, having created the foundations of human lan-
   guage,
in his solitude, having created a small parcel of LOVE,
having created, in his solitude, one short sacred hymn,
he meditated profoundly about who he should
make to participate in these beginnings of language,
about who he should make to participate in this small
LOVE,
about who he should make to participate in the series of
works that made up the sacred hymn.
Having meditated profoundly,
out of the wisdom contained in his own divinity,
and in virtue of his creative intelligence,
he created those who would be companions of his divinity.

VI.

Having profoundly meditated,
out of the wisdom of his own divinity,
and in virtue of his creative intelligence,
he created the valiant Namandu.
He created them all at the same time with the reflection of
his wisdom,
the Sun.
Before the earth even was,
in the midst of the mists from which all things sprang,
he created the large-hearted Namandu.

To be father to all his numberless future children,
to be the true father of the souls of all his future numberless
children,
he created the large-hearted Namandu.

VII.

Out of the wisdom contained in his own divinity,
and in virtue of his creative intelligence,
he instilled in the Namandu,
the true father of the future Karaí,
the true father of the future Jakaira,
the true father of the future Tupá,
an awareness of his own divinity.
He instilled in the true fathers of
all his future children, the true
fathers of the words/souls of his
future numberless children,
an awareness of his own divinity.

VIII.

Then the true Father Namandu,
Looking into his own heart,
instilled a knowledge of divinity
in the future mother of the Namandu.
Karaí Ru Ete instilled a knowledge of divinity
to her who was foremost in his heart,
to the future true mother of the Karaí.
Jakaira Ru Ete, in the same way,
looking into his own heart
instilled knowledge of the creator
in the true mother Jakaira.
Tupá Ru Ete, in the same way,
instilled knowledge of the creator
in the mother of the Tupá,
she who was foremost in his heart.

After they had assimilated the divine wisdom
of their own First Father,
after having assimilated human language,
after having understood the idea of Charity/Brotherly Love,
after having understood the words of the divine hymn,
after having understood and assimilated the fundamentals of
creative wisdom,
then we called them too true fathers of the words/souls,
most high true mothers of the words/souls.

3. The First Earth.

I.

Our true Father, Namandu, the First,
having conceived his future earthly dwelling-place,
out of the wisdom contained in his own divinity,
and in virtue of his creative intelligence,
he created the earth with his divine wand.
He created an eternal palm in the future center of the earth;
he created another in the dwelling-place of Karaí, the East,
he created another in the dwelling-place of Tupá, the West,
in the North/Northeast, in the place of the good
winds, he created yet another eternal palm,
and the last palm he created in the place of the first
time-space, the South;
he created five palms in all,
and the earth is held together by these five.

II.

There are seven paradises;
the firmament rests on four columns;
these four columns are totem poles.
Our Father blew the firmament across the heavens,
he pushed it in place with the winds.

First he created three columns in paradise
to stop its movement,
and then he put in place the totem poles of the
four-quarters;
then everything stood in its proper place
and all vagrant movement stopped.

III.

The first being that dirtied the house of earth was the
first serpent;
the serpents on earth now are no more than its mere
image;
the first serpent is now on the outskirts of the
paradise of our Father.
The first being that sang in the earthly house of our
First Father,
the first being that lamented the first lament,
was the "Yrypa," the small, colored locust,
the colored locust is in the outskirts of our Father's
paradise:
the locust we see is only the image of the
locust that dwells in the outskirts of our Father's
paradise.
In the same way the Y-amai, the lord of the waters,
the creator of waters, that exists here is not
the true Y-amai;
the true Y-amai lives in the outskirts of our Father's
paradise.
The one that exists here is merely a "shadow."
When our Father created the earth there were no fields,
merely forests.
Because of this, and in order for him to help create
prairies,
he sent to earth the green grasshopper.
Wherever the grasshopper set down there sprung up
fields of pasture and the grasshopper celebrated his

creation of pasturelands with his
"singing."
The first grasshopper is in the outskirts of our Father's
paradise:
the grasshoppers that remain here are nothing more
than its image.
Then with the fields had appeared
the first one to sing in them,
the first to celebrate their appearance
was the colored partridge, and this first colored partridge
now exists in the outskirts of our Father's paradise;
the partridges here are merely its "shadow."
The first animal to stir up the dirt in the house of earth
was the armadillo; only the armadillos
that live on earth now are merely the "shadows" of this first
armadillo.
The Mistress of Fogs and Mists is the Owl.
Our Father is the Sun, the Lord of the Dawn.

PART TWO

When our First Father was ready
to return to the depths of
paradise, he said:
—Only you, Karaí Ru Ete,
and your children, shall I put in charge
of the strands of inaccessible flame that
I leave behind,
you and your children, the valiant Karaí.
Thereupon he fixed them with the name
"the Lord of the Flames," and put them
in charge of the sound of crackling fire . . .

Then he said to Jakaira Ru Ete:
—You shall guard the words that I conceived in
my solitude, you and your children,

the large-hearted Jakaira.
And because of this the Jakaira still call themselves
"The Lords of the Mist of Inspired Words."

Then he said to Tupá Ru Ete:
—You shall be in charge of the great sea
in all its extent and totality . . .

Our true Father Namandu, the First,
when he was about to lavish
his own divine intelligence on the earth
in terms of "good science,"
to those who wear the male and
female emblems, he said to
Jakaira Ru Ete:
—Every spring, it will be your
duty, you and your children, the
large-hearted Jakaira,
to circulate the spring-mists/fogs
across the extent of the earth.
Only in this way can your sons and
daughters prosper.

—Karaí Ru Ete,
your beloved daughters and sons
shall be in charge of the sacred flames.
—You, my son, Tupá Ru Ete,
shall be in charge of guarding
moderation in the hearts of
our children.

Only in this way can the numberless beings
that spread across the earth,
although they may tend to stray from the idea of CHARITY,
won't stray, but will live in harmony.
Only through moderation
can the laws which I have promulgated

work, without excess or abuse,
in the future lives of our beloved sons,
in the future lives of our beloved daughters.
After Namandu Ru Ete, the First,
had given the right names to the
fathers of our future children,
to the true fathers of the words/souls
of our future children, and had allocated
each one of them his
place in the world, he said:
—Now, after having given thee thine names
and thy places in the world,
it will be up to thee to create
the laws that will prevail on earth,
over male and female.

And then he instilled in every man and
woman, in the first parents of the first
children, the first sacred
man- and woman-songs, in the first fathers
and the first mothers,
in order that mankind
might truly prosper as it spread across
the face of the earth.

4. The Flames and Fog of Creative Power.
In the center of the divine being dwells the mystery of
"The Flames and Mist of Creative Power."
It was Namandu, the First, who made the Flames and Mist
part of his being, *kuaa-ra-ra*, the creative power of his
wisdom.
On earth neither the best of men nor the best of women
can enter into this inaccessible mystery of
the Flames and Mist
unless they seek the Vision; only to the Vision-Seekers

will the gods reveal the mystery of the
Flames and Mist.
Because he, Namandu, was the first
to give voice and reality to "the
Flames and Mist of Creative Power,
the Sun of Divinity," because he
at the same time covered the earth and
the firmament with the light of his
heart and the Sun, so that no one could
escape from his sight,
because he created the Words/Realities
of the Flames and Mist,
because of this, Namandu was called the
First, the Beginning.

5. The Creation of "Guardian-Spirits"/"Familiars."
—When someone is about to be born,
male or female,
I will send a word-soul to be
incarnate in them,
said our First Father,
and in this way I will "direct"
mankind discreetly and without
its knowledge.
So go, son of Namandu, of Karaí,
Jakaira, Tupá,
fortify yourself as you descend to
the surface of Earth, and although
you will encounter horrors wherever you go,
confront them with valor.

6. The Flood.
The inhabitants of the First Earth
had become indestructible.
Those who prayed well,

who possessed understanding,
had attained perfection
and directed their lives toward the
future life . . .
Those who lacked understanding,
who were involved with "evil science,"
who transgressed against those who rule
above us,
assumed "low" and "fearful" forms
in the course of their
reincarnations.
Some became birds,
some frogs, some beetles;
Our Father had turned one woman thief
into a deer.
Only living according to the precepts
left behind by our good parents
can we prosper.
Lord Incest sinned against our First
Fathers:
he married his paternal aunt.
The waters were about to descend,
Lord Incest prayed, sang, danced,
and the waters descended
before Lord Incest had been
saved.
Lord Incest tried to swim,
he tried to swim with his woman,
in the water they danced, prayed, and
sang.
Inspired by religious fervor
at the end of two months they had
become strong
and reached perfection.
They created a miraculous palm with two leaves

and they rested in its branches before
leaving for their future home,
before becoming immortals.
Infamous Lord Incest
created the indestructible earth for
his future home
and became our Father Tapari,
the true father of the minor gods.

7. *The New Earth.*
Namandu Ru Ete speaks to a Heavenly Messenger about the
creation of a New Earth:
—Go, my son,
and ask Karaí Ru Ete
if he is disposed toward
the creation of a new
earth.
Karaí Ru Ete, to the Messenger:
—I am in no way disposed
to create something predestined to
vanish; what I feel like doing is leveling
my anger at the earth. Tell Namandu,
"Karaí has no intention of creating a new
earth."

Namandu to the Messenger:
—So be it,
go to Jakaira Ru Ete and ask
him if he is disposed to create a new earth.
Jakaira Ru Ete answers:
—I *am* disposed
to create a world for myself on
earth.
Although I see on earth bad
presages for all our children

until the end of humankind,
still I will spread my life-giving
mist over the surface of the
world; my sacred flames,
my mist must spread over all beings
still lost in imperfection.
I will create tobacco and pipe
for the salvation of our children.
I will gently illuminate all the
valleys in the jungles
with my thunderless lightning.

8. *The Populating of the New Earth.*
For the grandfather of the new earth
Jakaira Ru Ete created the Tatu Ai, the colored armadillo,
and he gave control of the earth to the dragon-snake with
heads on each end of its body.
Our father Pa-pa Mirí created the earth.
He decreed that the sacred songs of man
be sung.
He decreed that the sacred songs of men
would be accompanied by the sacred songs of
women, only before listening to the sacred songs of men
sung across the surface of the earth he
grew homesick for his heavenly home
and for his Great Mother, and
before he had set out his earthly home in all
its details, before having filled the world of man
with sacred song,
he returned to "heaven."

9. *How there was Originally Fire on the New Earth.*
The earth of our First Father had been destroyed
and a new earth had been created.
"Good, my son, Pa-pa-Mirí,

return to earth, rely on your own wisdom,
bring my word to those who wear the beautiful
feathered emblems of masculinity;
those adorned with feathers are my chosen
ones, they are the ones who shall work good on
the earth," said our First Father.
Having created it and put it in its proper place,
he delegated power to Pa-pa-Mirí
to illuminate those who wore feathers
and others of the earth,
telling them what they needed to know.
And descending to earth, the first thing that
Pa-pa-Mirí thought of was fire.
Talking to his divine frog son, his messenger,
he said, "I will play dead, and my enemies
will rise up against me, my enemies who now
possess fire; and we will take it from them
and give it to my children. So, Son Frog, hide, wait,
and when I get up and shake myself, drink the fire
down."
So he stretched out on the ground as if he were dead,
and our First Father thought that his son had died
and he said to Vulture who was not quite yet Vulture:
—Go to my son who is dead, who is dying, and bring
him back to life.

So the Vulture-not-quite-yet-Vulture came and saw the ca-
    daver,
saw that it was nice and fat, and lit a fire in order to roast it,
he along with his companions.
They brought wood and lit a fire under him;
then Pa-pa Mirí got up and shook himself at his
frog son, "Have you swallowed it yet?"
"No, not yet."
He lay down again, stretched out, pretended he was dead,

and the Vultures-not-quite-yet-Vultures gathered together
    again,
gathered firewood, lit another fire and our Father shook him-
    self
again, asked his frog son again,
"Have you swallowed the fire?"
"Yes, I have . . ."
"So take it out so the rest of
my children can use it, get some laurel, put the fire in
it, and get some lianas, put the fire in it,
'store it' for the use of those men who wear feathers,
'store it' so that the inhabitants of earth will always have it."

At this point the Vultures-not-quite-yet-Vultures returned to
our Father, and our Father, knowing that they had tried to
    roast
the body of Pa-pa Mirí said:
"Go and be changed forever
into beings that have no respect for
the dead . . ."

And the vultures cried,
because there was no way for them to ever
attain perfection.

10. Prayer to the Creator at Dawn.
Oh, true Father, Namandu, the First!
Celestial Sun,
Sun of Wisdom . . .
every morning we salute you with
eternal, indestructible words of
prayer whose pronouncing extends and
preserves our lives,
every dawn we orphans of paradise
pray to you,
Oh, Padre Namandu, the First.

WHAT THE WORLD USED TO BE LIKE
(*Chorti Maya*)

People used to tell long ago that the world, long ago, would be destroyed again and again. They say that the sea rose over the earth and filled all the earth with water. And the earth became mud, until it finished—it turned to water all over the earth, and the people were completely killed off by the water. Because—they ended up floating, the people who were on the earth, ended up floating like rubbish on the water.

And no birds remained, nor foxes, nor deer, nor buzzards, nor hawks; nothing remained, because all at once, everything was destroyed on the earth, because they say that long ago, there were no mountains on the—world. Because they say that the world was once just stretched over the water; there were no mountains like today.

But when God saw that the humans in the world were destroyed, then one day, when it was filled with water all over the earth, and it had become pure mud, all over the—world. And when it began to dry, it went, and that water, where it began to gather, went away, and began to wash away the earth. Then was when everything appeared: streams, mountains, and stones. Everything there is.

It all became visible, because they say that that water, where it dried away, and where it began to gather together, washed away the earth. And everything appeared, and the many rocks there are became visible.

But long ago they say that there was nothing. That all at once, all the places lay about on the surface of the earth. Today we see great mountains, and—there are many streams, because so, on that day, it was—the water, when it began to gather itself, completely washed away the surface of the earth and the many mountains became visible in the country.

Because the people used to tell long ago that the sea, from time to time, rose up, in its waves, and rose up standing like the clouds. And when it rose up standing, then it let itself come down, and covered everything on the earth. So they used to tell it, because long ago, they tell that the sea lay all around the edges of the world, and that is why it immediately covered over the world when it was rising in—the world. So they used to tell it long ago.

And they used to tell too that the sea was not all one. They say there was one sea that was red, and one sea that was white, and there was one sea that was sticky like tar. And they say there was one sea that was pure blood, perfectly red. But we did not get there to see. They say there was one sea which was very large, and just like milk, perfectly white; they say that they were stuck together, the sky and the sea.

And there lived the gods. And they say that at sea every day as every night, there was lightning. Because they say that there lived the gods. But we do not know if it is really true, what they tell. And they say that in the sea there were many animals, filling it.

And that is why there was a town whose name is Barrios—Guatemala—where—the sea lies—they tell that long ago that from time to time those animals tried to come out in—ships, wanting to fall on the town. But they were not allowed by the soldiers; they shot and they turned and went. But we didn't get there to see.

But so they tell it. They tell that—they used to say that beyond the sea there are people who have horns. There are people with four eyes. They say that there are other people whose eyes are behind their heads, and some in front. They say they have four eyes. And then those people who—they eat. They eat people. But they said that beyond the sea they are. And they say there are people who—they have no heads. And there are—people—whose heads are flat. They used to tell all this. That beyond the sea there are no people like—where we live.

And that is why they told that—if they were allowed to go out, by the government, they would destroy the people, but—they say that—they were not given permission. No—the people who are beyond the sea wanted to go out and—they were feared.

They told that there was a place named the United States. They say that the people in that place, the people had hair, and—their arms were big around. And they say that when—

they used to eat people, that their hair grew. And that is why long ago, they were frightening, people who came from distant places who were not known, they were feared, and they hid the children from them and—all the women they hid when they saw them. Once they made a—a war in a place.

They used to tell that those people where there was a war, when bombs were dropped on their heads, they say that they went into the sea, and there they were protected, and for that reason they were not killed. But they say that there came a day when poison was dropped in the sea; then they all died. But they say that when shots were fired they were not killed, because they went into the sea; not until the poison was dropped in—the sea did they all die. So they used to tell it.

II. TREN TREN, KAI KAI, AND THE GREAT FLOOD: THEME WITH VARIATIONS

TREN TREN AND KAI KAI (*Mapuche*)

Two Versions

A.

Tren Tren is a large mountain in a range which runs between Galvarino and Temuco. Kai Kai was a huge serpent with three arms, which were trees, and a tail that was rooted in the ground. There is a lake high up on Tren Tren, which was the house of Kai Kai. Kai Kai had the head of a huge ox. When its eyes were open, it was asleep; and when its eyes were shut, it was awake. People used to come every once in a while to hit Kai Kai's tail with sticks. Kai Kai would awaken, and its eyes would close. Kai Kai was the chief of all the animals. Then, one day, the people molested Kai Kai too much, and Kai Kai led all the animals away. Kai Kai led them into the air. They did not fly away, but just walked into the air. No one knows where they went, but they are the spirit protectors (pillan) of all living animals.

B.

Tren Tren was a hill and also a good spirit which helped people. Kai Kai was a sea bird, an evil spirit, who used to enjoy harming people. This is how Tren Tren saved the Mapuche and vanquished evil. One day Kai Kai decided to wipe out all the Mapuche, and caused the sea to rise until the land was flooded. Many people managed to climb Tren Tren with their animals, and the wild animals followed. When Kai Kai said "kai, kai, kai, kai," the sea rose until it nearly covered the top of Tren Tren and threatened all the people and animals thereon. Upon seeing this, Tren Tren rose still higher. This continued until Tren Tren reached its present height and all the sea water was used up. Kai Kai was beaten. Thus, all the people and animals that had climbed Tren Tren were safe. This shows how powerful Tren Tren was. He conquered Kai Kai and saved the people.

THE FLOOD (*Toba-Pilagá*)

Three Versions

A.

Rainbow does not like women to enter water when they are menstruating. Women with blood must not go near water.

Once upon a time there was a girl who was menstruating and who remained shut up in her hut. Her mother and her sisters had forgotten to leave water for her when they left to go to the bush. The girl was thirsty and went to the lagoon to drink some water. When her mother returned home, she told her what she had done. The mother asked, "Where did you go to drink?" "To the lagoon," answered the girl. "Tonight it will rain," said the mother.

That very night it rained heavily. It rained until the next day. It rained until all the people in the camp were drowned. When the water receded the dead people were all white. A chief, a great spirit came. He took a stick with a piece of cloth. Then it was night and it rained again. The corpses turned yellow and green. The spirit struck the water near the corpses with his stick. Birds of all colors, black, white, and green, flew up. There were no longer any people, only birds. This was the origin of birds.

B.

There was a menstruating woman who said, "I am thirsty, I wish to drink," but her mother did not bring her water. Being very thirsty, she went to a lagoon and drank. She returned home. Rainbow arrived. He is displeased when menstruating girls enter water, and for that reason he was angry. A strong wind arose, accompanied by whirlwinds and heavy rain. Rainbow caused the people to turn green and yellow and black. The water rose and rose. The people were drowned and all died. The white corpses of children floated over the water. A wak'ap' bird [a sort of stork] came and attached a cloth to a stick. He struck the corpses with it and they were changed into pumas and birds. Some were green, some yellow, and some black. The word of Rainbow was accomplished. He who had destroyed the village made the wak'ap' bird into a chief.

C.

There was a village which had an abundant crop of maize. An old woman happening to go there returned loaded with maize which had been given to her as a present. She told her relatives about this village with its abundance of maize, and the people of her village went to visit their friends there. They were well received and their hosts invited them to stay in their houses.

The chief said, "We will give them maize. They have lots of fish in their village and we shall visit them at another time." When the guests returned home, many men followed them to fish in their lagoon.

While the people were away, a woman who was menstruating went to the lagoon to fetch water. The Rainbow (Wosa'k) got angry and turned against the people, who were changed to yellow. The Rainbow opened his arms and made "Pffff," and the whole village began to sink into the earth. Many tried to escape, but the wind prevented them from flying. A cock crew while the village sank.

The parents of the menstruating girl escaped, but when they returned to their village they could not find it. It had entirely disappeared and the place where it had stood was covered by a hill. They joined the others who had gone fishing and told them about the sinking of the village. "We cannot return. The people are destroyed. Nothing is left. There is a hill on the village site." Then they mourned the dead, cried and gave vent to their grief, and stayed where they were.

THE DELUGE (Apinaye)

The big snake Kanĕ-rōti came up from the sea and made the Rio Tocantins and the Rio Araguaya. He left to his smaller companions the task of making the lesser streams and creeks.

Then it rained for many days. All the watercourses overflowed their banks; the flood waters of the Tocantins joined those of the Araguaya. For two days the whole world was flooded. Many Apinaye fled to the Serra Negra, a mountain behind São Vicente, toward the Araguaya, which for that reason is called Ken-klimati (mountain of the meeting). Others took refuge in high jatoba trees, still others clung to big bottle gourds, drifted hither and yon, and finally perished.

One married couple took three gigantic gourd bottles, put manioc cutting, maize, and other seeds inside, stopped the orifices thoroughly with wax, and tied the three vessels together. Then the two sat down in the middle and allowed themselves to drift on the water. The current drove their craft close to the Serra Negra, but it resisted the powerful whirlpool.

On the Serra Negra the water was already up to people's knees; quite suddenly at night it fell again. Those perched on the high jatoba trees were now unable to get down and finally turned into nests of chope bees and termites.

When the water had ebbed away, the couple with the three gourds looked for a dwelling site and started a farm there. The people of the Serra Negra, however, having no more cuttings, lived on palm sprouts and nuts. One day a boy there killed a dwarf parrot, which he took to his mother. When she prepared it, she found maize kernels in his crop. She asked the boy from what direction the bird had come and when she had found out everybody went there to search. Finally they found the couple's farm and stayed there till harvest time in order to acquire more cuttings and seeds.

THE UNIVERSAL FLOOD (Guarao)

It rained torrentially and without stopping for many days, even months.

The waters flooded the forests and rose up over the tops of the trees, and they rose up until you couldn't even see the tops of hills because the waters had covered them completely.

The Indians didn't know what to do.

They looked all over for some solid spot where they could stay, but everything had been covered by the waters which still continued to rise. Only a few here and there stayed on top of the waters in their canoes.

The winds were wild.

As the rains continued pouring down torrentially without letting up a moment, even the canoes, no matter how hard they tried to keep them afloat, sank. Everyone was drowned.

Only one Indian was saved, a poor old man with a black beard in a canoe with his wife, three daughters, and their husbands.

The Indians rowed with all their might, going around in circles in the water; the torrent continued and they trembled with cold and the rain made them shut their eyes. Finally the old man saw something above the waters a long way off in the distance. It was the top of a tree covered with leaves and they rowed toward it in silence, keeping it in view.

You can imagine their surprise when they got closer and found out that what they had imagined was the top of a tree was actually the top of a mountain.

The Indians got out onto the dry land when the waters began to go down. Seeing that the whole rest of the world was under water, lots of small animals had come to the top of this mountain seeking refuge and it was filled with deer and cattle, rabbits, tapirs, and all kinds of game. The Indians lived off of those animals as long as the flood endured.

The Indians say that we all descended from that old man and his family, and that all the other Indians drowned because they were evil.

THE STORY OF THE GREAT FLOOD (*Yagua*)

Very long ago, Nawa, the river, started to swell. When the dry season came, the people saw that the river kept on rising. Then they knew that there would be a great flood. They left their houses, which were on the lowlands of the forests, and built new houses on the higher places. Still the water came and the forest got very wet. All the people walked in water up to their knees. They strung the hammocks high in the house, but still the river grew.

Iwaoi, who was a very clever man, went to hunt. He hunted for a long time. During this time he ate very little, but collected all the meat he hunted, and his wife smoked it so that it would keep. When Iwaoi finally returned from the hunt, he cut down many balsa trees and made a big and very strong raft. His wife collected all the manioc she could gather, and put it on the raft.

The people were now walking in water up to their necks.

41

Risacsun was a great shaman. He saw the raft that Iwaoi built and made evil magic against Iwaoi. Iwaoi died and Risacsun took the widow as his woman. Iwaoi's widow and Risacsun boarded the raft, but Risacsun killed some of them by magic, and then nobody tried any more.

The rainy season started, the water rose, and a great many of the people drowned. Others climbed trees, but most of these died there from hunger.

Risacsun was on the raft, and ate well and slept. The river rose, and one day the raft broke away from the tree to which it was tied. Risacsun and his wife tied all their bundles to the middle of the raft, as there was too much movement and shaking. They floated on the water for a very long time. Everything around them was under water, and even the treetops were overrun.

As Risacsun ate too much, all the food Iwaoi had collected was soon gone, and then they were hungry. The birds had no place to roost, so they came to the raft and sat down. Risacsun waited until the birds had fallen asleep, then killed them and ate well.

One day a heron came to roost and Risacsun saw that its feet were muddy with clay. Risacsun then knew that there was dry land near, so he steered the raft in the direction from which the heron had come, and found there was land covered with mud. Risacsun tied the raft to a tree and went onto the land. He found dry land, and with the aid of his wife built a house on it.

The rainy season ended, and the waters went down. Risacsun and his wife then walked many days until they got back to the place where they came from. There they found very few people, as most of them had died in the flood, but the manioc grew well in the mud that remained on the ground when the water receded. The people had a lot to eat, they grew very fat, and had many children.

III. THE GREAT DARK

THE GREAT DARK (*Warao*)

God had already existed for a long, long time. Darkness did not yet exist; it was always daylight. But there wasn't any night.

God had two gourd trees in his house and he didn't want the Indians to touch them. One day an Indian asked him, "Why don't you want us to touch them?" "Because we want to be able to see you," answered God. So they didn't touch them in front of God.

Later, when God wasn't looking, they ran and touched the gourd trees, and inside the trees there was some kind of sound —something like water flowing. And then it got dark and God asked, "Why did you touch them?"

The Indians, when they looked around, couldn't see anything. They couldn't see far, they couldn't see near, they couldn't see their own faces.

Two men went and touched the trees. From then on it was dark and they couldn't see anything. And God said: "Now how will night be? I will that you all sleep." And they slept; and after they had slept a long time they woke up and it was still dark. They went back to sleep again and the next time they woke up it had dawned. It was day and everything was fine, and God said: "Wouldn't it be a good idea to let day come, and then night and then day again?" And the Indians answered: "Very good." And so God willed it to happen that way. "From now on you will sleep and wake up," he said to the Indians. Which is why he made us the way he did. If they hadn't gone to sleep the way they did, there wouldn't be any such thing as darkness. If the Indians had obeyed God in the first place, it would always be day.

Now it's not that way. The sons of God had to do what they

did; which is why everything turned out bad. And so ends my story.

THE LONG NIGHT (*Toba-Pilagá*)

Three Versions

A.

Early in the morning people went to look for food. They saw a big cloud which was coming toward them and was covering the sun. Darkness fell over the earth. The people shut themselves in their huts, for they were afraid of going out where they could not see anything. Their huts were situated under an algarrobo tree. They had almost no food left and they cried out to those who had gone hunting, but the hunters did not return. After a month their food was exhausted. They started to eat their own children. Those who did not have any children were changed into animals. A man who had three children ate them all; afterwards he was transformed into a deer. A woman also became a deer. A man who had five children allowed only one to live. People with eight children kept four. At the end very few people remained. When daylight returned, most of the men had been changed into animals— jaguars, deer, and so forth. Day broke. Those who were still men covered their eyes with their hands. If they removed their hands from their eyes too soon, they ran away in the form of deer. Those who remained men and women were the ones who had kept their eyes shut a long time. Then they slowly started to look, first down, then around. The first one who looked began to cry like an animal. He was an animal. They had to look gradually if they wanted to remain men.

B.

Long ago there was night and then morning. The sun got up and set at dusk. It is said that it was covered by a cloud. The women and children went to look for food. Darkness arrived and put out the sun. Those who were gathering wood or collecting food shouted. They were hungry because there was no light, but constant darkness. When they had eaten all their food, they ate their children . . . Those with many children did not die. When the darkness ended, many had died. When light came, a man and his wife were transformed into deer, an old woman was changed into an anteater, and a man into an ostrich. For those who opened their eyes slowly, all was well. They remained people.

C.

Darkness came over the sky. At noon the sun was covered and the people beat trees and yelled, making all the noise they could. Those who had gone to pick up mistol (*Zizyphus mistol*) were lost; others who were fishing could not see to return home. In the evening the darkness moved toward the north. Twenty men were missing. They had been eaten by jaguars.

IV. POPULATING THE VOID

THE FIRST INHABITANTS OF THE EARTH
(*Guarao*)

In the beginning mankind lived above the clouds while the earth itself stayed uninhabited.

One day a powerful Guarao priest shot into the air the "arrow of his thought" which, when it fell, pierced the pavement of heaven. When he pulled it out sand began to fall through the hole which kept getting bigger and bigger, and through it they saw the earth with its mountains, its seas and rivers.

The hearts of the Indians beat excitedly when they saw it and they decided to send a "commission" to take a look at the earth and report back what they found.

One of the Indians let himself down on a rope made out of palm fibers and he "landed" on one of the islands in the delta of the Orinoco.

He explored the island thoroughly and then climbed back up above the clouds and reported the news:

"The earth is truly good. It is surrounded by water and full of fish, birds and palms."

"Let's go down and live there," said one of the other Indians.

And on the appointed day they all began to descend, one after the other, from heaven down a rope made especially for that particular descent, and the last one down was that particular priest who had first penetrated the pavement of heaven with the arrow of his thought.

His wife started down in front of him. She was in the last month of pregnancy and so it was hard for her to get through the hole in the heavenly pavement. All the efforts of her husband, the priest, were useless. All he could manage to push through the hole was one leg up to her thigh . . . and her leg and thigh together turned into seven stars, plugging up the opening into heaven.

This group of stars the Guaraos call No-Ji-Ja-Basi, and they make up the Pleiades or the Great Bear.

WHEN IT WAS DECIDED TO MAKE MAN
(*Maya*)

I.

Here, then, is the beginning of when it was decided to make man, and when what must enter into the flesh of man was sought.

And the Forefathers, the Creators and Makers, who were

46

called Tepeu and Gucumatz, said: "The time of dawn has come, let the work be finished, and let those who are to nourish and sustain us appear, the noble sons, the civilized vassals; let man appear, humanity, on the face of the earth." Thus they spoke.

They assembled, came together and held council in the darkness and in the night, then they sought and discussed, and here they reflected and thought. In this way their decisions came clearly to light and they found and discovered what must enter into the flesh of man.

It was just before the sun, the moon, and the stars appeared over the Creators and Makers.

From Paxil, from Cayalá, as they were called, came the yellow ears of corn and the white ears of corn.

These are the names of the animals which brought the food: yac (the mountain cat), utiú (the coyote), quel (a small parrot), and bob (the crow.). These four animals gave tidings of the yellow ears of corn and the white ears of corn, they told them that they should go to Paxil and they showed them the road to Paxil.

And thus they found the food, and this was what went into the flesh of created man, the made man; this was his blood; of this the blood of man was made. So the corn entered into the formation of man by the work of the Forefathers.

And in this way they were filled with joy, because they had found a beautiful land, full of pleasures, abundant in ears of yellow corn and ears of white corn, and abundant also in innumerable fruits and honey. There was an abundance of delicious food in those villages called Paxil and Cayalá. There were foods of every kind, small and large foods, small plants and large plants.

The animals showed them the road. And then grinding the yellow corn and the white corn, Xmucané made nine drinks, and from this food came the strength and the flesh, and with it they created the muscles and the strength of man. This the Forefathers did, Tepeu and Gucumatz, as they were called.

After that, they began to talk about the creation and the making of our first mother and father; of yellow corn and of white corn they made their flesh; of cornmeal dough they made the arms and the legs of man. Only dough of cornmeal went into the flesh of our first fathers, the four men, who were created.

2 .

These are the names of the first men who were created and formed: the first man was Balam-Quitzé; the second, Balam-Acab; the third, Mahucutah; and the fourth was Iqui-Balam.

These are the names of our first mothers and fathers.

It is said that they only were made and formed, they had no mother, they had no father. They were only called men. They were not born of woman, nor were they begotten by the Creator nor by the Maker, nor by the Forefathers. Only by a miracle, by means of incantation, were they created and made by the Creator, the Maker, the Forefathers, Tepeu and Gucumatz. And as they had the appearance of men, they were men; they talked, conversed, saw and heard, walked, grasped things; they were good and handsome men, and their figure was the figure of a man.

They were endowed with intelligence, they saw and instantly they could see far, they succeeded in seeing, they succeeded in knowing all that there is in the world. When they looked, instantly they saw all around them, and they contemplated in turn the arch of heaven and the round face of the earth.

All things hidden in the distance they saw without first having to move; at once they saw the world, and so, too, from where they were, they saw it.

Great was their wisdom; their sight reached to the forests, the rocks, the lakes, the seas, the mountains, and the valleys. In truth, they were admirable men, Balam-Quitzé, Balam-Acab, Mahucutah, and Iqui-Balam.

Then the Creator and the Maker asked them: "What do you think of your condition? Do you not see? Do you not hear? Are not your speech and manner of walking good? Look, then! Contemplate the world, look and see if the moun-

48

tains and the valleys appear! Try, then, to see!" they said to the four first men.

And immediately the four first men began to see all that was in the world. Then they gave thanks to the Creator and the Maker: "We really give you thanks, two and three times! We have been created, we have been given a mouth and a face, we speak, we hear, we think, and walk; we feel perfectly, and we know what is far and what is near. We also see the large and the small in the sky and on earth. We give you thanks, then, for having created us, oh, Creator and Maker! for having given us being, oh, our grandmother! oh, our grandfather!" they said, giving thanks for their creation and formation.

They were able to know all, and they examined the four corners, the four points of the arch of the sky and the round face of the earth.

But the Creator and the Maker did not hear this with pleasure. "It is not well what our creatures, our works, say; they know all, the large and the small," they said. And so the Forefathers held counsel again. "What shall we do with them now? Let their sight reach only to that which is near; let them see only a little of the face of the earth! It is not well what they say. Perchance, are they not by nature simple creatures of our making? Must they also be gods? And if they do not reproduce and multiply what will happen at dawn, when the sun rises? And what if they do not multiply?" So they spoke.

"Let us check a little their desires, because it is not well what we see. Must they perchance be the equals of ourselves, their Makers, who can see afar, who know all and see all?"

Thus spoke the Heart of Heaven, Huracán, Chipi-Caculhá, Raxa-Caculhá, Tepeu, Gucumatz, the Forefathers, Xpiyacoc, Xmucané, the Creator and the Maker. Thus they spoke, and immediately they changed the nature of their works, of their creatures.

Then the Heart of Heaven blew mist into their eyes, which clouded their sight as when a mirror is breathed upon. Their eyes were covered and they could see only what was close, only what was clear to them.

49

In this way the wisdom and all the knowledge of the four men, the origin and beginning of the Quiché race, were destroyed.

In this way were created and formed our grandfathers, our fathers, by the Heart of Heaven, the Heart of Earth.

3.

Then their wives had being, and their women were made. God himself made them carefully. And so, during sleep, they came, truly beautiful, their women, at the side of Balam-Quitzé, Balam-Acab, Mahucutah, and Iqui-Balam.

There were their women when they awakened, and instantly their hearts were filled with joy because of their wives.

Here are the names of their wives: Cahá-Paluna was the name of the wife of Balam-Quitzé; Chomihá was the wife of Balam-Acab; Tzununihá, the wife of Mahucutah; and Caquixahá was the name of the wife of Iqui-Balam. These are the names of their wives, who were distinguished women.

They conceived the men, of the small tribes and of the large tribes, and were the origin of us, the people of Quiché.

There were many priests and sacrificers; there were not only four, but those four were the Forefathers of us, the people of the Quiché.

The names of each one were different when they multiplied there in the East, and there were many names of the people: Tepeu, Olomán, Cohah, Quenech, Ahau, as they called those men there in the East, where they multiplied.

Many men were made and in the darkness they multiplied. Neither the sun nor the light had yet been made when they multiplied. All lived together, they existed in great number and walked there in the East.

Nevertheless, they did not sustain nor maintain their God; they only raised their faces to the sky, and they did not know why they had come as far as they did.

There they were then, in great number, the black men and the white men, men of many classes, men of many tongues, and it was wonderful to hear them.

There are generations in the world, there are country people, whose faces we do not see, who have no homes, they only wander through the small and large woodlands, like crazy people. So it is said scornfully of the people of the wood. So they said there, where they saw the rising of the sun.

The speech of all was the same. They did not invoke wood nor stone, and they remembered the word of the Creator and the Maker, the Heart of Heaven, the Heart of Earth.

In this manner they spoke, while they thought about the coming of the dawn. And they raised their prayers, those worshipers of the word of God, loving, obedient, and fearful, raising their faces to the sky when they asked for daughters and sons:

"Oh thou, Creator and Maker! Look at us, hear us! Do not leave us, do not forsake us, oh, God, who art in heaven and on earth, Heart of Heaven, Heart of Earth! Give us our descendants, our succession, as long as the sun shall move and there shall be light. Let it dawn; let the day come! Give us many good roads, flat roads! May the people have peace, much peace, and may they be happy; and give us good life and useful existence! Oh, thou Huracán, Chipi-Caculhá, Raxa-Caculhá, Chipi-Nanauac, Raxa-Nanauac, Voc, Hunahpú, Tepeu, Gucumatz, Alom, Qaholom, Xpiyacoc, Xmucané, grandmother of the sun, grandmother of the light, let there be dawn, and let the light come!"

Thus they spoke while they saw and invoked the coming of the sun, the arrival of day; and at the same time that they saw the rising of the sun, they contemplated the Morning Star, the Great Star, which comes ahead of the sun, that lights up the arch of the sky and the surface of the earth, and illuminates the steps of the men who had been created and made.

V. EMERGENCE

EMERGENCE MYTH (*Cubeo*)

The people came out and shed their anaconda skins. They went on to the place of the star ray rock, where they crossed over the milky waters. They came to the rock where the minnows pass and then to the rapids of the four channels. They came to the rock where Bwü, the Agouti, jumped across the rapids at the place of the pepper plants. They came to the place of Kwákü the Ancient, and then to the place of Borikakü the Ancient, at the place where he spilled the milk of the tree as he was drinking it. They came to the place of the worm people, and to the tree across a stream under which Bwü passed. They came to the rock of the jaguar, which, failing to scale the high bank, took fright at the sight of an Ancient and dashed into a tree, where it became transfixed. They came to the beach of the kumari plant, where an Ancient cut down a kumari bush and it turned to sand. They came to the place of the war club, where an Ancient, coming for a drink of water, met a kinsman. They quarreled and the Ancient clubbed his kinsman to death. They came to the place called "milk of the tree," where an Ancient passed out a calabash of palm tree milk. There, at the rock called "drinking milk," they drank it.

They came to the place of rushing waters, a whirlpool of milk, to the rapids of the dove, where a dove dropped into the water and turned into a rock. They came to the beach of the many small fish, and to the rock where the amari tree grew. They came to the point of the rock, and there the Ancients crossed over to reside. They stopped here and made pottery vessels. Then they crossed a hill and there they resided, at the hill of the hán han bird. They paused at the rocky hill of milk, the place where the hán han birds played. They came to the rock of the marúku monkey, where they killed a marúku and it turned into a rock. They came to the high bank which the Ancients looked upon with the rounded eyes of wonderment. They went upriver and they passed through the passage of spume, out into the black waters at the head of the creek. Here an Ancient made a burrow and left in it a calabash of milk. At this place, called "the trail of milk," they left the river to reside on a high hill at the bend where the Cuduiarí enters the Vaupés. They went on and came to the stream of blood where the waters are reddened by the rays of the sun; there the Ancients arrived and there they lived. From there they explored upriver and then came back.

They returned and drank milk, the cold milk at the rapids from which they had emerged. There they came to live, at the place where the waters were like milk, at the lake of the yellow clay. Then they went on until they came to the place of the namúkoriba fish and then they passed a rapids that was like an urn of milk. There they came upon their in-laws. They were already at the greasy creek, at the place of the closed-off creek. Above them was the whirlpool of Guassi and the fast black waters. There, at the whirlpool of the tree trunk, at the place of parrots' wings, they portaged overland and they quickly arrived at the place of the butterflies, at the lake shaped like a container for curare.

They came to the place of many grubs, which they cooked into a stew. They came to the high bank where the water rushes in with a sucking sound, to the place of the tangle of roots. They came to the place of the jaguars, to the place of the bark-cloth fishes, to the creek of the mimikü bird, and then to the place of the pupunha trees. From there they returned and they came to the creek of the wakúdjari and then to the bank of the yellow clay, and then to where the creek of the red fish is, and then to the hill of the haku fish. Then, at a place called hororákipúru, they came to the high bank of mud, and then to the place of the parrots. At the creek of the parrots they came upon the circular trench called "the circle of women" (because it is the women who dug this trench). There an Ancient who had been tied up by his enemies managed to free himself and escape. Now they continued up the creek to the place of the sweet potato, and they came to the creek of the wild peccary and then on to the lake of the birds and the bird place.

From there they went up the creek of the sweet waters to the place of the doves. And then they went to the place where maize grew and then to the sharp jaguar rock. Here an Ancient, sitting down on the rock, pierced his rectum and died. They went on to the place of the milk palm, to the garden of the jaguar. They came to where Kwünkwü, the Ancient, decided to settle down, Bahúkiwa, who decided that he did not care to be human and turned himself back into an anaconda.

The Ancients moved on to the place of the háku and puño fish, to the place of Wari the in-law, the hill of the woodpeckers, to the rocky rapids where Komóri the Ancient settled down, then to the parrot beak rock, then to the place of the sloth, then to the city of the bark-cloth trees, then to the rocks of the manioc graters, then to the place of the deer, and then to the place of the small parakeets, where Opómbibekü lived, a dwarf with an enormous penis. Finally, they went to the place of the stone people.

VI.   THE CITY IN THE SKY

THE HOUSE OF THE CREATOR (Guarao)

Above the white clouds there exists a huge city called Burejanokosebe or the "City of Vultures," built on top of a huge mountain.

On one of the sides of this mountain is the House of Wasps, a large, high house all filled with angry wasps the size of hummingbirds.

Next to the House of Wasps is a bonfire that never goes out and a large pan that boils on and on without ever stopping.

Higher up, quite far from the City of Vultures and the House of Wasps, is Nabaida a Kuai, the huge, blue Upper Sea.

On the shore of this Upper Sea there are many pretty, well-constructed houses; and it is to this place that good Indians go when they die.

On this side of the Upper Sea, close to the City of Vultures and the House of Wasps, there is a special place where all the souls that leave this world first arrive. It's like a gate, a door, but still there are a few houses there.

When the souls of the dead first get to this gate they look and see how rough or calm the water is, to see if it is possible to cross over to the other side where the pretty cities are. If it's stormy and the waves are big, the souls don't dare try to cross over but stay on this side where the smaller houses are. Many souls live on this side, the souls of those who couldn't get across the water to the other side where the house of Nonatu, the Creator, is.

The souls of bad Indians fall into the pan that is always, always boiling. If they just stick their noses a little bit out of the pan the wasps come and sting them to death.

VII. SKY FIRE

THE GREAT FIRE (Toba-Pilagá)

Two Versions

A.

The people were all sound asleep. It was midnight when an Indian noticed that the moon was taking on a reddish hue. He woke the others, "The moon is about to be eaten by an animal." The animals preying on the moon were jaguars, but these jaguars were spirits of the dead. The people shouted and yelled. They beat their wooden mortars like drums, they thrashed their dogs, and some shot at random with their guns. They were making as much noise as they could to scare the jaguars and force them to let go their prey. Fragments of the moon fell down upon the earth and started a big fire. From these fragments the entire earth caught on fire. The fire was so large that the people could not escape. Men and women ran to the lagoons covered with bulrushes. Those who were late were overtaken by the fire. The water was boiling, but not where the bulrushes grew. Those who were in places not covered with bulrushes died, and there most of the people were burned alive. After everything had been destroyed the fire stopped. Decayed corpses of children floated on the water. A big wind and a rainstorm broke out. The dead were changed into birds. The large·birds came out from corpses of adults, and small ones from the bodies of children.

B.

Long ago Moon was attacked and wounded, and thus the Great Fire originated. As soon as people noticed blood on Moon, they started to chant and to shout and they struck their dogs to make them bark. Men discharged their rifles in the hope that the monster which was preying on Moon would be frightened and relinquish his prey, but all this was of no avail. Moon was far away and his weapons broke because his spear and his club were carved of soft yuchan wood (*Chorisia insignis*) instead of hard palo mataco (*Achatocarpus praecox*). A fragment of Moon fell down and caused a fire. Everyone rushed to a lagoon where abundant bulrushes grew. As the fire was spreading over the surface of the earth burning the grass and the trees, people entered the lagoon. Those who had taken refuge among the bulrushes were saved, but those who had remained in the open places perished in the boiling water.

FIRE (*Apinaye*)

A man found an arara nest with two young birds in a cave in a high and vertical cliff. He took his little brother-in-law along, chopped down a tree, leaned it against the wall of rock, and bade the boy climb up to the nest and catch the young ones. The boy went up, but as soon as he stretched out his hand toward the young araras, the parent birds rushed at him with fierce screams, so that he got frightened and did not dare to grasp them. Then the man got angry, knocked the tree aside, and left.

The boy, unable to descend without the tree, remained sitting by the nest for five days. He nearly died of thirst and hunger. From time to time he would softly sing: "He, piednyo padkō!" (Oh, brother-in-law, give me some drink!). He was completely covered by the droppings of the araras and swallows that flew above him.

Then a jaguar came past the foot of the cliff. He saw the boy's shadow moving and rushed up to seize it, but only caught the air. He waited till the boy again moved and again tried to seize his shadow, but in vain. Then the boy spat down, and now the jaguar raised his head and saw him. "What are you doing up there?" he asked. The boy told about how his brother-in-law had left him. "What is in the hole?" asked the jaguar. "Young araras," answered the boy. "Then throw them down!" ordered the jaguar. The boy threw down one of them, which the jaguar immediately devoured. "Was there only one young one?" he then asked. "No," was the answer, "there is a second one." "Then, throw it down, too," commanded the jaguar again, and when the boy had obeyed he ate up the second one, too.

Then the jaguar brought the tree there, placed it against the rock, and asked the boy to step down. He began to climb down the trunk, but when quite close to the ground he got scared: "Dydma kod-kab id-kre" (You are going to eat me up), he cried and hurriedly climbed up again. "No," the jaguar quieted him, "come down, I'll give you water to drink." Three times the boy almost got down, and three times his fear of the jaguar drove him back. At last, however, he climbed down all the way.

The jaguar took him on his back and carried him to a creek. The boy drank till he remained lying there and fell asleep. At last the jaguar pinched his arm and awakened him. He washed the dirt off him and said that, having no children, he would take him home as his son.

In the jaguar's house a long jatobá trunk was lying, which was burning at one end. While the Indians of that time ate only flesh dried in the sun, the jaguar had quantities of roast game. "What is smoking there?" asked the boy. "That is fire," answered the jaguar. "What is fire?" asked the boy. "You will find out at night when it warms you," the jaguar explained. Then he gave roast meat to the boy, who ate till he fell asleep. He slept till midnight; then he woke up, ate again, and then again fell asleep.

Before daybreak the jaguar went hunting. The boy followed him some distance, then climbed a tree on the road, where he waited for the jaguar to return. But toward noon he got hungry, returned to the jaguar's house, and begged his wife for food. "What?" she shouted, turned round toward the boy and, pointing at her teeth, cried, "Look here!" The boy cried out from fear and ran back to the tree, where he waited for the jaguar, whom he told about the occurrence. The jaguar took him back home and scolded his wife: "I told you not to frighten my son!" His wife excused herself, saying she had been merely jesting.

The next morning the jaguar made a bow and arrow for the boy. He took him outside and told him to shoot at a termite nest. He did, and the arrow pierced the nest. Then the jaguar ordered him to kill his wife with the arrow if she threatened him again, but to make sure of his aim. Then he again went hunting.

At noon the boy got hungry again, went home, and asked the jaguar's wife for a piece of roast flesh. But instead of answering, she threatened him with her claws and teeth. Then he aimed at her, and now in alarm she cried, "Hold on! I'll give you to eat!" But the boy shot the arrow at her side so that it came out on the other. Then he ran off, while she sank down with a roar. For a while he heard her roaring, then nothing was to be heard.

He met the jaguar and told him he had killed his wife. "That does not matter," answered he. At home he gave the boy a lot of roast meat in addition and told him to follow along the creek, then he would be sure to reach his tribe. But he was to be on guard: if a rock or the aroeira tree called him, he should answer; but he was to keep still if he heard the gentle call of a rotten tree. In two days he was to return and fetch the fire.

The boy moved along the brook. After a while he heard the rock shout and answered. Then he heard the call of the aroeira and again answered. Then a rotten tree cried out, and the boy, forgetting the jaguar's warning, answered it too. That is why men are short-lived; if he had answered only the first two, they would enjoy as long life as the rocks and the aroeira trees.

After a while the boy again heard a cry and answered. It was Megalo-kamdu're (me-galo, image, shade, soul of dead, bull-roarer). He came up and asked the boy, "Whom are you calling?" "I am calling my father," answered he. "Am not I your father?" "No, my father looks quite differently, he has long hair." Then after a while Megalo-kamdu're went away

59

and returned after a while with long hair, pretending he was the boy's father. But the boy refused to recognize him, because his father had big earplugs. Again Megalo-kamdu're went away and soon after returned with what had been missing, but the boy still insisted he did not look like his father. "Are you not by chance Megalo-kamdu're?" he asked. Then the man seized him and wrestled with him till he was quite worn out, whereupon he put the boy into his big carrying basket and went home with his burden.

On the way Megalo-kamdu're noticed on a tree a flock of coatis (*Nasua socialis*). He set down his basket, shook the coatis down, killed them, and packed them all on top of the boy in the basket. Then he took this on his back again by means of a tumpline. Then the boy, who had somewhat recovered in the meantime, called to him to make a trail through the woods first so he could carry the load better. Megalo-kamdu're accepted the suggestion, set down his basket, and cleared the road. In the meantime the boy slipped out, laid a heavy stone on the bottom, packed the coatis on top, and hurried away.

Megalo-kamdu're, having finished his job, came back to his basket and picked it up, but found it still very heavy. But at last he got home with his burden. He set the basket down and said to his numerous children, "There, I have brought a nice little bird!" Then one child took out a coati, raised it and asked, "Is it this?" "No," answered Megalo-kamdu're. The child took out another, "This?" "No." Then he took out all of them, one by one, and got to the stone. "Now there is only a stone here!" "Then I must have lost it on the way," said Megalo-kamdu're and went back to look for it. But he found nothing, for the boy had long made his escape.

Back in his village, he told about his adventures with the jaguar and Megalo-kamdu're. "Now let us all fetch the fire so we need not eat raw food any more!" he concluded. Then various animals came to offer their help: first the jaho', but they sent him away because he was too weak; he was to run in the rear and extinguish what blaze fell off. The jacu' was also spurned; but the tapir was considered strong enough to carry the tree.

When the Indians, led by the boy, got to the jaguar's house, he gave them the fire. "I have adopted your son," he said to the boy's father. Then the tapir carried the burning log to the village. The jacu', running after him with the jaho', swallowed a live coal that had dropped and thus got his red throat.

VIII. THE SKY PEOPLE

SUN AND MOON (Apinaye)

First Sun came down to earth. Moon followed, but missed the spot. But when he went hunting the next morning, he saw Sun coming from afar. At once he stooped under a palm and crawled into the bush on all fours to hide. Sun followed his tracks and called to him to come out, asking whether by chance he was afraid of him. "No," answered Moon. He came out and excused himself, saying he had not known who it was.

Sun now told him he had already erected a hut by a brook and stored fruit there. He took Moon along, but made fun of him on the way for having hidden. Then Moon begged him not to speak of it any more, saying he had hidden because he was ashamed of missing the place agreed upon.

Sun went ahead. When he came past a wasp nest hanging from a branch above the road, he passed it quickly, stopped at some distance, and said to Moon, "Do take the gourd bottle there along!" But as soon as Moon touched the branch, the wasps pounced upon him and stung him all over his face. Wailing, he ran to his comrade: "That was no gourd bottle! Something has stung me." "What could it be?" asked Sun with a serious face, "perhaps a branch fell on you?" "No," lamented Moon, "it hurts very much!"

His eyes were all swollen from the wasps' stings so that he was unable to open them. Sun had to lead him like a blind man. But when they came to a tree lying transversely across the road, he jumped over it quickly, while Moon stumbled and fell. "Oh," said Sun, "I had not noticed the tree at all." Thus he acted three times; then Moon did not want to walk further. Sun had to carry him on his back, but he purposely pushed him against all the branches. Moon wailed, but Sun comforted him, saying he would get well sooner thereby. He pinched Moon's testicles, and when Moon cried out in alarm he soothed him saying he had probably squeezed his testes against his back. At the hut he set Moon down precisely in a thorny shrub. Moon jumped aside, wailing he had been stung, but Sun said he had only stepped on some old dry twigs. At home Sun then pulled the wasp stings out of Moon's skin with his fingernails and gave him medicine so that he was cured. He reserved one side of the house for him, inhabiting the other himself and leaving a space in the middle for dancing.

Sun went hunting. He heard the woodpeckers at work pecking honey out of the trees, went to the old woodpecker and begged for some honey. The woodpecker called him to come and gave him his share. He wore a brilliant red headdress, which, however, was somewhat worn. A little further on, however, Sun saw another woodpecker wearing a beautiful brand-new one. He went there and begged him, too, for honey, which he obtained. Then he further begged for the headdress. The woodpecker at first refused, but was persuaded by the other woodpeckers. Thus he bade Sun step under the tree and warned him not to drop the head ornament. Then he rolled it up and threw it down. As it dropped it was like real fire, but Sun caught it and threw it from one hand into the other till it had grown cold. At home he stored it in a lidded gourd, which he opened the next morning before going hunting to make sure the ornament was still there.

Moon observed this, and when Sun was gone he opened the vessel, took out the headdress, put it on, and danced with it in the house. Sun heard him dancing from afar as he came home and grew angry, scolding Moon, who excused himself, saying he liked the ornament so much.

The next morning he begged Sun to help him get a similar ornament and importuned him until he finally took him along. They went together to the spot where the woodpeckers were at work on the bees' nests and asked first for honey. At first Sun got his share and ate it. Then when Moon, too, received his share, Sun murmured to himself, "Bee bread! Bee bread!" Then Moon's honeycomb had not a drop of honey, only bee bread, about which he complained bitterly. Then Sun begged the woodpeckers for another headdress, and at last one of them was willing to part with his. Sun prepared to catch it, but Moon suspected him of wishing to keep this head ornament too, and insisted on catching it himself. Then Sun stepped aside, and Moon took his position under the tree. But when he saw the ornament dropping upon himself looking just like fire, he was afraid of grasping it and allowed it to drop to the ground. At once the entire grass of the steppe was aflame.

The two fled from the flames as fast as possible. Sun crawled into a fireproof clay wasp nest, hiding there until the fire was over. Moon, seeing him, also hurriedly crawled into a wasp nest, but this was of pasteboard so that the fire drove him out. He tried a second and a third nest with the same result, and only succeeded with a fourth in sheltering himself until the fire was over.

Sun went through the burnt steppe and called his comrade, who at last answered from afar. He came up and stood still at a distance, blackened by the smoke and with his hair singed off. Sun called him to come nearer and scolded him harshly. He struck him on the crown of his head with the palm of his hand so that he toppled over and remained seated on the ground. Weeping, he declared he would never more take out the headdress without permission.

Thereupon Sun proposed to search the burnt steppe for beast that had perished in the fire. The Sun and Moon found quantities of game and each put up a griddle for broiling it. All the slices on Sun's griddle, when opened, proved very fat. But when Moon cut his open, Sun murmured softly to himself, "Nothing but skin! Only skin!" And all were lean. Three times Moon came to his comrade's griddle to complain. Then the latter at last angrily took a slice of capybara from over the fire and threw it at Moon's belly, burning his skin so that he began to wail aloud. "Run to the creek," cried Sun, but when Moon got to the bank Sun murmured "Dry! Dry!" At once the creek dried up. Moon picked up mud in both hands and rubbed his scalded abdomen. Then he saw a turtle lying in the mud beside himself. In the meantime Sun said, "Water, return!" Soon the creek bed filled with water. But the turtle bit into Moon's scalded belly and clung fast. He wailed aloud and bitterly complained of his comrade's malice, but Sun answered that it had happened merely by mistake.

At last they carried the game home, and there each made a grate to spread out their slices of flesh anew. But Moon made no fire under his, so his flesh got full of maggots. When he had gone away, Sun went to his grate and inspected the damage. He took down a piece of a wild hog and broke it into fragments on the ground. Then all the slices turned into all species of furry game. When Moon got home, he found nothing but the destroyed griddle and the tracks of game. Then he seized a slice of ostrich flesh from Sun's grate and knocked it against the ground; and forthwith the remaining slices turned into all species of game birds.

Sun went to the creek, where he found a burity palm with ripe fruits and ate his fill of them. Thus his feces acquired a fine red color. When Moon noticed it, he immediately asked whence the red color came, he wanted his own feces to be equally fine. Sun suggested that he eat the blossoms of the pau d'arco tree on an empty stomach. Moon did so, but his feces got black. Then he sneaked after his comrade and caught him eating burity fruits. He went up and charged him with his lies, but Sun only answered he should come now and eat his fill, too. But as Moon was plucking the fruits, Sun murmured, "One side hard!" And all the fruits Moon tried were only somewhat ripe on one side, the other being hard and inedible. Then Moon, angered, hurled one fruit against the burity trunk, which then was still so low that standing up one could reach the fruits with one's hands. At once the trunk of the palm shot up to its present height, and similarly with the trunks of all other fruit trees, which until then had still been as low as shrubs. In vain Sun cried, "Enough! Enough!" They all grew so high that henceforth no one could reach the fruits with his hands. Sun was very much annoyed, but Moon declared that was precisely the right way, for when thirsty a person could discover water from a distance by the tall burity palms.

Sun went hunting and found a nest with two young dwarf parrots, which he took along in order to raise them at home. He selected the one with more plumage, giving the other to his mate. They fed the little birds after returning from the chase, took them on their fingers, and taught them to speak.

One day, while both were out hunting, one of the dwarf parrots said to the other, "I pity our father. When he comes home tired from the chase, he must first prepare food for himself and us. We will help him." Then both parrots turned into girls and prepared the meal. While one was working, the other kept watching by the entrance. As Sun and Moon were returning, they heard the pounding of a mortar from afar, but then suddenly it ceased. As they entered, they found the meal ready, but the two dwarf parrots, as usual, were perched on their beam. They found human tracks, but to their amazement, only in the house, not on the road. This continued for several days. At last Sun said to his comrade, "Let us hide on both sides of the house in the bush, and as soon as we hear the pounding in a mortar each of us shall run to one of the two doors." They went each to his ambush and heard laughing and talking indoors. As soon as they heard pounding, they ran in and simultaneously entered by the two doors. The girls dropped their pestles, lowered their heads and sat down. They were very beautiful and of light skin, and their hair extended to their knees. Moon wanted to address them, but Sun prohibited it and himself first addressed one of them: "Is it you, then, who have been preparing our food?" The girl laughed. "We were sorry for you because you had to work when you came home from hunting. So we turned human and prepared your meals." Sun said, "Now you shall forever remain human!" The girls replied, "Settle between yourselves who is to marry whom!" At once Sun said, "You are mine!" And Moon said to the other, "You are mine!" They made platform beds for themselves and their wives and lived together with them.

Now Sun thought, if they had women they ought to make a plantation. He staked out a bit of the woods and divided it into two sections, for himself and his comrade. Then he called the woodpecker Dya'i, the snail Duwu'dn, and the quartz Klid, to start with the clearing. But Moon had slunk after him, and hearing the sound of work in the woods, he took a cudgel and hurled it in that direction. At once the three stopped work forever.

Sun and Moon planted bottle gourds in their cleared plots, and when they were ripe, Sun chose a quiet, deep spot in the creek and made a path thither. Moon did likewise a little futher downstream. The next morning Sun went first to his plot; Moon, who was still sleeping, followed later. They got all gourds to the bank and then threw them into the water by pairs, and as soon as they came up they turned into a couple of human beings, who would sit down on the bridge crossing the creek. When Moon had made four human couples, Sun caused his next couple to be blind and lame. Moon went to his comrade and complained bitterly on seeing the handsome people Sun had made. But Sun said that was the way it should remain. Then Moon, too, uttered a magical formula, and several of Sun's children also developed defects. Thus both continued till there were no gourds left.

Then Sun said, "Let us lay out a village for our children. They looked for a high site and laid out a circle, which Sun divided by an E–W line, saying, "I put my children on the N side!" "And I put mine on the S side!" answered Moon. Thus the two moieties arose, Kol-ti and Kol-re. Then Sun asked, "Who shall rule the village?" Moon answered at once, "Kol-re!" But Sun said, "No, Kol-ti!" And so it was. That is why the Apinayé chiefs are still of the Kol-ti moiety. They married off their children and gave them good advice: "You must take pains to multiply! Fetch wasp larvae and let your wives smear them on their bodies, then you will have many children!"

Then Sun said to Moon: "Now our children are all married. Come, let us go!" "Yes," Moon agreed, "let us go! You shall light up for them by day, and I by night!" Then they assembled all the people in the plaza and Sun spoke: "My children! Now I am going off with my godchild!" And Moon replied, "Well, then, let us go, my godfather!" Then both rose to the sky.

THE SUN (*Guarao*)

The sun is a fire in the clouds that will never go out. Once upon a time there was a little insect that the Guaraos called Jokoji a-rani, who took a little fire in its beak and flew up into the sky and left the fire stuck on a cloud. The little bit of fire set the cloud on fire and formed the sun, and it has never gone out. When the Jokoji a-rani sings a lot the sun heats up, and when it stops singing the sun is hardly hot at all.

At night the sun gives neither light nor heat because Jokoji a-rani, the Sun's Mother, isn't singing.

THE SUN'S WIFE (*Guarao*)

The Sun has a wife up in the clouds, at the very top of the sky where the Sun gets to at noon.

This wife gets his food ready for him.

When the Sun arrives at the zenith he eats, rests, and, once rested, starts on his way again.

But the Sun's wife, who is faster than the Sun, runs on ahead of him, and when he "sets," she waits for him open-mouthed and swallows him. And that's why it gets dark at night—the Sun has been swallowed by his wife.

SUN, MOON, AND STARS (*Guarao*)

Two Indians got married and less than a year later the wife had a child. The following year she had her second child.

One day her husband, in a fit of bad humor, told her:

"I'm tired of you, I'm going to leave you."

"And where do you think you'll be going then?" she asked.

He refused to answer her and two days later he grabbed his weapons and disappeared.

Arriving at the bottom of a very, very tall tree, he climbed to the top and from there leaped up to the clouds. Two days later the Sun appeared in the sky; until then there hadn't been any Sun at all.

When his wife looked up in the sky and saw the Sun she said to herself:

"No doubt about it, that's my husband."

Then she found out that she was pregnant again and remembered that before he had left her husband had told her:

"After I've gone and you want to find out where I went, just ask the child inside you."

As her husband didn't return, one day she went out looking for him up in the mountains. When she found the tall, tall tree she wondered about it, and asked the baby in her womb:

"Did your father go up this tree?"

"Yes, Mother, this is the one he went up."

Only she didn't understand the baby's language and she asked him again. This time he didn't answer her.

There was an old woman sitting at the bottom of this tree and the Indian also asked her about her husband:

"Have you seen my husband around here?"

"Don't ask me," said the old lady, "ask the baby in your womb."

"But I already asked him twice. The first time I didn't understand what he said, and the second time he didn't want to answer me. Listen, old lady, tell me the truth or I'll cut off your head."

"Okay, woman, I'll tell you. Your husband climbed up this tree."

"And how did he get up?" asked the Indian.

"Look for yourself, woman, crawling, like a cat. He got to the top, and from the top he jumped up into the clouds, and the clouds carried him up even higher. Try it yourself and you'll see how the clouds and the wind will carry you up to where your husband is."

So the woman climbed the tree too, to the top, leaped up, and the wind carried her into the clouds. And the next night the Indians saw the Moon appear in the sky.

Seeing the Moon, everybody said:

"That's the woman who disappeared from her ranch a couple of days ago. Her husband is the Sun and she's the Moon."

The child she was carrying, as well as others that were born up in the skies, all became stars.

THE MOON'S DAUGHTERS (*Guarao*)

In the beginning the Moon was a young man with two grown unmarried sisters.

Late one night when he came home and found his sisters asleep, he lay down with them without their knowing.

When they woke up they asked, "Who could it have been?" without realizing that it had been their brother.

One day they decided to find out who was violating them, and so they took some caruto fruit and boiled it to make a strong dye. Before going to bed that night they dyed their chests with the dye so that whoever came that night would be stained with the dye.

The next morning they woke up and found their brother all stained with dye:

"Who would have guessed it," they said, "it was our own brother."

When he heard them complaining the young man was so filled with shame that he flew up into the air and became the Moon.

The Guaraos think that all women are the Moon's daughters. And because sometimes the Moon has a bloody tint to it, they think that it's really bloody. And seeing that all women are daughters of the Moon and the Moon drips blood, so they, too, should drip blood.

THE ADVENTURES OF THE SUN GOD
(*Guaraní-Mbyá*)

The future mother of our father Pa'i was a child who had just "become a woman." She was going through the forest with a lasso trying to catch partridges when she caught an owl. She kept it for a pet, but when she wanted to feed it crickets it refused to eat them, and wouldn't eat butterflies either; all it would eat was dried crusts of corn bread. Every night her owl slept at the head of her bed and softly waved its wings over the head of its mistress; which is how its mistress got pregnant. Then the owl became a "person," our father, Pa-pa Mirí . . . who wanted to leave the earth altogether.

"Let us go to my house," he said to his wife.

"I don't want to go; your wife would be angry, the true mother of your children who are in paradise," she answered and refused to go.

"No matter how late you are, bring me my son," he said, and he returned to paradise leaving his wife, the mother of Pa'i, behind on earth.

Then she followed the tracks of her husband, carrying her son in her womb . . .

The place where our grandmother first lived was called the Place of the Surging Waters. The Place of the Surging Waters is the center of the earth, the true center of the earth of our father Pa-pa Mirí.

In this place there grows a miraculous palm tree, and when this miraculous palm flowered for the first time the first bird to drink its nectar was the piri'yriki. The footprints of our grandmother are still preserved to this day exactly the way they were in the beginning; and if we believe, if we pray the right prayers, then we will be able to see them.

Pa'i saw a lily and when he saw it he said:

"Pick it so that I can play with it when we reach the outskirts of Pa-pa's paradise."

His mother picked it, but when she did a bumblebee bit her. She became angry and said:

"Wait, wait it's not the time to play with toys, wait until we get closer to paradise."

And he asked his mother about which road his father had taken, but she didn't, wouldn't answer; she kept walking and walking until finally she got to the House of the Primitive Beings.

In the House of the Primitive Beings the grandmother of the Primitive Beings told the travelers:

"You'd better keep on your way, my daughter, the young ones here are perverse and dangerous."

But still the mother of Pa'i didn't leave, and the grandmother covered her in a big jar. When her grandchildren arrived from the jungle they called out:

"Look, our grandmother has been hunting!"

To which the grandmother replied:

"What do you expect me to have hunted when you've been out all over the jungle and haven't caught a thing?"

When the old woman's youngest grandson came in, the one with the sharpest nose lifted up the edge of the pot, took a good deep sniff, and found the mother of our father Pa'i.

Finding her he killed her, and when he was disemboweling her he found Pa'i inside her and he told his grandmother:

"Roast him and we can eat him."

But the spike of the spit wouldn't penetrate Pa'i's skin, so he told his grandmother:

"Let's barbecue him."

But they couldn't barbecue Pa'i either, and so he said:

"Put him in a mortar and grind up his bones."

But it was impossible to break Pa'i's bones, so he suggested that she take him and dry him in the sun, "So he can be a household pet for me."

When Pa'i had dried out, he started looking for a bow.

"String my bow for him," said the grandmother of the Primitive Beings.

And they strung her bow, and with it Pa'i killed butterflies and brought them in great quantities to his grandmother; later, when he had gotten both bigger and smarter, he hunted birds for her and killed them in great quantities too.

Eventually the younger brother, with the sharpest sense of smell, became Pa'i's companion, and he, from the power of his own divinity, created the Future Moon from a kurupika'y leaf.

When they had become thoroughly at home in the ways of the jungle, their grandmother warned them:

"Don't ever climb that blue mountain."

"Why doesn't our grandmother want us to climb that blue mountain?"

And Future Moon answered, "If you want, let's go."

"In spite of everything," agreed Pa'i.

So they went from one side of the mountain to the other and killed lots of birds. The younger brother found a parrot, shot at it, but missed. The parrot spoke:

"You are feeding those who devoured your mother."

And when Pa'i heard this, he leaned on his bow and cried, then let loose all the birds he had captured, turned his brother into a jayru bird and came back to his grandmother with empty hands.

Now, once Pa'i knew that the Primitive Beings had devoured his mother, he laid a trap for them.

Along came the older brother and asked Pa'i what he was doing.

"Making a tiger trap," he answered.

"That won't kill them," said the older brother.

"Get in and let's see," said Pa'i, and the older brother got in and died, and in this way he killed those who had devoured his mother.

Then our father Pa'i created a fruit tree out of the Primitive

Beings, pretending to invite those who had devoured his mother to sample the fruit. He brought some of the fruit to his grandmother and then begged her to eat yet more: "Come on, come on to the tree itself and eat all you want."

So he created a river and placed a bridge over it, threw bark into the water and out of the bark created water monsters: snakes and water dogs, boa constrictors, all of which devoured the women of the Primitive Beings.

He made the Moon cross over the river and hang on the other end of the bridge, and he told his brother: "When everyone is over the middle of the river, turn the trunk of the bridge over. I'll screw up my nose as a signal."

But Pa'i screwed up his nose before the time had come, and his brother turned the bridge over while it was still empty. One of the Primitive Beings who would have been thrown into the water if he'd waited just a little longer, leaped safely to the bank of the river.

"Monster!" screamed Pa'i, infuriated at seeing one of those who had eaten his mother safe and sound on the bank of the river, "May you fornicate with your mother and may your seed extend over the whole surface of the earth. May you sleep and wake up changed, you who from this moment forward shall 'haunt' the banks and coasts of rivers!"

If things hadn't happened in this way, there would never have been jaguars.

Then Pa'i, instead of letting the tree he had created stand as it was, changed it and left behind only its "image." He turned it into the Food of Iguanas, the Eugenia Myrcianthes.

After all these things had happened, Pa'i gathered together his mother's bones and told his brother:

"Go and scare a partridge."

He went and scared a partridge and Pa'i's mother said: "Listen, the little one is scaring partridges!"

And Jachy, the little one, said: "Mother! Mother! I wanted to be suckled . . ."

And the bones of the mother fell down again. Pa'i told his brother: "Go further and scare another partridge." And when he did, his mother spoke again: "Listen, the little one is scaring

73

partridges!" And the brother again screamed out: "Mother! Mother!"

He tried to suckle again, and again she fell apart, and now that Pa'i saw how impossible it was to make his mother's bones come to life again, he threw them in the jungle: "Sleep a deep sleep and come back to life in some way like my mother!" So the bones became a weasel, which is why, to this very day, when a weasel falls in a trap and is killed, the Sun doesn't come out—because of remorse.

Pa'i Rete Kuaray and Jachyra continued following the banks of the river, one on each side. Jachyra, Moon, found a guavira. "What fruit is this?" he asked.

"What does it look like?" asked Pa'i, the Sun.

"It's a colored fruit with a little rounded part on each end."

"Well, then, it's a guaviju; don't eat it . . . you have to 'smoke' it before you can eat it."

They kept walking along the banks of the river and Moon came across an aguai tree, and he asked his brother what kind of fruit it bore. "What does it look like?" asked the brother.

"The fruit is large and yellow."

"So it's aguai," he answered. "Don't eat it raw; you have to cook it first, and when you do, save the seeds, put them in the fire and squeeze them with your bow."

So, he put the aguai seeds in the fire and pressed them with his bow, and when he did they exploded, scaring him out of his wits. Jumping out of the way, he jumped across the river, landing on the other side next to his brother.

Then they got to a place where Charia was fishing. Kuaray went under the water and pulled on Charia's hook. Charia thought it was a fish, pulled hard, and fell over backwards three times. Finally Charia pulled Luna out of the water, hit him over the head with a stick, and brought him back home to his wife as if he were a fish.

While Charia's wife was cooking Luna, along came Sun and Charia asked him, "How about some fish?"

"I don't want to eat," said Sun, "Just leave me a little polenta/corn pudding. Don't throw away the bones, though, I'll pick them up later."

74

Then, having gathered together the bones, Sun took and remade them into his younger brother and put a soul back in him . . .

To this day, the reason why Luna disappears is because Charia had once eaten him; and it is only because his brother had brought him back to life that he ever comes out again as a new Moon. In the same way, when Luna is eclipsed, it's because Charia is about to devour him; Luna is eclipsed in his own blood.

Luna sneaked into the house of his paternal aunt—with the intention of fornicating. Wanting to know who it was who had gotten into bed next to her, she daubed her fingers in resin and during the night, while he was trying to touch his way to her, she daubed his face all over with resin.

The next day Luna went to wash his face in order to clean off the resin. It didn't come off; nothing he could do would get it off. All he ended up doing was just dirtying his face more.

And, that's why to this day Luna has a dirty, stained face.

Then the Sun said to his younger brother, "Shoot an arrow into the center of the sky." Which he did. "Now shoot another arrow into the back notch of the first one." Which he did. And he kept shooting arrows so that they stuck in the back notches of the arrows already hanging from the sky—until the arrows finally hung down all the way to the earth.

"Now climb up the arrows," said Sun.

He climbed up easily, pulled out the first arrow, climbed through the hole and entered heaven/the sky. His bow, of course, is still up in the sky, the bow we call Moon-Boy/Rain-Bow. Then Luna caused it to rain in order to try to wash off the stains he'd gotten from his aunt. Which is why it still rains today; it's Luna still trying to wash off the stains.

Now our father Pa'i had children. He made his little boy wash his feet when he wanted fish, and after he'd washed, all the fish died and he gathered them up and ate them. Later along came Charia.

"Lend me your son," he said, "I want some fish too."

He took him into the forest, hit him on the head, and dragged him to the river; he killed our father's little son. Our father Pa'i was infuriated; he fought with Charia—first he knocked Charia down, then Charia knocked him down. Charia couldn't beat Sun and Sun got up again—which is why to this day we have eclipses.

Afterwards our father Pa'i made a hamper for his daughter. She gave it to Charia and he took and raped her on the road, destroying his penis. For this he punished her harshly, and when he was finished he turned himself into a basket.

One day our father Pa'i made a feathered headdress. He made it out of fire and gave it to Charia. Walking through a prairie he smelled something burning—the feather headdress he was wearing. He jumped into a swamp and when he came out it was still burning. He jumped into a river and when he came out the headdress was still burning, and he ran across the fields burning himself up.

When he had finally burned himself up entirely, Nande Ru Pa'i blew over the ashes and turned them into "mbariqui," gnats, mosquitoes, and horseflies.

Charia's stomach exploded and a piece of it, when it hit the ground, turned into the Tataupa Partridge, the Mistress of Fire.

Our father turned Charia's soul into Tupa' Reko'e—bogeys, perennial agents of destruction. One of our father Pa'i's daughters wanted to look.

"Don't look," said Nande Ru.

But she looked anyhow and died. She was the first person to ever die, and because of her death we still die today.

THE STORY OF THE MOON (*Tukano*)

Moon, Muyhu, had a sister named Méneri-Ya. Muyhu fell in love with his sister and every hour of the night all night long he made love to her. Muyhu's father was called Mení.

Méneri-Ya thought it was some other man who came to make love to her, and so she did what she wanted and enjoyed herself and afterwards asked herself, "Who could it be who's coming to make love to me?"

She got pregnant and afterwards said to herself, "Tonight I'm going to try to find out who my lover is." And so she covered herself all over with black ink, and when Muyhu came that night she hit him across the face with her hand in order to leave a mark on him so she could identify him the next day.

Then the next day she saw it was her own brother. Muyhu was all covered with black inkstains.

It was just beginning to dawn and Muyhu went outside and vomited as a kind of remedy, "medicine," cleansing . . . He looked at himself in the river as if it were a mirror, and when he saw his reflection he was ashamed and he tried to wash off the stains but couldn't. So he jumped into the river, sank down, and drowned; his life was over. His body was washed up on the beach and his corpse rotted and there was nothing left of him but bones.

Then along came Otsó, the Bat, and started to eat these bones when they cried out—and from this time on Otsó started to eat human flesh.

It was at this time that the Adyába, the Creators, arrived and went to Muyhu's father, Mení. Mení, "Where are the things that the Adyába made out of these stones?" because he didn't know he was talking to the Adyába.

At that precise moment Mení sent an owl to look for Muyhu, an owl who was a shaman—which, incidentally, is why the owls have their eyes open so wide. The owl looked all over for cocaine (coca) but he didn't find any—it was all gone, all used up.

Then the Adyába went upriver and found the decayed bones of Muyhu. There wasn't any cocaine there either. The Adyába threw a ball of cocaine on the ground in order to start it growing again and it became today. "Do you think that maybe we're shamans and it's our turn to eat this cocaine?"

After they'd created cocaine the Adyába went to sleep, and the next day they went to look at the bones again and they looked at them and touched them. They went home again and then came back again to make fine cocaine. Mení sent someone to look for the Adyába. There were three of them: the older, the middle and the younger. Mení sent them to look for Muyhu again and told them: "You three should look all over until you find the body." And they answered, "We're not shamans, but we'll go and look for it."

When they found the bones they asked the ants (mahína) to help put them back together. They tied them together and they took tobacco leaves and molded them around the bones to make a kind of tobacco body. Then they lit a "cigar" and blew the smoke over the tobacco body (like Adam), and the soul came back into the body and it came alive.

The first one formed the body, and the second one said, "You were the one who made love to his sister," and as he did the body came apart again. They reassembled it and covered the bones with tobacco again so that the soul would return . . .

They lit the tobacco again, blew it on the body and life returned. They got together an armful of palm branches (cumare) and handed them to Muyhu and they told him to "Just tell everyone that you've been out gathering rope palms and you're just coming back now." They also gave him a little black lizard to take back with him.

So when he returned home he threw the palms on the ground and acted like nothing odd had happened. But his sister, Méneri-Ya, didn't recognize him because he had a different body now, and when she came out and saw the lizard she asked, "What does it eat?" Nothing but caimo fruit," he answered, and as there was a caimo tree right there, he asked her to climb up and get the topmost seed on the tree for his "pet." Which she did. But instead of stopping at the top of the tree, she kept going right up into the sky—which is where she stayed.

"Come back down," Muyhu called after her, "you've got to suffer the same as me. Come on back, come on back." But she stayed in the sky.

Then along came Méneri-Ya's pet bird, Umú, looking for

Méneri-Ya. He didn't find her anywhere. He looked for her in the West, the North, the South, and the East, but she was nowhere to be found. He took a bath and went out looking again, came back, rebathed, and this time he saw in the reflection in the water that Méneri-Ya was up in the sky, and the minute he saw her he flew up to her screaming the whole way.

A bee was stinging Méneri-Ya when Umú got there, and Umú killed it. Méneri-Ya asked Umú, "Do you love me?" and he answered that yes, he did. So Umú came back home again, took a bath in a water jar, and carried water back to Méneri-Ya. He threw the water all over her because she was dying from lack of water. Once he threw water all over her, she was fine. Méneri-Ya sent Umú back down to earth again to get her leg ring, and she told him it was in a box where she kept her feathers. He came back down, found it and she put it on while Umú started weaving a rope of cumare fiber so that Méneri-Ya could come back down to earth too. She started down, but when she was halfway down the rope broke and she fell into a field, landed on her feet, and then walked back to her house.

Muyhu was in the house when he asked her, "Back again? So you could come back just like me?"

Muyhu sent her to bring back a jarful of water, but the water dried out and the jar stayed empty. Several times she went to fill the jar but it stayed empty. While Méneri-Ya was carrying the water, Muyhu and his father, Mení, escaped and the house disappeared and there was nothing left but a hill. Mení broke everything in the house so that nothing could tell Méneri-Ya where they'd gone. All that was left was a little piece of pottery. Méneri-Ya came laughing with the jar on her head, and when she got to where the house had been the little piece of pottery told her, "Your father ran away down this path."

She followed the path until it split into two. It was here that Mení had put a jar and a turkey-feathered ornament that looked like people, that even moved like people. Mení had told the ornament that if his daughter came crying it should show her the right way, if she was laughing it should show her the wrong way.

The jar saw Méneri-Ya coming from a long way off, laughing. When Méneri-Ya was far away she was still laughing, but when she came closer she started to cry and she asked the jar which way her father had gone. The jar showed her the wrong path—which was the road of the tigers . . . So she went down the tiger road but they weren't there, only their mother, Oako, the sister of Mení, who asked Méneri-Ya, "What did you come here for? I have sons, but they aren't people."

The tigers were clearing the fields, and when they came home in the afternoon with their hatchets on their shoulders they were singing the Song of the Hatchet. When they came in they asked their mother, "Have any people come?" And she answered, "Nobody." But when one of the tigers started looking in a mirror at his face, he saw Méneri-Ya hiding on a platform up in the rafters in a wicker basket and he told his mother, "You said nobody had come, but I can see her."

The tiger started to play a song on his mukuki (ocarina) that went: "What a pretty woman I see, what a pretty woman I see." And, she thought to herself, "What an ugly, ugly man," and she spit, and her saliva fell in the tiger's hand and he licked it up.

Then the tiger went out into the forest again to get the rest of his brothers. When they came back home she painted them all with the same kind of paint she'd painted herself when she'd "caught" her brother. They started to dance and she grabbed the oldest one, but he didn't like her. And it was the same with the second—and the third. None of them wanted to dance with her. Finally she came to the very youngest, and he danced with her.

The youngest tiger danced with a palm branch in his hand, a palm branch that was the handle of an ax. When he went along banging on the ground with the ax handle he smashed one of Méneri-Ya's toes and then ate it. They kept dancing, and he smashed another toe and he ate that too. Little by little he ate her all up and Méneri-Ya died and went to heaven.

Méneri-Ya was pregnant. The tigers had only eaten her flesh, but not her insides. The insides they gave to their

mother. They took them to the door and took out the liver
and the guts, and there inside was a little boy. "The tigers ate
your mother," she said, "and when you grow up they'll eat
you too." And the boy asked, "Don't I have a mother?" and
he jumped into the water.

The tigers came up to their mother and asked, "Who are
you talking to?" "Nobody," she answered, "I was just saying
to myself that we've got a lot of butter in the house." Only
they didn't believe her. "You're lying," they said. "You were
talking about something else."

So they grabbed a bunch of nets and started looking in the
water where the boy had jumped, but they didn't find any-
thing. One tiger stationed himself on the bank, another one
dove down into the water, figuring that no one could escape
them that way.

At last the tigers became "water spiders" and the boy be-
came a little frog (umáma) . . . The other tigers heard the
little frog singing and said, "There he is," and they went
looking for him and found him. But the boy had already left
the frog; he had just left enough "soul" in it to enable it to
keep singing, and he'd gone back under the water.

The boy was called Warími Sué and he kept going down,
down, down under the water until he got to a house on the
very bottom. A lot of Mení's children were already living
there—and he stayed with them. All of Mení's children went
swimming just outside the doorway of the underwater house
and he went along with them. Some of the other boys carried
him on their backs.

Next to the door there was a whole pineapple patch and
Warími started to play with the leaves. He started drawing on
the leaves with sticks. Which is how the art of writing began.

Warími didn't want to go inside the house. He preferred to
stay outside. And when the other boys swam with him he
alway kept his distance. They were all his older brothers, but
they didn't know him. They'd never seen him before.

Warími started to pester the other boys, playing, touching
their bodies—which nobody did there. He carried water to his

brothers but never went inside the house; he stayed outside drawing on the pineapple leaves. He caught butterflies and painted some of them all over with colors and then let them go. The ones he didn't paint he ate.

Then one day when he went swimming the other children told their fathers that a strange boy always came to swim with them and the fathers hid in the bushes in order to see who he was. Warími went swimming with the children and he pestered them, touched their breasts. He dug a hole on the beach into which he put the biggest girl in the bunch, and there she stayed, all buried over with sand. The other children urinated on top of her, and when they did a whole flight of butterflies suddenly appeared. When Warími saw so many butterflies he came to play with them and he'd hardly sat down and started to draw when the girl got up and grabbed him. Warími turned back into a tiny baby boy and started to cry and wouldn't stop. Mení heard him crying and said, "Now my daughter has a child." And he came to comfort the baby, to stop him from crying. The oldest daughter took him in her arms, but he still didn't stop. Then one of the children took a turn carrying him, but he didn't stop until he was in the arms of the youngest of them all. When he stopped she started to blow on him and painted him with red dye and blew on him again and anointed him with beeswax and then he was all right, the perfect picture of calm.

Since then they've always blown on babies when they're born. This youngest girl kept Warími as her son, and Mení thought that he was his own grandson. Which is why he blew on the fish, the cassava bread, and everything else which the girl ate so that nothing would hurt her. Which is why they still blow on mother's food. Mení even blew on the girl's milk so that it would be all right for the child. And the child grew very quickly. In one night he got big, the next day he started to crawl, the next day he started to walk and talk. They blew on everything he ate and he ate everything.

Now that he was bigger he went into the fields to play alone. He had a blowgun and some cotton from the fields and he played with the blowgun. Then he invented a palm-branch blowgun, and when flies came to bother his grandfather he shot them with darts, then grabbed them, ripped off their wings, and used them to make a feathered dance headdress.

When he was ten years old he had another blowgun of pachuwa wood and he used it to kill the green birds that came and ate seeds; but one day he shot a different kind of bird, not a green one but a blue, and it started to fly away, fell into the fields and turned into a man and started to scream, "Ay, ay, ay."

Later Warími went into the forest and got some wicker to make a basket. He hit Mení, his grandfather, on the back with a piece of it. Mení grabbed it and it turned into a crab. With what was left over he made lots of baskets—and a fish trap.

When one fish got trapped in the fish trap Mení grabbed it, ripped out its guts, and put it back in the water. Which is what he did with all the fish he caught.

Then Mení ran home to cook the fish. The aunts arrived, Mení ate some fish and left again. He crossed over the head-waters of the River Pirá and turned into a dove, but when he got an oar and rowed back down the river, he turned back into a person.

Warími begged him, "Take me in your canoe." But the canoe was full of baskets,[1] and there wasn't anyplace to sit down. So they put the baskets all together in a pile and Warími sat in the "pilot's" place and they started down the river.

Mení asked Warími, "What are you doing here anyhow? The tigers ate your mother a long time ago."

It was exactly midday at this moment and they were moving into the territory of the tigers. They got out of the canoe, found someone "waiting" for them, and cut off her head—it was the Mother of All Fish. She was very greasy and with her grease they made gasoline and a motor and attached the motor to the canoe. Warími told his grandfather not to look, and when he turned around he started the motor and left.

They ate all the fish they had with them and then came upon another little "farm." There they found a rotten, bitter

[1] Balayes—Actually "sieve-like" baskets used for winnowing.

pot of yucca-leaf soup. They went further up the river and they made the motors very small so they sounded far away, although they were very close.

Warími went to the place where the tigers were. Before he got there he caused it to get very hot. The tigers couldn't stand the heat and came out of their house, so when Warími arrived nobody saw him. In the middle of their house was a huge mirror that Warími polished, and he then stretched out singing in a hammock. The hammock broke and he fell down on top of a jar of cassava flour—which also broke.

Warími became a baby again. He hung a tiny little hammock in the corner and stretched out again and stayed very small so that when the tigers came back they didn't see him.

Then along came Koné, the woodpecker, and knocked on every post that held up the house. The tigers asked, "Who is this bird?" "It belongs to my grandson," said the grandfather.

"Where is that bitter man?" asked the tigers, and at that moment in came the tiger who had eaten Warími's mother. Warími was sitting next to his grandfather. The tiger knocked on Warími's head and sucked on his finger, which was bitter.

The next day Mení went back to his house and Warími stayed alone in the tigers' house. Warími went and cut down some sugarcane and called the tigers, telling them to eat it. They came to eat and Warími told a riddle to each tiger in order for them to forget about the sugarcane.

The big tiger who had eaten Méneri-Ya came along and sucked on the sugarcane but didn't eat any. Then he spit up some of Warími's mother's blood which Warími saw. He asked himself, "Can that be my mother's blood?"

Warími turned one tiger into a guinea pig, another one into a tapir, all of them into different kinds of animals. And they all ate each other up.

The tiger who had eaten Warími's mother was on the edge of the little farm and he killed a big armadillo, carried it to his home and ate it.

The tigers were playing with a top made out of Méneri-

Ya's head, and when the head said, "My won . . ." Warími kicked it with his foot.

One tiger told Warími to come and sleep in the same hammock with him—which he did. The tiger was barely asleep when Warími got out and put a bench in his place. The tiger woke up and ate the bench.

In the morning, as soon as they got up, everyone started playing with the top again. Warími gave it a kick and it fell right in the middle of a field of platanillos.[2]

Warími decided to go into the forest to pick mirití fruit where the tapirs lived. But suddenly he changed his mind and instead sent Water Spider. Together they took the mirití shells and put teeth on them and the shells turned into Pirana fish. The tapir came to eat the mirití fruit and Warími gave it a kick and kicked it into the river where the Pirana ate the tapir.

Afterwards he went to another little farm in order to tell them to make "corn liquor." At the other farm they were already making corn liquor for a fiesta. Warími went to the fiesta in order to sing the Song of the Hatchet—and the tigers sang along with him . . .

Afterwards they started to dance; and the next day the tigers decided to go to another farm carrying Méneri-Ya's head and they went out in a long row singing, "Now what's happening is that fish are eating tigers."

Then Warími made a bridge and when everyone was in the middle of it, he turned it over and the tigers fell into the water and were eaten by Pirana. One of the tigers, though, had one paw in the water and the other out, and the fish ate the one in the water and left him with only one paw. This was the tiger who had eaten Warími's mother.

Warími went to where his grandfather was, burned down the house, and left. Warími killed everyone and went and told his grandfather. These people were tigers and he killed them because they'd eaten his mother. Mení agreed with him, "Of

[2] Platanillos—A term applied to many different kinds of plants throughout Latin America. Plátano is banana. Perhaps the meaning here is to a banana-related plant. See F. J. Santamaria's *Diccionario General de Americanismos* (Mexico, 1942), II, pp. 500–1.

course you had to kill them," and Warími lied, "I didn't kill them," showing Mení his body full of self-inflicted wounds. And Mení said, "Let's go kill them." And the two of them went to see the tigers.

There were dead tigers everywhere and Warími made all kinds of marks in the dust with his foot so it looked like, instead of the two of them, a whole "army" had come to see the dead.

They got to a place where there once was a house and they looked and found a piece of stick that they once used to dance with and they started to play with this stick; they played to the East and they played to the West and to the North and the South and inside the earth and in the sky, and Hikániké came back down from heaven and told Mení, "Warími is the one who killed us."

Mení told Warími, "Don't come around here; go someplace else."

And he went all over, into the jungle to hunt and fish, and then he came back and ate and hung around, going from house to house, wherever there were people. Warími went to the jungle and met Watsóa, the Guansoco seed which had just fallen on the ground and was looking up while an animal kept eating away at it. The animal's name was Watsóa Wehéro.

"Hey, my friend, throw a seed down to me," Warími said, and Watsóa Wehéro made a ladder with a stick and told him, "Come on up." So Warími went up to eat the seed; but he'd barely gotten up into the tree when Watsóa Wehéro took away the ladder and left; Warími couldn't get down. For days and days he stayed up in the tree and there was no way for him to get down.

When Winter came the cranes arrived and Warími begged them, "Please, help me get down," but no one helped him. They told him that other people would be coming right away, people with dance headdresses, with cocaine, with tobacco you can breathe out through your nose. And when they did come they gave some to Warími and he blew it out through his nostrils. They came with dance feathers, and Warími didn't have any. They told him to make some wings with feathers, and he made them with cotton and looked just like a crane. They told him to try to fly, but he couldn't, so stayed on a branch . . . They gave him some tobacco and he blew it out through his nose and then he tried to fly again, and at last they all flew together and they went around flying and singing.

There was a place there where there was a trap just like a pair of scissors, and whoever tried to walk through it was killed. But Warími knew all about the trap and stuck a stick in it so that the scissors couldn't close and everyone could walk right through the blades without any problem.

They got to a "candle farm" and they couldn't get past the flames. Whoever tried to pass through the flames never made it through. Warími jumped right into the flames, it started to rain, and the rain put the flames out.

All kinds of different birds were flying along with them, ducks and coro-coros . . . whole flights of birds. And they were all going together to the house of Rumí-Kumú. When they got there, Rumí-Kumú gave them food, bread and fish.

As more and more people arrived, Rumí-Kumú asked them, "Is there anyone among you who is 'different'?" "No," they answered, "we're all the same." And he gave them all food.

Warími squatted down to eat peppers with the others; but he was hidden behind all the rest. He didn't take anything out of the pot, but people passed things to him. He ate a lot very quickly and he wanted to eat some more cassava bread. When the others took a piece of cassava off the round loaf it immediately filled in again and stayed a complete circle. But when Warími ate it started decreasing in size, and when Rumí-Kumú saw this he said, "Before, when I made cassava bread it never got used up; now it's disappearing, so there must be someone 'different' among us."

The next day they had a party for Rumí-Kumú, and they gave him some fish. These people sang the Song of the Scissors. They sang, it dawned, and they went back home. They left and Warími stayed alone in Rumí-Kumú's house. Then he took off his feathers.

Rumi-Kumú came along sweeping and when she saw

Warími she asked herself, "Isn't that an orphan there?" Warími was sleeping next to the door. He touched her body and she got frightened and said, "I knew that must be you there."

Later she went to her father's house. Her father, Rimáhinó, was sleeping. There were lots of stoves lit and Rumí-Kumú took a piece of clay pot in and heated it up and put it on her father's chest—but he didn't wake up. The second time she did this he woke up a little and she told him, "I came to bring you some food."

"Who's with you?" he answered. "Nobody," she said at first, and then admitted, "An orphan."

"He must be my grandson," said Rimáhinó. "Leave him with me so he can help me and light candles." So she left Warími with Rimáhinó and went home. Rimáhinó went to swim just outside the doorway. He had a machete in his hand. Afterwards he came and spit at the foot of each candle, and each one he spit at turned into a person.

"Okay, orphan, light a candle," Rimáhinó told Warími. There was so much smoke he couldn't even see. The people who had emerged from the spit were answering. Rimáhinó went around hitting the air. Warími decided it was time to turn himself into a flea and he started biting Rimáhinó in the back. Rimáhinó hit himself in the back, grabbed the flea, and popped it into his mouth.

The flea got into Rimáhinó's stomach in order to steal poison and Rimáhinó couldn't kill it. Rimáhinó closed his mouth and the flea couldn't get out. It climbed up into his nose, but he put his hand over it. Then the flea made Rimáhinó sneeze and managed to get out. It escaped with the poison, ran away, and wanted to drink a little.

Warími then changed into a bird. He flew up into a tree and started to sing. Rimáhinó, thinking it was one of his birds, left it alone. After a while Warími changed again, this time into a parrot, and went to where Rumí-Kumú was. Rumí-Kumú was in the fields planting yucca. Warími as a parrot flew down low over her. She wanted to hit him, but he was too fast for her. She realized that he was the one she'd left with her father and that he'd escaped. Warími turned back into a person again and he went to where the Mother of the Serpents was. Warími put poison on the serpents' food in order to kill them. There was another Serpent Mother who was pregnant. Warími cut down a very big palm nut that fell on top of her and killed her.

Then he went down the road until he split into two. There at the junction were two snakes. Warími turned himself into a butterfly and flew over them and saw that there was no way that he could kill them, so he borrowed a blowgun from Eagle, made a dart, poisoned it, and then killed them. At least he killed one of them, the one with the four noses (Gahóabo); the other one, the crocodilish one, got away by jumping into the water . . . and to this day crocodiles still hide in the water.

Warími kept walking and finally got to where his grandmother—Mení's wife—was. She was crying, looking all over for her grandson. It was spring, the season of the Chontaduro palm, and she was up in the trees picking Chontaduro fruit. Warími turned himself into a bird again, flew up into a Chontaduro palm, and started to sing. The old lady didn't believe that it was him and said, "Damned bird, coming here to sing when my grandson isn't here."

Then Warími asked her to come down from the palm tree, and he put a scorpion into one of the palm fruits so that when his grandmother picked it the scorpion bit her. Warími turned himself into a person again and said hello to his grandmother. She answered, "I'm here, my grandson, a scorpion just bit me." Warími took the scorpion off of her and she got better.

Warími was cooking poison when Yúo, the wife of Green Lizard, came out and said, "You're always cooking poison." Warími became disgusted with her and killed her with an "arrow" made of poison foam.

He kept cooking poison and stuck his finger in it, tasted a little—and died. Then many snakes came to steal the poison—which is why snakes to this day are still poisonous.

Later Warími came back to life again and scared the snakes. When he'd finished cooking he got a little tipsy in order to kill more people, and he went to all the different tribes.

Ramé, the Eagle, ate everyone who was alive.

A little bee went and flew into the eagle's nostrils to see what parts were the most delicate in order to figure out how it would be easiest to kill the eagle. Then he came out and told Warími. Warími went to kill the eagle. He climbed up on top of a mountain and shot. The eagle was on another mountain. Warími got inside the blowgun itself.

Then he went back to where his grandmother was and had some Chontaduro beer. After it was wounded, the eagle started to bleed and the blood turned into a kind of cane called Ríiyá. Still bleeding, it flew to the top of another mountain and its blood formed another cane of sugar . . . the eagle kept bleeding and lots of fish ate the blood, which is why those fishes have so much trouble nowadays . . . When the eagle died lots of other people came to "smoke." The eagle was very, very large and went all over the world and then came back home—which was where he died. When he died they took feathers from his face for the sacred songs and dances. Which is why there are so many singers here. The eagle showed them how to sing.

THE STORY OF THE STARS (Tukano)

A moon of this earth went to the door of his house and laid down on the stone threshold. The stars—who were women—came down and took him back with them to the sky. When they got up in the sky they called him "Cousin" and they had a party and got all dressed up in feathers. The man didn't dance, but the stars did—and they were all the same size. Afterwards, the stars plowed up a whole bunch of big fields in one night. They ate—four little jars of yagé, a little cocaine, and a pot of mingao.

Afterwards the man returned to the earth and had a star for a wife. When he descended they gave him a "rattle spear" and told him, "Carry this spear with you and when you plow a field; never plow a little, always plow a lot. First clear the land and then plant coca (cocaine) and tobacco. After you've cleared the land, put this spear in the middle of the field and leave it there overnight."

At four in the afternoon the people of this earth started to plow the fields. The spear was strong as a machete. It helped a lot, did a lot of work. At three in the morning they were finished.

Later, when the sun was up, the star-man went to look at the field to see if it was finished—and it was . . . everything was already grown. He retrieved his stick and the pots of mingao, tobacco, and cocaine and went home. He went home because it was day; but it was night for them and they slept.

The following year he did exactly the same: plowed up a big field with his spear, planted mingao, cocaine, and yagé, started at three in the morning, finished at five, picked the crop, and returned home.

In summer the stars came and poisoned the rivers and caught and ate a lot of fish at night—which was their day. Only the star-man was sleeping.

The next year he did the same. He plowed at night and finished at five in the morning. Then the third year he made the fields just a little smaller, and the year after that a little smaller still. He planted mingao, yagé, and tobacco, and stuck the spear in the middle of the fields.

Everyone started to work at three in the morning, but they got lazy, stopped, and refused to move. Afterwards the star-man went to see how big the field was, and all that was there was yagé, mingao, tobacco, and a little jar. The workers were stars and they had left and taken the spear with them. After he lost the spear he had to plow up everything alone—he suffered because it was such hard work.

EARTH, SKY, AND WATER (Maya)

I am going to tell a story which I heard told long ago. The old people used to tell about the world where we live. They said that under the—world which we live on, farther down, they say that there is just water.

And they say that under the water there is another place. Like here. And they say that that place is filled with people called evil. And they say that that place is the home of the evil ones. Because they say that that place is just like a town, that it is large and filled with many people, but they say that they are evil, that the evil are "different."

They say that when the sun sets here, and the night grows dark, that in that place it is growing light, and things are becoming visible. And here it is dark, and that when the sun passes through that place, over the heads of those men, that its heat is stronger.

And they say that those people don't know what to do because of the heat of the sun. They think that there is another place, under the earth where we live, and the sun passes there when it is dark here.

Well, we think that there is another sky below. And they say that that place is the place called hell. Because they say that the place which is called hell, that there go all those who have committed sins. All who know how to curse, who have killed, who have stabbed, have made sport of their fellows, who have thought lies and all sins, they say they alone go to fill up that place. They say that that is the place, hell, where there is a fire lit, and that it doesn't go out. They say that there go all who die.

But their beliefs about the place, hell, are not all the same. There are those who say that some who die in a year, the angels come to take them out of that fire. And there are some who say that it is a resting-place from which there is never an exit for those who die who have sinned greatly, because they say that there is another place where those who were killed come, and those who died in water, those who fell from tree branches, those who fell into caves, they say the place where they stay is separate. Because they did not meet an ordinary death, and that the place where they stay is separate. They say that that place is where all the people who were sinners stay.

They say that when the man dies who kills or if he has stabbed someone, when he comes there he is shown the head of the man whom he killed, or if he has stabbed someone they say that he is shown the blood which he drew, when he arrives.

And they say that there are some who hurt their friends, so

they die; they say that there are those who die by what their
friends do, who are witches, and when they die, they go to
rest among the evil ones there. And when they arrive, on the
day they die, those whom they killed are taken out.

And they say that those who know how to hurt or are
witches, they say that when they die, they are tied over the
fire, and there they hang, for all time, and that there is never a
payment for all they have done. There they hang, with smoke
in their eyes. From the fire where they are hanging. They say
that those who know how to tell lies hang over the fire, and
their tongues are roasted by the fire.

Because they say that a great sea is under the world. There
is a white sea, and there is a red sea. They say that there is a
sea like milk, that we float on a sea.

And that is why they used to say that if the world which
we live in would be made to flex suddenly, and go into the
water, we would be finished. Because they say that there is
just water under the earth. And we are floating on the water.

They say that where the edge of the world remains, which
we live on, and at the edge, they say, there is just water which
is called the sea of tar. They say that it is called the sea of tar
because it is where the edges of the world and sky join to-
gether. And nobody goes there, neither ships nor planes can
go there.

At the edge of the world at the edge of the sea, there live
the angels. And if any of the earth-dwelling people come
there, they are immediately struck with lightning by the an-
gels, and they bring down any plane that happens to fly along,
because they say that there is a sealed heaven, which we call
the sky, and the earth. Because they say that the world and the
sky are like the back of a wasp, coming together at a joint.

So the sky, above, which we see here, they say is mountains.
Green. And farther up, beyond the heavens above, there is a
place, a town like we see here; they say that there live all who
die here and that there they go to live in that place. And far-
ther up there is another place, that there live the gods.

That is why long ago when there were those who prayed to
God, they said, "Where you are standing, where you live be-

yond the heavens," because they believed that the sky which we see above is not the dwelling-place of God, but that the dwelling-place of God is farther up. And that is why they thought thus, that below there is another place where there is a sea.

And they say that where the sky is joined to the world which we live in, and where everything is we know, that the world joins together. They used to say that Our Father God lives way beyond the sky above and that all the places, the sea and the world where we live, are held by the sole of his foot, and that is why they say that if it flexes that the world will immediately be flattened with us and we will be destroyed.

Because they say that the world is just floating with us, like foam floats on the water when we are cooking, and we are just floating, rippling on the water; they say that so, too, the world is just floating, rippling with us, and held by Our Father God with his foot. And that if he makes it flex with us, then immediately this world will be consumed with us, and the water will rise over the earth, until it becomes sea all over this earth.

They say that the sea of tar which we know where the sky is put together with the world, glistens beautifully. That is why some say that it is the sea of tar and some say it is the crystal sea. Because they say that its surface glistens beautifully.

And they used to tell of the dry wind which blows over the earth here. And it doesn't rise to a very high altitude. They say that farther above there is another wind which blows that does not let it pass above the wind that blows over the earth. Because the wind which blows here is bad. Not sacred. Because the wind here blows everything over the earth and whatever is on the earth, everything bad that there is on the earth is blown by it. But they say that the wind which lies farther up does not let the evil pass above. And they say that farther up, there is another wind lying, that that wind is called the sacred wind, because there is no evil in it.

The wind which lies in the sky is called the sacred wind, and there is no evil in it. Because the sky is supported by it.

And they say that the wind which lies above, which is stuck

94

to the sky cuts off the fire of the sky. Because if it weren't for that wind, this world would be burned up by the fires of the sky, which pass above. Because the sun which we see above is fire. And if there were not that wind to cut it off, then the world would burn up.

That is why the wind always blows down here, because the wind which blows here is a great shelter, and it was left by God to blow in front of us, and to cool the earth, so that it does not catch fire, and so mankind does not die from the fires of the sky. That is why they say that the dry wind which blows here at no time goes away. Because the dry wind lies separate all the time, separate from the wind which comes with the rain.

The wind which comes with the rain, is the protection of the one which brings the rain, which is raised up by the angels into the sky. But the dry wind which lies all the time blows on us so we are not burned by the fires of the sky.

Long ago the world was destroyed with mankind. Because there was an angel and they say that the angel did not obey his father, who is Our Father, that he wanted to cause a quake, shake the braces of the world, or its cornerposts.

They say that that angel, when he decided to shake the cornerposts of the world, that the world immediately went into the water, and all the world with the human beings was engulfed and the world was destroyed.

But they say that one time, when Our Father God was tired, here and there he formed the world, with people on it. Then God destroyed mankind and said to them, "You do not leave the human beings, whom I have raised and whom I formed on the earth, where they are living. And you, you flooded them everywhere. Now fix them up, since you had the power to destroy them, so you have the power to fix them up."

They say that those angels got up and that they hardly knew what they were doing. They went and got earth and poured it on the water, and they say that that earth fell and fell, and dissolved, and went into the water, and you couldn't see where it was going. And they were berated by Our Father God; he said to them, "What is this? You have the power to destroy, but to make again, this you cannot do!" Then they say that there came another angel, whose name was San Raimundo.

The angel San Reimundo went and took a little earth and dropped it on the water. And they say that as that earth fell on the water, it swirled all over the water, and the water was covered over by it, and it immediately began to harden like foam on the water. They say that it went on floating on the water, until it thickened all the water of the sea; the world came back again and the people increased upon it; they say that from that day, the world has never been destroyed again with mankind. And that is why they say that today there are many people.

They say that that destroyer of people, some of those he destroyed turned completely into fish, that fish appeared because people were destroyed everywhere, and those people who were destroyed, and the world with them, were covered by the water and became fish. Fish were people.

There were some who used to tell that the corners of the world had cornerposts. And they say that at those cornerposts were angels standing, holding them. They say that when the angels shook the cornerposts of the world, it quaked all over the earth and that they were going to destroy it.

But they were not given permission by Our Father God above, but they were tired, standing there, holding on to the cornerposts of the world. And they wanted to destroy the world. But they were not given permission by Our Father God to destroy it, because Our Father God loves us, the human beings, and will not destroy us.

There was another little old man who began to say that the world here that we live on and curves around, that when it is dark here, they say that the sun above passes underneath. And in that world it rises. And when it passes below the other world, then we see the sun above.

He began to be asked, "How come we don't feel it when we are turned over?" He used to say, "How are we going to feel that we are sinning? We don't know! And such is the power of God over us. And that is why we don't know when we are turned upside down."

Some used to say that the world is turning with us. They used to say that the sun which passes above is like a train with a light.

They used to say that what there is today in the world we see—the lights that are in the towns, that it was God who gave to the people on this earth the knowledge to make them, because that's the way it is where God lives, and that the lights in the sky are electric lights. Because it is a town.

IX. "TAMING"/"FORMALIZING" THE SACRED

HYMN TO VIRACOCHA (*Inca*)

Root of all being, Viracocha,
God always near,
Lord of Dazzling Vestments,
God who governs and preserves,
Who creates by merely saying
LET THERE BE MAN
LET THERE BE WOMAN,
May I whom you created
Live free and without danger.

Where shall I find thee,
Beyond or in this world,
In the middle of clouds
Or in the middle of shadows?

Listen to me,
Respond to me,
Let me live for many days
Until my hair is white,
Lift me up,
Take me in your arms,
And in my weariness
Help me
Wherever you might be,
Father Viracocha.

INCA PRAYER FOR ENLIGHTENMENT

Imminent Creator,
Root of Being, Viracocha,
Light of the world,
God of life and death,
Viracocha of the rocks,
Viracocha of rituals,
Imminent Creator,
Who gives the gift of speech
And unites all men
So that they might learn
With the force of your light,
Wherever they may go.

HYMN TO THE SUN (Inca)

Viracocha,
You who say,
"Let there be day,

and let there be night,"
You who say,
"Let there be light,
and it dawns."
Make your son, the day,
follow you across the sky,
surrounded by peace and well-being,
so that his light may help
man, whom you created.
Father Viracocha,
Inca of the day,
Together with the Moon
Give your light
In peace and good fortune,
To man, your servant,
Fed by you,
Freed from evil,
Maintained in
Peace and well-being.

PRAYER FOR THE INCA

Oh, Viracocha,
Viracocha, root of being,
You who instill new life into creation,
Viracocha,
Creator Viracocha,
Preserve the Inca
You who created him
In the power of his monarchy,
Preserve him in peace and
well-being.

May his vassals be numberless
And his enemies defeated
Until the end of time.

May you preserve your sun
And the people of his world,
May his joy
Last forever.

HYMN OF THE INCA RUKA

Still come, Oh, Lord,
Omniscient Lord of Heaven and Earth,
Creator of all that exists,
The beginning of all things.

Creator of man,
I will worship you ten times
With my unveiled eyes
Fastened on you.

I shall humiliate myself at your feet;
Look at me.
All the rivers
And waterfalls
And birds
Are filled with joy.

Never let me walk alone;
And above all
Help me in my cry
With all the strength of your voice
That I may carry out your intentions.

It is enough that we remember you
To give us joy
To honor us
And going thus sheltered in the thought of you
Numberless
We invoke your name.

THE INCA WASKAR PRAYS TO THE WAK'AS

Troublemaking Tempter,
Savage and adverse Demon,
In my hours of danger
Evil-doing
And perversion,
You, adversary
Of mighty Cuzco,
I adore.
With my total being,
With all my energies,
In fire and festival
I sacrifice all to You,
Lord of Thieves.

Perhaps you are he
Who the rabid enemy of the
Supreme Creator has
Sent to tempt us.
This is how I, my children and my
Grandchildren have always spoken to you,
You Powers.

This submissive servant
Of Viracocha, the
Light of the World,
Always has detested
You All.

PRAYER TO THE MOTHER OF THE GODS
(*Aztec*)

Yellow flowers open wide:
It is Our Mother, She of the Masked Face.

—You who have come from Tamoanchan.
Yellow are your flowers:
It is Our Mother, She of the Masked Face!
—You who have come from Tamoanchan.
You whose flowers are white.
It is Our Father, She of the Masked Face.
—You who have come from Tamoanchan

The Goddess is atop the round cactus,
Our Mother, Obsidian Butterfly.
See her in the Spring Fields
Nourished by the hearts of deers.
It is Our Mother, the Queen of the Earth,
Adorned with new clay and new feathers.
From the four quarters they break lances:
She is transformed into a deer.
Over the stony ground Xiuhnelli and Mimich
Come to see you.

MOTHER MOON (*Inca*)

Moon, Queen, and Mother,
We weep,
We suffer
For the bounty of your waters,
For the love of your rains.

The saddest of your children
Cries to you
Out of hunger
Out of thirst.

Father, Lord of the World,
Where are you,
In Heaven,
On the Earth,

Or on some other close-by world?
Bestow your rains on me,
Your servant
Who implores you.

HYMN TO THE WORLD TREE ("Wanka")— (Inca)

You were shade,
Life-road and
Torrent of Life-Water,
My heart nested in your branches,
My joy flowered in your shadow.
How is it possible for you to go so alone?
Won't you come back to open my eyes?

Why do you have to leave, leaving me
Without even opening your lips?
Where shall I find shade now?
What water will sing to me?

How can you have left me so alone?
The world will be a desert for me now.

LACADONE PRAYERS FROM CHIAPAS (Maya)

*1. A Game of Bow and Arrows Offered to the Gods When a
    Boy Reaches Puberty.*

Take me, oh Lord,
To redden your bow and sheaf of arrows.
Look at my son's bow and arrows,
When he grows
He will give you an offering of paper,
Oh, my Lord.

2. *Eclipse of the Sun.*

Oh, most excellent Lord,
Do not permit this fire to disappear.
Let Thy heat burst forth and
I will fulfill my duties to you,
Oh most excellent Lord.
I have not strayed, oh Lord,
I am not tied to anything,
Not even to my own family,
Oh Lord.

3. *Evoking the Name of the God Whose Presence Is Desired.*

I do this, I move my hands for him whose name is in the sky,
For him, whose name is in my hand.
Do not allow a false name in my hand.
Take me, receive me, give me your name,
Do not permit a false name in my hand.
For him whose name is in the sky, in the sky-house,
I say his name with my hand,
I say his name in the sky.
Do not permit my hand to lie.
In the sky-house tell me your name.
In the sky-house receive my spirit.
Take me.
Within is the trunk, the root of (here you say the name of the
    god whose presence is desired) . . .
For him, I speak his word with my hand.
May my hand not disappear.
It speaks true.
He is finishing his word here in my hand.
He shall elevate it if it is well said.
He finishes his word in my hand.

4. *Guessing the Name of the Offering the Gods Want.*

An offering of Pozole[1] if you want it, oh Lord.
An offering of Pozole if you desire it, oh Lord.
Something that will be your gift if you want it, oh Lord.
What do you want?
An offering of Pozole?
What do you want?
An offering of Pozole?
Arise, awake, come forth in vigor.
I will make my offering of Pozole for you.

5. *A Gift of Beans Burned in the Name of the Gods.*

Here are the first beans!
I give them to you, oh Lord.
I shall eat them.

6. *An Offering of Pozole.*

My offering of Pozole is for you, oh Father!
In front of you I empty, I again pour my Pozole into your
    mouth,
For your well-being,
So you will come and bless my children,
So that you will descend from above.
Wait a moment to drink my offering.
My offering is for you, oh Father.
I give it to you so that you may offer it to the Father.
My offering is for you, oh Father,
I offer it anew before you, for you, for your happiness.
Take it, it is for you.
Take it, it is for you, it is your offering.
Take it and give joy to my children.
Take it and give me joy.
I alone sacrifice to you.

[1] Pozole—Corn liquor.

7. An Offering of Pozole Offered to the Fires of Usucún.

I empty my cup, I pour my offering into your mouth, Usucún,
Oh Lord,
I give you my offering of Pozole.

*8. An Offering of Pozole Made to the East of the Sacred
    Fields.*

This is the most important part of my offering,
For you, oh Lord.
It is for the good of my children, oh my Lord.
It is for the good of the spirit of my wife.
Eat and drink,
Accept this offering of Pozole, it is for you,
It is your offering.

9. Palm Leaves Distributed to the Participants in the Rite.

Receive these leaves,
Oh heat of fire,
They are yours.
I am going to clean your
Gifts.

10. Palm Leaves Held Over the Smoke of Burning Incense.

Before you I inhale your smoke,
Which is why I am well.
I enjoy life.
I perform sacrifice to you.
Neither snake nor tiger bite me.
May there be no pain nor fever,
May pain not bind the spirit of my children.
May fever not bind the spirit of my children,
Neither the spirit of my children nor that of my wife.

11. *Song for a Small Child, with Palm Leaves Consecrated in the Smoke of Incense.*

Preserve my child, oh Lord,
May he not suffer pain nor fever.
May his feet be without pain or fever.
Do not punish him with the bites of snakes
Nor with death.
My child plays and is happy.
When he grows up he will offer you Pozole,
He will offer you Copal.[2]
When he grows up he will give you Tortillas.
When he grows up he will give you paper.
When he grows up he will sacrifice to you.

12. *A Gourd of Pozole Distributed to Each of the Participants.*

Sit down,
Drink my offering of Pozole,
It is for you.

13. *An Individual Offering of the Pozole Offering.*

His spirit is coming,
The spirit of the Lord.
My offering of Pozole is for you,
For the spirit of my children.
I offer my sacrifice for you, oh Lord,
For the spirit of my wife.

14. *Song Sung During the Fermentation of the Sacred Drink.*

The bark of the Balche[3] passes through my hands,
The bark of the Balche passes over my feet.
I am the chief priest.
I help in the ceremonies.

[2] Copal—Incense.
[3] Balche—Tree used to prepare the sacred liquor.

I am the one who gives you heat, who makes you boil.
I am the one who boils you.
I am the chief priest.
I am the one who stirs you with a spoon.
I mix you.
I am in charge of your preparation.
I cure pain with green chili,
I cure with green chili,
I will get drunk
and lie.

15. The Purification of the Ceremonial Drink Contained in the Hollow Trunk.

May you break!
May you open!
I incense you,
I incense the tree.
May it break.
I am he who alleviates pain,
Who takes away headache.
I am he who keeps the wood of the
Hollow trunk dry.
I am he who gives grace to the movements of the
Flesh.

16. Purification of the Grains of Copal.

May you break, fall apart!
I burn you. Live! Wake up!
Don't sleep! Work!
I am the one who wakes up life.
I am the one who raises up life.
I am the one who restores you.
I am the one who wakes you up.
I am the one who makes your bones.
I am the one who makes your head.
I am the one who makes your lungs.

I am the one who makes you—your maker.
For you this sacred drink.
For you this offering of Balche.
I am the one who raises you to life.
Wake up! Live!

17. An Offering of Balche and Coco Hang in Front of the Fire.

I serve you face to face, I spill the sacred Balche,
Which is for you along with this Coco.
Standing in front of you I give you this sacred water;
It is for you, carry it to the Father.
In front of you I make this offering of sacred water.
It is for you, for you.

18. An Offering to the Gods of Handmade Bark Paper.

Here it is.
Accept my paper.
I wrap your head with it again,
For your happiness.
It is for you, that you may guard my children.
When they grow up they will sacrifice to you.
Accept the paper, it is for you,
Offer it to the Father.
I wrap your head with it,
So that you will watch over my wife
Who makes Pozole and Tortillas.

19. Balche Poured into the Fire in the Name of the Gods.

I pour the sacred Balche into the fire, into your mouth.
I gave you the sacred Balche for your well-being,
It is for you, offer it to the Father.
I spill and serve sacred Balche for you,
I pour it into your mouth,
It is for you, for you, come and see,
Descend, look.

In front of you I make my offering of sacred Balche.
It is for you,
So that you will drink it for your well-being.
I pour sacred Balche into your mouth.
Feel good, my children,
I give you sacred Balche.
Feel good, my wife.
I pour sacred Balche into your mouth again.
I begin to live again,
I alone perform sacrifice for you.

20. Tamales Offered to the Fire in the Name of the Gods.

For you these Tamales, these heavy Tortillas,
This offering of Tortillas, many Tortillas,
Tortillas wrapped in leaves, a heavy offering of
Wrapped Tortillas, cut in two, cut in three,
For many days, for many years.

21. Balche Offered to the Fire in the Name of the Gods.

Accept my offering, please, please accept my offering,
The scent of the vanilla has ascended into the skies.
May it please you,
May life enter into you,
May the spirit enter into you,
For many days, many years.
May life enter into you,
May the spirit enter into you.
May the scent of the vanilla please you
As it ascends into the skies.

*22. Grains of Copal Offered to the East of the Ceremonial
    Garden.*

I lift up my gifts for you, for you,
That you may descend and see my gift.

Before you I take my gifts in my hands,
So that you will descend, see them and
Acquire wisdom.

23. *Grains of Copal Offered to the Fire in the Name of the*
    Gods, Within the Gardens of the Sacred Ceremonies.

You yourself are in the censer, full of copal, full of resin.
You are in the censer, full of copal and resin,
When the day is virgin, when the night is virgin,
When the day goes, when the night goes,
The day is descending, when the night is descending,
At midday, at midnight,
When the day goes, when the night goes,
When the day is virgin, when the night is virgin,
When the sky is clear, when it is full of clouds,
For many days, for many years . . .
Full of resin and copal,
The spirit is your gift.
I put the censer at your feet.

24. *An Offering of Meat Hung in Front of the Fire in the*
    Name of the Gods.

I offer you this meat,
For you,
Offer it to the Father,
I give it to you for your well-being.
It is for you, for you.
My offering of meat is for you.

25. *A Little Ceremonial Drink Given to the Head of the*
    Family.

I have this in my hands for you,
So that you will drink it again for your happiness.

26. *A Gift of Meat Offered to the Fire in the Name of the Gods.*

For you yourself is this meat.
I have given you meat before,
It passes through the fire, oh Lord.
For many days, many years.
Good meat for you, well cooked.
This offering of meat, this offering of meat,
Oh Lord, for many days, many years.

27. *An Offering of Tamales Burned in the Fire.*

I hold my offering of thick Tamales over your mouth,
Oh Lord.
Again the meat for your well-being,
My offering of thick Tortillas for you,
My offering of meat for you, oh Lord.
I give my thick Tortillas to you,
My offering of meat,
Again for your happiness,
Again so that my children might thrive,
Again so that my family may live.

28. *An Offering of Meat and Tamales Offered to the East of the Ceremonial Garden.*

I give you the best part of this meat,
These Tamales, oh Lord.
Take the meat
And let my children live,
Let my wife who makes Pozole and Tortillas
Live.

29. *The Offering of Meat and Tamales Offered to the Participants.*

Again I offer you a little meat,
For your happiness,

Again I offer you Tamales,
For your happiness.

30. Individual Offering of a Piece of Meat and Tamales.

I offer you the most important part of my Tamale,
Oh Lord,
I offer you the most important part of my meat,
Oh Lord.

31. The Last Offering of Pozole to the Old Brazier.

I pour Pozole into your mouth.
I pour Pozole into your image.
It is for you, that you rise up into your place of rest.
Your Coco is all finished.
Your Pozole is all finished.
My sacrifice to you has finished.
I have offered all that I am going to offer to you.

*32. The Old Braziers Are Cleaned and the Figures Are
Removed from Where They Were.*

I am cleaning away the ashes, oh Lord.
I always clean away the ashes with palm leaves for you.

*33. The First Offering Made on New Braziers and the
Figures Put in the Vases.*

Look, I pour it, I pour it into your mouth, oh Lord!
Receive it, I pour it into your mouth.
I put your new image in your new vase.
The palm leaves of my house are for you, oh Lord.
Look, I change the palm leaves in my house for you,
Over your new vase
I offer anew for your happiness.
I do it for you.
I put resin in your new vase.
Into your new vase I pour Balche.

It is my gift for you, again for your happiness.
I wrap your head in paper in the new vase,
Again for your happiness.
I offer you honey and Totopostles.[4]
My sacred drink is for you,
I offer it to you in your new vase,
For your happiness.

34. *An Offering of Pozole for the New Braziers in the Name of the Gods.*

I stand before you and offer you this Pozole.
Come and see your vase, descend to see your vase,
Oh Lord.
Live, oh vase, I perform sacrifice to you.

35. *An Offering of Balche Given to the Ceremonial Pot.*

I pour my sacred Balche into your mouth,
Balche pot,
It is my gift to you.

36. *A Gift of Tobacco Given to the Fire in the Name of the Gods.*

Here is the best part of the tobacco, oh Lord!

37. *A Gift of Pozole Offered to the Fire in the Name of the Gods.*

For you my offering of Pozole.
This offering.
For many days, many years.
Many days will pass, many years will pass.
For you this offering of Pozole.

38. *Song Used on Taking a Day Off.*

May the serpent and the tiger not bite me.
He who goes is (here you put in the name of the person).

---

[4] Totopostles—Usually Totopostes, a very fine, thin kind of tortilla.

May his feet hold out,
And may he never be cut with a sharp splinter.

OFFERTORY PRAYERS FROM QUINTANA ROOS (*Maya*)

1.

I set the virgin table
In front of you, Lord God.
I offer you thirteen jícaras,[5] cold and virgin words.

2.

Kanleox, Beautiful Lady, and you,
Beautiful Lady Magdalene, and you,
Beautiful Lady Veronica, and you,
Beautiful Lady Guadalupe.
Here I assemble you where the
Majesty of the Holy Lords is:
Lord Zaztunchac, God of the Rain,
Transparent Stone of the East,
Yaxpapatun, The Green Stonebreaker,
Chacpapatun, The Red Stonebreaker,
Kanpapatun, The Yellow Stonebreaker,
Ekpapatun, The Black Stonebreaker,
Kakalmozonikob, Gods of the Fire and Whirlwind,
Mizencaanchaac, Lightning-Flash that cleans the sky,
Ah Thoxoncaanchaac, Our God of the Rain of the Third
    Heaven . . .
Boloncaanchaac, Rain-God of the Ninth Heaven,
Lelemcaanchaac, The God of the Lightning Rain-Whip,
Hohocaanchaac, Rain-God of the Fifth Heaven.
Be glorified.
As my words fall for the protectors of the earth,

[5] Jícaras—Fruits.

The protectors of forest and plain and mountain,
Thus I make my words ring out to where they live,
Where they dwell.

3.

Three greetings when my word falls there in Punab.
I direct my words to the protectors of all the earths,
There where the Great Ones receive them in majesty,
From here, the village of Tusik.

4.

I offer to your right hand these thirteen fresh loaves,
And nine fresh loaves and thirteen jugs,
And huge fresh loaves, and the first fresh, virgin offering.
Ask nothing of our Holy Lord God
If the Lords in Majesty don't permit it.

5.

Here I offer this drink, Zaca,[6] to the South Wind
And to the Whirlwind of Yellow Fire, and to the
Great Wind from the East.
From the four corners of my fields I make my offerings
To the Lord Jaguars, to the North Wind, to the West Wind,
To the South Wind
To the Great Lord God.

6.

Holy sacred drink, first excellent sacred drink
Offered to the Lord God
In front of this table, Lord God.
First table, first altar,
For the first rain from the Great East,
For the four Great Jaguars
Of the four corners of the sky, cloud paths,
For the Rain God in his dominions of Coba to
The Great East,
Protect us, four Great Jaguars,

[6] Zaca—An offertory drink made out of cornmeal and water.

Three greetings when my word falls there, in Chichen.
Here I bring my word, four Great Rain Gods,
In front of the table of the Lord God . . .
First table, first altar,
For the four cloudy corners of heaven.
Three greetings when my word falls in Chemax.
Here I bring my word, in front of the table of my Holy Lord God.

7.

Here I kneel so that the Priest Idzac
May offer his overflowing cup, here in front of the table of One Chac.
There in the Great East . . .

8.

It is the hour for offering the first cup, in the name of The Lord God.
It is time for the second cup to be offered.

9.

Three greetings when my word falls there, in the Great East,
There in Coba, for the three Great Rain Gods,
For the four Great Jaguars.
Here I bring my word,
Here in front of the table of the Lord God,
. . . in front of the table of One Chac, there in the Great East.
Three greetings when my word falls at X-katak-chucumil,
Three greetings when my word falls there in Chemax.
Three greetings when my word falls at Nahcuche,
For the Rain Gods, for the Jaguar Gods
In the four corners of the sky.
Three greetings when my word falls in the great city of Zaci.
Three greetings when it falls in Pixoy.
Three greetings when it falls in X-katbe, in Uayma, in Sah-
    cabchen . . .

Here I bring my words for the four Great Chacs, Rain Gods,
In front of the table of our Holy God the Father.
Where was equaled the word spoken at Ceteac?
How can the word spoken at Maní ever be forgotten?

10.

Three greetings when my word falls, Lord . . .
So that I may make my offering to the Guardians of the
Fertile Earth,
To Those Full of Majesty, for the Guardian of the Seed,
For the Guardian of the Sprouting Plants, he who nourishes
them.
So that he may water the seed, for the Guardian of the Moun-
tain,
For the Whirlwind of Fire and the Guardians of the Fertile
Earth,
For the God of the Forest,
For the Lord Black Pahuatún,
Our Lord Red Pahuatún,
Our Lord Yellow Pahuatún,
Our Lord White Pahuatún,
Those of the Four Quarters, the Four Cloudy Quarters.
Three greetings when my word falls in the place
Of the God of the Shining Lightning Water,
Three greetings when my word falls in the place
Of the Rain God of the Lightning Whip.
Three greetings when my word falls in the place
Of the Rain God of the Heaven Thunder.
Three greetings when my word falls in the place
Of the Rain God of the Rain and Lightning Whip.
Three greetings when my word falls in the place
Of the Beautiful Lady of Corn,
Three greetings when it falls in the place of the
Hungry corn plants,

In the place of the Rain God of the Ultimate Heaven.
Three greetings when my word falls in the right hand
Of the Great Rain God,
And in the hand of the Great Jaguar,
On the first table of the Great God of Heaven,
On the right side of the first altar
Of our Lord God, whose blessing is given
Above this sainted table.
My offering be carried, great and holy,
To the Guardians of the Fertile Earth,
Because it has been offered by me the same day it has been
Prepared, offered to the Four Quarters of the Heavens,
The Four Cloudy Quarters . . .

11.

Three greetings when my word falls
Before the Guardian of the Fertile Earth there in the
Water of the May Flower
Which is performed for the Guardians of the Fertile Earth
For the first time in three years.[7]
I make my offering to the Rain Lords
Who cover the seeds with dew,
Who refresh the fields.
And for the Great Chac, Rain God,
That he may protect the corn . . .

12.

Oh, my beautiful Lord, my beautiful, my beautiful Lady Na-
tivity!
I offer a holy and great offering to you,
My saint, on this day of days of men . . .
To the Lords of Majesty,
Into the hand of our Lord God,
Who gives us his blessing.

[7] The ceremony should be performed yearly. Here the man making
the offering has been truant in his duties.

I offer a great offering
To the right hand of the Rain Gods,
To the Great Jaguar, to the Great Chac . . .

13.

In front of your table I offer you, Lord God,
Four loaves of bread, again the first holy loaves,
And five loaves for the Jaguar God . . .

14.

I offer a nine-layered holy bread
And a large holy bread for the Guardians of the Fertile
    Earths,
For Those Full of Majesty, here in the village of Chan Kom.
I bring my word. The Gods come to receive it at the large,
Holy table,
At the four corners of the table.
All the Lord Guardians of the Earth
And Those Full of Majesty come.
And thus they receive a large and holy table
On this earth . . .

15.

The Priest Idzac kneels and offers
The offering here in the sacred vessel,
At the table of the Great Lord of the Earth,
Here at the Four Quarters of Heaven,
Into the right hand of the Lord God . . .

OFFERING TO THE EARTH SPIRIT (*Chorti Maya*)

There is a celebration held in the place where I live, and not
only in the place where I live—in all the villages they hold
that celebration.

On the fifteenth of January, when people are coming home

from the celebration in Esquipulas, there are some who make an offering at the support of the house where they live, on the very afternoon when they come back from the celebration; they begin to grind the *chilate*; they grind until it gets to be seven or eight o'clock.

When the *chilate* has been prepared, and completely mixed with water, they begin to carry it to the arbor. There are some who put out as many as fifty bowls, some thirty, some twenty-five, some forty. When they begin to carry that *chilate*, it is stood in front of the cross where the arbor is, lined up. Bread is thrown in on top, and the chocolate which we call cacao. And then come two little gourds, alike, with neither sweetening nor bread. Those two gourds they say are for the angels. Because they say that the angels do not drink much. One large bowl is set down, which holds a lot of *chilate*, and then everything in the arbor is ready.

When all the *chilate* has been set out, and the legs of the tom and hen turkeys have been tied, and the chickens, and everything is ready, then they begin, some who were invited to conduct that offering, begin to pray. They go on praying until it gets to be twelve midnight. Because he keeps on praying, sitting there, because that "priest" was especially invited by the giver of the celebration. But some, who themselves know how to pray, do not invite someone else. But if the giver of the celebration does not know how to pray, he invites another of those who knows. And that "priest," when he is there praying, he speaks to what they say is—the spirit of—the earth.

He speaks like this: "Our Holy Mother, where you were left by Our Master God, who is living in the sky, and you, He left you, and we are living here, we—press you. We are doing everything to you. You see us sinning. We are sinful; you see everything we do. But do not let you—do not let your patience end. You see us; bless us, do not turn your face from us. Bless us, and today, we human beings are bringing you to mind with our poultry, where we raise it. And we want you to bless us; do not let disease fall on our children and on us, on all our poultry which we put out. We bring it here, our poultry; it is your payment, and with it we entreat you. Look on us with open eyes, and give to us what we eat with open hands."

That man sits praying. His prayer is long. He asks that disease not enter, he asks that the chickens not die, he asks that the children not die, that no disease fall on the house, because they say that is what the payment is for, with the incense, the turkeys, and the chickens. They say that it is the payment so that he does not let disease enter and fall on the house.

When the praying is finished, then they begin to go out to the nearby paths with coals and the censer. They walk along censing the path, carrying each a gourd of *chilate*; they pour it on the paths, and they carry a few with the incense to pour out in the holes where they dug them. Those holes they dug just as the sun was setting. They began to go to dig the holes in the nearby paths. One is dug for the *chilate* to be put in, and one is dug for the coals to be put in where the incense is to be burned.

And they say that those little holes which—the *chilate* is poured in and where the coals are placed with the incense, they say it is like an enclosure, so that the master of disease does not pass, or any spirit who—wants to enter the house, but they say that the—*chilate* and the incense are like—they are placed like a fence so that nothing may pass inside. And the four corners of the paths they walk, pouring *chilate* in them and the incense on the coals. They say it is like a fence which encloses the house within itself, so that disease does not enter.

But the most important place is where the arbor stands. Because there stands a cross which is planted on purpose by them. And at the foot of that cross there they pour the *chilate* and cut the throats of the chickens, the tom and hen turkeys. And they pour out a whole bowl of *chilate* which they call white *chilate*. And the two small gourds they say are for the angels they pour out there at the foot of the cross. And then when all is finished, they begin to offer the *chilate* which is stood there by them, the *chilate* which is made with sugar and bread on top; they begin to give it to the people.

When that sharing is finished, of the *chilate* with the people, there are some who go home and some who remain. They sit down, because they do not sleep, because the man who was invited to pray to the earth does not sleep, because he was invited on purpose to conduct that celebration. All the incense which there is has to be all burned up, until it gets light on the earth. And if there is much incense, he burns it until seven o'clock the next day.

Then the turkey which is being killed and the chicken, when the praying is finished, then it is carried, all the tom turkeys which were killed are carried over to where the—they say is the kitchen, where it is full of women, so it will be prepared. And they begin to make tamales. And those tamales when it grows light on the earth are cooked; then they begin to be distributed to the people who stayed up there for the celebration.

Then, when all that distribution is finished, then the man who was praying goes out and goes to his house. He is given a jug of *chilate* to carry to his house and he is given a whole chicken to carry away, and he is given tamales. Because they say that since he was invited especially, he is given a lot of everything that was put out.

X. BIRTH

NAHUATL BIRTH-CEREMONY SONG (*Aztec*)

The midwife, having finished with her main duty, cut the newborn child's umbilical cord. Next she would wash it and while doing so she would speak to it, and if it were male, she would say:

"Lord, our master, she of the jade skirt, he who shines like a sun of jade. A male has been born, sent here by our mother, our father, Lord of duality, Lady of duality, he who dwells in the nine heavens, he who dwells in the place of duality."

XI. NAMING

NAMING CEREMONY (*Cubeo*)

People of our soil
The milk that is from this place that causes to grow
People who are our offspring
They are given milk
Milk of our soil
Milk that causes to grow
People who are being grown
People of our soil
People who are our younger sisters
Milk of the calabash
Milk that makes one grow quickly
Milk of our soil
People of our soil
People who are our younger brothers
The first one to grow fat
He also will grow fat
Milk that is nourishing

Milk that is nourishing that will make him fat
People of our soil
Urahana who was the first to grow fat
Milk that is nourishing
He will grow fat
Milk that is liquid
Milk that is nourishing
The manioc gruel that is nourishing
Milk of our land
People of our land
Urahana was the first one
The manioc gruel that he ate
The milk that was given to him.

Milk of our soil
That our offspring may grow
That we may all grow
Milk of the calabash
The offspring of Urahana
The calabash of Djuredo
When she Djuredo saw the birth
Milk to make it grow, she gave it
Milk of the calabash it drank
A child was being born to Urahana
The offspring of Urahana
The calabash of Djuredo
When she Djuredo saw the birth
Milk to make it grow, she gave it
Milk of our soil
She saw him grow
The son of Hihedu
Her fat offspring
Milk of our soil
She saw them grow
Milk of the calabash

Children of our soil
She saw them grow
Son of Hihedu
Grew big and fat
Son of Urahana
Grew big and fat
This milk of the calabash
He drank and grew
She saw it.

XII.   CURING

CURING (*Chorti Maya*)

When the curers are curing, they proclaim, name by name, everything found in the divining.

They speak like this: You judgments from above, where you are coming to play in the blue ring, the white ring, of San Gregorio of Water, with the rainbow of your appearance, the rainbow of your expression, the warmth of your appearance, the warmth of your expression, the heat of your appearance, the heat of your walking.

Where you pile yourselves up, coming into the blue basin, the white basin, the child San Gregorio is playing there, with the reflection of his appearance, the reflection of his expression, the beams of his appearance, the beams of his walking, the warmth of his appearance, the warmth of his expression.

Where you have come to play, with the water dam of your walking, the water dam of your running, the numbness of your hands, the numbness of your feet, the hallucination of your appearance, the hallucination of your expression.

With the hardening of your walking, the hardening of your running, the lassitude of your expression; with the jaundice of your walking, the jaundice of your running, the jaundice ghost, the bone-breaker ghost, the dizziness ghost, the water-drip ghost, the water-slosh ghost.

You come with the trembling of your running, the trembling of your walking, the vein distance of your running; with the impaling of your walking, the impaling of your running, with the thick mucus of your presence, the thick mucus of your coming, with the bloating of your presence, the bloating of your coming, with the nausea of your walking, the nausea of your running, with the panting of your walking, the panting of your running, with the itching of your presence, the itching of your coming, the tickling of your presence, the tickling of your coming, with the body-burning of your presence, the body-burning of your coming, with the mucus-dripping of your presence, the mucus-dripping of your coming, the coldness of your hands, the coldness of your feet, with the body-draining of your walking, the body-draining of your running.

Where you are playing, you come and are playing your ghost beams, you are playing your ghost Hol Txan, the Hol Txan of your appearance, the Hol Txan of your expression, the jaundice of your appearance, the jaundice of your expression, with the desiccation of your presence, the desiccation of your coming, with the bone-bending of your walking, the bone-bending of your running.

Where you are tossing end over end the angel of this little creature, you are playing cat and mouse with his ghost, his spirit; you who are deceivers, deceiver your coming, deceiver your arrival, deceiver ghosts, deceiver spirits, where you are guiding the ghost of this little creature.

And now you are diminishing his ghost, you are diminishing his spirit, when you toy with it. You carry his ghost on a litter, you carry his spirit on a litter, there you are already meta-morphosing over his head. You are becoming beasts of prey over his ghost's head, you are becoming beasts of prey over his spirit, like you who become beasts of prey over the head of this sick person.

You are clutching at his spirit, you are clawing at his ghost, you are softening his ghost, you are softening his bones when you waste away the healthiness of his appearance, the healthiness of his expression. You are trampling on his ghost, you are trampling on his vitality.

When you tug at this little creature, you are making his soul pant with the warmth of your appearance, the warmth of your walking, the sweat of your appearance, the sweat of your expression, with the roaring of your walking, the roaring of your running. As you are all crowding together, gnashing together over his head where he lies whipped and punished by you.

You make him unconscious where you crowd together, snorting beside this little creature. His appearance is made sorrowful, his expression is made sorrowful by you. He has no vitality, no protection because of you.

Truly, you are the kings of death, the kings of disease, the kings of all evil spirits. You are now hovering, sickening, casting your beams over mankind, over the earth, since you seek the Silent Day, the Silent Hour so as to transform yourselves, to Hol Txan over mankind, since your walking is like a thief's presence, your running is like a thief's presence.

But today, this is the hour, this is the day; in the name of all the gods which we are proclaiming over the head of this sick person here, this day let there be protective power over the head of this little creature, so you will release his angel, release his spirit where it lies threatened and punished by you.

But today I deliver you spirits of disease into the hands of the angel Holy Spirit, and all the angels. So, they chase you running, throw you to the King Mountain. So, Lightning Aimer, Thunder Aimer carry you away.

XIII. EXORCISM

EXORCISING THE XIXIMAI (*Chorti Maya*)

There is a ceremony performed in July. But they say it is a se-
cret ceremony. They do not want people to gather. Because
not much is set out: only a bowl of *chilate* and twenty-five
discs of incense, and two balls of *chilate* paste; and they lay
down a large tortilla. They dunk them in the *chilate* standing
on the quern where the grinding is done.

Then they begin to cense the whole surface of the quern,
the fireside, over the stone supports, the pots, the bowls, and
the jugs. They cense the logs where the corn is, and all around
the back of the house they go censing. They gather up all the
children, everything which is in the house.

When all the back of the house has been completely censed,
they cense all the corncribs. Then, so that the *xiximai* in the
house will go out, the woman goes out, walking backward.
The man is censing the ankles of the woman, swinging the
censer all around the edge of the path where the woman is
walking backward. They say that that woman, it is as if she
were the *xiximai*. It is being ejected from the inside of the
house. It is being scolded. It is carried out.

It is told: "Lady Ancestor! King Ancestor! Boy Ancestor!
Girl Ancestor! Today, when I am paying you, abandon my
house where you live. You are using up what I eat in my
house with my children. You do not know how much fatigue
I find in my work. And you appear the same; you are still
using up everything inside my house. By you alone, hunger is
binding the bellies of my children at my house. But today I
give you your payment, your leave. I make you flee with the
name of the gods above." He is talking and censing the path
where the woman is walking.

He says to the *xiximai*: "This is your payment, your leave,

Lady Ancestor, today you remain in the hands of the angels, you remain in the hands of Lightning Aimer, Thunder Aimer. Where you stay, you are using up everything in the place. But the angel San Gabriel, the angel Santo Tomas, archangel San Miguel, when we are invoking your names, over the heads of those eaters. Today when I am placing them in your hands, make them flee, Lightning Aimer, Thunder Aimer, let them go take shape in the great mountains, the green mountains.

"And if they do not take shape where it is good and green, then let them collapse to the ground, collapse flat. Since if there is abundance, they eat everything, and if there is not they are hungry, the Lady Ancestor, the King Ancestor. In the name of all the angels, I chase you out of my house. Where I am, your appearance is already gone. Your expression is already gone, where you dwell.

"You are using up everything in their houses and in all the places among the human beings on earth, Lady Ancestor, Predecessor, Lord Ancestor, Predecessor, Boy Ancestor, Girl Ancestor. See your road toward the sunset, in the great mountains, the great peaks. There take shape for all time, because we cannot endure you, and we cannot stand to feed you, because you go as spirits, you do not appear and mingle with the human beings.

"But we place you in the hands of the spirit gods. This speech is to put you to flight, retracing your steps."

Then the woman returns to her hearth.

EXORCISING DISEASE (*Chorti Maya*)

When the disease is raised by a were-animal, man or woman, then the diviner traces it out with his gift of divination until he finds out from where the master of that disease was summoned. Name by name he divines to see from where that disease was summoned, whether from the wheel San Gregorio, or from San Antonio of the Earth or from San Antonio the Servant, or from Santa Magdalena of the Earth, or from San Manuel Monte de Oro, or whether that disease was summoned from hell.

Because they say that there is another place below, under this earth. And that town there is filled with many evil ones. There lies the Evil King. They say that when one of those evil ones is called as master of the illness, then he who does not believe neither cures nor prays.

Then a great curer is sought who knows the names of the masters of those diseases. That curer divines to see how it will be necessary for that disease to leave, if it must be paid for to the gods. Then he says that incense is to be bought, small candles, and two large candles.

When the candles are ready, and the incense, he divines to see if the discs of incense are to be burned. Because they say that that incense is payment to the gods above, and the angels, for putting the master of the disease to flight. The large candles they say are like a light, to show them the dwelling-place of God above, that they are to abase themselves before him. Those candles, one they say, is for God, and one is for strengthening the spirit of the sick person. The prayer-sayer passes that candle over the head of the sick person where he lies. Then he begins to pray.

He says in his prayer, "You are our God. We, the human beings on the earth, great is our need of you. Now we pray your name in five Our Fathers and ten Hail Marys, since you have left it written that so you are to be prayed to." Then he says the Our Father five times and the Hail Mary ten times. And in the midst of that prayer he names all the gods and angels.

He says in his prayer,

> "Oh Our Divine Eternal One,
> Oh Our Lord Jesus Christ,
> Oh Our Father Holy Spirit,
> Oh Saint Michael Archangel,
> Oh Angel Holy Spirit,

"Today we name your name in one Our Father and two Hail Marys.

"In your names, gods above, today we chase all were-animal spirits where they crowd together playing over the head of this little creature, where his angel lies punished, his spirit whipped, where they crowd together preying like beasts on the spirit of this little creature.

"You know where the human who works evil dwells, the black heart, the infernal heart, where he stays in the silent day, the silent hour, where he stays imploring his infernal friend. Since he is your friend, he is the Evil King, the King Lucifer, Don Juan of the World, Dona Juana of the World, the King San Manuel Monte de Oro, the King San Antonio of the World, the King San Reimundo, Dona Reimundo, Queen Santa Magdalena of the World, Don Juan Dembute, Dona Juana Dembute.

"Since they are playing on the five-hundredth level of hell under the earth, and they are coming to play in the wind of the lake, they are joining themselves with the fighting men, fighting king, serpent men, serpent king, viper men, viper queen, Sesimite men, Sesimite king.

"But today, in your names, our gods, we put to flight these were-animal spirits, they run away, since they are spirits of the evil ones under the world. But you put them to flight, Lightning Aimer, Thunder Aimer. Conjure them where they rose to come here, under the earth.

"Today give them their leave immediately where they lie dominating this little creature. Since it is the dust-breath, the blight-breath, the rainbow-breath, the tiger-breath, the were-animal-breath where they are blowing, the black heart, the evildoer. But you stand as an advocate over the head of this little creature."

Then he gets up, where he was crouched to pray. He goes out backward with the censer. And in his prayer he calls the witch by name, and censes all the outside of the house, until he goes out to the walk.

XIV. VISION QUEST

OTOMI VISION-QUEST HYMN (Nahuatl)

To thee, the Cause of All, to thee I cried out in sadness, my sighs rose up before thy face; I am afflicted here on earth, I suffer, I am wretched, never has joy been my lot, never good fortune; my labor has been of no avail, certainly nothing here lessens one's suffering; truly only to be with thee, near thee; may it be thy will that my soul shall rise to thee, may I pour out my tears to thee, before thee, O thou Giver of Life.

Happy are those who walk in thy favor here on earth, who never neglect to offer up praise, nor, leaving till tomorrow, neglect thee, thou Cause of All, that thou mayest be known in all the earth; I know that they shall live, I see that they are established, certainly they have drunk to forgetfulness while I am miserable, certainly I shall go to see the land of the dead, certainly we shall meet where all souls are contented.

Never were any troubled in spirit on the earth who appealed to thee, who cried to thee, only for an instant were they cast down, truly thou caused them to rule as they ruled before: Take as an example on earth, O friend, the fever-stricken patient; clothe thyself in the flowers of sadness, in the flowers of weeping, give praises in flowers of sighs that may carry you toward the Cause of All.

I array myself with the jewels of saddest flowers; in my hands are the weeping flowers of war; I lift my voice in sad songs; I offer a new and worthy song which is beautiful and melodious; I weave songs fresh as the dew of flowers; on my drum decked with previous stones and plumes I, the singer, keep time to my song, as I take it from those dwellers in the heavens, the zacuan bird, the beautiful tzinitzcan, the divine quechol, those melodious birds who give joy to the Cause of All.

XV. HERO'S DEATH

POEM ON THE VALUE OF DEATH IN BATTLE (*Nahuatl*)

They are emeralds; your clay and your feathers
Are turquoise,
Oh Giver of Life!
Death by the obsidian blade
Is the luck and wealth of princes,
Death in battle.

XVI. RITUAL SONGS

THE SONG OF THE COLIBRÍ/THUNDERBIRD (*Chiripá-Guaraní*)

What do you have to tell us, Colibrí?
Colibrí, throw lightning!
Has the nectar of your flowers gotten you drunk,
Colibrí?
Never mind, throw lightning, throw lightning!

RITUAL SONG OF GOD THE GRANDFATHER
(*Paí-Kaiová-Guaraní*)

Nothing else but my Grandfather existed,
the primitive first father,
Before he had even set up the center of the earth,
he *was*, my Grandfather, the primitive first father.
Before the earth had even been established,
he *was*, my Grandfather, the primitive first father.
Before the earth was even covered with forests,
he *was*, my Grandfather, the primitive first father.
Before there even were souls in heaven,
he *was*, my Grandfather, the primitive first father.
"I still haven't made the earth,"
said my Grandfather, the primitive first father.
"I still haven't made the flaming earth,"
said my Grandfather, the primitive first father.
"I still haven't made the earth, with the help of *jasuká*,"
said my Grandfather, the primitive first father.
"I still haven't made the earth by means of the *jasuká's*
luster, I still haven't made the earth with the help of the
jasuká's flames,"
said my Grandfather, the primitive first father.

"Now I have designed the earth,"
said my Grandfather, the primitive first father.
"With the help of the *jasuká*, I have designed the earth,
with the help of the *jasuká's* brilliance I have
designed the earth and the heavens, with the help
of the *jasuká* I have designed the heavens,"
said my Grandfather, the primitive first father.

My Grandfather was mighty and absolute,
"But the earth," he said, "looks like a slice of bone,
there is no thickness to it,
there is no thickness to it so that I can walk on it,
this shining earth still isn't thick enough for me to

rest my feet on it," said my mighty and absolute Grandfather.
"I still haven't given final form to this earth,"
said my mighty and absolute Grandfather,
"This earth is about to take form,
it is about to take form with the help of
the *jasuká*."
"I made the earth stretch,"
said my Grandfather, the primitive first father,
"With the help of the *jasuká*,
I made the earth stretch with the
help of *jasuká's* 'light,'
I made the earth stretch with
the help of *mba'ekuaas'* 'light,'
with the help of the 'light' of the
jeguaká, I made the earth stretch.
I made the earth stretch with the
help of the flames of the *jeguaká*,
with the help of *nanduá* I made the
earth stretch, with the
help of the 'light' of *nanduá*
I made the earth stretch,
with the help of their fire,
with the help of their thunder,
I made the earth stretch;
with the help of *kurusú*
I made the earth stretch,
with the help of *kurusú's*
flames and thunder
I made the earth stretch," said
my Grandfather, the primitive first father.

"Now we are walking on the earth,
now we are walking on the shining earth,
now we are walking on the flaming earth,
the thundering earth,
the perfumed earth,
now we are walking on this gleaming perfumed earth,

now we are walking on this flaming perfumed earth,
now we are walking on this heavily perfumed
death, this earth weakly illuminated by the
light of eternity,
now we are walking on the earth very weakly
illuminated with eternal light by the
jasuká, jeguaká, mba'ekuaa and *kurusú*," said
my Grandfather, the primitive first father.

The creator returned to the depths of his
primordial paradise and there my Grandfather, the
beginning of all things, sat thinking of his future
home;
with tenuous eternal light he illuminated his future
home,
came quickly toward it,
now it was brightly lighted
and my Grandfather, the primitive first father,
was looking for a throne to sit on,
a small flame-adorned throne,
a small thundering throne
on which to sit,
in order to sit with his own law,
in order to sit with his own light,
in order to sit with his own flames,
in order to sit with his own thunder,
in order to sit with his own word,
in order to sit with his own gleaming word,
in order to sit with his own flaming word,
in order to sit with his own thundering word.

RITUAL SONG OF TACUARA (*Paí-Kaiová-Guaraní*)

Our Grandfather, the primitive first father,
issued forth from the *jasuká*.

Our Grandfather ate the *jasuká's* flowers and grew.
Tupá Arasá, Soul-Who-Crosses-The-Heavens,
issued forth from the *jasuká*.
After our Grandfather had issued forth the
parents of all souls issued forth
and gathered together in great number
and *Tupá Arasá* came to where the *jasuká* was and
asked,
"How are you going to duplicate/multiply yourself, Pa'i?"
"I don't know," said our Grandfather, although he
knew, he said he didn't know.
"Pull up the center of your ritual cap and make a
woman," said Tupá Arasá.
He pulled up the center of his cap, blessed it,
charged it with power,
called it *Jeguakávy*, Ornament, and created
our Grandmother out of it,
our Grandmother, Takua Rendy-jú Guasú, Flaming
Divine Great Bamboo.
Our Grandfather lived with our Grandmother
and she became pregnant and so Papa Réi
came visiting.
Our Grandfather was out preparing the fields
for planting when along came Papa Réi to the
house and when our Grandfather
got home from the fields he could see that Papa Réi
had been there.
Seeing our Grandmother pregnant he thought the
father was Papa Réi and so he left home
again in a fury of
thunder and lightning, calling out to the Shaman
Sun inside the womb of our Grandmother:
"If you are my son you will be able to follow
my rays; come to my house, if you are really my
son," and he started to war with our Grandmother,

sent a hurricane wind against her;
Our Grandmother didn't get angry, simply
stopped him.

RITUAL SONG WITH WHICH OUR GRANDMOTHER THRUST ASIDE THE WINDS OF THE HURRICANE (*Paí-Kaiová-Guaraní*)

My true mother was truly perfect
when she brandished her baton,
when she brandished her baton
for the first time, dancing with her baton,
dancing for the first time with her baton,
lifting her baton up in her hand.
"Sing long songs for Karavié Guasú first," she
told the baton,
"Sing long songs for Pa'i Namói,
sing long, beautiful songs for Arary Vusí,
sing long, beautiful songs for Tanimbú Guasú,
for Japarié Guasú,
close to this earth, still without forests,
sing long beautiful songs,
close to this earth, still without foundations,
sing long, beautiful songs,
close to this miraculously created earth,
sing long, beautiful songs,
close to the divine souls, still with nothing to talk about,
sing long, beautiful songs,
close to souls that still cannot reproduce themselves,
sing long, beautiful songs . . .
leave me alone and let this
affliction pass over me."

XVII.   THE YEAR-ROUND

SOLSTICES AND ECLIPSES (Maya)

When the eleventh day of June shall come, it will be the longest day. When the thirteenth day of September comes, this day and night are precisely the same in length. When the twelfth day of December shall come, the day is short, but the night begins to shorten. When the tenth day of March comes, the day and night will be equal in length.

This annulus in the center of the disc is white and indicates the course of the sun. Between the two rings the black spots indicate the face of the sun, which goes over the large black one and descends to the small black one. Thus its course here on earth also. On the ground it is thus manifested plainly all over the earth also. The progress of the sun is truly great as it takes its course to enter into the great Oro extended over the world. This is the record of the motion of the sun as it is known here on earth.

To the people on the sides of this half section, the sun is not eclipsed; but for anyone who is in the middle, it is eclipsed. It is in conjunction with the moon when it is eclipsed. It travels in its course before it is eclipsed. It arrives in its course to the north, very great. It is all the same with eclipses of the sun and moon before it arrives opposite to the sun. This is the explanation so that Maya people may know what happens to the sun and to the moon.

ASTRONOMY (Chorti Maya)

There is one large star and one small one when it becomes dark over the mountains. We do not see them by day, until the sun sets and it is already becoming dark on the ground. Then that star appears in place over the peak. The old people used to say that its name is San Ramon Watcher-over-the-Earth. Those old people, I used to see them praying to it. When it grew dark, they bent over behind their houses with their candles. They prayed to it as they did to the moon.

There is another . . . another star that rises when it has just become dark. At about seven o'clock. That star, every night it travels across the sky. When it gets to be four o'clock, it is already about to get light. That star is already setting over the peaks where the sun sets. When it gets to be five o'clock, that star has already set behind the peak. That star has been named by them as San Oromán Watcher-over-the-Earth.

It is said that it was set in place by God as a watcher over mankind. They used to say that those stars had been left on purpose as watchers over mankind so that not even for a moment would man remain abandoned on the earth. And so, behind the one comes another. And behind that one, already comes another. Because it is said that they are fellow runners with the sun, and mates of the sun, left by God Our Father. So they used to pray to that star.

There are times when it unites its body with the moon. And people say, "When that star unites its body with the moon, that is a sign that someone is going to kill himself in the villages. If not, a war is going to be made in the towns." So they believe, because this is what the old people believed, that those stars which travel are watchers over mankind on earth.

And those which we see not traveling are said to be fires, so that it does not become completely dark on the earth. Because it is said that if it gets completely dark, all of the animals of the master of the peaks will come out, and finish off man on the earth. It is said that that is why those stars were left, as a sign in the sky.

When it is just about to grow light, at about four o'clock, another comes out. They call it Child San Pascual. The old people, just as that star came out above the peak, used to begin, with their candles, behind their houses, to pray to it. There they bent over until it became light, because that star there, just behind it came the sun. They prayed for nothing to happen to them or their children. They prayed for all men on the earth.

The stars we call Star-group, because they go together, people say that those seven stars travel joined together. They rise just at daybreak. When it becomes light, those stars have already set.

And those which do not move, at times we see them fall down from the sky. Like coals, it is said that they move in the sky.

The eclipse is feared by people when it lies in the sky. Because it is said that . . . that eclipse, if given time by God, that eclipse would eat the sun or the moon.

And so, they say that when the sun or the moon is grabbed by the eclipse, then the moon offers up mankind on the earth, so as not to be eaten by the eclipse. Because it is said that if one day passes, or two days, there will be no sun; it will become dark on the earth. All the animals there are will rise up in the peaks, in the seas, and all the spirits who are dead, just like those who are completely dead. And those spirits will come to life and eat the people who are alive on the earth.

BIRTH OF THE SUN (Chorti Maya)

Another festival is held on the twelfth of March. They say that on that day is the birth of the sun which illuminates us on earth. They say that the sun has not just one name. The one which is best known by people continues to be Jesus Christ. They say that when it is just getting light its name is Child Redeemer of the World. One name is San Gregorio the Illuminator. One name is San Antonio of Judgment. One name is Child Guardian. One is Child Refuge. One is Child San Pascual. One is Child Succor. One is Child Creator. They say that at each hour, one of these is its name.

The moon's name given by them is Queen Santa Maria. One is Queen Piety. One is Queen Charity. One is Queen Succor. Queen of Judgment, Queen Guardian. Because they say that the moon is married to San Gregorio.

They say that when we die, we men, they say that it is the Queen who whips us, we who are men. And the women are lashed by Jesus Christ. They say that when the whipping is finished they are thrown into the fire which is called Purgatory until a year has passed since death.

When they have finished paying for all their sins, then the Angels come and pick them from the midst of the fire, so they can be with God. Because they say that that fire is set by God, and that it burns and cleanses all the sins which we have. They say it is left by God; it is the place where all sins are paid for which were committed while on earth. That is why they pray and pray, praying to Him. They say that it is so they will not be whipped much when they die.

Long ago, those who were already grown men prayed day after day. Long before it began to grow light they rose from their beds and went to kneel behind the house. They lit candles, and began to pray to Him. Because they used to say that He is the master of all there is. And so it is until today.

That is why on the twelfth of March there are many who perform that ceremony. They fire rockets, they set out candles, incense, and *chilate*, and cut the throats of turkeys.

ESQUIPULAS—BEGINNING OF THE YEAR
(*Chorti Maya*)

I

The first celebration in the beginning of the year is on the fourth of January. The people begin to go to the Esquipulas celebration.

When it is time that we go to the celebration, our wives begin to get out the brittle tortillas, which we call "crackbacks," so that we can carry them along to the celebration. We carry many, so there will be enough for us to eat until we come home. When night falls, so that we can go right on, she has prepared a chicken for us to eat on the road, wrapped up some stuffed tortillas, and has ground parched cornmeal.

When everything is there, she fills up a net with it, which we carry along on our backs.

When we arrive in the town of Olopa, we buy candles and go in with them, in front of our Mother, the "Pastora." We show them to her because they say that she is the wife of the "Milagroso." Then we leave, and go to San Juan Creek to sleep. There we eat the chickens which we took from our houses. The bones of those chickens we do not leave behind; we wrap them in corn husks so as to return them to our houses, because they say that where we leave those bones, the spirit of the chickens remains in that place, and ours do not thrive.

As it grows light, we go out to where we are going along the road. We are already looking for our firewood. We lay it flat across the tops of our nets, so as to make a fire with it where we are going to stay in Esquipulas. We arrive at Santiago Creek, and everyone bathes, because they say that we cannot come before the "Milagroso" if we have not been bathed.

When we arrive at the edge of town we begin to pray. We are praying until we enter his sanctuary. When we have finished praying we go out and look for where we will stay. We begin to boil our beans.

The next day we go stand among the people, where they are lined up, so that we may pass behind Our Father, the "Milagroso." Because in that town there stands a God whose name is "Milagroso."

II

They say that that God was found in a flat clearing. He was standing, with his clothing glittering beautifully. They say the people gathered together so as to see him. But that God did not allow himself to be touched. Because, they say, some wanted to bring him, to stand him up in his house.

III

When his house began to be built, on that clearing, they say that he didn't want to remain there. Because there was a big lake at the edge of the clearing.

They say that when it was light the next day people went to look in his house, which had been built so that he would remain in it. There was nobody when they went to look; there he was standing at the edge of the lake. Time after time he was carried and put in his house. He did not remain.

IV

Those people said, "How are we to build the house of Our Father here? Because the lake is large. It can't be done, because if we bother the serpent who is master of the lake, he might get us."

V

But they say an old woman was caused to have a revelation by the master of the lake. She was told, in her dream, "If I am paid as I desire, they may build the house."

VI

Those people began to gather together; they put out chickens, turkeys, incense, candles, and bread. They gathered together, the women, and began to make *chilate*, and some, to carry water. When everything was there, they poured the *chilate* into the jugs, they began to wrap the turkeys in nets. The chickens they carried to the banks of the lake.

They had the old woman kneel, she who had dreamed, so she would pray to that serpent.

VII

The old woman began to pray. She said to the serpent, "Holy Queen Snake, King Snake, you who are ruler and master of this lake here; we, the human beings, sons of the Highest God, we are coming to entreat and move you, with the poultry of Saint Magdalene who is mistress of our poultry, and with the milk of the trees blessed by our Master, God. This is your payment. Do not turn your face away; take it with open hands. Hear our prayer. We, our need is that you give us a place where we may raise a house by your side. Because the God who appeared before us likewise will rule over you."

When the old woman came out with that speech, the lake thundered like the sky.

VIII

They say that that snake was frightened when he heard the name of the ruler. When the old woman had finished praying, and when they had finished cutting the throats of the turkeys and chickens, the old woman rose and spoke. She said to the people, "After eight days, begin the work."

IX

They began to measure out the supports of the house. They laid out its trenches, where they were to line up the stones, and which went into the ground, as the "risers" of the house. But with the night, the lake kept lapping, and completely undermined everything. When it became light, there was nothing. It was entirely eroded and gone into the water. When it became light the next day they went to look, and nothing they had done was there. And so, every day. They began to speak of it. They said, "We are just wasting ourselves. It hasn't come out the way this old woman said."

X

The old woman dreamed again. She was told in her dream that the master of the lake wanted servants.

When the old woman had dreamed again, all the people who were working gathered together. They told the old woman to seek by divining to find out how that snake wanted his servants, whether alive or dead. It appeared from the divining that live ones were wanted.

XI

And when it became clear that the serpent wanted live people, then those people who were working said, "It is necessary that we go and stand, some of us here, in the mortar, alive." Because they say that the people of olden days used to say that that house, when it began to go up, had its roots in the ground. They say that two by two, men were stood up in its corners, alive they say. Those men were inserted, standing up, in the mortar, where the cornerposts rose.

When they had done that, then the house rose before them. When it was ready for them to complete, a mason fell down to the ground. His picture, put there by them, is there to this day. They say that that man was a Spaniard.

They say that that serpent accepted. And so that town appeared. That is why people say nowadays that that church is standing over a lake. They say that when the place had just been completed, it thundered all the time, like the sky, until the neck of the serpent was tied by the "Milagroso," and he gave up thundering. Today the wire is visible, hanging down, coming down over the church and going into the earth. Because they say that there is that serpent, lying, tied.

They used to say that a long time ago, at the celebration, many people remained each time there, men, women, and children. Because they say that when they were passing behind the "Milagroso," they say there were those under whom the planks slid away. They fell and went into the lake. Others' necks turned themselves backward. They say that they were those whose thoughts were not pure. They say that by the "Milagroso" their necks were wrung. They died.

When they are passing behind the "Milagroso," where he hangs, all leave their money in front of him. Some leave a candle beside him. They say that is so they will be given more life by that God. Because they say that that God has the authority to take away every sin which exists in man.

Therefore to that celebration many people come and do penance, so that they will be saved from their sins. Upon arriving at the edge of town they crawl along on their knees, where they are walking along, kneeling, in the street. Some of those filling the street walk along, laying out their jackets on the ground; others, their headcloths, others their sheets, for them to pass over them, those who are going, kneeling, on their knees.

Some, when their jackets are free, quickly go and stretch them out ahead, until they bring them to where the "Milagroso" hangs. But there are some who die from fatigue. They say that they are the ones who have much sin; therefore they die.

XVII

Therefore, when they go out of their houses, they say prayers so that nothing will happen to them on the road. There are crosses standing on the road, as they go along. They see them from quite a distance. They begin to break off flowers from the bushes. If not, pine branches, with which they lash their ankles. They leave them lying in front of the crosses, so that they will not get tired.

Those who do not find something with which to lash their ankles grab their hats, and lash their ankles with them. If not, one grabs a rock, sets it on his shoulders, so as to lay it in front of the cross. And likewise when they have turned back toward their houses.

XVIII

That celebration begins on the first day of January. He who goes on the fourth, comes back to his house on the eighth. He who goes on the eleventh comes back to his house on the fifteenth.

We leave on our way to Esquipulas on Tuesday, and the *chilate* makers, the day when we are away in Esquipulas, on Thursday, throw the corn in the water for *chilate*. On Friday they break up the corn grains. And the next day, which is Saturday, they begin to grind it fine when it gets light. And when night comes they begin to boil it.

On Saturday they have a lot of work. Because the women are making the *chilate*; others are beginning to grind the dough for tamales, others are fixing turkeys and chickens. And the men: some are looking for firewood; some are going banana-leaf cutting for tamale wrapping. Then, when every-

148

thing is there and all of the turkey is cut up into pieces, the women begin with the tamale wrapping. The tamales, when it is daylight, are yellow.

Then the men who are there, one of them goes out along the road with the tamales and *chilate*, for those who are coming back from the celebration to eat. And immediately he returns to the house, so as to order the cross taken out. And the women begin to put on their clothes, which are washed.

They cradle the crosses and go out on the trail, so they may be bowed to, and for the sign of the cross by the men who are coming back from the celebration, and the prayer leader. The woman cradles the cross and the man swings the censer with the incense, so the smoke of the incense spreads itself all around.

If nobody goes to meet them on the road, they fire a rocket, from the place where the houses are first visible, so that it is known by those who stayed at home that the celebration-goers are about to come back. All around, people are clustered. Along the road they are waiting, so as to go to the houses with those who are coming home from the celebration. Because they want to eat tamales, and want to drink *chilate*, and in order to assist those saying their prayers.

They go out on the path with the cross which was adorned by them inside the house, for them to pray before. They cense it with incense until they bring it inside. For they say that the spirit of the "Milagroso" comes with them when they arrive at their houses.

When they are going inside, the woman who is cradling the cross and the man who is censing it walk very very slowly with it. When they have arrived at the door, the woman enters with the cross, and then the man who is censing it. Behind enters the one who is saying the prayers, and the one in charge of the celebration. Behind the prayer-sayer and the one in charge of the celebration, all the many people who are assisting in the praying jam themselves together entering. Those who do not, remain on the house plot. They wait until the praying finishes because they are *chilate* drinkers and tamale eaters.

149

They arrive; the woman comes to the edge of the altar of the cross and stands the cross on its support. And they let themselves fall to their knees, all of them. And also the man who is censing the cross, until the praying is finished. There they kneel; they do not get up until the prayer is over.

XIX

When the praying is finished, everyone who was working is gathered together with the *chilate* makers; they go in one by one for the candles to be rubbed against the heads of all the little children. Because they say that it is the blessing of the "Milagroso" that they are praying will come. He is separating out those who did not go to the celebration. When this is finished, then the tamales and *chilate* are taken out. When they see it is becoming twilight, they begin with the burning of copal. All the villages fire rockets and bombs. With the firing of rockets when night falls it comes to be as late as twelve o'clock at night before they rest.

XX

Because when they are burning incense, that is the time when they pray. They ask for everything that they want: their health, their corn, their beans, their chickens, their cattle, those who have some, their coffee trees. They ask that they not be dried up by the heat.

They say to the "Milagroso," "Where we are coming, we see you. Give us what we want, so that there is an abundance of what we eat in our houses. Let there not be a scarcity for us. Give us a healthy appearance, healthy expressions. Do not let disease enter our houses. All the evil spirits: you are dominant over them. Throw them into the mountains, where there are no human beings."

XXI

It is that evening, on the fifteenth of January, that some celebrate on their house lots, which is called "Limosna." When the light falls on the peaks, the *chilate* grinding begins. It is ground until night falls. When it comes to be nine o'clock at night, they begin to go back and forth carrying *chilate* to the bower. Then at twelve o'clock at night the praying ends. They begin to distribute the *chilate* among the people who are there. When it gets light the next day, all the people begin to be fed. They are given tamales. When the tamale eating is finished, the people begin to disperse, going to their houses.

BLESSING OF THE FIRST FRUITS (*Paí-Kaiová*)

Hail, Chirú, adorn my body
like your own;
Mburuvichá first adorned your
body;
may he also adorn mine.
May Mburuvichá who first adorned your body,
also adorn mine.

SACRIFICIAL HARVEST CEREMONY AND PRAYERS (*Mapuche-Araucanian*)

1. Sacrificial Harvest Ceremony

Now the sacrificial ceremonials begin. While the two old women beat their kultrugn, the sergeant hands a yellow hen and a pipe filled with tobacco to the captain—pipes at the gnillatun must be of wood or clay. The hen has been resting near the place where the banners were set; the pipe was there also. The captain, holding the hen by the feet and swinging it skyward, says a prayer of petition: he prays for favorable weather, for an abundant harvest, for health for the people and their animals, for an increase in animals, and for whatever else he wishes. After the prayers are said, the sergeant breaks the neck of the hen or tears off her head, drops her on the ground, and sits by until she has died, drawing drafts from the pipe and blowing smoke skyward. The sergeant now throws the hen on the holy fire where it is completely consumed. If anyone else has brought a hen to be sacrificed, it, too, has been killed and may now be thrown on the fire.

Next, sheep and calves and maybe a young horse, which have all been hitched nearby until now, are prepared for sacrifice. There are two ways in which the blood of these animals may be offered: the animal may be killed and the blood squeezed from the heart and sprinkled about, or the pulsating heart of the living animal may be pulled forward and the blood allowed to squirt about at each pulsation. In either case, the captain holds the heart for all to see, while he prays, "Hear us, Chau! We are all united in this prayer. Hear us, Father in the far above and woman with him. Hear us! Give us blue skies so that we shall have a good harvest."

"Today," added Huenun, "many families sacrifice only hens because they are poorer than formerly. However, as poor as I am, I sacrificed a calf six years ago after my eldest daughter had died—she was the seventh of my children to die. A machi told me that someone was doing me harm and that my remaining children and my wife would also die; already the evil with which to kill them had been prepared. She said that if I offered a calf at the gnillatun, their deaths might be averted. I offered the calf. My wife and children are all living."

While the large animal is being consumed by the holy fire, every father walks around it and dashes a pinch of flour into the fire. He may do this as often as he is moved to do so, and each time he does, he prays Chau to bring to a favorable harvest all that the people have planted. After the men have made their offerings, mothers of families are invited to do the same, but only those come forward who have brought flour with them and who have an inclination to offer some—usually these are only old women. No children are permitted to participate in this ceremonial. While the flour is being offered, the captain, smoking the pipe and blowing smoke skyward, begs Gnunechen to grant favorable weather and an increase in animals. He prays also that families, especially those participating in the gnillatun, be maintained in good health and that sickness bypass them and go elsewhere. After this, all again dance as before, but this time around the stalks with the banners.

And now the caciques—or if there is only one present, he and some of the older men—meet to the north of the fire and encourage each other to keep intact the customs of their forefathers; they make it a point to say that they are doing so right now by celebrating the gnillatun. They then ask God to bless crops and families. "There is really much talking going on among them," said Huenun. "It is not unusual for them to talk for an hour. We sometimes wonder what they are talking about." Following this, the captain prays again while the cacique and people stand by in close formation.

Next, two men on horseback, each with a trutruka, take position to the north of the holy fire; the captain and one of the two girls are mounted on horses to the right of them; the other man and girl, also on horses, to the left. These six now stand in line facing the holy fire. Back of them and also facing the fire, are all other participants who came on horseback. The sergeant now rides back and forth, four times, in front of the line of six, each time ordering all to yell "Ya-ah!" All nonparticipants—usually these have come as observers or with old persons who participate—arrange themselves in similar formation to the south of the fire, but outside the ellipse—nonparticipants never enter the ellipse. "These are invited Mapuches," Huenun explained. "No gringos or Chilenos blancos are ever allowed to be present—only invited Mapuches are permitted there." After the "Ya-ah!" has been yelled, the line of six exchanges position with those on horseback who are behind them. This exchange of positions takes place four times; each time, when it is completed, the sergeant rides back and forth and exhorts all to yell "Ya-ah!" With this the ceremonial ends.

Women now leave for the sun shelters—each family or several together have erected one outside and to the east of the ellipse. Participating men and boys seat themselves in a semicircle where the banners are standing, that is, within the ellipse to the south and west. Women serve them mudai and toasted wheat here, and sometimes tortillas and roasted meat also. Invited men and boys, nonparticipants, go to the sun shelters to eat; all women and girls eat there, also.

After all have eaten, the konchatun is performed; it is an integral part of the gnillatun and should never be performed except at the gnillatun, and then only after the meal. Huenun was emphatic about this. The konchatun takes place in the northeast part of the ellipse, where all gather.

At the konchatun, Huenun continued, one man reciprocates an act of friendship another man rendered him at some time. These two men stand facing each other; if they wish it, another man may stand alongside each of them. The reciprocating man cuts a sheep completely open at the underside, from neck downward, takes out the heart and, while it still pulsates, hands it to his friend, expressing words of gratitude to God for having granted him the good fortune of having this man as his friend. The two together then flip some blood of the sheep skyward and toward the holy fire. Following this, the reciprocating man gives the slaughtered sheep to his friend, who cuts off the head and right front leg and asks someone present—probably the man who has been standing by his side, if there has been one—to take the remainder of the sheep and put it in his (the recipient's) sun shelter. Later the recipient takes it home. From then on, these two friends stay close to each other until all depart for home. Huenun seemed to like the konchatun, and regretted that in recent years it is sometimes omitted at the gnillatun. "Our young men do not want to learn how to perform it," he said in slightly angry tones. "Eventually it will die out. I am glad you are recording what I tell you, because I know that what I tell you is the truth. It is most important that generations of Mapuches yet to be born can learn the truth.

"By now evening has come," Huenun went on to say. "All prepare to leave for home, but before doing so, there is a grand finale. All men who came on horseback ride around the elliptical track four times, while those with pifulkas fife them, those with trutrukas blow them, the two old women beat their kultrugns, and every man, woman, and child fills the air with 'Ya-ah's!'"

At the very end, mudai is put into a pottery vessel and is buried where the banners are planted. "Now," said Huenun with enthusiasm, "at the next gnillatun—maybe in a year or two, or three or four, although there should be one every year —this container will be unearthed, and if the mudai has turned to kernels of wheat or corn or if it is still in liquid form, it is a good sign and indicates that we shall have a fruitful year. If it has turned to earth or has disappeared, it is a sign that we shall have a bad year.

"Should it happen," added Huenun, "that so many animals are brought for sacrifice as to warrant a second day of ceremonials, the sergeant wakes at the holy fire all night to keep it smoldering. Families who live close by go home, but those who have come from far stay in nearby rukas. All make their appearance again the following morning for a repetition of the ceremonials. Every day the ceremonials are the same as the first day. I have attended gnillatuns that have lasted five days," he added.

"The last day of the ceremonial must end when the sun is there [at an angle of forty-five degrees] because the people have to be home before dark, since there is always danger of attacks by pumas after dark.

2. *Harvest Prayers*

(I)

Here you are, Lord of the Earth,
Today we celebrate the Gnillatun in homage to you.
Favor us with foods, with wheat, peas, and potatoes.
Thou shalt preserve us and say of us:
"My lambs still pray to me."
Have pity on us because you have created us.

(II)

I have entered once more into the field of prayer.
I have said to myself, "Time to do a little business,
Time to ask again."
I am alive on the earth and
I ask again for calm skies and cloudy skies.
My heart is clean and I beg again to receive

155

The fruits of the earth.
I make my prayer with a clean heart, oh God.
You created me.
You make me a priest, you gave me the job.
So once again I hoist my sacred banner.
My blue acolyte and my old wife will help me,
Because God has given me this rite
To obtain my sustenance, the fruits of the earth,
Wheat, peas, green beans, barley, potatoes, corn,
Black beans, pigweed,[1] for all these things I pray, oh God,
Sow well, look at me while I have my heart in my hand
Like a pearl, like a drop of dew.
Give me all the different kinds of grains
To sustain my sons and daughters,
To sustain my large family.
Which is why I say of you today:
"He will be generous with me." . . .
The Chief of this tribe has asked me,
"Pray for me, so that my large family may live."
The season is far advanced, which is why I want quiet
    weather
and rains.
Be good to me, God, you have created me, made me the way I
    am.
Send me rain, may my seeds sprout,
This is our way of asking, these are our customs.
All my numberless people, all the Mapuches, have these
customs . . .
God, creator of all men, who has power over men and animals,
You have given us all animals, horses, cows, sheep,
chickens,
You have created them all for us and told us,
"Pray for these things."
Which is why we pray.

[1] Pigweed—In Quechua *quinoa*. Used as a "tonic" like cocaine.

Here is your chicken, your immolated/ sacrificed heart.
Receive it again today.
Today, as the sun rises up, I offer you your chicken,
And your heart as precious as pearls, drops of dew.
Here is your holocaust,
Receive it today, I beg you, please receive it from me.
My good father has died, my grandfather,
Many of my family, my good relatives, my grandmother.
I beg, God, for me, take your part of the seed,
I want to reap all that I sow.
Which is why the Chief asked me to pray today.
For this I pray, God,
So many of my ancestors prayed on their knees in this same
holy field.
Have mercy on me, oh God,
Give me that which I ask,
Give me today what I ask.

(III)

Favor me, oh Father.
We live for you. For you we care for our crops.
You give us oxen.
Sheep exist created by you,
Horses exist created by you.
Favor me, God my Father, favor me.
I will be good.
May my boy live,
Give me your good luck, God my Father who is in heaven.
This prayer in your commandment, your power.
You have instituted all prayers, all petitions.
They are different kinds of prayers . . .
The prayer we are praying today was sent to us by you.
You are the creator of all the people here.
This prayer was known to our ancestors.
The prayer we pray today is not my prayer but the
Prayer you taught to our ancestors.

Hardly had people been created when you said,
"This is the way that I want the Mapuches to pray,
With the blood of animals, with the blood of lambs, with
mudai,[2]
That is how you pray."
Hardly were people made when you taught them how to
  pray,
Which is why I pray to you today, God, my Father.

HARVEST SONGS OF ANGASMAYO (*Quechua*)

1. Joining hands and running across the straw.

Let us go around, let us go around,
Clap hands
Let us follow the crowd, let us follow the crowd,
Clap hands
Beside this threshing floor,
Clap hands
Beside this threshing floor we will have a circle,
Clap hands
Let us have rods of ribbons,
Clap hands
Let us have armfuls of ribbons,
Clap hands
Let us increase, let us stretch out with the shawl,
Clap hands
We will spread out with the matting, let us spread out,
Clap hands
Like rain let us shower down, let us shower down,
Clap hands

Like rain let us spread out, let us spread out,
Clap hands

  [2] Alcoholic drink made of grain.

To clap, to run, is to learn how,
Clap hands
Like rain let us shower down, let us shower down,
Clap hands
Like rain let us spread out, let us spread out,
Clap hands
Let us shower down, let us shower down,
Clap hands
Strike at it, strike at it,
Clap hands
Dance more, dance more,
Clap hands
Beside this threshing floor, beside this threshing floor,
Clap hands.

2. Guavas[3]—Sung after turning over straw with forked poles.

Guavas, guavas, guavas,
unmarried girl would you like,
guavas, guavas, guavas,
unmarried girl would you like,

Ay sweet lime of my memories
you have talked with another in my absence,
in what ravine have you talked,
in what ravine have you conversed.

By night we will meet one another,
when it shall be black, we will meet one another,
may God grant you shall want
for us to meet by night.

You have spoken with a knife,
you have spoken with a razor,
just here, just here, we will go around,
just here, just here, we will tumble down,

[3] A very common fruit in Latin America.

We will tread on it, we will tread on it,
we will strike, we will strike,
face, with our face,
until the finish, we will tread on it, we will tread on it.

Like dust, we will make it like dust,
thus, so that they say of us,
we make an evening of dust, we make an evening of dust,
thus, so that they say of us.

Like a branch we will be burdened,
like a branch we will fall down,
like an earthquake we will shake,
like a thunderbolt we will sound.

3. Green Olive Tree—Turning the straw over again.
We will turn around, we will turn around,
with your painted forked pole,
it is true what you say,
from your mama your trimmed pole,
beating, we will let ourselves go,
we will join the dull bull talk,
boasting, boasting, with your mouth of roses,
that is true, to say it is roses,
your hole of a mouth,
boast, boast, with your sweet stem of a throat,
it is true to say that it is a bragging stem of a throat,
we will turn around, we will beat,
with the talk of an unmarried girl.

4. Little Lizard—Dancing on the straw, hands interlocked.
Stone, stone, it is your house,
little lizard, little lizard,
thorn, thorn is your house,
little lizard, little lizard,

Paint labors
in a book of silver,
little lizard, little lizard,
paint the S
in a book of gold,
little lizard, little lizard.

Mask of cabbage,
walking cane of onion,
coriander your headpiece,
parsley your clawpiece,
cut-out wood your tail,
look, take care,
little lizard, little lizard.

5. *The Bagre Fish*

In the depths of the river, there is a bagre,
in the depths of the river there is a bagre,
look, look, how I warn you, bagre,
look, look, how I speak to you, bagre.

The old guitar is coming,
the old guitar is sounding,
look, look, how I warn you, bagre,
look, look, how I speak to you bagre.

In the depths of the river, there is a bagre,
in the depths of the river, there is a bagre.

6. *Cerbaschay*

We will go to Tarma, running, running,
Cerbaschay
We will go to Tarma, running, running,
Cerbaschay
Seize me, seize me,
Cerbaschay

At the side of the threshing floor,
Cerbaschay
Threshing, threshing,
Cerbaschay

Like the sparrow hawk, we will flap wings, we will flap wings,
Cerbaschay
Like the sparrow hawk, we will hover, we will hover,
Cerbaschay
Like the condor we will turn around,
Cerbaschay
At the side of the threshing floor we will turn around,
Cerbaschay

By the edge of the ribbon,
Cerbaschay
Seize me, seize me,
Cerbaschay
By the brim of the sombrero,

Cerbaschay
Seize me, seize me,
Cerbaschay
Seize me by the hand, seize me,
Cerbaschay.

7. *Bachelor*

Spring at the foot of the quishuar, weaver of belts, bachelor,
spring at the foot of the quishuar, weaver of belts, bachelor,
Choose, if you say I will choose, bachelor,
weave, if you say I will weave, bachelor,
at the side of this threshing floor, bachelor,
at the side of this threshing floor, bachelor,
like the painted gourd, we will paint, bachelor,
like the gourd not painted, we will not paint, bachelor,
a shawl of colors we will carry, bachelor,

white silver we will carry in the pocket, bachelor,
half unfastened we will leave the girdle, bachelor,
a ten-cent piece we will put at the girdle, bachelor.

8. Lima-Lima Flower[4]

Ay, lima-lima flower,
Talk with him, you have told me,
in what cove have we been talking,
in what hollow have we been talking.

At this hour he may appear—
to pound him like jerked mutton!
At this hour he may appear,
we will tread on him like a frozen potato!
At this hour he may appear,
like ground chili we will leave him!

Ay, lima-lima rose,
Talk with him, you have told me.
with me, you have not talked,
with me you have not conversed,
(perhaps you have a knife placed for me?)
(perhaps you have a razor placed for me?)
with me you have not talked.

From Lima a letter has come,
who can answer?
When my mother comes to know about it
she will say it is from your sweetheart,
when my father comes to know about it
he will say go to the convent,
who can answer?
If I could answer, I would answer,
if I could respond, I would respond.

[4] The Lima-Lima or Talk-Talk flower grows up in the cold, mountainous regions. The Indians believe it can cure the mute.

When there is paper, there is no one who can write,
when there is someone who can write, ink will be lacking,
when there is ink, penholder will be lacking,
when there is penholder, pen I will not have,
when there is pen, envelope will be lacking,
when there is envelope, stamp will be lacking,
when there is stamp, there will be no post office,
when there is post office, there will be no train,
when there is train, I will deliver it.

Ay, lima-lima flower,
Talk to him, you have told me.

9. *The straw has been ground down by the dancing. During*
   this song the boys sing louder and louder and the boys beat
   time faster and faster with their feet.

Continue the round, continue the round, continue the round,
continue the round, continue the round, continue the round,
like a wheel we will revolve,
like a wheel we will revolve,
at the edge of the threshing floor, they are telling us,
at the edge of the threshing floor, they are telling us,
like a wheel we will revolve,
at the edge of the threshing floor we will revolve,
beat your feet, bachelor,
strike, bachelor.

Like dust, like dust we will make it,
like cornmeal, like cornmeal we will leave it.

Why are you frightened, bachelor?
why are you afraid, bachelor?
You being free, your partner feels lost,
you being one, your partner feels lost,
where she is, I would not feel lost,
where she is, I would not feel lost.

We will form, we will form, like a file we will file,
how ugly you are, boy, how ugly you are, young man,
why do you weep, why do you feel sad?
Ay, poor boy, ay, poor bachelor!
what is your heart saying, what is your heart saying to me?
As for me, my heart is palpitating,
as for me, my heart is palpitating.

Ay hummingbird, hummingbird, we will sing, hummingbird,
ay hummingbird, hummingbird, we will whistle, humming-
    bird,
how pretty, how pretty, heavenly little poncho,
how pretty, how pretty, little poncho like the dawn,
ay hummingbird, hummingbird, son of a hummingbird,
ay hummingbird, hummingbird, daughter of a hummingbird.

Higher than the graveyard the shepherd's horn, it cries,
higher than the house of Samaniego, the shepherd's horn
    moans.
What says your heart, what says your heart
does it not palpitate, your heart, does it not palpitate, your
    heart?
Ay poor boy, ay poor bachelor,
for you, for me, too, it will be our star,
ay poor boy, ay poor bachelor,
these people have been the cause,
the sons of these people have been the cause
of our meeting each other on this threshing floor.

10. *Majordomo*

Majordomo, majordomo,
you are worthless, majordomo.
Captain, captain,
you are worthless, captain.

Where is it, where is your bull,
where is it, where is your cow?

This is bull, this is cow,
it is worthless, this your cow,
good bull, you have said to me,
good cow, you have said,
Is this good bull,
is this good cow?
The bull of mine, it is son of good bull, of good cow,
it is son of a good milk cow.

You are worthless, steward,
of dirty water you made chicha,
you give only one cigar,
the leaves of the tanquis is your coca,
you are worthless, steward,
let us gather at your place, let us all get together.
Black, we will be black, we will be dark,
you are worthless, steward.

11. Traveler

Traveler to another town, what says your heart?
As for me, my heart trembles,
as for me, my heart palpitates.
Trumpet of the countryside,
trumpet that cries,
trumpet that moans,
trumpet that cries.

Ay poor boy, what says your heart?
Ay poor boy, what says your heart?
Like the street of Concepción, black, we will be black,
like the street of Concepción, dark, we will be dark,
like the bridge of Mejorada, rocking, we will be rocking,
like the street of Huancayo, black, we will be black,
like the bell of Huancayo, ringing, we will be ringing.

We are not going to love a widower man,
if you like, a field-working man will like you,

a widower man, he is like a barn of green peas, which are
    spilled,
a widower man, he is like a barn of broad beans, which are
    spilled,
like the cookstove of the blacksmith, he is black,
he is dark like the cookstove of the traveler.
A widower man you are not going to love,
in the plaza of Chupaca his coarse face,
in the plaza of Huancayo without a cent.

HOLY WEEK (*Chorti Maya*)

One celebration happens in April, which is called Holy Week.
Many people go again to Esquipulas. Anyone who didn't go in
January goes then in April. Leaving the house on a Tuesday,
he arrives on Wednesday, so as to be there.

Thursday at eight o'clock the Nazarene is carried and shut
away in a house far out on the edge of town. That house
serves as a prison. There they stand him and shut him away.

At that time, when they shut away the Nazarene they say
that the Glory is shut away. There it stays shut away during
the whole evening and until the next day. On Friday they take
him out at eight o'clock. They take him out and parade him
around in all the streets of the town.

He is scolded by the Priest when he is being paraded
around. He is called "Burro! Horse! Long-Ear!" because they
say that he sold his father. And behind him come three boys.
They are poking him with canes which they carry, with nails
stuck by them in the ends of the canes. They are walking and
poking the backbone of the Nazarene.

And when they reach a place where they stand him to rest,
a man comes with a sponge in his hand; he moistens it with
dye and suspends it at the mouth of the Nazarene. So they
carry him until they reach the house which is called the
prison. And his torso is bound by them with rope, and with a
cross on his back.

And when that day is here, when Jesus Nazarene is carried,

that is the time, at seven o'clock, when the Glory is shut away. On that day nobody can work, nor bathe, nor gather firewood. They say those who do help the evil ones kill.

That is why whoever wants to bathe and wants to gather firewood, in the evening they gather firewood. Then they can bathe. When they hear the sounding of the bell in the town, they say that the Glory is already being shut away.

At that time nobody can work, nor can he bathe, because they say that if he bathes, his ears are plugged up, because the Glory is shut away. They wait until the next day, on Saturday.

Friday comes. On Friday, the Holy Corpse, which they call *San Manuel de Mesías* is crucified.

When it gets to be eight o'clock, they take him out and parade him in the street. They carry him and crucify him on a cross. They wait until it gets to be four o'clock. They take him down from the cross and carry him on their shoulders to stand him in the church.

At three o'clock in the afternoon, two Virgins leave, and Apostles. They are carried along to the parish, where San Manuel lies. And that is the way they spend the duration of the afternoon, until five o'clock in the afternoon, when San Manuel is taken out again, and the Virgins and Apostles. All together they go out, being carried along on shoulders, humbly, humbly.

They say prayers in front of them at every house on the street whose doorway is decorated with pine branches. And a table was placed by them. And they come and those Gods which they are carrying around are stood up. It comes to be twelve o'clock at night when they enter inside the sanctuary.

When he is put back into the church, the people gather themselves into a group. They pray. There is a custom they believe in. There are some who bring corn whose grains are blood red, so as to hang them on the arms of the cross where San Manuel hangs. Others bring squash, looking for one with a curled neck. He hangs it beside where he is tied, hanging. Another brings dough which he dips out in front of him, because they say that he is the master of all that is.

That is why people, when they are dying, save their corn, which has beautiful grains. They look for those with beautiful white grains, with black corn, with red corn. Because they say that that is the blood of Jesus Christ.

Because, they say that with the blood of Jesus Christ there appeared all the beans, corn, squash, sugarcane, and bananas. Because they say that the devil met Jesus Christ one day. He said to Jesus Christ, "Let us perform a test. We will see whose blood is better."

They say that the devil cut himself. And from the blood of the devil there came out all the animals which are evil: snakes, poisonous lizards, iguanas, worms, lizards. And then, the blood of Christ. There came seedlings, beans, sugarcane, squash.

That is why people believe until today. Because so the old-timers used to believe, a long time ago. But in each celebration they always use incense, candles, and *chilate*. In that celebration, when people are coming home from Esquipulas all around, grouping together, they walk along praying to the houses. And all around the peaks thunder with the many rockets and bombs where they are bursting in the villages.

And they say that is a promise they make with the "Milagroso," so that he will give them everything they ask for. They say that so there will be abundance in the house. That is why they put out all those things.

XVIII. SNAKE-PEOPLE/PEOPLE-SNAKES—WITH FROG, WHALE, AND OTHER AQUATIC VARIATIONS

THE HORNED SERPENT (*Chorti Maya*)

There is another story that is told about the serpent that is called Txan. They say that at one time, about the river that passes by the edge of the town of Jocotan, they say that that river, at one time, rose until it went into the brush. The water carried off absolutely everything—the cane, the bananas, whatever was planted near the banks of the water.

It carried off everything and carried off the houses that—the houses which were found near where the water passes. It carried everything off; it grabbed and carried off the pigs, the chickens, horses, and cattle—everything that it found where it was overflowing, near the banks of the river. It carried everything away. And the houses. Because they say that the serpent came out of a mountain named Sesekmil.

We don't know the place but so it is said, that that is what the mountain's name is, where the serpent came out. And for that reason the people say of the serpents, when they grow within the mountains, that their horns come out.

And then when they grow, then the serpents which still aren't—still aren't Great Serpents, when they grow, they say that they go like people; they look for their wives, to mate with them. Well, they say that when there is a landslide, that that is the serpents coming out; they say that they go looking for their wives to mate with them. And, therefore, they come out of the mountains where they live, and go crawling to another mountain. But where they come out they make great landslides, and they destroy the place.

People today say that not all come out and go to where they want to go. Because they say that that serpent was found lying here on the banks of the stream. And he remained lying in the water, on top of a big rock. And there he lay. Because they say that he was smitten by the gods because it was seen that he was causing great destruction in that place. He carried off the houses, and then he was smitten by the gods. And, therefore, the people say that the serpent may not come out, if he is not given permission by God.

There are some that come out without causing a landslide, or they do but do not destroy any houses. And then they go wherever they want to go. But if the serpent destroys many things, like houses where he comes out, he is not allowed by God to go wherever he wants. He is smitten, and killed right there. Because they say that that serpent was smitten by the gods; and there he lay in that stream where his path came out, passing by the villages.

It has come to be said that that serpent lay there for eight days. Because nobody came by where he lay and saw him. Because they were frightened. And they say that the serpent, in his tail, went around carrying two bags. They say that they were filled with money.

And, therefore, they say of that serpent that when he was found, lying dead, people filled the banks of that stream. They wanted to go chop off his tail and take out the money. But they were afraid because they say that the wind of the serpent's passing is very great. That wind suddenly throws one down into the river. And one cannot get out. And, therefore, the serpent is feared.

Well, that snake they say it was lying there for eight days. No one came to its side because they say that although dead, it still had the wind of its passing. And that didn't let people come up beside it. But people watched it because, they say, it was a great deal of money. It came out carrying it when it emerged, when it wanted to go mate with its fellow serpent, in some other mountain. It took all its money along. And they say it was a great deal.

And then the people wanted to take it out, but they were

frightened. And they say its horn was all full of money. Its horn, they say, was like the horn of a bull, but very large. And that is why they said the serpent had money.

When the water began to dry up, he remained lying on dry land. Then they say that many vultures began to gather, and he began to be eaten. But he lay there a long time. He was being eaten by the vultures because they say that that serpent was very large.

And that is why it took a long time for the vultures to eat him all up. But I didn't see it, since I didn't go see where he was lying dead. If I had seen it, maybe I would have taken his money.

TRUTH FROM THE SERPENT (*Maya*)

Once there was truth, which we drew from the Serpent in ancient times, from the clear unclouded heavens to the evil-knotted earth beneath. But when the enemy warriors came, the folds of death became the swaddling clothes of our babies.

Now it should be said of the four gods, the four Bacabs, that they stretched out the earth. And when they had finished stretching out the earth, they planted the red Imix tree.

They receive a handful of offerings as a token of their having stretched out the earth. These Bacabs shake the tree. Perhaps the moon germinates the plants.

And they planted the white Imix tree in the north. Perhaps they will grant us a sign, a symbol of the stretching out of the earth.

Although they place a black Imix tree at the west of our land as a sign of their having stretched out the earth, the black face of this black Imix tree in our midst will frighten the multitude.

The yellow Imix tree stands to the south of the land as a sign of the stretching out of the earth. It stands there, yellow, to tell the news.

Finally there is the green Imix tree in the middle of the country, to commemorate the stretching out of the earth. The people are instructed concerning the origin and existence of the katun. So be it . . .

Sweet was the ancient fruit, and succulent on the tongue; sweet to soften the hard heart, to mollify the angry passions! Chac Vayab the Bat, he it is who sucks honey from the flowers . . .

Let the flowers spring forth from the bowl!

The Maya people learn about the gateway to the house of flowers. The priests smell the flowers. The lords smell the flowers. The warriors smell them. This is the treasure of the Lord of Flowers which he brought when he descended. Is not life the burden of the flowery katun, and of the previous stones?

The penances dear to the heart of Ku Mitnal, God of the Underworld, did not arrive, either, when the Nine Wisemen, the Bolon Tzacab, descended for the penance of the flowers.

Now the wizards vie with one another in taking the shapes of the blue heron and of the hummingbird. Then flowers descend from the source and from the folds of the hand, nine flowers. When the hearts of the flowers appear, the priests place four branches of flowers on the burning altar of the sun . . .

No longer are there stones which speak a little. He does not sit down to rest with his burden, the gifts of the nine gods. The seven devils descend, bringing a condition of ruin, even utter darkness.

This is the burden of the katun in the days of the Christians, in the days of the lascivious men, when such terrible suffering came . . .

When the invasion came during Katun 11 Ahau, even the heavens pitied themselves. They blamed it on the moon when our warriors cut their own throats. Great numbers assembled and they all sang together to the gods.

There was he who advises about new moons; and he who advises about attaining man's estate; and he who advises about buying and selling; and he who advises about the prime of life; and he who advises on the problem of marriageable daughters.

Your expectation is from the gods and from your elder

brothers. Lest your visitor, the god of the white face, make you change your manner of dressing and turn you into effeminate fellows, you must cut off the white, bearded strangers from Ichcansiho. Whip them from the land!

And the priests of the living God, the true God, shall write in the sacred book of the universe concerning the earth when He descended and His effulgence grew brighter and brighter.

Gradually in this land there shall be no more sculptured Temples of the Jaguar for you, when these men extend their sway among the heavens.

The lords were vanquished, and there was much praying for their lives and shedding of tears at the end, as they lay stretched out on the mats trying to staunch the flowing blood, or lying flat on their backs in heaps.

The true men work miracles to protect the people. The priests, Ah Kin, work wonders. The searchers, Ah Bobat, work wonders. Nobody will be left out. They thoroughly cleanse the lords, their faces and their hearts. Will you, the foremost division of earth-dwellers, be taken captive lying flat on your backs, while your feet are still able to carry the whole of you?

Should meditation during the day, and meditation during the night, be considered the sin of the day, and the sin of the night?

Great is the tenderness of the hearts of Ah Bobat, true men, when alas your arms are laden with burdens like stones and, without houses, without parents, you look upon yourselves and your feet are confused.

Men with trumpets are making the rounds of the country. Only seven days remain to our government. Then come the men to dig to the very bottom to fill their baskets. They lay waste the property of our people, making destitute the houses of our rulers. The holy symbols on the altars will allure them. They will covet the precious masks.

These men will laugh in the faces of our countrymen and of the people of the province, and of our rulers and lords. Having at heart the welfare of Pop and Zam and of the government, true men will deny, when they are asked, that they have any property.

A wave of disgust sweeps through the house of the gods because you forget life, you forget your own ancient teachings. Within your very doors, the avaricious lords are your punishment in the living katun.

The mouths of our white oppressors declare the things pertaining to the year to be only wind. They even go so far as to say that there will not be a throne in the heavens, shining like the sun, to be adored in its majesty.

The ancient people strove to attain perfection. In olden times they recognized the miracles performed by the heavenly Hunab Ku, the One God. Formerly, Ichcansiho knew how to protect all the people.

The security of our land, the security of the province shall return! Our faces shall be set free! Our hands shall be set free! Our feet shall be set free!

If the earth is shattered, if there is pestilence, if destruction comes to the rulers, they will forget the sight of the stripping bare of the altars of Pop and Zam. Then their necks were stretched, during the three days of government, the three days of Zam, mourning again for their eternal homes, lamenting the invasion, mourning for the casting of lots before starting on a journey. We will find Zam and Pop in the heavens.

There are some who deny their ancestors, who deny their ancient houses when the covetous sons, the covetous sons arrive. Ropes descended. Clay descended. When the descent of the hills came, as was customary, they were resentful.

The lust of the belly, the lust of carnal sin, the lust for noble family, the sin of arrogance, all these are vices which come quickly . . . So be it. The sculptor of the gods . . .

The surface of the earth will be moved. How can the people be protected, thus disturbed in the midst of the earth, in the sculptured land of Ichcansiho, when all around us there are beggars soliciting alms? They will appropriate the idols and the vestments of Pop and Zam from the lords. The burden of our land will be: how much will it take to satisfy these avaricious rulers?

The sons of the sun are sorrowful, and wisely so, for they lament the intruders, and they feel poignantly the ridicule of the casting of lots. They doubt that protection of the people will result from scoffing at the Bacabs.

According to the omens above the earth and the prophecies, the disturbers of our land shall eventually turn back, after the years of avarice have passed and our sons have used concealment after concealment.

The lords watch for the coming of Hunac the Knower, Hunac the Artist, Hunac the Enchanter. He will teach the priests the complete magic of Zam and Pop. And the Jaguar will measure out the six magic formulas of government: these involve good chiefdoms, a good aristocracy, good men, and good sons, throughout the earth. He will bring food and water on his back, regardless of borrowed Pop and borrowed Zam. When they arrive each day in the midst of the land, they will find themselves in an uninhabited desert.

When good men are oppressed and their towns destroyed, there will be no more mountain lions in the land, no more foxes, no more ferrets in the ravines. There will be no niggardly king. There will be no deliverer to save his kingdom. There will be no licking of the feet of rulers.

No longer will the theft of our idols continue: "There will be the majesty. There will be the nobility. There will be the religion." But if they do not merit life, the pestilence will come to end the deception.

When an end finally comes to the troublesome days of the troublesome katun, He-who-crushes-the-rocks will bring to pass six good years followed by six bad years, in order that once more there may be an intercessor in our midst. The wicked knife of the warrior will wound grievously and destroy. We look forward to the good things when happiness will finally come to the land.

There will be no more foxes, no more towns, no more ferrets in the ravines. There will be no more noble descendants adorning the lion's den. It will be better if the world comes to an end.

One looks at the face of Citbolon or at the face of the sky of Citbolon, one at the sun, one at the forests, one at the trees, to determine what kind of remedy the heavens will provide, to be written down in the Book of the Katun for future years: "The business of life will be difficult, and retaining the breath of life full of sorrow."

The lords bind up their faces in pain because true men swelter in toil, and hunger is their burden, and because of their bad conscience about protecting the people.

They are agitated by the drums. The bat is awakened by the drums. The four Bacabs ride to earth on the back of a green rainbow. One by one the stars fall.

The lords hold their breath in the throat and make true their promise about setting Pop in order. It has become perverted by this time, a stain on the good name of our people. When the bearer of Katun 10 Ahau arrives, there will be great sorrow among the lords on account of the year-bearer . . .

The warrior will employ his prowess on nobody. When they are taught about the abundant life, they will have compassion on the fields. They will have compassion on the mountains. They shall be followed for the benefit of all concerned, so that there shall be no more sorrow in the fields, no need for distress in the mountains because the whole province and the entire earth were stretched out by the Bacabs . . . away from the insolent and lawless men, and from those who look with scorn upon our ancestors and upon our noble lineage. This is the offense of the lords of Chichen, the lords who came from the sea.

The Bacab who lives in the northern land; when our rulers shall presently fulfill all their obligations, perhaps there will descend arrows, perhaps there will descend shields to shelter the homeless ones.

Our sons sprinkle with their tears the majesties of the altar of Zam and the altars of the Pops. They take delight in the words concerning the path of truth, recollecting the furious speeches at the solemnities on account of the cupidity of the lords.

Then as in ancient times parting the sky, Sip will arrive. Now let true men be revealed to the people. They will break the necks of the lords of creation, because they secretly scoff at the altar of Zam and at the altar of the Pops.

However, when the country is on the point of being turned upside down, the humiliation of the overturning is a great evil in itself, the denial of perfection. They lament the invasion. They mourn for the casting of lots in order to learn the path for arriving at the divine goal.

They die, he who is of Pop and he who is of Zam. If true men cut their own throats, to the people will be left only what resembles the approach to a blank wall, a being left on the outside. Since no one ever arrives who travels by an evil road, the people weigh their words, whatever they may be, lest there be almost no end to lies.

When trees grow in the land, when rocks grow in the land, when it happens for the third time that they dwell in peace and serenity of life in Chacmitan, then there will come a recompense for the ancient hunger.

Three times for government they will have the authority of Zam, three times the authority of Pop. In the fourth tun they shall see an increase in the prosperity of the state and in the prosperity of the lords. Finally a day will come when there will be no more uprooting in the land, when it has been overthrown once again. There will be no more festival days to honor the authority of Pop and the authority of the Zams . . .

The gods give us the bread of heaven in their mercy. Let there be obedience to their laws. Is not the desire to obey, is not obedience itself the duty of the lords? Their throats will be silent when the life of abundance comes to an end, and with it esteem for one blood relationship. And there will no longer be obedience through veneration for one Western tongue in the land of Pop and Zam. The pestilence shall be their burden.

When discord comes among the rulers may the gods forbid that true men among the people shall perish! The vomit of blood shall be the burden of the katun. The day shall come when you will withhold the bread of life from these white-skinned effeminate fellows, from their very teeth.

Our descendants shall pierce them with the lance. Our ancestors shall pierce them with their hands tied together. The chanter of news shall pierce them. The horse shall strike them down with despair. The horse shall pierce them in secrecy. It is decreed.

At Chichen one half the katun shall be good; one half shall be without good. There will be the majesty of the throne of him who speaks the magic language of the stars of heaven submerged in blue water. Likewise the pestilence will enter our houses . . .

In order that our people may recognize deception when it comes, we have written down the auguries of the days of the katuns one by one, telling by what signs the burden of each katun may be recognized, and the manner in which the count of the bearer of future events is safeguarded when he comes; also the road by which the wisemen shall arrive on the day when they come, that it may become the road of the believers themselves. In the katun of trouble the warriors quietly blacken their faces.

Alas for us when the great ones, the bearded ones, the sons of the sun, the white men came along the trail! On that day we became the victims of their evil desires.

The bearded ones, the ones who shoot—this is the signal of the white god—were arriving. Six sons of heaven, some aged and infirm, came shouting to announce the news, spreading it over the country. They were present in every clump of trees, behind every heap of rocks, the friars, all exactly alike in appearance, negotiating for our souls and haranguing us about the "true god."

When you tried with all your hearts to emulate them they obstructed your efforts to protect the people. At our ceremonies we prayed to the gods above, asking intercession for our brothers, when they arrived.

You meditated on the words of God, never deceiving us with regard to the road of the future still to be made firm, the road of bondage. The Father of Heaven and Earth will hear your prayers, when you come to cast lots in the presence of the people in the matter of the tuns.

Little by little we began to grow weary of the maiming of the people by the Christians, when I should have liked to protect the people and guard the country. They gradually began to plant a church in the middle of Tiho. This did not do much harm to the katun treasure.

Gradually, they began the hangings again for the second time, and they kindled the fire on the stone. The offenses of the white people are all alike, even against those who surrender themselves or their relatives, everywhere they go. Brothers plead for justice in their throats. Gradually we discover that the Christians are great liars. Little by little we realize that they are great cheats.

Little by little, whether they take seven sacraments or not, their prayers are heard by their powerful God. You cast your lots. The people come. You set in order the enchantments . . .

Gradually the hanging of the great men among us began to take place, the extinction of noble lineages. Gradually began our sorrow for our daughters, our sorrow for our sons, for the foolish behavior of our daughters and the foolish behavior of our sons, made purposely so.

The omens of the gods must go, the omens of Kavil must go, and those of the Sky serpent, of Canhel the Sky serpent, alas!

Little by little began the offering of prayers to the Devil. Little by little came the days of spying and lying, when we began to go hungry and our feet were bruised with much walking for the protection of the people.

When they lifted up the necks and held in their hands the heads of nobles of high lineage, when they held up the neck of Chac Ahaucan of the lineage, when they began on the two priests of Zam and the two priests of Pop, and on Balam the Fox, Balam the interpreter of wonders, the Dog, then our hearts were broken when we heard the news.

The wretched man inquired minutely again and again as to how to be able to recognize the days of the moon count, and the katun-bearer, and the prophecies of the gods above.

When you descend to covetousness and avarice and the invocation of the Devil, then you reach the lowest abyss of falsifying the words of Hunab Ku above. The swindlers ridicule the year count of the Jaguar. The white men invent a system of spying on our great ceremonials, on the cherished rituals of the Jaguar Balam.

The stonings, the grievous hangings, all the cutting down and the wearisome bearing of heavy burdens have exhausted and bruised and pierced us. And when the katun-bearer arrived seven years ago, we made enchantments for protecting the people. And the mourning for the threefold learning, and the great yearning for a return to the occult teachings, kindled a fire which finally burst forth in Ichcansiho. The fact that the flaying of the mountain lion in the open plaza has been forbidden brings us to stony ground. We have burned great quantities of copal on account of the hangings.

When the katun-bearer finally arrived and the burden of our afflictions was unfolded, we saw the look on the faces of the two priests of Zam and the two priests of Pop, when they read the prophecy of the katun which does not lie, the words of the God in the holy heaven. And you, my brothers, mourned for the casting of lots and lamented the coming of the intruders . . .

Alas, three prophecies, three precepts, three hindrances to meditation, three hindrances to seeking the wisdom of the Sculptor of the Squared Stone, before the faces of the lords, when he polished his words concerning the other affairs, the other teachings.

There will be deep distress in spite of our yearning to protect the people, and they will be disturbed by divisions. There will be agitation in the midst of the land when "Justitia" descends upon the teaching of our sacred religion, and upon the words of the true God, and our obligation to protect the people from the abyss.

A thousand scaly warts descended when we were bitten by the serpent seven years ago. When we were bitten by the serpent seven years ago, a thousand scaly warts appeared after they came.

Shame descended on our fields when the spectacle of battle arose, the spectacle of war when it descended. We suffered from the absence of the venerable ones, the representatives of our people.

O Lord of Council, Lord of Strength, grant that the abundant treasures of the sandy beaches and the treasures within the ocean may not come to an end, when they descend! Be with us!

When those who pour out libations come face to face with dangerous warriors, they cut their claws and hang them up in a row. When the wolf descends with the burden of taxation, when the Christians arrive, when ropes descend from heaven, when great avarice comes, and the pestilence and the vomit of blood.

Mourning for our leaders, mourning for the casting of lots to determine the road by which the katun approaches and where its resting-place shall be. One by one the mysterious flowers fell when we reached the end of the concealment of the katun bundle, in the prayer for completion and the longing for the gift of perfection, when the avaricious hagglers intruded upon the katun ceremonies.

When the power descended with great force, sprinkling the faces of fierce warriors, they trembled and shuddered with fear. Immediately their hearts were grieved at the condition of affairs here on earth in the katun of perplexity, in the majesty of the katun, the lordship of the katun, the words of the katun, the food of the katun, the holiness of the katun, the march of the katun, the occupation and purpose of the katun, the great sons of the katun, the great daughters of the katun, the children of the katun, the warriors of the katun, the young men of the katun.

When they came, demanding entrance into our houses and assuming the power of government, on one day there was one cell for Zam and Pop, in the current katun. Oh the wretchedness of a country when trees and rocks rise up and join in the battle . . .

When the present government came into existence in the interests of the people, there happened to be many Maya who ridiculed their kindred. The conditions of local affairs throughout the country will rapidly reach a very low ebb. It will be a katun for shooting arrows, a katun for discharging muskets in battle. There will also be the shooting of our mischievous sons and daughters. In the course of time, when the prophecy of the katun ends in exhaustion, when the remedy comes and the gods descend, what kind of sculpture shall be unveiled?

With regard to the internal affairs of the country, the omens appear black indeed, because of the entanglement of the katun. Little by little, the government of the people will be divided, when the rulers keep asking them for money.

There will always be those who labor. There will always be wisemen. Yes, they spring up in this land of trees, in this land of rocks. The lords will take counsel together. They will cut the claws of those whom they will hang up in a row, then they scratch the bowed backs of the wolf and the foxes. They will burn fiercely on the altars. Then there will be no more foxes, no more wolves.

Then there shall be the great life, the life of the katun, the spirit of the katun, and a benevolent government. There will be rejoicing in the people's welfare. From the mouth of the sea they will obtain och fish. Then the katun, the flower of the Tree of Life, shall be established. After that, drought and blood vomit will bring happiness to an end.

They shall redeem the standard of the temple, Ah Kantenal. They shall redeem the vomit of blood for the fourth time. They shall redeem Kukulcan, carried on the backs of the Itza priests in four ceremonies.

In the assemblage of people they shall open the sealed katun. At dusk they will smell the fragrance of the flowers. Day shall be turned upside down. Their faces shall be disturbed. The genealogical tree shall descend. Stones shall descend and heaven and earth shall be universally consumed by fire.

They shall make a divination concerning the living and the dead: "The dead shall live! Dying from old age, they shall immediately ascend into heaven. They shall ascend quickly by good roads. Evil roads descend, spreading out on the earth."

At the end, in the final days of the katun, we will hear the words of the father of heaven and earth regarding the government of Katun 13 Ahau during his days, at the completion of the katun.

LANDSLIDE (*Chorti Maya*)

I'm going to tell another story. There is a town whose name is Ocotepeque . . . in Honduras. Of that town, they say, that once upon a time the town was large, and there were many people in it. And the houses were very pretty to look at. But there came a day it was destroyed, when that town was destroyed in the year 1932.

Not long ago that town was destroyed. And they say that when that town was destroyed, an old woman began to go around. The whole town was told that it should leave. They say that the old woman said, "Get out now! Because today this town no longer has any protection. Because this town . . . today is the day that it will be destroyed, and those who leave running will still be saved, and those who do not will be done for."

But the people did not obey. They said, "This old woman, she's just out of her mind, going around talking." Because they say that that old woman went to all the houses, and began to warn the people, but they said that "This old woman has just gone crazy." They did not believe what the old woman said.

But when evening came, the rain began to fall and it fell until day came. Another day dawned—it didn't stop. And then when the next day broke, at the moment day was breaking, the mountain thundered up above. Because that was a great mountain. It all slid down and buried the town, because we went there and saw the landslide which had come and buried the town.

The people say today, those who were there, they say that when the town was destroyed there were still people who began to flee, from that town; they went and stayed in a place far away.

But there was a stream that ran by the edge of the town, where it was destroyed. And they say that to that stream came a great deal of mud, which was brought by the landslide above. And they say that—there were those who began to get out their money then. They began to put it away, far away, where they thought that the landslide would not come. Because they say that that landslide little by little began to slide

184

down; they heard its thundering. It is said then—they said that —"There is danger we may truly be destroyed, because that is a real landslide coming, up there."

Then all the many people of the town began—they got out everything that was in their houses, and put it far away. And some worried about their money and began to take it away in their bags. They began to take it to put it away. And some— who began to carry it away, they say that they turned back to get other things they were getting out of their houses. The place where they were going was buried because that landslide came down from above.

And there where they were running down that ravine they were buried. And that money which was beginning to be taken out and put far away, where the landslide did not reach.

And its owners were buried when they turned back, so they could get out more of what was in their houses. And there they were buried. When, it is said, they heard all the earth coming down on their heads, there they were finished. And they could not return to see their money where it was left.

And, therefore, the people of that town, Ocotepeque, say that there many people began to gather up that money, and because of that, today they have money. Because many people began to get out their money to put it far away where the landslide did not come. But that was not a safe place because that was where they came back to their houses, wanting to bring away again what they had been bringing, and they did not get out because the landslide coming down from above buried them.

Then they saw that they were not able to go down the ravine, because the ravine had completely filled with mud. Then, what those who were still there, back in the town, did, was to gather together, in a house which was very high. There they were safe.

But there were those who still began to move things. So as to get their—things out that were in their houses, their money, their clothes, everything they still wanted to take far away. And there they were done for. On the path where the great landslide came down. And so the whole town was filled with mud that buried all the houses, completely covered with mud.

185

But only one house remained at the edge of the town on top of a high place. There it was filled with people who were safe.

And when that landslide was done, then a plane came and dropped bread on that house where they were shut up. And it went on, dropping the bread where the others were still there, in that house. But all the people were buried in their houses. Because the town was buried all at once by the mud. And the water began to rise very high.

And today the town of Ocotepeque is not where it was in the old days, but another town has become Ocotepeque. And, therefore, that town's name is New Ocotepeque.

But they say that the town that used to be, they say, was a big town, and the people that lived in it had money. But they were all destroyed. At that time. The people say that town was destroyed because a serpent came out of the mountain.

And, therefore, today the serpent, the people say that the serpent is the snake, the great snake lying inside the mountain. And when they come out, then they cause great avalanches. And places are destroyed by them then and there.

SNAKE-WOMAN/WOMAN-SNAKE (Chorti Maya)

There is another story they tell about the same snake. The river which runs by where we live, the Jocotan . . . it is said that when that river appeared—that snake came with it.

And they say that when she came, that snake laid out the river here. They say that all night long they heard her playing, like the playing of a marimba. They heard her playing and all the people were afraid. They said, "Well, what can this be? I wonder if we aren't going to be destroyed now." Because all night long the place was lying in a hammock, swinging back and forth. And all the people were afraid.

And then when day broke they came out and saw, on the high ground the river lay there. And the people were scared to death.

They saw that the great river lay there. And for two days then it happened that the news went out that the snake had come, because there were houses which were near where the river passed; they say that they saw that snake's body pass. It was as big around as a house. And its horn was very large.

And with it she plowed the earth as she went, and all the water with it. They say that when she went floating in the water, when she went through the great water, they say it was like a thunderbolt, as it thunders in the sky when rain falls. And it crashed.

And then she came to a place named Conacaste, where there stands a big rock. And when she came there, she was not able to pass by the rock because it was a big rock.

And they say that it wasn't because she could not pass by it, but rather it was her friend's house. And since it was her friend's house, there was no way for her to knock it down. Then she passed to one side of it, and near the village named Conacaste.

It is said that those people all came out running, to go up higher. Because they saw that many mountains were crumbling because of the snake, and they came out running and left their houses and went high up. Their houses were carried off but they were not. And when she had passed, they began to build their houses again.

And that snake came to a place called Santa Barbara. But the place is called El Encuentro. Because they say that that snake and another snake which came by way of Ipala met one another. And the water passed near the town of Chiquimula. There the water passed, and they say that—those snakes had come for just one day.

And—and she came to that place and they joined themselves together, the two snakes, because the snake that came there by way of Ipala they say was a female, and the other was a male.

And when they met they began to play, writhing together. And they came farther down. There stood a big rock. And there, they say, they arrived. The horn of the big snake, which was the male, broke. Because he began to play with the female snake his horn broke.

So the people even to today call that rock Stuck-horn. Because they say there the big snake whose horn broke stuck his horn. But the people say that if he hadn't turned back to look at the female, and if he hadn't gone with her, and if he hadn't

187

left off being embraced by the female, he wouldn't have broken his horn.

But they say that because he turned around to look at the female that's why his horn broke. And then when his horn broke he could not go where he had wanted to go, because they say that he wanted to go to the West.

But since his horn was broken he didn't go where he intended to go, but instead went to one side. He didn't reach the place he had intended to reach. But they say that he let himself be embraced by the female.

But we didn't see them start to play. Because the sea, the sea they say is all full of snakes. And that is why the snakes that come out of the mountains go there and mate because there they find each other. Some are taken for daughters-in-law. Some are taken for sons-in-law. And that is why they say that the snakes, those which are growing, go looking for their fathers-in-law so as to take a wife. And, therefore, the people say that there are those that stay in some mountain at the source of the waters, and there are those that go as far as the sea.

But what the people say is that the snakes that do so much damage to the mountains and destroy the houses, cannot go where they wanted. But those that don't, they are given permission by God to go wherever they want to go. But those that lose out before God do not arrive. That's the way people tell it: that snake began with the female snake and broke his horn.

THE UNDERWATER WORLD OF THE NABARAOS[1] (Guarao)

Two Songs:

I.

My husband is a Nabarao
and I want to live with him;

[1] Nabaraos—A kind of water god/demon.

but my older sister prevents
and mistreats me because she
hates Nabaraos.

He lives at the bottom of the
river and I want to be with
him, only my sister prevents
me because he is a Nabarao . . .

In spite of her I'll return
to him, if she dares to mistreat
me more,
I'll return to my Nabarao husband.

2 .

He treats all children like they were
his, like he was their father,
the Nabarao, my husband, he treats
all children like they were his.

He sleeps at the bottom of a whirlpool,
inside of his house,
and when he comes for me I'll go with him.

THE SNAKE'S SWEETHEART (*Quechua*)

She was the only daughter of a married couple. Every day she
used to go to the hills looking after the cattle. Her father and
her mother had no other children. Therefore, they used to
send her day after day to pasture the cattle. The girl was al-
ready marriageable, well developed and handsome.

One day, on the hilltop, a very refined, very thin youth
approached her.

"Be my love," he said. And he went on talking to her about
love.

As he was tall and vigorous, the young woman assented.
From that day on they used to see each other on the hill; there
they made love.

"I want you always to bring me toasted flour," said the youth to the shepherdess.

She fulfilled her lover's request. And she brought him toasted flour every day. They ate together, each serving the other.

Thus they lived for a long time. The youth walked and ran face downward, crawled, as if he had many tiny feet. This was because he was not a man. He was a serpent. But in the eyes of the girl he appeared always a thin, tall, young man.

The girl became pregnant and said to the youth:

"I am with child. When my parents learn of it they will scold me and will want to know who is my child's father. We must decide whether to go to my house or to yours."

The youth replied:

"We must go to your house. And I will not be able to enter it freely—that is not possible. Tell me whether there is a hole in the wall next to the millstone of your house. Isn't there always a hole near the millstone where the rag for cleaning the stone is kept?"

"Yes, there is such a hole near the stone."

"Take me there," said the youth.

And the young woman asked:

"What will you do in that hole?"

"There I would live by day and by night."

"You could not fit in it. It cannot be; it is a very tiny hole."

"I shall go into it. And it will serve me as living quarters. Now I want to know in what place you sleep: in the kitchen or in the granary."

"I sleep in the kitchen," said the girl. "I sleep with my parents."

"And where is the millstone?"

"Our millstone is in the granary."

"When I go there you shall sleep on the ground next to the millstone."

"And how can I separate myself from my parents? They will not want me to sleep alone."

"Pretend to be afraid of thieves robbing the granary. 'I shall sleep there to watch it,' tell them. And enter by yourself to grind the millstone; do not let your parents do it. Every time you grind flour throw a little into the hole in which I will be living. I will feed only on this. I will not eat anything else. And so that they do not see me, cover the opening carefully with the cleaning rag."

Then the girl asked:

"Can you not present yourself freely before my parents?"

"No, I cannot," he replied. "Little by little I will make my appearance before them."

"And how are you to live in that hole? It is very small; a chunk of wool barely fits into it."

"You will have to enlarge it from within."

"Very well," she said. "You probably know how to fix yourself up in there."

"But you will have to take me there. And you will leave me behind the wall of your house. During the night you will take me to the granary."

"All right," answered his sweetheart.

That night the girl went to her house alone; she sneaked into the granary and enlarged the opening near the millstone. The next day she left for the hill to pasture the cattle. She found her lover in the usual place.

"I have already enlarged the hole for the cleaning rag," she told him.

At nightfall they went together to the sweetheart's house. She left the youth in the corral, behind the house. And she came for him in the night. She took him to the hole near the millstone. The youth glided noiselessly into the hole. The maiden said to herself as her lover moved into the hole: "Impossible! He will be unable to enter!"

That same night she told her parents:

"My father, my mother: it is possible for thieves to steal everything we have in the larder. From now on I am going to sleep in the room where we keep the food."

"Go ahead, my child," assented the parents.

The girl moved her bed to the larder and placed it on the floor, near the millstone. The snake glided to the bed and the lovers slept together. From then on they used to sleep together every night.

When there was need to grind the millstone the young

woman would let no one else do it; she would go, and throw handfuls of flour into the cleaning-rag hole. Before leaving she would cover the hole with the piece of rawhide which was used to clean the millstone. In that way, neither her parents, nor anyone could see what was in the hole. Her parents suspected nothing; it did not occur to them to uncover the hole and look inside. Only when they realized that their daughter was pregnant did they worry and decide to speak.

"It looks as if our daughter is pregnant," they said. "We had better ask who the father is."

They called her and questioned her:

"You are pregnant. Who is the father of your child?"

But she did not answer.

Then the father and the mother each asked her, first the one, then the other. But she remained silent.

Until she felt the pains of childbirth, one night, and then another night. Her parents attended her. And the serpent could not slide during those nights into the maiden's bed.

The serpent no longer lived in the hole. He had grown a great deal, he had become enormous and could no longer enter the hole in the wall. Sucking the young woman's blood, he had grown fat and was swollen and reddish. He dug under the base of the mill, made a hole there and transferred his living quarters. It was a kind of cave under the mill, a big nest, the new home of the serpent. He had grown fat, round and wider; he was bloated. But in the eyes of his lover, he was not a snake, he was a youth. A youth who had grown rapidly.

The lovers could no longer cover the hole which they had dug under the millstone. That is why every morning the girl would fold the covers of her bed and hang one on top of the other over the stone foundation. Thus they were able to hide the serpent's nest from the eyes of her father and her mother when these two entered the granary.

Faced with their daughter's stubborn silence, the parents decided to find out; they asked the people of the village:

"Our daughter has appeared to become pregnant from nothing. Have you not seen her speak to someone somewhere? Perhaps in the fields where she was pasturing the cattle?"

But all would answer:

"No, we haven't seen anything."

"Where do you make her sleep?" some asked.

"At first she used to sleep with us, in the same room. But now she insists on sleeping in the larder; she has her bed there next to the millstone. And she alone wants to grind; she permits no one to go near the millstone."

"And why does she object to your coming near the millstone? What does she say?" they asked.

"'Do not go near the millstone, dear parents; you might soil my bed; I will grind by myself,' she says," answered the parents.

"And why does she not want you to go near the mill?" they asked.

"She has already suffered the first pains of childbirth," the parents replied.

Then they said:

"Go to the sorcerer. Ask him to seek and find out. We common folk cannot know what is happening. What could it be!"

The father and the mother went in search of the sorcerer. They took with them a small bunch of coca leaves. They asked him to look into their daughter's case.

"My daughter doesn't feel well. We don't know what ails her," they said to him.

The sorcerer asked:

"What is wrong with your daughter? What hurts her?"

"She has become pregnant. We do not know by whom. It's been a long time since she began to suffer pains, night after night. And she cannot give birth. She does not want to tell us who the father is," the woman said.

The sorcerer consulted the coca leaves, and said:

"Something, there is something under the millstone in your house! And it is the father. Because the father is not human, it is not a man."

"And what can it be?" the aged couple replied fearfully. "Divine everything, divine well, we beg you."

Then the sorcerer continued to speak:

"There, inside is a serpent! It is not a man!"

193

"And what are we to do?" the parents asked.

The sorcerer thought for a moment, then continued to speak, addressing the father:

"Your daughter will oppose your killing the serpent. 'Kill me first before you kill my lover,' she will say to you. Send her far away, to any place that will require a day's journey to reach. She will object even to that order. Say this to her, mentioning some town: 'I know that in that town there is a remedy for giving birth. Go, buy that remedy and bring it to me. They tell me that with that remedy you will be able to give birth. If you do not obey me this time, I will beat you up, I will beat you to death,' say to her. Only thus will you get her to go. At the same time hire people armed with cudgels, machetes and heavy sticks. Then make your daughter go and carry out your order. And when she is far away, everyone enter the granary and push the millstone. There, underneath, there is a big serpent. Beat it to death. Beware of the snake leaping towards you because if it leaps, it will kill you all. Behead it well; dig a grave, and bury it."

"Very well, sir. We shall carry out your instructions," the father said, and he left; his wife followed him.

Immediately he went looking for people, strong men to help him kill the beast. He hired ten men, well armed with cudgels and sharp machetes.

"Tomorrow, when my daughter has left, come to my house, walking without letting anyone see you," he told them.

The next morning they ordered the young woman to cook her food. They made her get up early. They gave her money to make the request seem real, and told her:

"With this money you will buy the remedy for giving birth. In Sumakk Marka, that town on the other bank of the river, you will find the remedy."

But the girl refused to obey. "I cannot go," she said, "I don't want to." Then the parents threatened her.

"If you do not go, if you do not bring the remedy, we will beat you to death. We will beat you until we destroy the fetus that you carry in your womb."

Frightened, the girl left.

They saw her walk until she was out of sight. When she had disappeared into the distance, the hired men went to her father's house. They all gathered in the yard. They divided their ration of coca among themselves; they chewed for a while, and then entered the granary; they transferred to the yard all the things that were there; finally, they removed the woman's bed.

And they armed. With their cudgels on their shoulders and gripping their machetes, they entered the granary; they surrounded the millstone and waited. They pushed the millstone aside; a thick serpent was stretched out there; it had a large head, similar to a man's; it was getting fatter. "Wat'akk!" On finding itself discovered, the serpent leaped, its heavy body made a noise as it straightened out. The ten men struck it and wounded it. They divided it into several pieces. Its head was hurled out, on the pampa. And there it began to struggle; it wriggled and rolled on the ground. The men followed and pounded it, they went to wherever it fell and tried to finish it up. They struck it from above; its blood ran all over the ground; it gushed out in spurts from the mutilated body. But it could not die.

And while they were beating the serpent's head, at that moment, the woman arrived, the sweetheart. On seeing people gathered in the yard, she ran to the granary, to the millstone. The stone was covered with blood. The serpent's nest was empty. She turned her head to look at the yard; several men were pounding the head of her lover with cudgels. Then she let out a deadly scream.

"Why, why do you destroy my lover's head? Why do you kill him?" she exclaimed. "He was my husband! He is the father of my son!"

She screamed once more; her voice filled the house. She contemplated the blood and was horrified. And due to the effort she had made in screaming, she had an abortion; a multitude of little snakes wriggled on the floor, they covered the ground in the yard, leaping and crawling.

They finally killed the big snake. They also killed the little snakes. They pursued and trampled all of them. Then, some of the men dug a pit in the earth and the others swept up the blood. They swept the blood from the whole house, they gathered it near the pit and buried the serpents and the blood-drenched mud. And they led the maiden to her parents' room. There they cured her. They returned the things from the granary to their original place. They cleared and put the house in order. They carried the millstone to a waterfall; they placed the stone under the fall and left it there. And when everything was in order, the young woman's parents gave each man his just reward for the work he performed. They received their wages and left.

Later the parents asked their daughter:

"How, in what manner could you live with a serpent? Your husband was not a man; he was a demon."

Only then did the maiden confess her story; she told of her first meeting with the serpent. And everything came to be known, and was clarified. The parents cured their daughter, they took care of her and made her whole and sound of body and soul. And then, much later, the young woman married a good man. And her life was happy.

THE MAN WHO BECAME A SNAKE (Kayapo)

A man turned himself into a snake. His wife stayed an Indian, but he became a snake, and together they went to live in the forest. The bananas in the man also became a snake.

Another man came into the forest looking for them and asked his wife,

"Where is your husband?"

"He's out hunting," she answered. "And where are you going?"

"I'm going after you."

"My husband turned himself into a snake," she said.

"Really?"

"Yes."

"Could I see him?"

"I'll hide you."

The snake-man brought home a tapir and a wild pig.

"What kind of people have you prepared for dinner?" asked the snake-man.

"There's the meal I made for you," she said.

"So I'll eat it," said the snake-man.

And the snake-wife served up the meal for the snake-man and he ate it.

During the night he started talking in his sleep. His belly was the belly of a snake, his mouth was that of an Indian—and so was his head.

When day came, the Indian got up and left and returned to the village. When he got there he told everything that had happened.

Then another man went to see the snake-man and his wife—to look at them—came to the house, sat down, and waited until snake-man came home with a deer and ate the visitor up. Next a whole delegation of villagers came looking for the lost man and asked, "Where is the man who came around looking a couple of days back? Has he already left?"

"He was eaten up," said the wife . . .

They talked things over. More villagers came. The snake-man ate a village. Still more came and when they looked for him, his wife said he went to bed. And the villagers killed the snake.

The snake-man's wife was pregnant and when she gave birth she gave birth to a bunch of snakes. And she hid the snake-children in the corn.

"The Indians killed your father," their mother told them. "May snakes from this day forward bite people so that they may die in pain."

"We are going to kill all the snake-children," said the Indians, and they began to cut down the cornstalks with their hoes and kill all the snake-children. The snake-children made bigger holes and crawled in them, and the men couldn't kill them but they bit the men. In the old days there weren't any snakes. And then an Indian became a snake, and the Indian snake-man began to have children.

And since then there are many snakes in the forest. Then the snake-wife returned to the Indians.

THE STORY OF THE DEVIL FROG (*Tukano*)

Wmá Watu, the devil-frog's wife, was called Waí Masá. They didn't have any children, and one day she ran away from him. Then Devil-Frog went to the house of his older brother, Yebá, and while he was swimming outside the door he hid under a guinea pig that was upside down in the water—so that nobody would see him.

Then along came Híno and hit the guinea pig . . . Devil-Frog wanted to grab Híno and he hid himself for three days but he never saw him.

There was a bird who knew where Híno was and who had seen him going to bed with Devil-Frog's wife. The bird came and told Devil-Frog that his wife was sleeping with Híno and she never gave out with a word of complaint.

"When she goes out to pull up some yucca tomorrow and goes to the door to wash it, go and see what's going on. Don't you know that someone else has your wife?" said the bird.

"Why didn't you tell me before?" Devil-Frog asked.

"I've been whistling for you every day," the bird said.

"Make a blowgun," said Devil-Frog, "and fill it with poison darts."

The next day at noon Híno was on top of Devil-Frog's wife making love to her and the bird called Devil-Frog. Devil-Frog got inside the blowgun and shot way up into the air and came down stuck in Híno's back.

"What bit me," asked Híno, "a horsefly? That's what it was, a horsefly." And he started to die.

"Why are you dying?" she said. "Don't die."

Híno was lying on his chest. He was beautifully adorned with beads and leaves and feathers, painted all over, very handsome.

Híno died on top of Waí Masá. They pushed him off of her, carried him to the Cano Colorado and made a dam out of sticks and hid him among the sticks. She was afraid of Devil-Frog and she thought she'd get away without seeing him. She pretended she was swimming and came home and didn't say a word.

The day before she had been very happy and talked and laughed a lot. But now she was quiet and didn't say anything.

Devil-Frog was sitting quietly thinking and he asked his wife,

"What's wrong with you? My wife doesn't talk to me. Yesterday you were happy and today you don't say anything. Why?" And he told her to go make dinner.

Devil-Frog went to the door to take a bath and started looking for Híno, but he didn't find him. Finally he did find him and he saw his penis, cut it off, and wrapped it in leaves like you wrap up fish and he went home.

His wife was making casabe bread,[2] and there was a big fire lit and Devil-Frog put the penis into the fire in order to roast it. Devil-Frog ate all the bread and was so filled up that he didn't eat any fish. "What did you put into the fire to roast?" his wife asked. "I'd like to eat it because I'm very hungry."

"So go ahead and eat it," he said. "I'm eating coca."[3]

She took it out of the fire, unwrapped it and started eating it. It seemed just like a fish. She'd eaten half of it along with a piece of bread when Devil-Frog said, "You're eating penis because of all the days you slept with Híno."

She stopped eating, went to the door, vomited, and threw away the rest of the penis.

When Híno didn't come home his father started looking for him and found him in the water outside of Devil-Frog's home. Devil-Frog tried to get away as fast as possible. He was a Payé, a Shaman. He went to his older brother's house and abandoned his wife.

Yebá, his older brother told him, "You killed people. You killed one of the children of Híno's father."

Devil-Frog replied he hadn't killed anyone, and anyhow, if he was going to kill someone, he could do better than kill the Waí Masá people, Híno's father's children.

These Waí Masá people were all fish. They came after Devil-Frog and tried to kill him, and finally caught up to him in the Pirá River, just below Cano Colorado.

[2] Made from yucca root.
[3] Coca—cocaine.

Devil-Frog was alone and only had a bow and arrow. They shot lots of arrows at him, but none killed him. He shot his arrows and killed five in one day and escaped by way of the Cano Tatu with the fish still after him.

THE HEROIC MARIA-GUARI (*Guarao*)

I.

Maria-Guari had two beautiful sisters and, to protect them against the danger of Nabaraos when they went to bathe in the river, he had a little pond dug next to his house for them to bathe in. He fenced in the pond and covered it with little clay people-statues in order to scare away the Nabaraos.

One day when he went off to fish he told his daughters, "Even though you have your pond to bathe in, wait until I get back."

But after he had gone the older daughter said to the younger, "Little sister, let's go swim in the pond."

"But Maria-Guari forbade us," said the younger.

But the older one went swimming anyway.

When Maria-Guari came home he asked the girls, "You haven't been swimming, have you?"

"No, brother."

"You're sure you haven't been swimming?"

"Absolutely certain."

"I hope so," said Maria-Guari. "We'll know in a couple days."

And in a few days the older sister was pregnant.

"And you expect me to believe you weren't swimming?" said Maria-Guari.

"Brother," asked the younger, "how can our sister be pregnant without a husband?"

"Because she went swimming when I wasn't here," he answered. "Only wait awhile . . . maybe she's not pregnant after all."

The older daughter got more and more restless. She couldn't sit still; she'd go up in the hills and sway back and forth and forth and back . . . endlessly.

And then one day when she came home she brought back an enormous basket of fruit, and her brother, now very suspicious, asked her, "How in the world could you, being pregnant, climb up in such tall trees and pick so much fruit? I'm going to find out who was doing the picking for you."

II.

And so, without his sister knowing it, Maria-Guari followed her up to the mountains and here's what he saw! When she got to the foot of the tree she squatted down and out of her womb came an enormous snake that climbed up into the tree and threw down fruit to her.

"Little Mother," the snake told her from time to time, "this fruit is big and ripe, eat some."

When she had her basket full, the snake came down and got back into her womb.

As soon as he got home Maria-Guari started to make a good bow and a pile of arrows.

"Why are you making those arrows?" his sister asked him.

"Just for fun," he answered her. "Something to keep me busy."

But the Indian suspected that he was making the arrows to kill the snake that she carried in her womb. The next day when the Indian went back to the mountain to pick fruit she told all the birds she met on the way:

"If you see my brother following me, let me know right away!"

She got to the foot of the tree and the snake came out just as it had before, but when it was up at the top of the tree throwing down fruit the birds warned the Indian: "Your brother is coming!"

The Indian yelled at the snake. "Come down, my son; your uncle is coming to kill you."

But there wasn't time, and while the snake was coming down Maria-Guari shot an arrow and the snake fell dead.

"Ay, ay, ay," wailed the Indian. "My son dead, my son dead!"

This was the first heroic deed of Maria-Guari.

THE VENGEANCE OF MARIA-GUARI (Guarao)

When Maria-Guari killed the snake, the son of a Nabarao and his sister, he felt his heart swell with the courage and bravery of the world's great heroes.

He had a very cute little boy and his sister was always wanting to bring him to the House of the Nabaraos: "Maria-Guari, my brother, let me take your son to the house of his uncle so he can get to know him."

Finally one day the sister took the child and brought him to the House of the Nabaraos. But Maria-Guari followed right on their heels . . .

When he got to the house everyone was asleep and he looked all over for his son. He saw lots of big pans upside down but didn't see his son anywhere.

He turned one of the big pans over and found his son under it. And then he really got mad and cut all the ropes of the hammocks the Nabaraos were sleeping in. Many of them broke their heads when they fell, and the rest ran away.

This was the second heroic deed of Maria-Guari.

The Indians were especially afraid of a bird called in Guarao the Tokoyo, a kind of owl, because it was a "Witch-Bird"/Bird with the Evil-Eye.

Maria-Guari chased the Tokoyo down, drank its blood and ate its heart, and so took on all of its magic powers. The first thing he did was to go to a wasp's nest with a "broom" of dry leaves and kill all the wasps. But even that didn't "satisfy" him and every day he got angrier and angrier. In those days the Caribs were habitually cruel to the Guaraos, so much so in fact that even to this day the Indians talk of "Carib-ghosts" who pester and bother the Guaraos. So one night Maria-Guari attacked one of the nearby farms and didn't leave one Carib alive. He then decided to go wherever there were Caribs and kill them all with his own hands.

"Don't come, little brother," he told his son. "The Caribs will eat you."

But the little brother wanted to go and so he went with him. Maria-Guari told him: "Listen, it's okay if you come with me,

but don't be afraid, because Maria-Guari doesn't have any-
thing to do with sissies. Just stay close to me, and I'll take care
of you."

II.

They got to a Carib ranch and Maria-Guari started to kill
Caribs, but in the heat of battle he forgot his brother, and
when he turned around he saw that the Caribs had already
killed and eaten him. All that was left was one little leg.

Maria-Guari's anger knew no bounds. In order to revenge
his little brother he started to kill Caribs on the left and right,
and no matter how hard they fought back they didn't have a
chance against the Guarao hero.

When the chief of the Caribs saw that they all were going
to be killed he begged Maria-Guari: "Cousin, let the rest of us
live; there are only a few of us left."

Maria-Guari was tired and so he accepted the truce, stopped
fighting, and allowed the rest of the Caribs to flee to the
mountains.

And this is why the Caribs disappeared from the territory
of the Guaraos.

XIX.   TRICKSTER STORIES

FOX TAKES A WIFE (Toba-Pilagá)

A little rain fell and Fox came back to life. He arrived at an-
other village, this time in the guise of a good-looking young
man. At night he sang in a disguised voice. All the women of
the village flocked to hear him, but no one recognized him. A

girl fell in love with him because his appearance was not that of Fox. They slept together. The girl, who was in love with him, scratched and tore him with her nails. "Don't scratch me like that," cried Fox, "or I shall leave you. It hurts!"

"How can I stop scratching you? I scratch you because I love you."

"Listen, I come from a country where women do not scratch. So you had better stop."

The girl paid no attention to his words and went on scratching him. When she scratched or pinched him hard, Fox groaned, "Ay! ay!" She scratched harder and harder. Fox cried until his cries were those of a fox. In this way the girl found out that she had been sleeping with Fox, and then she left him.

FOX TRICKS HIS PARENTS-IN-LAW
(Toba-Pilagá)

The following day, Fox took another form and sang another song. Many people came to hear him. Another girl fell in love with him and slept with him. As she did not scratch him, they slept together until morning. Fox said, "I shall go look for some food." He left the girl at home. In the bush he collected sachasandias (elke', *Capparis salicifolia* Gris.) and empty honeycombs. He put them in a bag and returned home. The girl's mother took the bag and hung it on a post. She said, "I am going to get a gourd and mix water and honey in it and let it ferment. I shall prepare mead for my family. What is left will be for my son-in-law." Fox said to his wife, "Call your father and keep him busy with the gourds. I am going to take a walk and will come later."

Fox's parents-in-law opened the bag, looked inside, and cried, "This is not honey, these are sachasandias. Look! This fellow is not a man, nor the son of a man—he is Fox." They threw the bag away. The father-in-law wanted to take revenge on Fox because he had been put to shame.

FOX BECOMES A GOOD-LOOKING YOUNG MAN AND IS ABOUT TO MARRY, BUT IS UNMASKED BY CARANCHO (*Toba-Pilagá*)

In the morning it rained and the rain fell until evening. Fox got up. He changed himself into a good-looking young man. During the day he walked and walked. Nobody recognized him. A woman sent her friend to tell him, "I love you, you delight me. Tonight I want to be with you." The woman spoke with Fox, and they stayed together. The woman said, "I never loved anybody, but when I saw you and learned you were a bachelor, I wanted to be your wife. Will you be my husband?"

"Yes," said the Fox, "I have no wife."

The woman said, "Tomorrow let's go to my father's house."

"Yes," replied Fox, "I would like to go with you."

They spent the morning together. Later on they went to the father's house. On the way Fox frightened the woman by shouting, "Look! a serpent." The woman jumped and was pricked by a thorn which she could not pull out. Fox took a reed, split it, and tried to get the thorn out. The woman said, "Don't cut me. Let it stay. It will rot and will be easy to get out." Fox carried the woman on his shoulders. When he came to the house of his father-in-law, he said, "Your daughter has a thorn in her foot. I cannot take it out." The father answered, "Nobody here can get it out. Let's go and see Carancho. He can do it. If he can't, we shall call on Fox." The father-in-law did not know that his daughter's husband was Fox.

The father-in-law went and called on Carancho. "Carancho, my daughter has got a thorn in her foot," he said. Carancho went with him to his house.

"Where is your daughter?" he asked. She was sitting beside her husband.

Carancho said, "You did not look where you put your feet, that's why you were pricked."

"Yes, I was walking, and he scared me with a serpent. I jumped and this thorn stuck in my foot."

"Look, Fox," said Carancho, "you are fooling people again.

205

A few days ago I scolded you, and now you are playing tricks on this poor woman."

"Am I Fox?"

"Of course you are. Do you think I don't know it?" asked Carancho.

The father-in-law said, "Yesterday I said that he was a fox, but nobody paid any attention to me."

Fox stood up. "Where are you going?" asked Carancho. "I tell them I am Carancho, but not you. I don't change my shape. You change your shape to make love to women."

Fox answered, "I change my shape because I can do it, but you are unable to transform yourself."

Carancho was wiser. He warned them, "If someone you don't know comes along, scratch him. If it is Fox, he will cry like a fox; otherwise he will cry like a man."

The people listened to Carancho. They struck Fox and killed him.

XX.   FABLE-HISTORY/SCIENCE

THE VULTURE KING'S DAUGHTER (Guarao)

A certain Indian learning guisiratu,[1] smoking a lot and eating very little, got so thin that the wind practically blew him away. He was in such bad shape that he actually lost his will to live and so he lowered himself into a sandpit, half-covered himself with sand, and waited for the vultures to come and eat him.

[1] Guisiratu—Guarao yoga.

But the vultures didn't come, but rather one of the daughters of the tow-headed vulture Bure Kuamana, who has his house above the clouds. The girl gave the Indian a sort of "flying apparatus" and told him: "Put on these wings, brother, and come with me. I'll take you to my father's house and there we can get married."

The Indian tied on the wings and soared up above the clouds, following the girl, and they arrived at the city of the vultures where the two-headed vulture Bure Kuamana had his palace.

"Wait for me out here a moment," said the girl to the Indian, "while I say hello to my father."

And she went into the King Vulture's house and said: "Father, I've just returned from the earth and I've brought with me a man to be my husband."

"Good, good," said King Vulture, "but first he has to take all the water out of that well with this basket."

Which the Indian tried to do. But it was impossible to empty the well because when he tried to take the water out it would leak out through the holes in the basket.

He was getting to the point of desperation when the spirit of a certain bird arrived in the form of a young man, and, grabbing the basket, emptied out the well until it was dry.

"Father," the girl said to King Vulture, "the well's dry. Now we can get married."

"The well may be dry," said the two-headed vulture, "but because he was helped by someone else he still can't be my son-in-law. First he has to cut down that tree on that hill over there."

The Indian tried to cut it down; but at the first blow he realized that it was flint and the ax wouldn't cut into it. Then along came an evil-eyed woodpecker witchbird, and he knocked the tree down with his beak.

"Okay now?" the Indian asked King Vulture. "The tree is down!"

"The tree may be down," answered King Vulture, "but you received outside help. If you want to be my son-in-law you have to carve a wooden statue of me that portrays me exactly the way I am."

The Indian turned to King Vulture's daughter:

"How can I carve a statue of him if he doesn't let me see him and I don't know how he looks? What I'm going to do is turn myself into a lizard and climb up on the roof and I'll be able to see him from there."

He turned himself into a lizard and started to crawl up the zinc-plated house walls. But as he was climbing he made so much noise that he frightened King Vulture. King Vulture hid and so the Indian didn't get a chance to see him.

Next he turned himself into a tiny little ant, and because he was so small that he didn't make any noise at all he climbed to the roof unnoticed and peeked inside and saw King Vulture—a vulture with two heads.

He stayed on the roof a good long time looking at King Vulture and then came down and made a perfect likeness of the king. When his daughter presented it to him, King Vulture said:

"The statue is perfect, flawless. But the artist was on the roof turned into an ant, taking his time getting a good look at me. Fortunately this disqualifies the work itself. Tell him that if he wants to be my son-in-law he has to make me a house at the entrance into the white clouds."

The Indian went to look at the site and gather materials to make a house.

But Bijibiji, the Devil's Little Horse, came and told him: "If you make the house, your father-in-law won't be able to refuse you his daughter's hand and so he'll have you killed and he'll eat you. It's better if you run away and go back to earth."

He handed him a kind of winged jacket and said: "With this you'll be able to fly back to your own country."

The Indian put on the wings and flew down to earth, but when he'd descended to treetop level he saw the Vulture King's daughter flying after him screaming: "Why are you running away, brother? Don't you know that my father and I love you?"

"I'm not going back," said the Indian, "because your father is evil and cruel and he wants to kill me. I'm better off here on the earth."

208

"But if you stay here," replied the vulture angrily, "I'll eat you when you die."

To which the Guarao answered: "After I die you can do what you want with me."

Which is why vultures eat the flesh of the dead, which at first they didn't do.

THE FROG AND FIRE (*Guarao*)

At the beginning of time all the fire in the universe was gathered together in one enormous bonfire. But one day a frog approached the fire and started to lick it with his tongue until he'd swallowed it all. And so fire disappeared from the surface of the earth.

Because there was no fire no one could cook anything. People used to put fish out in the sun to "toast" it and that's the way they ate it—raw.

After many years, an Indian decided to bring fire back again, only it wasn't possible because the frog had it in his stomach. One day while this Indian was out walking around in the hills he came across a *curcurito* palm covered with fruit, grabbed a handful of fruit, and gave it to the frog.

"Fantastic!" said the frog, tasting the fruit. "Where can I get more?"

"Come with me," said the Indian, "and you can eat as much as you want."

When they got to another palm tree covered with fruit, the Indian told the frog:

"You wait here at the bottom while I climb to the top."

The Indian climbed to the top of the tree and called down to the frog:

"Listen, they're really ripe; I'm going to throw you as many as you want so you can really stuff yourself."

The frog looked up while the Indian cut the branch free; but once it was free it fell down on top of the frog and killed him right there.

Once the frog was dead the fire that he had locked up inside him burst out and set the whole forest on fire.

Which is why the Indians have a saying that "There's always been fire in the forest."

THE STORY OF THE PUMA AND THE FOX
(*Quechua*)

A puma caught a beautiful llama, ate his fill, and then buried the rest for dinner. A fox who was spying on the puma, after he had left, dug out the rest of the llama and had himself a magnificent breakfast. When the puma came back at sunset he got furious when he saw how his food had disappeared and he went in search of the thief.

Walking around without any clear idea of where he was going, he came upon the fox sound asleep. The clownish puma, wanting to ask the fox about the thief, decided to wake up the fox. He made a bundle of straw and started to tickle the fox's nose. The fox, thinking that what was tickling him was flies, yelled out in his sleep, "Get away flies, I just took the dinner out of his mouth. Imagine what I'll do to you!"

So the puma knew the whole story, grabbed the fox by the throat and, punishing him for his daring, strangled him to death.

MORAL OF THE STORY: The braggart condemns himself with his mouth.

THE NIGHT BUTTERFLY (*Quechua*)

Once upon a time there was a couple living happily together with their first son. The husband had to go away a lot on business, and when he left his wife was always in tears, spending the nights waiting for him, all the time spinning.

Then one night the son woke up and asked his mother, "Who is that moving next to you?"

"It's my lover," she said frankly, "my sweetheart who comes to keep me company."

When the husband came home his wife had just gone out and he asked his son what his mother did on the nights when he was gone. And the son told him that her lover came every night and that they stayed up until very late talking and that the lover had talked to him too.

As soon as the husband heard this he went looking for his wife and he threw her over a cliff and killed her.

One night while he was sitting up thinking, remembering, staring into the light, his son woke up and started to scream, "There's my mother's lover, there's the one who is always with her," pointing at the butterfly that used to come and visit his mother at night.

The husband, when he realized the gravity of his error, keeled over dead with desperation.

THE MURDERER AND THE SHEPHERD
(*Quechua*)

A man was walking along at night through the mountains alone except for his beautiful dog. The man, sunk in his own thoughts, went one way and the dog another, and suddenly out of a cave came a killer who stopped him and threatened to kill him.

He begged him not to do him any harm, and finally when it was obvious that all the begging in the world wasn't going to do him any good, he stopped and asked that he might sing one last song of farewell to the world he was going to leave behind.

"Okay," said the killer, and he began to sing:

"Salt and pepper, I'll never see you again!
  Salt and pepper, nevermore will I taste you!
  Salt and pepper, no more will you season my food!
  Salt and pepper, my cold cuts will miss you!
  Salt and pepper, farewell forever!"

Salt and pepper was the name of the Indian's dog, and when he heard his master's anguished calls he came like the wind, freeing him from the killer's hands, grabbing the killer by the neck, and strangling him.

THE CONDOR AND THE FOX (*Quechua*)

A condor and a fox got into a heated argument about who was better suited to the tough, punishing weather of the Andes.

"What are you talking about, strength, when I see you on a rainy day all rolled up into a ball inside your cave, you and your children, gnawing on bones and dying of hunger?"

"And you, brother, up in your nest like a vulture on its last wing, you think you're any better off than I am?"

"All I have to do is fold myself up in my wings, whereas you . . ."

"I've got my tail to keep me warm and protect me."

And so they went on, really not going anywhere, until finally the fox suggested . . .

"I'll tell you what, let's both spend the night outside and whoever goes inside first loses and becomes the winner's dinner."

"Okay with me," said the condor. "Only it has to be a bad night."

"Agreed." And they both chose spots.

Along came the rainy season, and one day with the clouds swirling around like whirlpools of smoke, the condor went in search of the fox. And it began to storm, lightning lit up the skies and cut through the clouds, and there, lit up by the lightning, the condor saw the fox, its hair all on end, trying to get away as fast as he could. Only when he heard the condor calling him, he had to stop and get ready to go through with the wager.

It was a crazy, wild night, like sitting under a waterfall and all the fields were flooded, but there they were determined to wait out the night. The condor perched up on a little rock and without further ado stuck out his naked neck and, lifting up one wing, stuck his curved beak inside it. And the fox, squatting on the wet ground, stuck his nose between his legs, extending his tail over himself as much as he could.

While the condor wasn't really all that badly off under his waterproof feathers, the poor fox was soaked through, with the water running down over his stiff, pointed ears. He was soaked, his skin was all goose pimples, he hated himself, and from time to time he'd whimper to himself, "What cold! I'm freezing to death."

Which the condor thought was very funny, and when the next morning the condor "unfolded" himself and walked majestically over to see how his rival had fared, he found the fox dead—he had literally died from the cold.

What a sad end to obstinate presumption!

THE STORY OF YEBÁ (Barasana)

Híno was drunk. His daughter grabbed a finger that he had between his thumb and index finger and ripped it off. She only ripped off the one branch, because he had a lot more on this arm.

Every tribe ripped off a branch. Edúria grabbed the heart finger, Súna grabbed the ring finger. Hanéra took the arm itself. Which is why Hanéra knows how to dance and sing so well.

These were the first blades of Kahí Mé—Yagé.[2] All the first people—Yebá, Warimi, Adyába, Mení, are on top of Úmea Gatséro.

A priest walking along threw tobacco up into his nose and put out a ladder so that the people could come down. Everyone came down and stood outside the house. The only one who went in was Yebá. Yebá taught everyone how to dance and tell stories. He brought food and gobbled it down. Which is why everyone gobbles their food and talks . . .

Yebá was all dressed up with feathers and different adornments. He was angry because there wasn't any food. Which is why men complain to the women when there isn't any food.

[2] Yagé—Hallucinogenic drug.

There was a house but no men, only women. The husbands were only "guiós."[3] The girls were very pretty. There wasn't any food, only seeds. There was no yucca bread, no fish, no tobacco, no cocaine. And then along came Yebá, my grandfather. He was very evil. First he didn't say anything, and then he asked,

"Where's the food? I want something to eat. Where are the husbands?"

He got rid of all the "guiós" and that night slept with all the wives. He was very evil.

Because there wasn't any food for him he went out and jumped in the water and two hours later came back with some yucca bread. Then he went out and brought back some tobacco, but he left the seeds outside and they robbed them. Later he brought back Yagé.

Everything looked good, everything was plentiful . . . Yebá ate the yucca that was already on the "farm."[4] At first he ate it raw and got sick; then the women cooked it an hour, two hours and he could eat it without any problems.

Yebá had never used tobacco. One of the women gave him a little tobacco and he thought it was a fish. He ate it. It was night and he began to feel very sick. He was "drunk" with the tobacco and it gave him diarrhea but he couldn't defecate.

One of the women carried him into the middle of the house where he had green, watery diarrhea. Then she carried him to one side and then the other side of the house so he could defecate in both places. Then he did it in front of the house and behind the house and all the time it was still green.

Then he felt better and sat on a bench in the middle of the house. The women looked at where he'd defecated and green tobacco had appeared.

"Now the tobacco is good," she said.

He didn't look at the tobacco, only at the women. They were taking care of the tobacco, looking at it, and he told them,

[3] Guiós—Large watersnakes.
[4] The original here is Chagra/Chacra. It's not really a "farm," something smaller, a house with a garden around it, maybe a couple of pigs.

214

"Don't let anyone come in here and steal the tobacco."

It grew very, very rapidly.

The women were tired. Yebá told them to keep guard. But some people came and robbed the tobacco and worms ate the leaves. Yebá hadn't kept guard.

At dawn Yebá went to see how things were and then sat down and slept an hour. The women came to tell him that they were keeping guard and they were angry because he was asleep. While he was sleeping more people had come and robbed other sprouts of the tobacco, and the worms had eaten what was left of the leaves. Yebá hadn't even been aware of what was going on. Finally he woke up and got rid of the robbers and the worms, and when some more people came later on he told them that the tobacco had already been robbed.

But Hanéra already had some good tobacco because when Yebá had gotten up he'd picked some of the leaves, toasted them in a broken piece of pottery, and then ground them up.

While Yebá was making the tobacco, the women made some very potent corn beer. Yebá started to drink and by six in the evening he was good and drunk.

Yebá had a number of boys who were birds. He was their "patrón"—boss. They didn't get drunk and told him, "All we drink is pure water." But he answered them, "Lies!"

They said that all they'd done is grab a few leaves, no tobacco—and the women said the same thing. They claimed that all they'd had was a little "nip" of *chicha*/corn beer, but by six in the evening they were completely drunk.

Yebá's first wife was a bird, but she didn't make any food so he started looking for another wife. There was an old woman who was Yebá's grandmother. She was a great shaman. Everyone was drunk except a woman named Yawirá and the old woman wanted to give her tobacco. "Let me see how you take it to see if you know how." The birds, Yebá's people, said that the old woman didn't know how to take tobacco, that only men knew how to take it.

So the old woman got mad and told Yebá, "You think you're the only one who knows how to take tobacco. Well, today I'm going to take it too." She started to gulp it all down and she gave some to the bird-men and bird-women. She gobbled down a bunch of meat. The first meat was people, only now it's just meat.

She grabbed some "snuff" and gave it to the boys and the women. She got drunk and vomited and went outside and disappeared. Yebá's women said that they hadn't gotten drunk and that the tobacco of the old woman was very weak (pure leaf) and that her corn beer was only water.

Then everyone went up into the hills, the birds, the long-tailed monkey, and Yawirá. Yebá breathed some powdered tobacco up into his nostrils and got drunk—he learned how to get high and to dance. The old woman taught him.

The tobacco that the old woman breathed was called Munó Hotí Bukú. She kept it in a feathered box. She also took "thick" tobacco—tobacco not powdered.

Yebá learned how to smoke, sing, and dance. Even today when there's a party everyone smokes tobacco because that's the way they were taught.

Yebá didn't eat any pepper or meat or fish. A shaman has to "breathe" everything in. If he doesn't breathe it in he gets sick, gets a fever. If you don't breathe in the tobacco it's ugly and it hurts. If you breathe it in it's good.

Then afterwards he ate some roast and bananas. Yebá's wife escaped with another boy in order to see the world. She escaped with Yuhká, who is a buzzard who eats rotten things.

Yebá was wifeless and he set out to find her but he didn't find her. Then finally some other people told him, "Yuhká robbed your wife."

Yebá said, "I'm going to look for my wife," and he made a whole bunch of darts for his blowgun and made some cumare poison.

When he got to Yuhká's house there were lots of other people there besides his wife. They gave him food but he didn't want to eat it. His wife asked him, "Why don't you have some breakfast?" She had a hard time looking at her husband at all.

She ate lots of yucca bread, but all he ate was the moldy pieces. Because the river was low there was lots of fish and Yuhká invited Yebá to eat some spoiled fish and everyone left.

Yebá went slowly, behind everyone else. Yuhká's people went far away. In the middle of the road Yebá grabbed his wife and brought her home. When they got home he broke up and threw out everything: the house, the roof, the jars, the cuyas,[5] the baskets, everything.

On the roof there was a black cuya but Yebá didn't see it. Afterwards he left and the black cuya ran and told Yuhká that Yebá had taken his wife back. Yebá was sitting on the ground next to his fields and when people came, he started shooting at them with his blowgun and he killed them all. More people came and he killed them too . . .

They went along the road and the sun was very hot—it was a very hot day. They came upon a monkey that had some water and Yebá was so angry that he didn't want to give his wife any of the water. But finally she grabbed it, spilled a little, and said, "I want a lot."

"Climb up in this tree," he said. "You can get some up there."

There was a trunk with a hole in it. She climbed up and put her head into the hole and Yebá said, "I love you a lot and you escaped."

And he pushed her into the hole and while she was drowning she said, "What are you so mad about? I came with you, didn't I? Grab my hand."

And she died. She turned into a frog. She became the night frog that every night croaks, "Eu, Eu, Eu."

Yebá kept walking and finally came to his home. No one else was there. He grabbed a bunch of yucca and the leaves rotted. He went into his house and there in the middle of the floor was a pile of rotten leaves.

He got in under the leaves and covered himself all up—with his arms outstretched so that he could grab whoever came in. Along came Yuhká and started to take off the leaves until he got to Yebá. Yuhká thought that Yebá was a leaf, sampled him, and thought he was tasty.

When he started to eat him in earnest, Yebá grabbed him by the feet.

[5] Cuyas are little guinea piggish animals people raise and eat.

"Don't kill me," Yuhká said. "I gave you your wife back. You killed your wife, not me. You killed lots of people. I don't kill anyone."

And Yebá answered him, "That's right, I kill, I'm very brave."

Then Yebá cut off Yuhká's feathers and left him naked and featherless.

Yuhká waited on the farm for a long time until his feathers came back and he could fly. First he flew into a nearby tree and then into one a little further away and then disappeared altogether.

Yebá stayed alone, without a woman, and then started to look for a new one. He went to look for the daughter of his old wife, Yawirá, in the house of the Híno, the watersnakes.

Yawirá's father told him, "Take this cuya all painted with black paint." His daughter was inside.

Yebá said, "But where are the girls?"

And her father answered, "When you get home look inside the cuya and sniff a little tobacco. Along with the smoke sniff the house, and the farm, and then my daughter will talk to you because she is inside the cuya tied with *bejuco* rope."

Yebá had thought that the cuya was only a cuya. Halfway home he was exhausted because the cuya was so heavy.

"I don't want the cuya," he said. "There's no one inside."

Then he cut the ropes and she came out of the cuya. It was Wetá-Rohi. She went flying. At first he was speechless, and then he started to scream after her, "Don't go, don't go, come with me, let's go home." But she kept flying away and he went home alone and threw out the empty cuya and gave up the search.

Yebá made another house. There were only tapirs and Yetá Bekú, who came to ask him, "Do you have any Yagé?" And they went to take Yagé at Yetá Bekú's house because there they danced a lot.

The first day they danced the Dance of the Rubber Tree Fruit, the next the Dance of the Tapir, then the Dance of the Fish, then the Dance of the Yucca Bread, then the Dance of the Mochilero,[6] then the Dance of the Shirt, the Dance of the Incense Tree, the Dance of the Shrimp, of the Maracas, of the Pan Pipes, the Table, the Doves, the Ink, the Worms, the Lizards, and the Hatchets.

THE GIRL AND THE "ACHACHILA" (Aymara)

Once upon a time there was a beautiful, hard-working, happy Indian girl. All the other girls loved and admired her for her sweetness. The young men considered one glance from her a real reward, a boon.

Every afternoon this young girl, before cooking or weaving, went with a jar down to a stream near her home in order to get some fresh water. One day when she was bent down over the stream she saw her reflection mixed with that of an old man with brilliant eyes, white hair, and a long beard. For a moment she thought she was seeing things, but turning around she saw an old man sitting on the bank of the river, old but *simpatico*.[7] In his eyes burned a blue flame. She tried to focus her eyes on him and suddenly she found herself facing a little man who hardly reached her knees. She tried to run away but a graceful, sinuous voice called her back:

"Don't be afraid, I'm the Achachila who lives in this stream during the day, and at night I go and sleep in my cave in the mountains. I'm the one who makes young girls happy. Ask for whatever you want and you'll get it."

All the young girl could say was, "Just fill up my jar; I'd better get home."

The Achachila disappeared and the girl went into her house carrying the jar of fresh water.

The next day a fox ran across the path of the girl, which cheered her up because a fox always means good luck. A little further down the road she saw a young man she'd never seen before. He playfully threw a pebble at her and she threw one

[6] Mochilero—A bird.
[7] *Simpatico*—Pleasant, easygoing, easy to get along with.

back at him, and before she knew it he was kissing her and carrying her off to his cave where they passed the night singing and drinking.

"We'll always be happy," he told her. "You stay with me and no one will ever hurt you. I'm good, sweet, and kind like the Achachilas. You'll have everything you want. Stay with me and you'll never die."

The girl's parents, seeing that she didn't come home that night and being afraid that something awful had happened to her, looked all over for her until they finally found her in the cave. She was dead and magnificently naked, smiling with her hands over her breasts, lying back in a languishing attitude of ecstasy.

Her parents were horrified. They understood. This was the cave of the Achachila who changed himself into a fox and a young man in order to seduce young girls.

THE ORIGIN OF THE CHINCHILLA (*Aymara*)

A very snooty and proud vulture had two daughters. The older one was great around the house ("nest") and the younger loved to sit around, clean her feathers, and do nothing else at all.

One day the father condor left to look for food, and forbade his daughters to go out while he was gone—especially the coquettish, lazy one. When he returned he found his older daughter desperate and bathed in tears. Her sister had gone out, disobeying her father's orders, and she'd disappeared. The old condor hardly seemed worried, and went to sleep and slept until the next morning. At dawn he flew up over the mountains and started to look for his daughter. Finally he saw her with her wings all spread out comfortably in the nest of one of his worst enemy's sons.

"Why did you run away?" her father complained. "What did you lack at home?"

"Nothing," tearfully answered the daughter. "But this condor told me he loved me and promised to go with me on long voyages to the regions of the dawn, promised that he'd give me all kinds of beautiful feathers and make me a nest of silk, and that we'd live in total luxury always surrounded by the most beautiful sights in nature."

"So live in luxury, in the middle of silks and feathers," answered the father angrily. "Be a living jewel yourself. Only you won't live on the heights any more but in the depths of the earth. Instead of nests that shine next to the sun, you'll live in dark underground caves . . ."

He then turned to the condor who had seduced his daughter, "And you, you'll live with my daughter in the depths of the earth. You'll have no more nests out in the open air but in underground palaces carved out by your teeth. You won't be condors anymore but rodents living underground, although you'll be the most beautiful and exquisite rodents that have ever lived."

And after he'd finished talking, the old condor flew up into the middle of the sky and watched while his daughter and her lover flew down to earth. The daughter never flew again after that and lived under the earth surrounded by silks and soft feathers. She became the Queen of the Rodents in the Andes— the Chinchilla.

THE ORIGIN OF COCA (*Aymara*)

In one of the most beautiful regions of the Andes there once lived a woman who combined magnificent beauty with perverse coquetry and sensuality. She was a goddess who liberally spread around her charms when she descended to human form. This sort of prodigality stimulated both the jealousy of other women and the cry of "Immorality" from the elders. The two groups united and threw the woman off a cliff, where she fell onto a piece of fertile land that was constantly rained on. Out of the woman's ashes grew a little bush whose leaves had very special properties. They were full of power, they alleviated pain and made life optimistic. And that's how the woman they had killed revenged herself; all the boyfriends and husbands of the world from then on were tempted by these marvelous leaves which quietly put to sleep their sexual desires.

XXI.   SPIRIT WORLD

THE BAISANO: THE JAGUAR GHOST
(Guarao)

"Let's go fishing," said an Indian to his wife.

And he grabbed his harpoon and his lance, his wife grabbed the fire and put it in the canoe, and they went up the river at high tide.

"Let's go down this little channel; there has to be a lot of fish here," he said.

So they went down the little channel and on the first run they caught one fish, then another, and in a short time they'd caught six altogether. Which the wife thought was plenty.

"Six is more than enough. Let's go home."

"Not yet," said her husband. "As long as there's so many, let's catch some more and salt them."

On the next time around they came across a tree that had fallen over the channel, blocking the way.

"Careful now, let's not make a lot of noise and scare away the fish."

But the boat wasn't going right; it veered and turned around in the water as if no one was steering it at all. The Indian turned around to see what was wrong with his wife—who was supposed to be steering!—and he saw that an enormous tiger had grabbed her. The tiger was standing on top of the fallen tree and he had the Indian's wife by the throat; she was hanging there from his mouth so she couldn't scream.

Seeing his wife in the tiger's mouth, the Indian paddled away as fast as he could and went home.

"How come you're back so soon, brother?" asked the other Indians. "Is something wrong?"

"I wish I was dead myself, because a tiger has eaten my wife."

"Are you sure you didn't kill her and now you're making up this story?"

"Okay," said the wife's father, "if it was a tiger, you're not to blame, but if it was you, just get ready; you'll have to pay for her life with your own."

The Indians all grabbed their arms and set off in three canoes accompanied by the father and husband of the dead woman. They turned into the same channel and when they got to the fallen tree the Indian told them.

"It was here."

"I'm convinced," said the wife's father, "that it was a tiger and not you who killed my daughter; and now the tiger has to die too."

They started following the tracks of the tiger and walked for hours into the bush without finding him. Then the woman's father, who was a guisiratu (priest), asked the spirits about the tiger, and the spirits, the Jebu, told him that he still was a long way away.

The spirits told the father: "No matter how much we run after him we'll never get him, because the tiger that killed your daughter isn't a tiger like other tigers, but a spirit tiger, a Baisano."

And so they all went back to their homes.

TALKING TO THE SPIRITS (Carib)

Alemunwa:le, the night of the drinking my father talked with the spirits. Next day I stayed in the *to:kai*, and the following night nothing happened. The third night my father spoke again with the spirits. The following days I did nothing. I thought, slept, and smoked *ulema:li* cigars. My body was still painful. I was not allowed to drink or eat much. I drank a little bit of water, ate some manioc cake, very thin it was, I ate fish but only very small ones. I was very lean when I left the *to:kai!* The songs I learned afterwards.

Kuma:nda, Most of the time in the hut I did just nothing, I slept a lot and smoked. My father spoke with the spirits every second day. He talked to the spirits of the *ta:kini* tree, was kind to them and tried to attach them to his pupil. The spirits, at first angry because they were disturbed, are formed together with the pupil into a working team. I learned songs towards the end of the period of seclusion. My stepmother brought me food, manioc porridge and small fish. Big fish are forbidden, they have a strong smell and the spirits hate that.

Kabula:i, The first day I did nothing, just lying in my hammock, I felt sick. I stayed a week in the *to:kai* and learned songs every night. My teacher sang a particular song and I tried to repeat. The same with the spirit words. I had to fast, my wife brought me only some watery manioc porridge and water.

ITSEKES, MALIGNANT SPIRITS (*Kalapalo*)

Naki's wife kept nagging him because he had many lovers and had just arranged to marry a second, much younger wife. One day he decided to get away from her by going on a long fishing trip by himself. On the river, Naki saw a school of fish and drew his bow in order to shoot, but as he did so, the fish changed into human shapes.

Another time, Naki left Aifa before dawn to fish, accompanied by his daughter and his wife's son by another marriage. As they walked in single file, Naki leading the way, the little girl, who was in the rear, said, "Father, who is that following us? I hear someone's feet on the path." They stopped and listened, but saw no one. A second time, the girl heard footsteps, but again they saw nothing. The third time, just as Naki turned around, he saw a human figure on the trail far behind them, but as he looked, it vanished.

Another time, Naki went out at night to play the ceremonial trumpets (kagutu), which are kept in a small house in the center of the village. He went inside this house and began to play in such a way as to call other men to join him. As he sat waiting, Naki noticed a strong light coming from outside, so he walked outdoors to see what was happening. The moon had become very large and its light filled the entire sky. As he watched, the moon grew bigger and bigger until the darkness had completely gone and it seemed like daytime. Frightened, Naki ran inside the trumpet house to try once more to call a companion. Shortly thereafter Taguwaki arrived, but by that time the moon looked normal again. Naki told Taguwaki what he had seen, and they both became worried, because it meant Naki would probably die soon.

A "GHOST" STORY (Mapuche/Araucanian)

In the environs of Pitrufquen, there lived a rather wealthy man who had many animals. He also had a witranalwe to guard them in his absence. Near this wealthy man lived two of his brother's sons, who were poor.

One day the rich man visited his nephews' house. They all began to drink a lot of wine and became a little drunk by late afternoon. They began to feel hungry, but the nephews had nothing to serve the old man. They decided to steal a couple of sheep from the corral of their uncle. One said to the other that he was a rich old man and that stealing one of his sheep, perhaps even two, did not matter much. They went to the uncle's corral together, leaving the old man in their house drinking.

When they arrived, they saw a huge figure on horseback. The man wore a very large, black hat. He had a large mouth and long, sharp teeth, and a big, penetrating set of eyes. He wore a Spanish poncho, also large and black; and he had a set of silver spurs with great rowels. Upon seeing him, one of the nephews ran away, but the other, who had a sheep under his arm, stood stock-still before him. He fearfully asked, "Who are you, caballero?" The answer came in a very low and deep voice: "I am the partner of the owner of these sheep." The nephew then said that the owner of the sheep was his uncle, and, therefore, "Señor, we are like kinsmen."

After this, the young man took a little more courage and spoke further to the witranalwe: "Señor, why not let me take this sheep for the fiesta in my house? My uncle is a very wealthy man, and the loss of one little lamb, which he himself will eat part of, will not matter to him." The witranalwe answered in a very deep voice, "All right, but I want a bowl of blood when you kill the animal."

The young man assented to this demand, at the same time asking the witranalwe to help him carry the sheep back to the house. As soon as they arrived at the young man's house, he told the witranalwe to return in a little while for the blood. The nephew killed the sheep and drained the blood into a wooden bowl. He set both the bowl and a pitcher of wine outside the house for the witranalwe. The witranalwe approached at a gallop, drank the blood at one gulp, and then tossed off the wine. When he finished, he galloped off to the uncle's corral to keep watch over his master's sheep. He never revealed the secret to his master.

THE STORY OF MAYAKOTO (Guarao)

Mayakoto lived with his two wives and his two sons, one by each of his wives. He went out every morning to fish and never came back without bringing ten *morocotos;* which is why they nicknamed him the Morocoto Carrier.

When he went out he always carried with him a kind of flute, a *Jarijariesemoy,* or as the Indians called it, a Toucan Flute; and when he was coming back from fishing he always played the flute so that his wives knew he was coming back and bringing *morocotos* to eat.

When they heard his flute his wives got up and started the fire in the kitchen. Then each one of them got her grill ready so that they could start cooking the fish as soon as Mayakoto came in.

But one day when Mayakoto had gone out very early in the morning the "duende" (goblin) Jajuba appeared while he was fishing and swallowed him and the ten fish that he had caught.

The Jajuba got into Mayakoto's canoe and went to Mayakoto's house. He didn't know how to play the Toucan Flute, so on the way to Mayakoto's house the fluteless Mayakoto called out to his wives: "Wives! Where's the road? I can't see anything."

His wives looked at each other confused and said: "Who can that be who doesn't know the road? Mayakoto knew it very well; and besides, he always played the Toucan Flute when he came home."

Jajuba finally got to the house, went to sleep, and the two wives cooked the *morocotos*. Jajuba woke up after a while and told the women: "Bring me my sons."

One got up and brought him her son; then the other got up and brought him hers. Jajuba looked at them, put his arms around them, then went back to sleep and began to snore. Only his snoring was different from anyone else's; he snored through his nose and it sounded just like someone playing the Toucan Flute. And in fact it was.

One of Mayakoto's wives said to the other: "Sister, this isn't our husband. He's a goblin who has eaten Mayakoto, and Mayakoto is inside his throat playing the flute."

To which the other one answered: "It is just possible. And he has our children in his arms. How can we rescue them?"

"Cut me a pole," said the first one.

And the second one brought the first one a pole, and armed with it she carefully came up behind the goblin and got her son on the end of the pole, and the second one took the pole and did the same; they put their two sons in their *Guenepes*[1] and they ran at full speed into the jungle.

While they were running the older wife said to the

[1] *Guenepes*—Little baby-carrying "slings."

younger one: "Sister, it seems to me that we're being followed."

"Let's stop and listen," said the younger wife.

And they stopped and listened a moment and they *were* being followed; they could clearly hear the peculiar "U, u, uuuuu" Toucan Flute sound coming out of the nose of the goblin.

"So what should we do?" asked the younger one. "Don't you have any long hair?"

"Of course I have long hair," said the older one. "I have all kinds of hair."

"Okay, pull some out and spread it out over the ground."

So the older one pulled out a thick tuft of her hair and scattered it over the ground while the other said: "May all these hairs turn into a thick fence of spines that the Jajuba will not be able to get through!"

And they listened again and could hear the Jajuba calling them: "Wait, wait, my wives. Where are you going . . . wait for me . . ."

Only the scattered hair had become a fence of strong spines that the Jajuba couldn't get through. The two wives kept running and running up to the top of this mountain until they got to a house that was all closed up in which lived a woman called Guauta.

The two women stood in front of the door calling: "Grandmother, open the door."

"I don't want to open it," came the voice from inside.

"Open it, we're being chased."

"I won't open it. Go someplace else; you smell so awful that I'm dizzy from the stench."

The older one turned to the younger: "Little sister, what are we going to do?"

"Let's hit our babies on the ear so that they'll scream. Maybe when she hears them . . ."

So they both gave their babies a sharp slap in the ear and they started to scream and Guauta came up to the door and asked from inside.

"That baby, what is it, a boy or a girl?"

"A boy," answered the younger.

"And the other one?" asked Guauta.

"It's a boy too," answered the older.

"In that case come in," she said and opened the door, and as soon as they were inside Jajuba came up to the door screaming: "Grandmother, have you seen my two wives around here?"

"I haven't seen anybody," said Guauta. "And get away from here; you smell so badly that I'm getting nauseated."

"Come on, Grandmother, open the door a little, just so I can be sure that they aren't inside."

"There aren't any women here," said Guauta. "But if you like I'll open the door a little; see if you can stick your head inside."

And all the time Guauta had an ax hidden in her hand. She opened the door a little and Jajuba stuck his head through the crack. Guauta banged the door shut and caught Jajuba by the neck, took her hatchet and cut off his head.

The goblin ran headless down the mountain and the head fell to the ground, jumping around and screaming "Ayyyyyyyyyyy!"

A couple of days passed and Guauta told her visitors: "You'll have to go and pick some yucca. Leave the boys with me, I'll take care of them."

After the women had gone out, Guauta grabbed the two boys and stretched them, and when she had stretched them she turned them into two young men, and to one she gave a flute, the other a bamboo whistle.

When their mothers were coming back with the yucca they heard the flute and the whistle and they thought some more people had come and said to each other: "I'm ashamed to meet anyone right now."

But they came back to the house anyway and two young men came out; and the mothers didn't know the sons, the sons didn't know the mothers. In fact, when they asked the old lady: "Grandmother, where are our sons?"

"I don't know," said the old lady. "They've been gone for a long time. I think they went after you."

"They're not with us," said the two women, "and those two young men, they're called Jaburi, and we don't have any idea who they are."

The next day Guauta gave each of the boys a bow and arrows and sent them out hunting. The Jaburi hunted all day and got together a huge number of birds, and came home that afternoon.

"Mama Guauta, here's our catch," they said, handing her the birds. To which she answered: "Take the big birds for yourselves, and the little ones. After you've sprinkled them with urine, give them to these women to eat."

And the women, because they were very hungry, ate the birds in spite of the fact that they'd been urinated on. And Guauta, on the other hand, had a feast eating all the big birds: turkeys and ducks and cashew birds.

And the same thing happened day after day after day. Then one day when the Jaburi were out hunting, after they'd shot a huge pile of birds, they saw a *Kirikiri*, a kind of parrot, up in a tree, shot at it, missed, and the arrow stuck in the tree.

Jaburi, after cleaning out his bowels, climbed up the tree to get the arrow, but while he was climbing a bunch of young people came along, all happy and noisy and full of fun.

"It smells awful here," they complained. Of course it smelled awful. The Jaburi had cleaned themselves out. And the feces couldn't be those of anyone else but people who had outraged and insulted their own mothers, urinating on the miserable food that they gave them. On the other hand, they gave the best food to someone who wasn't even their mother!

"Look around, he has to be here somewhere."

So they looked up and there he was crawling around in the tree.

"Come on down," they shouted contemptuously. When he came down they told him: "When you shit throw it far away from here. How dare you do it inside our pots?"

You have to realize that this bunch of young people were really otters in human form and they had their cooking pots on a grill at the foot of the tree.

Afterwards they asked: "Jaburi, where is your brother?"

"I'm here," he answered.

"Listen, oh Jaburis, you are both insulting your mothers. Those two women that you give the hunt leftovers to all wet with urine, they're your real mothers. Your father who was called Mayakoto, the Great Fisherman, was swallowed by the goblin Jajuba when you were just little kids. One day when your mothers were running away from Jajuba they came to Guauta's house, who sent them to dig up some yucca, and they left you with the old lady. But Guauta stretched you and turned you into two young men; since then Guauta has pretended that she was your mother . . . and now you know the truth."

Then they told the oldest boy, "Your mother is the oldest. And yours," they told the younger one, "is the younger."

Then they added: "So from now on when you get home from hunting, give your mothers the biggest birds and give the smallest ones to Guauta—after you've urinated all over them. After all, she was the one who tricked you."

The Water Dogs disappeared and the boys returned home. When they got home the older boy took and gave the bigger birds to the older woman and told her: "These are for you, Mother. Until today we didn't know that you were our true mother; but now we know the truth."

Then they gave the rest of the birds to Guauta after they had urinated all over them.

Guauta started to cry and carry on: "Oh, Jaburi, Jaburi, my son, who has twisted you all up inside? You've changed, you've changed . . . Oh, my son, Jaburi . . ."

Jaburi told his mother: "Mother, I'm going to make a great big strong canoe and then we can leave Guauta's house."

"My son," said his mother, "make the canoe, but first listen to the true story of what really happened. Your father was an excellent fisherman, but Jajuba swallowed him one day when he was fishing. Without your father there we ran away from Jajuba, carrying you two with us. You were tiny little things at the time.

"We came to Guauta's house and one day she sent us out to dig yucca, and we left you two with her. When we got back

231

you were all big and grown up. Only how did this happen? Could it be that Guauta 'stretched' you like the otters said?"

Jaburi made a huge canoe. Only he'd made it out of clay and so the next day it melted in the tidewaters. So he made one out of black wax, only the next day it too was all broken up. He made one out of *cachicamo* bark, and when he came back to see it the next morning, it was still perfect; he made paddles for it and at dawn they got ready to leave.

Guauta was furious. She talked with all the pitchforks on her ranch, with the palm leaves that made up the roof and the walls of her house, and with her parrot: "Tell me when Jaburi is going to leave."

She left, and Jaburi left right after her; and when he did, the pitchforks began to scream: "Guauta, Guauta, Jaburi is leaving . . ."

But Guauta didn't understand because it wasn't her language. Then the leaves of the roof and walls began to scream: "Guauta, Guauta, Jaburi is leaving . . ."

Only she didn't understand them either. So the parrot screamed in bird language: "Guautaaaaaa, Guautaaaaa . . . Jaburi is leaving, Jaburi is leaving."

This she understood and she came running. When Jaburi saw her he pushed his canoe into the river so she couldn't get at it, but she grabbed it and pulled it to shore. Jaburi banged her on the fingers with one of the oars and she screamed: "My son, Jaburi! My son!"

The two mothers urged him on: "Come on, come on, before she drowns you."

He pushed off and started to row, but Jaburi didn't really know how; instead of grabbing the oar by the handle, he grabbed it by the paddle.

A bird passed overhead singing, "Kobokobore! Basaya, basaya," which the Indians interpret to mean, "You hold the oar by the handle and put the paddle part in the water."

"Ah, that's how you do it," said Jaburi and grabbed the oar by the handle and from then on didn't have any trouble with it at all.

After they'd gone on for a while they got to a certain beach and saw a beehive up in a tree. They chopped down the tree, and when she saw the beehive, Guauta said: "Oh, how I'd like to have a little honey out of this beehive."

"So get out and try a little," said Jaburi.

Guauta hung face down over the tree and started lapping up the honey, but Jaburi threw the trunk of another tree down on top of her and left her trapped there. The canoe continued on in its course toward the sandbars in the river, while Guauta, imprisoned under the tree, kept crying and screaming: "Oh, Jaburi, my son, oh, Jaburi, my son!"

After a while Guauta got mad and leveled this curse at Jaburi and the others: "May all those who have continued on their course, leaving me here, be shipwrecked when they reach the sea! And may the canoe in which they are traveling, as soon as it reaches the gulf, be turned into a rocky crag!" and she kept on cooing, "—M—auka. Jaburi! Ja . . . ! Ja . . . ! Gua . . . ! Gua . . . ! Guaaaaaaaa"—which means, "Oh, my son, Jaburi . . . Canoe, canoe, canooooooooooo-e!"

The Jaburi continued on down the river, but when they got to the gulf they sank, and the boat and all its crew was turned into a rock. The rock is still there in the Gulf of Paria between Trinidad and Venezuela, and it's called Rooster Rock or Soldier's Crag.

THE GREAT GOD, THE DEAD, GOOD AND BAD SMALL GODS (*Aymara*)

At the top of the Aymara pantheon is Viracocha, the supreme creator of the universe . . . for the Aymaras Viracocha is a powerful, fearful spirit who supports and protects mankind . . . Viracocha, like all high gods, is demanding of his worshipers, and he can get away with his demands because he controls whatever goods or evils come into an individual's life. He is an intimate participatory part of everyone's life . . .

The minor Aymara gods are directly derived from nature. There is a God of Mountaintop Snow, called Khunu, a Thunder God called Khon, and a Lightning God called Jilpa.

Another important part of Aymara religion is the Cult of the Dead. For the Andean Indian, death is just another kind of life . . . The body dies but the soul continues on its daily life. When the body dies the goods, the objects that belonged to the dead person, also die and have to be buried with him. They believe that the dead soul hovers about the body, which is why the body has to be buried three days after the person has died . . . for the Aymaras a tomb isn't just a depository for the body, but also for the soul. The whole business of a Death- or "Soul"-cult revolves around the idea of maintaining a link between the living and dead. They believe the dead want to hear their names spoken and receive messages of remembrance. The Aymaras also believe in a kind of "corporeality" of the soul, that it can suddenly appear, make itself manifest—or be conjured up by magic. They believe that the newly dead are visited by the souls of friends and ancestors— which is why they sprinkle ashes in an empty room during a wake. The visiting souls leave their footprints in the ashes, which enables people to tell the visiting souls' sex and age.

Here is a typical Aymara prayer to the dead recorded by José María Camacho:

Oh dead soul, leave, leave,
Go where you're going and rest,
But don't forget the family you leave behind,
Your fields and the rest of your goods.
Dead soul, leave, leave.

The Aymara believe in the resurrection of the flesh and in eternal punishment and look upon the next life as a kind of mirror image of this. The dead, once they had reached Upamarca, the World of Silence, keep doing what they had done before they died.

Aymara religion also has a demonic side to it. Demons like Supaya and Auka cause all earthly ills. In a sense, Aymara demonism is just another aspect of the Cult of the Dead; it not only explains death but all the evils of life in terms of the constant, malignant presence of demons.

The anti-demons in Aymara lore are the Achachilas. The

spirit of the Achachilas is the spirit of nature that lives in mountains, rivers, and lakes. The Achachilas are protective spirits; they are expressions of the Universal Good and they are forever helping out mankind against his ills and sufferings.

The Aymaras are always trying to find ways to find links between the gods and mankind. Man offers the gods his sacrifices, his food, his drink and in return he is blessed. The temples of the Aymaras were called Huacas; their priests, Huillas; their confessors, Ichuns; their Sacrificers, Huilano. The Aymaras even had a sacred oracle at the Rock of Iticaca, and later the name was changed to Titicaca, which in colonial times finally found expression in the Sanctuary of Copacabana. The priests, who in a sense "carried out the will" of the Divine, were called Laikas and Yatiris.

Prayer is at the very center of Aymara religion, usually prayers prayed in groups. They believe that in order for God to listen to them, the best intermediaries are children, and in order to pray for rain or to avoid epidemics and the famine that they believe is brought by eclipses of the sun or moon, they beat their children, whose cries and screams supposedly pleased the gods.

XXII. THE DEAD

WHEN ALL THE DEAD COME DOWN (Maya)

There is another custom where I live. On the first of November, they say it is a great festival for all the dead. That is the day that all the dead come down, but that day is a great festival for the people in my village.

They celebrate. They put out tamales on the table, they put out *xepes*, they put out sour *atol*, they put out sweet squash, they put out oranges, they put out bananas, they put out *guicoy* squash, they put out sugarcane, they put out tobacco on the table, so the dead man will smoke it, and they order that chicken with rice be put out, and a gourd bowl of chicha be set on the table. They buy bread and put it out when evening comes; they line up benches all around the house. They say that is for them to sit on as they are waiting for the dead man.

There was a man whose name was Dolores Felipe. When he was celebrating the Day of the Dead, he took his bench and sat down on it in his doorway. He ordered the benches to be placed in line all around the house—he sat down at the door. He called by name all the dead: his brothers, his cousins, his nephews, or his friends, his grandfathers, all his relatives he called by name to come inside. He did not see them. But, since he knew—what the names were of the men who were dead, he called them by name to enter, he went and gave a bench, and raised his hand: they say—he was giving a greeting with it to those who were coming in there.

Because they say that on that day everyone—the dead men who are dead, long ago would come down—they would come down to visit their families where they had left them. And that is why they are awaited on that day. They say that it is a great festival for them.

All around the house they fill it with everything they put out. Because they spread a cloth on the ground, washed, and on top of it they set *atol*, sweet squash, bananas, everything they want to put out, they put out together. Because they say that many are coming to visit there.

And—what is put out there when the prayers have been finished over the—tamales, then they offer them to the people who come to see the celebration; they are given bananas, sugarcane, chickens, tamales, everything that is put out they are given. Because they say that only the spirit eats—the dead man who comes there who is awaited. But—the—real tamale which is there they do not eat, and that is why they put everything out to eat, those who are waiting.

The one who was brought says prayers all night; he walks saying prayers until it gets light the next day. And many people walk with him because where he comes, the tamales which are put out he offers to the people. And that is why people follow along behind where he walks saying prayers.

Then, when it grows light, the prayers are finished, and then when there is chicha they begin to drink the chicha, and when there is music, with a violin—a guitar, with an—accordion. They dance. They get drunk as the evening passes because they say that they are happy because they are celebrating. They are awaiting the dead men, all who are dead; their fathers, their brothers, all who are their relatives, they are awaiting. And that is why they buy many candles and light them.

There are some who have many candles because they say that for each one of the dead whom they are awaiting there is a candle for him. And that candle, they say that it is his light for him to come before God with.

They say to him that "We were awaited." And that is why they buy many candles, each for each. They light them for each dead man who is being awaited. And in the town, the church, the bell is tolled until it comes to be ten o'clock of the day when the Day of the Dead comes. Because they say that that bell is the elevator of the dead who are going to their families, their relatives. And then they are raised up by the bell. That is why the bell in the church in the town is tolled from when it grows light; it is tolled until ten o'clock comes. Because they say that they are raised up with that bell.

There is a village called La Mina. And that village, when the Day of the Dead dawns, all the people celebrate it. And when it grows light, they carry tamales, flat tortillas, they carry them up to the cemetery where the dead are buried—everyone who has a dead man buried there, they carry the flat tortillas and put them out. And there they offer them.

People fill the cemetery when the Day of the Dead dawns, of those who were dead. And that is why when it gets dark on the Day of the Dead and a drizzle falls, the people say that "They are bringing down the drizzle." But nowadays, if the drizzle doesn't fall on the Day of the Dead, well, we say that maybe the dead didn't come down there, and so the drizzle didn't fall. Because long ago they say that they came down with the drizzle when the drizzle fell in the evening, but today, when the Day of the Dead comes without drizzle, well, we say that maybe they were not allowed to come down there, because they did not bring the drizzle.

And that is why there is no second harvest, because there is no drizzle the dead bring. Because they were used to saying that the dead who died, just like the soldiers of the government shut up for a year and when a year has gone, then they are allowed to come out, they visit their families which they left because they can't get out just any time because they dwell in the hand of God, and there is no way for them to get out.

THE VILLAGE OF THE DEAD (Kalapalo)

The Kalapalo believe a person's shadow travels upon death to a village located in the sky, far to the east near the point where the sun rises. After the body has been buried, that night the shadow visits the grieving family for the last time in their house and consumes food which the family has prepared for him. The next day he leaves the village and travels to the east (in the direction of the sunrise) until he reaches the sky. Still traveling east, the shadow approaches the entrance path to the village of the dead. Here he first encounters a side path leading to a smaller settlement. The shadows who live in this village always try to persuade the newly deceased to join them, and if the traveling shadow turns to look at them as they call to him, he is compelled to live in their village without ever seeing the main one.

If he is successful in avoiding this detour, the shadow then comes to a stream, over which are placed logs covered with a thick layer of moss. The shadow has difficulty walking over this slippery bridge and must be met by a deceased relative (frequently a parent or a sibling) who assists in the crossing. Finally, the shadow is conducted to the plaza of the village of the dead, where he is seated on a stool and presented to Sakufenu, out of whose body all men originally came. Sakufenu has one breast swollen with milk (some say she has only one breast, the other having been cut off by her creator, Kwatini). The newly arrived shadow drinks from her breast or from a gourd dipper into which the milk has been squeezed. Then a seclusion chamber is built, and the shadow enters for as long as it takes to grow strong again. During this period of isolation, the male shadows are visited by Sakufenu, who has sexual relations with them. Female shadows are visited by the men of the village. Finally, when the soul is strong once more, he or she joins the rest of the community in continual ceremonial dancing and singing. Sakufenu, rejecting the newly strengthened shadow, takes as her lover the next newly deceased man who arrives. The people of the village of the dead are able to spend all their time singing and dancing in ceremonies, for they do not have to cultivate manioc. In the center of the village is a large manioc silo, filled with flour, which never becomes empty. Although the village is very large, consisting of several concentric rings of houses, no one ever goes hungry because of this magical silo.

ARAVUTARA: THE FATE OF THE DEAD
(Xingu)

Aravutará had a friend who was his inseparable companion. They hunted together, fished together, went to the gardens together, worked and took walks together. They never left each other's side for a single moment. They were great friends. The two were always talking about what they would do if one of them died. And they decided that when one of them died, the other would go after him. Aravutará said, "If I die, you search until you find me. And I'll do the same for you, if you die first."

"We cannot remain apart because we wouldn't be able to stand the loneliness."

This conversation took place daily between the two friends.

And they always said that the one who went on living should make bow and arrows for the dead one, so he could fish and hunt up in the sky. One day Aravutará's friend fell ill and sent for him, "Friend," he said, "I am very ill and I'm going to die."

Aravutará, saddened by what he heard, tried to cheer his friend up, saying that his illness was nothing, he was going to get well. But the sick man was not convinced and said, "No, it's hopeless. I really am dying."

Two days later Aravutará's friend died. Just as they had planned, Aravutará went to look for his spirit everywhere he used to go when he was alive. Every day Aravutará visited these places, and he kept calling to his companion over and over. Tirelessly he went from place to place in search of his missing friend. One day there was an eclipse, and Aravutará told his mother that he was going to find his friend. "My friend asked me to look for him when one day the sun went out. That is why I am sure I will find him now." He said this and left. He walked along a trail, and there at a spot he picked, he sat down and began to wait. Night fell, and still Aravutará was sitting and waiting. At dawn he started to talk to himself, "My friend is taking a long time. It must be very hard for him to appear." After waiting a long time, he went home.

Very early the next day he went to the trail again. When he was dripping with exhaustion, he began to whimper softly. Just then he heard the laugh of the mamaés, the spirits of the dead, who were approaching. Shortly afterward, the mamaés began to pass by him. Since they can't stand the odor of living people, as they passed him, they complained about his odor and said, "There are people here that smell bad, that still have a body."

Each of them said the same thing as he went past Aravutará. They came all adorned with feathers and carrying bows and arrows. Aravutará looked for his friend among those who crossed in front of him. Since he could not find him, he said to a mamaé who was passing by, "Will my friend be along?"

"He's back there, bringing up the rear," the mamaé answered.

And the mamaés kept going by, one after another. Aravutará's friend was the last of them all. He came along laughing. Aravutará could hear him. When he got close, his friend's spirit spoke, "Well, friend, didn't we agree that if one of us died, the other would go look for him?"

"That's why I'm here. I came to look for you."

They stood talking to each other. Then Aravutará asked his friend, "Where is this group going?"

"They are going to a festival to do battle with the birds."

"I'll go with you."

"It's very dangerous. You shouldn't come."

"I'll come anyway. We're friends, that's why I have to go with you. I must go anyway because we always walk together."

"Come along then. Do you have any arrows?"

"No, I don't."

"Then go get some."

Then Aravutará said, "Don't leave me, friend. Wait for me here."

As Aravutará was leaving, his friend's spirit asked him to bring a lot of bast mats to keep the bird's feathers in. Aravutará went home and returned right away. When he came to the spot where he had left his friend, he started to call him, "My friend, are you here?"

"Yes, here I am, waiting for you."

Aravutará had brought bow and arrows and a bamboo flute. They began to talk to each other.

"To get where we're going, we have to sleep on the way. But you must not go to sleep," said the dead man.

After walking some distance, they came to the place where they would pass the night. The friend's spirit said to Aravutará, "Let's pass the night here and tomorrow we'll get there early."

Aravutará was hanging up his hammock and fixing the campsite. His friend's spirit warned him again not to go to sleep. "Don't go to sleep, my friend. Lie down, but don't fall asleep."

He said that and sat at the edge of the fire. After a while he said to Aravutará, "My friend, would you like me to lie with you in the hammock?"

Aravutará said yes. The friend lay down and said, "Don't be afraid of me."

And there they lay, stretched out together. In spite of his friend's warning, Aravutará slept for a short time; then he woke up and got out of the hammock. Then he got back in and went back to sleep. A little later he roused himself and got up again, but right away he lay down and fell asleep. When he woke up for the third time, he looked at his friend and saw that he had turned into a snake. Aravutará started with fear and said, "What's this snake doing, lying here with me?"

Saying that, he turned the hammock over. The snake fell out beside the fire and said, "What's this, my friend? Are you trying to burn me up? I'm your friend. I told you not to be afraid of me."

Having said that, he went back to being a spirit. All mamaés turn into snakes when they go to sleep. After being thrown on the ground, the spirit of Aravutará's friend would not come back into the hammock with him. He remained by the fireside. Aravutará fell asleep, and when he woke up, he saw that his friend had turned into a snake again. He also saw that the rest of the mamaés had turned into snakes. The next day, the mamaés continued their journey. Along the way, they came to an area overgrown with sapé grass and were afraid to step on the pointed sprouts. They were afraid of injuring themselves and dying completely. This was why they didn't want to walk over it. Mamaés may not wound themselves, or they will die completely. So they came to a halt and waited for Aravutará. Aravutará arrived and asked his friend what was going on. He explained that there were prickly spines ahead.

"These spines are harmless, wait and I'll go in front of you," said Aravutará.

Leading the way, he trampled a path through the sprouting grass. The mamaés followed behind. Farther ahead they came across the frogs, who terrified them. The arutsams carried cudgels in their hands. The mamaés retreated. Aravutará came up and asked what was going on.

"They say that there are large animals in our path," his friend's spirit answered.

"Let's have a look. That's ridiculous," he said, when he saw that it was nothing but a bunch of frogs.

He picked up a piece of wood and went about killing the frogs, till he had killed every last one. Aravutará's friend, seeing this, observed, "How about that, my friend? If you hadn't come along, we would have died once and for all at the hands of the frogs or in the grass back there."

When the trail was free of frogs, the mamaés marched on. Farther on, they ran into the crabs, who were armed with big clubs and lying in wait for the travelers. This brought the spirits up short.

"What's the matter now?" asked Aravutará, when he caught up.

"There are some huge beasts ahead waiting to kill us," his friend explained.

"That's nonsense," Aravutará said, seeing the crabs.

And he stepped on them, killing them all. When the trail was clear, the mamaés went on their way, until they came to a ravine that had no bridge. The mamaés put a log across the ravine, but it was not very steady and kept rolling this way and that. Afraid to cross, they retreated a little. Aravutará caught up and asked why they had turned back. His friend explained that a fierce beast was at the root of it. Aravutará had a look and saw the log bobbing up and down in the water. He went a little farther on and made the bridge secure. When he was done, he said, "It's ready, my friends, now you can go across."

The mamaés went across and continued the journey. Farther on, they came to a fire and stopped. Aravutará put out the fire, and they went on. It was still early when they neared the birds' village. When they saw the mamaés coming, they flew toward them.

Aravutará's friend asked, "Who's going first?"

"You spirits are," answered Aravutará. "I want to see how you fight."

The mamaés went to meet the birds. In the clash, the birds started to kill off the mamaés by pecking at them. They were dying one after the other. Aravutará said to his friend, "We must spread charcoal over our bodies to scare away the birds."

So the two friends smeared themselves with charcoal and joined the fight. When the mamaés had almost given up, the friend's spirit asked Aravutará to shout. "Shout, my friend, to scare the birds away for a while. My people can't stand any more."

All kinds of birds were there: eagles, parrots, macaws, toucans, all of them. Aravutará started to shout, but he too had no strength left. He was all bitten, scratched, hairless, and wounded. The birds were pulling everyone's hair out for themselves. The charcoal was almost all gone from the friends' bodies. The friend's spirit said, "Friend, play your flute to get rid of these birds."

Aravutará started to play the nhumiatotó, running back and forth. He played on and on because he did not want the birds to kill all the mamaés. At the sound of the flute, the birds flew off, but it wasn't long before they fell upon the spirits again. Then Aravutará's friend said that his people would fight only once more because they couldn't stand any more. He said, "This time we will kill only the big birds."

After this battle, the chief of the birds told his tribesmen to quit fighting because they were being killed at an alarming rate. It was Aravutará who was mainly responsible for the deaths. So the birds quit fighting and retreated. Aravutará gathered up all the birds he had killed: eagles, macaws, toucans, jabiru storks, parrots, congo kingbirds, and many others. He cleaned the feathers off all the birds and put them in between the mats. He filled all the feather holders.

His friend said to him, "How about that, my friend? If you hadn't come along, the birds would have killed all of us."

"That's exactly why I came," answered Aravutará.

The birds, whenever they killed a mamaé, would carry him off to the giant eagle to eat. He ate every one they brought. They went on killing and carrying them to him.

"Look, my friend," said the spirit, "right before our very eyes they're carrying people off to the eagle."

And the two of them watched the birds carrying off the dead.

"That's what they do. They kill people and give them to the eagle. That's what happens here to all of us."

After his friend finished explaining, Aravutará said, "Now let's leave. I looked for you because I was very lonely for you. We were friends always."

And the mamaés began to turn back. Only Aravutará was carrying feathers. The mamaés had come only to make a festival, which is their battle with the birds. The festival is always held when the sun becomes dark in the daytime. The souls that die in the battle are finished forever.

When they reached the spot where Aravutará had once gone to wait, his friend said, "Now don't look, because I'm going to disappear."

After that, Aravutará could only hear the footsteps of the mamaés, but he did not look at them. When the mamaés had gone away, Aravutará, alone now, thought about them. Why had he gone with them? And he went back to his village. At midday he was nearly there, but he didn't go in until nightfall. Outside his house, he could hear his mother weeping. When he went inside, his mother stopped weeping and was very happy. Aravutará said to her, "I told you that when my friend died, I would have to go look for him."

He said that and started to weep over the loss of his friend. Then the weeping turned to vomiting. When he stopped vomiting, he passed out and remained senseless. The shamans brought him back to his senses, and after that he was all right. Then he told the people everything that had happened to him. His brother asked him why he had vomited. Aravutará answered, "I couldn't stand the smell of the mamaés any more. I was sick of the stench."

And he went on with his story. He told the people everything. There was one who did not believe him and said that he was lying. But Aravutará went on telling his brother everything that had happened to him from the very beginning, from the day he went to wait for his friend on the trail, up till his encounter with the spirits, their trek to the birds' village, and the battle against them. When he finished telling them everything, he drank a special liquid to make himself vomit, to cure himself completely. The next day he sorted out the eagle feathers and brought them to the center of the village to distribute them among his tribesmen. While he handed out the feathers, Aravutará kept saying that he had been a great friend of the dead man and that they had never quarreled.

"That is why I went to look for my friend," he said, "and after I found him, I went with him to the festival of the spirits."

After these words, Aravutará revealed to the people what happens to the dead, saying that in the battle with the birds, the mamaés who die are carried off to a giant eagle who eats them.

"It is he, the eagle, who finishes us off once and for all."

Then he said that whoever goes to the feast without a bow and arrow is easily killed by the birds, but those who bring these weapons don't die quite so easily. It's much more difficult for them. He said that whoever covers his head with one of his body ornaments will not die easily either. The women must take a spindle to defend themselves with.

At last Aravutará told them how he had played the nhumiatotó flute up there, and added, "When you down here shouted at the sound of the nhumiatotó, the birds backed off. From here, you helped me very much up there," Aravutará concluded.

XXIII. AMAZONIANS IN THE AMAZON

THE IAMURICUMÁ WOMEN AND THE JAKUÍ
(Xingu)

The Iamuricumá women played a flute called the jakuí. They played, danced, and sang every day. At night, the dance took place inside the flute house, so that the men could not see. The flutes were forbidden to the men. When the ceremony was performed during the day, outside the flute house, the men had to shut themselves indoors. Only the women were allowed outside, playing, singing, and dancing, decking themselves out with necklaces, feather headdresses, armbands, and other ornaments today worn only by the men. If a man by accident saw the jakuí, the women immediately grabbed him and raped him. The Sun and the Moon knew nothing of this, but in their village they were always hearing the chants and shouts of the Iamuricumá women.

One day the Moon said they had to go see what the Iamuricumá were up to. They decided to go, and they went. They came close to the village but stayed a way off, watching. The Moon did not like to watch the women's movements: the old ones playing the curutá and dancing, others playing the jakuí, still others shouting and laughing out loud. To get a better view, the Sun and Moon went into the village. The women were having a festival.

As the Sun and Moon came closer, the chief of the women said to her people, "Don't say anything or they'll do something to us."

As soon as they got there, the Sun said to the Moon, "I can't stand to hear women playing the jakuí. This can't go on."

Then they discussed how to solve the problem, and the Sun said to the Moon, "Let's make a horí-horí, bull-roarer, to frighten the women away."

"Let's do, and stop this thing. This is a dreadful state of affairs."

Having said that, they left to make the horí-horí. It took them an entire day. When the bull-roarer was ready, the Moon asked who would attack the women with it, to frighten them.

"Let me take it," said the Sun.

And he began to adorn himself with feather armbands, headdresses, and other things. After covering himself completely, he went off in the direction of the Iamuricumá women. The Moon waited in the village. As he got close, the Sun started to whirl his giant bull-roarer over his head. The women went on dancing, but they were starting to get frightened by the approaching roar. When they turned around and saw the Sun making his frightful horí-horí roar, they were terrified. The Moon shouted to the women to get inside their houses. They abandoned everything on the spot and ran inside. The men, in turn, came out of their houses shouting with joy and grabbed the jakuí. Seeing what was happening, the Moon said, "Now everything is all right. The men will play the jakuí, not the women."

At that very moment the men began to play and dance instead of the women. One of the women, who had left something in the middle of the village, asked them from inside her house to bring it to her. When the Moon saw this he said, "From now on it will always be like this. This is the right way. Women should stay inside, not men. They will be shut away when the men dance the jakuí. They may not go out, they may not look. Women may not see the bull-roarer either because it is the companion of the jakuí."

The men learned everything that the Iamuricumá women had known: the music of the jakuí, its songs and dances. At first only the women knew these things.

THE IAMURICUMA WOMEN: THE WOMEN WITHOUT A RIGHT BREAST (Xingu)

The Iamuricumá women held a great festival for the ear-piercing of the boys. After the festival, one part of the village went fishing. The fishermen took along a lot of beijus to eat. The fishing area was far from the village. When they got there, they pounded some poisonous liana into the water and began to catch fish. The days went by and the fishermen did not go home. It was taking them a long time. The boys whose ears had been pierced were in confinement, waiting for the fish that their fathers had gone to catch for them. More than a moon passed, and still the fishermen were gone. In the village, a man who had not gone fishing decided to go after the fishing party and see what had happened. He had some beijus made for the trip and went off. When he arrived at their camp, the fishermen hid their fish. They did not want him to see them. His people were making a frightful racket. They were all turning into wild pigs and other forest animals. The young man did not like it and went home. Back at the village he said the fishermen would be a few more days fishing. But he told his mother the truth and said his father and the other people were turning into things, animals of the forest.

The chief's wife then ordered the women to get ready for the festival and to cut their sons' hair, the boys whose ears had been pierced. When everything was ready, the women set up stools in the center of the village, where their sons would sit while their hair was cut in the ceremony. After it was over, the chief's wife told the other women that they could not stay there any longer. They had to leave that place because their husbands were not people any more, they were turning into animals. All night long, the women talked about it, repeating over and over that they could not stay there any longer. The chief's wife spoke endlessly; day and night she carried on about the need for leaving at once and for abandoning the village forever. Then they all began preparing to leave. They spent two days getting ready, gathering their things, preparing

249

everything: ornaments, necklaces, cotton yarn to wrap around their arms, all things that their men wore.

The chief's wife, before anyone else, began to adorn herself with feathers, armbands, necklaces, and to paint herself with urucu and genipap. After adorning herself exactly like the men, she began to sing. By herself, she sang and sang continuously. Singing, she climbed on top of a house and there went on singing. The men who were left in the village started to complain and curse, but the singing went on. Another woman, adorned the same way, climbed on top of another house and began to sing too. After a while, still chanting their songs, the two women came down to the center of the village, where the other women, by now also adorned and painted like men, joined in the song. Then they started to spread poison over their bodies, to turn themselves into spirits. That is why today, in the place where the Iamuricumá lived, no one is allowed to remove lianas, roots, or anything else from the forest. Whoever does goes mad and gets lost, never to be seen again. They also drank the poison they rubbed on their bodies.

The songs and dances in the village lasted for two whole days. Then the Iamuricumá women, without interrupting their song, slowly began to move away. But before this, they grabbed an old man and dressed him in the shell of a tatu-acu.[1] They put beiju spatulas in his hand and told him to lead the way. As he set off, the old man said, "Now I'm not a person any more. I'm an armadillo." Saying this, he took the lead. After taking a few turns around the village, the Iamuricumá women, still singing, followed behind the tatu-acu, who went ahead, burrowing. He kept taking dives into the ground. He would plunge down at one spot, only to bob up ahead of them. Farther on, the women went past their husbands, who were still fishing. The small children were being carried. The fishermen asked their wives to stop, so the boys could eat some fish. The women would not listen and went on their way. Singing, adorned with feathers, and painted with urucu and genipap, each day they traveled farther, following the armadillo, who went along opening tunnels in the earth. Farther

[1] Tatu-acu—Armadillo.

on, they passed the Macao-acap village. It was midday. The local chief asked his people not to look, so as not to be taken away by the Iamuricumá women. The women did not obey and looked, and the Iamuricumá women carried them all off. Their husbands, who went after them, were also captured. Farther ahead, they passed another village called Etapemetáp. The chief gave his people the same warning, but they would not obey either, and they too were captured.

The Iamuricumá women went on with their journey, traveling forever. They walked day and night without stopping. The small children were thrown into the lagoons, and they turned into fish. The Iamuricumá women are walking still today, ever adorned and singing. They use bows and arrows and do not have a right breast, so they can pull back their bowstrings more easily.

CANNIBAL WOMAN (Toba-Pilagá)

There was a bad woman who had taken another woman's husband. One day they went to a bush to catch parrot fledglings. The man climbed a tree and threw the fledglings to his wife, who was to put them in a bag. When he could find no more birds, he called to his wife, "I don't see any more fledglings."

"Well, get down," said the woman, "but you have only caught a few."

The man climbed another tree on which he found a great many birds. When he threw them to his wife, he noticed that she was eating them raw. He became afraid. He threw her a fledgling which was able to fly, and while she chased it, he got down and started to run away. The woman pursued him and finally caught him. She broke his neck and cut him into pieces. She put his head at the bottom of her bag, the meat above, and covered everything with grass. Then she returned to the village. There she said to the women, "Don't open my bag; later I will share my meat." She went to the river to fetch water. People noticed even then that her form was changing and that she was getting claws.

The woman cut the meat and boiled it in several pots. While she was cooking, her mother-in-law came and inquired about her son. "He wounded a deer, and followed its track. He will be here tonight," the woman replied. When the meat was cooked, she roasted tasi[2] to eat with the grease, and then invited the people. She had roasted a few morsels on a spit. Several people thought that the meat had an unusual taste.

"It tastes like human flesh," they said. "Maybe it is the meat of the man she took with her."

A man came to her and asked, "Where is the man who set out with you this morning? How is it you returned alone? I think that this is the meat of the man who went with you."

The woman replied, "Yes."

A woman grabbed her hair, but the Jaguar woman seized her and broke her neck. Everyone ran away. They all seized their weapons and tried to kill the Jaguar woman, but they failed. Though they pierced her through and through with their spears, they could not kill her. The people deserted the village, and spread the news around.

A shaman, called Katakiaranarai (the drum player), told the people, "Dig a deep ditch and cover it with palm trees." He also said, "Dig out a yuchan [*Chorisia insignis*] and hide in it when the Jaguar woman comes." One shaman hid in the ditch, another in the yuchan. One of the shamans said, "I shall make magic. After that you must rush out. The people in the ditch will help you." The Jaguar woman arrived and shouted, "Why do you hide in the yuchan? This will be of no avail to you. I shall eat you in the yuchan."

The shaman told his people to sharpen their knives and their axes. Meanwhile the Jaguar woman began to open the yuchan with her claws. She made a deep groove in the wood. A woman inside the yuchan howled with fear. The shaman made magic so that the claws of the woman would remain stuck in the wood. The medicine man chanted, "I shall kill the woman who eats people. I shall kill the woman who eats men and women." The chant was finished. Jaguar woman's claws remained stuck in the wood. When the people inside the

2 The fruits of a creeper, Morrenia odorata H. *et al.*

yuchan cut them, Jaguar woman fell down. The shaman led his people in an attack against her, and finally killed her.

The people in the ditch said, "If you had not killed her, we would have destroyed her by forcing her to put her head in such a position that we might have crushed her."

The people cut the Jaguar woman into pieces, which they burned. Everyone danced with joy.

THE KUPE-NDI'YA, ALIEN WOMEN'S TRIBE
(*Apinaye*)

This story happened in a country far in the east, toward the sea. The single women of the village went to the beach to bathe. A big jacaré (*Caiman niger*) came up out of the water. He was quite tame, and the women got friendly with him. One after another lay down on the sand to cohabit with him. The next day they went to the same spot. They had brought meat and pies with them and cried, "Mi-ti, we are already here!" The jacaré replied, "Ho!" and came up the beach. Thus they continued their intrigue with the animal for a long time.

Then one day a man chanced to come to the same spot to shoot fish. Hearing the women coming, he hid and looked on unseen. He told his comrades what he had discovered, and the next day all hid in ambush by the shore. One of them, disguising his voice, cried, "Mi-ti! We are already here!"

"Ho!" answered the jacaré, came up, and vainly looked for the women. Then the men enticed him again, then he ran after the voice, got to the ambush and was killed by the men. They roasted him there, ate him, and heaped up the bones and the plates of his armor beside the fireplace. Then they went home.

When the women came they vainly called the jacaré. Then they noticed the fireplace and the remains of the men's meal and recognized what had occurred. They wept bitterly, but each made herself a club. They hid in ambush by the road near the village and one of them called from afar, "Kwa-kwa-kwa!" When the men of the village heard this cry they at once ran to the spot unarmed. The women rushed out of their ambush to assault them and killed them.

After this deed they moved on. First they came to the Coati People, then to the Bee People; they moved further and further and formed the tribe of Kupe-ndi'ya consisting only of women, who kill all male infants they bear.

Now two brothers were living in that village. Long after the departure of the Kupe-ndi'ya, one of the brothers wanted to dance one day, but he had no anchor ax and his brother would not lend him his. Then he recalled that his sister, one of the Kupe-ndi'ya, had taken an anchor ax along. He resolved to go in search of her, and his brother was willing to go along.

They walked thither and got to the Kupe-wako', who offered them earthworms for food. The brothers asked them about the Kupe-ndi'ya, but were told their village was still far away. Then they came to the Kupe-ganga'la and learned that they were only one day's journey away.

The next morning they actually got to a big village, for each of the women had her own hut. They inquired for their sister's dwelling and visited her. She had several anchor axes hanging in her hut and gave one of them to her brother.

The following morning two young Kupe-ndi'ya invited the brothers to bathe with them. They answered that they were not now interested in bathing, but in cohabitation. The two girls consented on condition that the brothers outrun them in a race. Accordingly, they raced with them from the village to the water hole. One of the brothers lagged far behind his opponent and had to rest content with that. The other beat his and at once went to cohabit with her in the woods by the bank of the stream. The next day the brothers started the homeward journey.

XXIV. HISTORICAL "AGES"

THE LEGEND OF THE SUNS (*Aztec*)

This is the accurate oral history of
how the earth was first founded,
how its foundations were formed,
How the first Sun began 2,513 years ago—
Set down this day, the 22nd of May, 1558.

This Sun, 4-Jaguar lasted 676 years,
and those who lived in this first Sun were
eaten by Jaguars. This was the time of Sun 4-Tiger.
And what they ate was our food, and they
lived 676 years.
And they were eaten in the year 13.
And then they all were destroyed and the Sun was destroyed
along with them.
On the year 1-Reed. They began to be eaten on the day
    4-Tiger,
and everything ended and they were destroyed.
This Sun is called Four-Wind.
Those who lived in the second age of the world were
carried away by wind. Under Sun 4-Wind they were
blown away and became monkeys.
Their houses, their flowers, everything was
blown away by the wind.
And what they used to eat was our sustenance. The date
was 12 serpent, and those who lived under this Sun lived
364 years.
And then they were destroyed; in a single day they were
blown away.
They were destroyed on the day 4-Wind.

And the year was 1 Firestone,[1]
Then came the Sun 4-Rain.
And those who lived under 4-Rain also were destroyed.
Fire rained down on them and they turned into turkeys.
And the Sun burned too,
all their houses burned.
Under this Sun they lived 312 years,
and then they were destroyed.
One whole long day it rained down fire.
And what they ate was our food.
The dates were 1-Firestone and 4-Rain,
and those who perished were young Princes,[2]
which is why today turkeys are called pípil-pípil—young
boys/princes.

This Sun is called 4-Water; and the
Water, the Flood lasted 52 years.
And the people who lived then lived in the time of Sun
4-Water, which lasted 676 years.
And then they perished; they were drowned and
became fish.
The heavens collapsed on them and they were destroyed
in a single day.
And what they ate was our food.
The day was 4-Flower and the year 1-House.
They perished and all the mountains perished with them.
The water lasted 52 years and then their years ended.
We are now in the Sun 4-Movement and under this Sun
there will be earthquakes and famine, and we shall all be
destroyed.[3]

[1] Firestone—Flint.
[2] There is some punning here in the original. Pípil-pípil in Nahuatl
means young boys (*knaben*), princes (*prizen*), or turkeys.
[3] The account of our present sun I have adapted from León-Portilla's
Aztec Thought and Culture.

XXV.   QUETZALCOATL: THE PLUMED SERPENT

THE SONG OF QUETZALCOATL (*Aztec*)

I.

Quetzalcoatl was considered a god,
he was adored as a god and prayed to in olden times at
Tula.
His temple was tall,
many-stepped, narrow-stepped.
There he lay with his face covered,
monstrous, his face like a huge stone,
heavily-, long-bearded.
And his people, the Toltecs, were artisans
Who cut stone and worked feathers,
craftsmen who had learned their craft from Quetzalcoatl.
There in Tula stood his green stone house, his gold house,
his coral house and his shell house, his house of beams,
his turquoise house, his house of feathers.
Nothing was far from the Toltecs,
they were swift,
they were called *tlanquacemilhuime*, those who walk a whole
day without tiring . . .
All the Toltecs were wealthy;
they were never poor . . .
And Quetzalcoatl performed penances,
he cut his leg with thorns and bled for penance . . .

II.

Then Quetzalcoatl and the Toltecs grew slothful
and three evil sorcerers, three demons came to Tula:
Huizilopochtli, Tlacahuepan and Titlacahuan,
and Titlacahuan began casting a spell.

257

He turned himself into a little old man,
His hair was white and silvery, he was bent over,
and he went to Quetzalcoatl's palace and asked to see him,
but they wouldn't let him in; he persisted,
and finally Quetzalcoatl relented:
"Let him come in, I've been waiting for him
for a long time."
And the old man said,
"How is my grandson, how is your health?
I've brought some medicine for you, here,
drink it."
And Quetzalcoatl answered,
"Come here, old man, you're worn out
with traveling. I have been waiting for you
for a long, long time."
And the old man answered,
"And truthfully, how is your health?"
"I'm sick all over, no part of me is well."
"So drink this medicine, it will cure you;
and you'll weep, your heart will be troubled,
you'll think about your death and where you will go."
"And where will I go, old man?" asked Quetzalcoatl.
"To Tollan-Tlapallan, where an aged guard awaits you.
And you shall talk together and when you
return back here you'll be a child again."
Which greatly moved Quetzalcoatl; and the old man urged
him again,
"Cheer up, drink the medicine."
Only Quetzalcoatl refused, and the old man reasoned with
him,
"So don't drink it all,
drink just a part of it,
taste only a little."
And Quetzalcoatl took a little,
and then drank the rest down.

"What is this medicine, I feel so much better.
The pain is gone. How can I be so well so fast?"
"So drink some more," the old man urged, "the
more you drink the stronger you'll get."
And he drank it down until he was drunk,
and he was roused up, his heart quickened,
and he realized that the old devil had
tricked him,
he had given him white maguey-wine,
and so had gotten him drunk.

III.

Then Titlacahuan turned himself into a stranger
and walked into the marketplace with his penis uncovered
and sold green peppers.
He went and sat naked in the marketplace
in front of the palace, and when
the daughter of Uemac saw him naked
she flamed up with desire.
"What has happened to my daughter? What has
gotten her so wrought up?" Vemar asked the woman who
guarded his daughter.
"The stranger who sells green peppers
has caused all this passion."
And her father commented,
"O Toltecs, bring the green-pepper vendor
to me, let him appear before me." . . .
They looked all over for him,
but he had disappeared—and then he
reappeared when they least expected him,
right back in the marketplace where he
had appeared in the first place.
And immediately they told Uemac and
Uemac invited him in and asked him,
"Where are you from?"
"I'm a stranger," Titlacahuan answered,

"I sell little green peppers."

"Cover yourself; put on some clothes."

"But where I come from this is the way we dress."

"But," answered Uemac, "you are the one who
has inflamed my daughter; you must
be the one who cures her."

"What do you mean, my dear lord," answered the "stranger,"
"It's better to kill me right now.
I'm not the only one who sells green peppers."

"No," said Uemac, "you will heal her."

And they fixed Titlacahuan's hair and bathed
and annointed and clothed him, and when he was ready
Uemac told him, "Go into where my daughter is guarded."

And he went and lay with her and she was "healed"
and the "stranger" became the chief's son-in-law.

IV.

Now the Toltecs were angry that Uemac's daughter
had married a stranger and they mocked and spoke ill of him,
and the chief called them in and said,
"I have heard all you've said
against me behind my back, but I have a plan.
Go to fight at Cacatepec and Coatepec and in
the midst of battle abandon him."

So the Toltecs announced war
with the intention of abandoning Titlacahuan
in the midst of battle.

And Titlacahuan went off to war with all the
dwarfs and cripples . . .

And Titlacahuan cheered on his
army of hunchbacks and dwarfs,
"Have no fear. We shall conquer them;
they will meet their doom at our hands."

And the rest of the army abandoned Titlacahuan
to his fate and returned home and told Uemac.

Which cheered up Uemac, who was ashamed
of his son-in-law . . .
Only when Titlacahuan was attacked he wasn't
defeated but defeated the enemy,
slaughtered them all, and
Titlacahuan came home in triumph and Uemac told him,
"Now the hearts of the Toltecs are satisfied that
you are my son-in-law. You have done well,
welcome home."

v.

Now Titlacahuan worked to destroy the Toltecs
from inside,
and Quetzalcoatl was troubled and he decided
to abandon the city of Tula,
had everything burned: his gold house
and coral house . . . and he buried his other
treasures in the mountains,
all the fabled wealth of Tula.
He sent away the precious birds and
changed the cacao trees into mosquitoes
and they started on the road to Anahuac . . .
And he worked wonders as he went along the road:
he wept and his tears pierced holes in stone,
he sat on a rock and left the imprint of his hands and seat,
he planted maguey fibers in the ground,
built a ball court,
balanced a huge phallic rock so that
one person could push it with his little finger,
and many men couldn't move it at all.
And when he had done all these things he went down to the
sea and fashioned himself a raft of serpents and set out
across the sea and sailed to the kingdom of Tlapallan.

XVI. "MYTHIC" HISTORY

VITI-VITÍ, THE ORIGIN OF THE DITCHES
(*Xingu*)

Viti-Vití was a person. He had a nose. He had a mouth. He had ears. He had eyes. He had everything that people have.

Viti-Vití was married to a woman of his own tribe. He had a brother-in-law, a mother-in-law, and a father-in-law. Viti-Vití decided to go get honey out of the hive. He went as it was getting dark because the bees were very fierce, Viti-Vití took his wife and brother-in-law. They went into the forest. When they got there, Viti-Vití said, "Brother-in-law, who's going to climb the tree, you or I?"

"I'd rather you went," answered the brother-in-law.

The wife had brought a large clay pot for the honey. Viti-Vití climbed up in the tree, carrying a shell to bore holes in the hive, to pull out the honeycombs. From up in the tree, Viti-Vití told them to bring the pot close to the tree to catch the honey in, but he was doing nothing of the kind. Viti-Vití was using the shell to turn his right leg into an animal's leg. With the shell he was cutting his leg, or rather scraping it to make it thin and end in a point. On the gound, his wife and brother-in-law kept asking him to throw down honey. Viti-Vití threw honey down to them. But what was falling into the pot was blood from Viti-Vití's leg. As it was dark, they could not see that it was blood. The two of them, wife and brother-in-law, ate up all the blood Viti-Vití had thrown down to them. Suddenly Viti-Vití's brother-in-law began to smell blood. He became suspicious and went to check the pot. Discovering that it was actually blood, he said to his sister, "This is blood. What can he be doing up there? He must be going crazy. We'd better get out of here and leave him alone. You go ahead and I'll be along shortly."

Viti-Vití's wife went off. Up there in the treetop, Viti-Vití continued to work on his foot. He asked his brother-in-law, "Well, have we got enough honey yet?"

"We have half a pot."

The brother-in-law knew that the half a pot was Viti-Vití's blood and said, "I'm moving just a few steps away. The bees are getting ferocious and biting us. We can't take any more."

He was talking and waving his hand in front of his face at the same time. Saying that, he began to move away slowly. When he was a little way off, he started to run. That left Viti-Vití all by himself, but he thought his wife and brother-in-law were down there, waiting for him. Meanwhile, he had given his leg the shape he wanted. From up there, Viti-Vití shouted, "Brother-in-law, oh, brother-in-law!"

Since he got no answer, he said to himself, "Where could they have gone?" As no one answered, he climbed out of the tree and on the ground continued calling to the two of them. Before she left, Viti-Vití's wife had dumped all the blood out of the pot. Viti-Vití kept calling, but no one answered. He decided to go home to get the two of them. When he reached home, he found everything shut up. Out of fear, his brother-in-law had closed the entire house. Viti-Vití from outside ordered them to open up. His brother-in-law did not want to open because he knew if he did, Viti-Vití would kill him with his pointed foot. It was his weapon. Viti-Vití peered in from outside, but he could not see his brother-in-law, who was hidden.

"Where are you, brother-in-law?" he asked.

The brother-in-law did not answer and would not let his sister, Viti-Vití's wife, answer. Viti-Vití got tired of calling to his brother-in-law and his wife. As nobody had answered him, he decided to leave that very hour for the forest, taking with him all his people. Everywhere he went that seemed like a nice place to stay, Viti-Vití would make long, deep ditches and leave part of his people there, and he himself would continue traveling. He advised all of them to build their village outside the ditch, within the semicircle described by it. The ditches were almost always arc-shaped, and one end always led to or away from water. The ditches, Viti-Vití recommended, should be used when it became necessary to protect themselves against cold winds. In almost every habitable place he found, Viti-Vití left a few of his people and a deep ditch for shelter. Viti-Vití still lives today with some of his people on the shores of the Great Kauikúru-Ípa lagoon, at one end of a ditch, where it meets the water.

At night Viti-Vití's footsteps can be heard. They make a dry sound when he steps on the ground with his pointed leg: toe, tim, toc, tim. That is the sound.

THE CONQUEST OF FIRE (Xingu)

The Indians did not have fire. Kanassa decided to search for it. He walked around a large lagoon. In his fist he was carrying a firefly. Tired of walking, he decided to go to sleep. He opened his fist, took out the firefly, and put him on the ground. As it was cold, he crouched down to warm himself in the firefly's light.

The next morning Kanassa came to the land of the curassow and found him making feather ornaments. The curassow was aware that someone was approaching. Recognizing Kanassa, he said, "Kanassa, some wild Indians are showing up around here."

"Nonsense. I just came from over there and didn't see a thing. That's only my people over there. There's nothing at all."

"I'm making this ornament so as to be ready when the wild Indian comes and I have to fight him."

"How are you going to wear this?"

"On top of my head."

"Then put it on so I can see."

The curassow put the ornament on top of his head and strutted around to show Kanassa. Kanassa stretched his arm out toward the curassow and said softly, "This ornament will never come off his head; it will always stay there." Then Kanassa left in a flash. The curassow started to take off the headdress but he could not. And from that moment all curassows wear headdresses. Kanassa kept moving till he came to the land of the cuiará, the small alligator of the scrublands.

The cuiará, seeing Kanassa, said, "Hey, Kanassa, are you taking a walk? Listen, there are wild Indians around here, so watch out."

"No, there is no such thing. There are only my people wandering around here."

The cuiará was making a manioc grater, and Kanassa said to him, "How are you going to carry this grater?"

"On my back."

"Then put it on so I can see. Put it on your tail. It won't work on your back."

The cuiará, as Kanassa suggested, put the grater on his tail and pranced around to show his guest. Kanassa stretched his arm out toward the cuiará and said softly, "This grater will never come off his tail. He'll be like this all his life." From that moment all cuiarás have had flat, rough tails, just like a grater. Having said this, Kanassa left in a flash, leaving the cuiará in a fury, trying to pull the grater off his tail.

Kanassa still had the firefly clutched in his hand. It was the only light he had. Kanassa kept moving till he came to a beach. There he met his relative, the saracura. Kanassa was glad to see her. Looking at the water, Kanassa said to the saracura, "How can I get across the lagoon? I think I will make a clay canoe."

And that's what he did. He made a big canoe and climbed aboard with the saracura. They made clay oars and pushed off. After a while they came across the duck, who was also crossing the lagoon with his entire family, his wife and five children, in a small canoe made of jatobá (courbaril tree) bark. They met midway, in the center of the lagoon, just when the banzeiro (large wave) was about to start. Water was already coming into the duck's boat. Kanassa liked the duck's canoe but didn't say a word, thinking, I'll figure out a way to get that canoe. And he said, "Where are you headed? I fear your canoe is going to sink, with so many people in it. If you want to trade, I wouldn't mind. My canoe is big and strong. Yours seems very dangerous."

"All right, that makes me happy. You are a good man, Kanassa," the duck answered.

The duck did not realize Kanassa's canoe was made of clay. Kanassa, aided by the saracura, grabbed the bark canoe and rowed away energetically. From afar, Kanassa stretched out his arm toward the duck's canoe, blew hard, and said, "Sink, canoe. Sink now. Banzeiro, be strong."

The duck's canoe could not stand up against the banzeiro and sank to the bottom. The duck was screaming with rage. "Kanassa, bring back my canoe. You lied to me. This one is no good, it's made of clay."

The duck and his family were terrified of the water. They did not know how to swim. When their canoe began to sink, they screamed and screamed, and kept struggling on the surface of the water. Suddenly it occurred to them that they weren't sinking, and they began to enjoy it. Today all ducks like being in the water. Kanassa and the saracura got to the other side of the lagoon.

Kanassa drew an arraia (ray or skate) in the mud at the water's edge, but as it was dark, he couldn't see and stepped on his own drawing and was wounded by it. As soon as she stung him, the arraia plunged into the water. Kanassa was mad at the arraia and complained, "I just made her, and already she's hurt me. It's all the firefly's fault because he doesn't give any light."

Kanassa started to throw away the firefly, but then he remembered something and said to the saracura, "Blow on the fire."

"What fire? There's no fire here. The fire is over there with its master."

"Who is the master of the fire?"

"It is the king vulture."

"What is this king vulture like?"

"He's a kind of ordinary vulture, but very large and hard to find. He has two heads. He will live only in high altitudes. And he will come down only to eat people."

"How would a person go about catching him?"

"The only way is to kill a large deer and hide under his hoof till he rots. When the ugúvu-cuengo comes, the thing to do is grab his foot and never let go till he gives you fire."

Kanassa decided to follow the saracura's advice, but he did not have to kill a deer. Instead he drew a picture of a big deer, hid under his hoof, and stayed there. For three days he hid inside the carcass, waiting for the master of the fire. After a while the ordinary vultures began to arrive. The ugúvu-cuengo was perched in a tall, dry tree. The vultures, making a terrible racket, shouted to him, "You can come. It's all right. We're waiting for you to come so we can start eating."

The ugúvu-cuengo, suspicious, was watching the carcass from above, stretching his neck to get a good view. Down below, the others went on shouting, "Come down. It's all right. Hurry up because we're starving."

The ugúvu-cuengo shouted back, "Drag the carcass over here to the tree trunk."

The vultures obeyed, but when they started to pull it, they saw Kanassa hiding.

Kanassa said softly, "Psst! Don't say a word. Get him to come over here."

The vultures went on shouting at the king vulture until he flew down from the big tree to the ground. With him came a great light. On the ground the king vulture examined the carcass well and, seeing nothing, started to eat. He told everybody to eat with him. The deer was very big, and they all began to eat it from back to front. When they got to the forepart, Kanassa, who was hidden in the dead deer's hoof, grabbed the king vulture's foot and said, "O Chief, I've captured you because my people need fire and only you know where it is. Don't be afraid. I'm not going to do anything with you. I only want you to show me where there is fire. You are the master of the fire."

The king vulture was not very angry. He called his son, a little black bird, and said, "My son, you must go find some fire up there in the sky. I'm caught here by Kanassa, who wants to know where there is fire. Go get it in the sky. Put fire in pindaíba fiber and take your time coming back. If you fly too fast, the fire will go out."

The bird went to get the fire in the sky and drifted down slowly to keep it from going out. But he brought only an ember. When he arrived, the urúvu-cuengo told him to blow on the ember and light the fire. Afterward, the urúvu-cuengo gave it to Kanassa, who immediately released him. When the fire was lit and burning bright, lots of frogs came out of the water and gathered around. "Where did this come from? Who brought it?" they asked.

The frogs had water in their mouths. As they were leaving, they squirted it on the fire and fled to the water. But this did not put the fire out completely. Kanassa revived it quickly. The frogs came out of the water again, but before they had a chance to reach the fire, Kanassa frightened them off.

The king vulture had already flown back to his dry tree nearby. From there, before flying off into the distance, he said, "Kanassa, when the fire goes out, break an arrow into pieces, crack them in half, tie one on top of another securely, and stick them fast in the ground. Afterward, find an urucu branch and stick one end into the pieces of arrow and spin it hard until you make the fire spring up."

From way up, the king vulture was still shouting to Kanassa. He was so far up that almost nobody could hear him. "Find a liana at the edge of the water, cut it open, and put it out to dry. It is very good to help you light fires with."

Now Kanassa had to carry the fire over to the opposite shore. For this he summoned the snakes, poisonous and non-poisonous, to carry the fire to the opposite shore of the lagoon. The snakes entered the water, carrying the fire, but in the middle of the crossing, one by one they got tired, and they lost the fire in the banzeiro. Only one, who was very speedy, was able to reach the other shore: the itóto. Kanassa crossed the water too, and on the other shore he gave manioc drink and beiju to the itóto, the snake who had borne the fire.

HOW PEOPLE WHO WANTED TO KILL RAINBOW WERE CAPTURED AND CHANGED INTO ANIMALS (Toba-Pilagá)

Rainbow (Wosa'k) is a large water serpent who stops the rain. He appears in the sky only when he is angry at people.

In the bush there is a black, pink, yellow or green substance which has the appearance of onions but is quite soft. The Indians call it Wosaylatik, Rainbow's excrement. This stuff has magic power and the Indians are eager to collect it in order to carry it in small bags suspended from their necks. It is not easy to secure the Rainbow's excrement. You have to approach it with great caution, taking detours and hiding; otherwise Rainbow will pursue you and send wind and rain on your trail. When Rainbow is angry, he drives men into holes situated in desolate tracts where nobody lives. If you succeed in collecting some of his excrement, you must put it in a grass bundle, urinate, and then run home retracing your steps so as to blur your tracks.

A man who had secured some of Rainbow's excrement told his people that Rainbow had almost caught up with him before he escaped with his booty. Somebody said, "Let's go and kill Rainbow." In the morning the men of the village left with bows and arrows. They gathered branches of palo santo and quebracho colorado. At noon they went to the hole in the ground in which Rainbow lived because they knew that at that time Rainbow was there. They piled up the branches at the entrance of the cave and built a big fire on which they threw earth to make it smoke. When the smoke reached Rainbow, a big noise was heard, "Brrrmm, brrrm." Rainbow was choking, but managed to escape through another hole. The men saw him and cried, "There he goes." Rainbow stuck out his tongue, and the men sank under the ground on the very spot where they stood. Other men, who had not seen what had happened, came to the same place and built another fire. Thunder roared under the ground. Rainbow emerged among these people, stuck his tongue out and turned it around his head, and everybody was swallowed by the earth. Thus Rainbow escaped. On the spot where all these people had disappeared caraguatá (*Bromelia*) plants grew. All the young people had vanished; only old men remained. Rainbow had not been killed, and those who had planned to harm him had disappeared. Rainbow said to himself, "Let's see whether the villagers will eat their own people!"

The old men went in search of the ones who had disappeared, but they did not find a single sign of them, not even their bones. They did not even know where to look for their lost relatives. They searched and searched without success. Rainbow left for some other region.

A rider passed through the place where Rainbow had his abode. The people under the ground spoke to him, "Who are you?" they asked. He said, "I am looking for the people who have disappeared." "Here we are," they shouted, "but our forms are changed. We cannot come out because we have been transformed. Caraguatá plants are growing where we were." Rainbow heard them and became angry. He unleashed a storm that pursued the rider to his village. When he got home he said to the people, "Your children are under the ground. They have been kidnaped by Rainbow." The people said, "Let's run away, Rainbow will soon be here." The old men were against this advice and said, "We'd better remain here and see whether or not Rainbow will come." Rainbow arrived in the midst of a storm. A man shouted, "Come, all of you, to my house and we will see what will happen." They burned honeycombs and wild pig hair for Rainbow and the storm ceased immediately.

The men of the village went to the place where their relatives were kept underground. One man shouted, but received no answer. The men said to each other, "This man has fooled us." They stayed for a while talking to each other. The rider who had informed them said, "Certainly they are here." Notwithstanding this, the other men left. Looking behind them, they saw an ostrich (Rhea). "There is an ostrich, let us catch it," they cried. They concealed themselves and started the hunt. When they approached the bird they noticed that it had large teeth. They shot at it with bows and arrows and struck it. Everyone ran to pluck its feathers. They gathered around a fire to roast the meat. From the middle of the fire leaped a big snake who said, "Why did you kill one of your own children? The ostrich was a man who was taken underground and then changed into an animal." The rider who had heard the voices said, "Yesterday they spoke, but now they have changed their forms." Suddenly they saw Rainbow, who came in the form of a wheel. He asked, "What are you looking for?" "We are searching for our lost people," said the people. Rainbow warned them, "Don't look at me or you'll become one-eyed." The men obeyed. Never point at a rainbow lest your finger remains crooked.

If somebody in your family dies and you have some of Rainbow's excrement, nothing bad will happen to you, but if you don't have any, misfortune awaits you. When Rainbow meets a dead man he bleats like a goat.

STAR WOMAN (*Toba-Pilagá*)

There was a man who was born in a pot. He used to go fishing. His house was set off from the rest of the people, and he did not live with the owner of the pot. When he was grown up he slept in the village, but he had no wife. He asked the sky to give him a wife, a star woman whom he saw in the sky. At night he slept alone, talking to himself, "I would like one of those stars to come down and marry me. If she took me to the sky I would not mind because I am a good-tempered man." He fell asleep. In the middle of the night a woman came. She touched his hand and his hand was frozen. The man was afraid, thinking it was a toad. He asked, "Who are you?" "I am Star Woman. You called me, so I came." "I love you, and I don't like the women here." "I shall stay with you if you have no wife." "No, I have none." The man returned to his hut, but he did not make love to the woman because she had said to him, "Let us sleep quietly." The man obeyed, for he did not know the woman since she was a foreigner.

The following day he went out. A man came and asked, "What about your wife?" "Who says that I have a wife?" "All the people." "But you know that the women do not like me." A big chief came and asked, "Have you a wife?" "Here she is." "Where did she come from?" "From the sky." The men sent the women to fetch fruits, but there were none. The chief told them to look for fruits of the tusca (*Acacia aroma*).

The women said, "Let's look for tusca." Ten women went with the Star Woman. Star Woman said to one of them, "Let's go together." When they were a little distance away she said, "Tell me where there is a plantation here." Her companion told her there was a plantation not far away. Star Woman asked, "Are there corn and pumpkins in it?" "No, everything is dry," answered the woman. They went and arrived at the plantation. "Where are the watermelons?" asked the Star Woman. "They are all gone." "Let us see." The woman showed Star Woman the dry stalks of melons and watermelons. Star Woman recited a charm and then stepped on the stalks of the melons and watermelons. She moved her foot and suddenly a big melon appeared. She moved her foot again and a big watermelon appeared. Star Woman sat down to eat. Nobody knew what had happened. Star Woman ate only a little. When she had finished, she shook the watermelon stalk and melons, watermelons, pumpkins, ancos, corn, and beans grew up. Star Woman said to her companion, "Don't tell anybody what you have seen. I came from the sky and no other woman can do what I do." They left because they had plenty of food to carry. They returned to the village and showed everyone what they had. Star Woman cautioned the men, "Don't eat this food without saying an incantation. First recite a charm and then eat." Those who listened to her found the fruits sweet; the others found them bitter.

The woman said to the man, "Tonight I shall sleep with you, and every night from now on. I shall also get food for you. Where is there an algarrobo tree?" "There is only one tree over there," said the man. "It doesn't matter if there is only one tree." Star Woman touched the trunk with her foot and already-pounded algarrobo pods fell down. They filled three sacks with algarrobo meal. They returned home. Star Woman said to her husband, "Tonight I shall go back to the sky. You shall go too." The man replied, "How can I go, it is so far!" "It is not far; in a short while we shall be there." "Let us go." They arrived there in a short while, and they found a beautiful hut. Nothing was lacking in it. Star Woman said, "I shall go first to prepare food and the rest. You wait near the door. Remember, you must eat everything I make, otherwise it will be bad for you." As she started to leave, she added, "Don't look below lest you fall." The man did not look below.

They were in the sky. The man looked down and everything was dark. He stood near the door. When the fire was lighted the woman came to tell him that his bed and everything he would need was ready. The man said, "Let's go." They went in. The woman cautioned him, "You may sit on the bed though it is very cold, but do not move." The man entered the hut, but the woman left. In the hut there were many people who looked at him with amazement. They said, "How is it that he has not been torn to pieces?" The man was very cold, his feet ached. His wife had warned him, "Do not touch the fire even if your feet ache. If you touch this fire something bad will happen to you. This fire is not like other fires, it is not good." The man sat down near the fire and he tried to warm himself, but he became colder and colder. He poked the fire to make it burn, but it did not help him much. The fire exploded and the man was covered with burns. He cried, "My wife! my wife!" The woman was listening, but did not answer. After a while she came and asked, "What has happened?" "This fire has burned me and I cannot get warm. There is some trick to it," complained the man. "You see," said the woman, "you shouldn't have touched it. I warned you. This fire is not like those on the earth. You must never touch it even though your hands and feet ache, for the fire will burst forth and I shall not be able to live with you." The man said, "If you cannot live with me, you had better send me back. I shall go back alone and free. I am a man." The woman replied, "I shall take you back, but I cannot marry you if your feet are aching and if you are frozen." The man returned to earth. He told the others, "This woman with whom I went to the sky gave me a frozen bed. When I tried to warm myself at the fire I noticed that it was not fire. It exploded and I was badly burned. I did not have nerve enough to go on freezing."

STAR WOMAN (Apinaye)

A young man's wife had died. He allowed his hair to grow long and slept in the bushes behind his mother's house. As he was lying there, he noticed a pretty little star above. He thought to himself how nice it would be if this star came down to him. But when he looked up again after a while the star had disappeared. Then a frog came hopping to his bed and jumped on his body. He threw it aside, but it returned and leaped at him. He hurled it far away into the bush; then he fell asleep. When the frog noticed this, it assumed the form of a girl and lay down beside him. The man awoke and asked, "Where have you come from?" "From there," answered the girl. "What has been the matter with you?" "A frog twice jumped on my body." "That was I! Did you not see the star directly above you?" "Yes, but now it is gone." "That was I, too. I am Kandyekwe'i."[1] They remained together all night, and before daybreak she returned to the sky.

The following night she came again, bringing a bowl full of sweet potatoes and yams, which she ate together with her mate, to whom these plants were as yet unknown, for the Indians then had no cultivation, but ate rotten wood with their meat.

At daybreak the man hid Star Woman in a big lidded gourd, which he carefully tied up. When his comrades later called him to a log race, he first opened the vessel again and looked in, and Star Woman smiled at him. He fastened the cover on carefully and joined the others. His younger brother, however, observed him. In his absence he opened the lid and saw the girl, who lowered her head for shame when she saw that it was not her mate. The brother hurriedly closed the cover. When the man returned from the race, he at once opened the lid of the bottle, but Star Woman kept her head down and would not look at him. So he took her out and now publicly lived with her. She was very beautiful and light-skinned.

Star Woman went bathing with her mother-in-law. When

[1] Kandyekwe'i—Female star.

274

they got to the water she transformed herself into a little opossum and jumped on the old woman's shoulder, but was thrown aside. She jumped a second time and was again pushed away by the old woman. Then she jumped up a third time, saying she wanted to tell the old woman something. She called her attention to a thick tree on the bank of the creek, which bore all manner of maize cobs, and explained that the Indians were to eat this maize instead of rotten wood. As an opossum she climbed up and threw down quantities of cobs. Then she reassumed human shape, packed the cobs together and carried them into the village. There she showed her mother-in-law how to make maize cakes. They ate of the new dish, also giving some to a boy. When he came eating across the plaza, where the men sat in assembly, they called him to ask what he was eating. The boy gave them some of his cake, and all liked it extremely well.

Then the men resolved to chop down the maize tree. They went to work with a stone ax and had got the tree near the point of falling when they got tired and sat down to rest. But when they were about to go to work again they discovered in alarm that the notch they had cut had closed again.

They sent two boys to the village for a better ax. On the way the two discovered a steppe opossum, which they killed and immediately roasted and consumed, though this animal is taboo to boys. Hardly had they finished their meal when they turned into senile, stooping old men. Another messenger found the boys who had been sent in search of the stone ax. He led the two into the village, where an old magician-doctor undertook their rejuvenation. He washed them and poured water over them till they were all but suffocated. Then they turned back into the boys they had been.

When the men had finally felled the tree with great difficulty, Star Woman advised them to make a clearing and plant maize. The Indians did so, and since then they have had their cultivated plots.

Star Woman, however, later returned to the sky after her husband's death.

CARANCHO TEACHES MEN HOW TO MAKE FIRE (*Toba-Pilagá*)

People of old ate the fish they caught raw. Once the chiefs said, "Let us go to gather algarrobo husks." The women filled their carrying nets and pounded the husks in their wooden mortars. This is how fermented drinks were discovered. A man refused to eat the algarrobo flour mixed with water which his wife gave him. He left the dish untouched for many days before his door. His father-in-law called on her. "My daughter," he said, "why don't you give your husband something to eat?" "I gave him food," answered the woman, "but he didn't like the mush I made for him." The father-in-law tasted it and found it delicious. He called someone else to taste it, and this man also found it quite good. They added some more water to the mush, and then called their friends. Others stood around watching them drink the new mixture. The father-in-law and his friends started to laugh and shout, because they were very drunk.

They said, "Tomorrow we shall go to get more algarrobo husks and we shall make more beer." They pounded the husks, put them in big calabashes with water. By midnight the beverage was fermenting. At dawn it was fermented. "Let us drink," they said. They were drunk in a short time. While they were drunk, they grumbled and spoke much nonsense. "We are poor, we have no fire and cannot roast anything." The women drank too. The chief also made a speech, "Do not copulate with your wives at dawn because you never will have time to finish. Copulate with them in the evening so that you may separate on the following morning. If you desire a woman, make love to her, do not take girls against their will. Allow women to remain with their lovers. Don't be indecent like dogs. We are not animals even if we lack fire."

The people said, "You are wise, O Chief, you know best and we shall obey you." "Yes," said the chief. "You better do as I have said. I am very much ashamed because we still behave like dogs."

Another chief came to visit these people. He asked, "Haven't

you any fire?" "No, but we would like to have some because
we have to eat our meat raw." "Why don't you ask Carancho?"
"We cannot, we are surrounded by water." "Well, but I suc-
ceeded in getting here." "Yes, but the water does not allow us
to pass through. The water is armed with clubs to kill us. Why
don't you go and speak to Carancho? Have you fire?" "Yes,
but I did not bring it with me because I thought you had it.
Carancho will come. When he is here, you must obey him or
he will put out your fire." The second chief left, and
crossed the water without any trouble.

The first chief said, "Now we must wait for Carancho, who
will come soon." Others said, "We'd better look for honey."
"No, it is better to wait here. Carancho won't be long," said
the chief.

The second chief went to speak to Carancho, "Listen,
Carancho, there are people over there who have no fire. They
need it badly because they have to eat their food raw."
Carancho said, "I shall go there tomorrow." "You and I have
equal power," said Fox. "I'll fly over there." "Have you
wings?" "Yes I have, and I shall fly high into the sky." Fox
flew higher and higher, but his feathers (fixed with wax) were
falling out. The people said, "Look at this poor fox, he is los-
ing his feathers." Carancho said, "This fellow will soon fall.
Let him." The people called, "Fox, come back!" Fox was high
in the sky. He heard the people, but answered, "These are not
my feathers, these are my hairs." He lost all his feathers, fell
down, and broke his neck. Carancho said, "I foresaw it. I am
the only one who can help people, and nobody else. Tomor-
row I shall go to see these people."

At dawn Carancho left to visit these people. He said to him-
self, "I shall teach these people and bring them here." He
walked until he found the water. "Water, why do you behave
like this? Why do you put out the fire?" The water explained,
"This is the order I received. We have a master, it is Wien the
water serpent." Carancho said, "I came in behalf of these peo-
ple for whom I feel sorry because they eat their meat raw. I
shall kill you and your master too." "You can kill us only if
you bring fire. Otherwise we shall kill you."

Carancho came near the village and saw the people who were eating raw meat. They said, "Who is coming? Who is this man?" "I am Carancho." An unmarried girl cried to Carancho, "Carancho, come into my hut and I shall tell you everything that has happened here." "I shall come, but first tell me if you have a husband. Anyway, I cannot get to your house because I cannot cross the water. Tell me something about this water and its master and what I have to do." The girl replied, "Give me fire. There is plenty of water here, but no fire, and we cannot cook our food. Help us. I can still speak, but the others have lost their speech because they are about to be transformed, since they have no fire." "If you obey me, I shall do something for you. Do as I say," said Carancho. "Yes." "Bring as many fish as you can," ordered Carancho. Carancho was nice to everybody. They brought the fish. "Now," said Carancho, "bring me branches of the pi'tala-dik and of the kuwak'á."[2] The people came back with the wood. Carancho was busy; he bored a small hole in the middle of a stick, inserted another one into the shaft of an arrow. He twirled this stick rapidly, and after a while the wood smoked and glowed. He took some caraguatá tinder and built a big fire. He heated the heads of his spear and arrows and plunged them into the water. The water dried up. The Master of the Water died and the people could make fire. Carancho stayed in the village. They made more fires and grilled their fish. Carancho stayed with these people.

HOW MANKIND RECEIVED FIRE (*Taulipang*)

In ancient times when mankind still didn't have fire, there lived a woman named Polinosamóng. She carried a lot of fire-wood home and put it in the fireplace. Then she bent over and fire came from her belly out of her behind and set the wood on fire. She baked up a whole pile of manioc cakes while the rest of mankind was still doing the best they could baking them in the sun.

[2] Wood used for making fire drills.

One day a young girl saw how the old woman made fire and she told everyone else. They went to the old woman and begged her for some fire, but Polinosamóng, the old toad, didn't want to give them any and claimed she didn't have any herself. But the people wouldn't be put off by the old woman's lies and they grabbed her and tied up her arms and legs and they gathered a huge pile of firewood, put the old woman on top of it, and pushed her belly: fire shot out of her rear.

The fire turned into firestone,[3] and even today people can get the fire out of flint by striking it.

THE UNDERWORLD (*Apinaye*)

Below our earth there is another world. It is said to be very beautiful: it is all pure steppe and the burity palms are very low. There are people there and game; the wild pigs come up to us from there.

Once an Indian was digging out an armadillo. He dug deeper and deeper into the ground after his quarry. His comrade vainly called to him to leave it alone and come up. At last he pierced the earth and tumbled down into the underworld, coming to lie on the leafy top of a burity palm. His comrade went back to the village weeping and reported what had occurred. Then a medicine man offered to bring the lost man back to the upper world. After four days he really succeeded by conducting him up along the road of the wild pigs.

THE VISIT TO THE SKY (*Apinaye*)

While a man was lying sick with a fever an ant crawled into his ear and bit itself fast there. Then he broke out all over his body in stinking wounds. His kin went hunting far away and abandoned him in the village. A hummingbird came to the

---

[3] The German is much less ambiguous than the English here. Feurstein=Flint.

deserted man and, seeing the cause of his ailment, pulled the ant out of his ear with his beak. But a flesh fly flew to the sky and told the urubus (carrion vultures), who came in great flocks.

The vultures laid him on their wings and while some of them flew below to support him, they carried him up to the sky. When they arrived and the man was permitted to open his eyes, he saw the earth far below and his wife and tribesmen camped by a brook. The vultures vomited carrion and served it to the man for manioc gruel. The tapir, who had eaten fruits, offered him his droppings; but at last a falcon fed him with roast meat.

Then the Thunder (nda-klag) summoned the man, who at first was very much afraid, for he saw it lightning all the time in the house, and above the door was suspended a wasp's nest. But at last he went in to Thunder, who was painted black like storm clouds. When he swung his sword club, there was lightning and thunder. The man stayed there a long time and was hospitably treated. In parting, Thunder gave him a sword club like his own. Then the carrion vultures took him back to earth as they had brought him up.

The man's kin had returned to the deserted village some time after their departure to look after him, but had found only traces of the carrion vultures. His wife had in the meantime acquired a lover, whom she would not drop even after her husband's return. While her husband was hunting, her lover came to her, but the sword club hung up beside the platform bed caused a stroke of lightning, so that the pair were terrified and postponed their meeting until nighttime in the steppe. But as they were embracing in the bush, the club sent a scorpion, which stung them in their genitalia. As soon as the husband got home, he openly charged his wife with adultery and told her he had someone watching for him. He left the unfaithful woman, and when she went into the woods with her paramour the sword club sent a swarm of wasps which pounced on the couple and badly stung them.

XXVII. STRANGE NEIGHBORS

THE KUPE-KIKAMBLEG[1] ("Alien Red-haired Tribe") (Apinaye)

In the easternmost end of the world, where the sun rises, there lives a red-haired people. Since the sun rises close to them, they suffer severely from his blaze and live in bitter enmity with him. Every morning at sunrise they shoot arrows at him, but with averted faces, since they cannot bear the light and the burning heat. But the sun rises very rapidly, so they always miss him.

So they decided to fell the post that supports the sky in order to make the sky topple down and prevent the sun from following his course thereafter. They chopped and worked away till the pillar was worn quite thin. Then from fatigue they had to stop, and when they returned to their task the chopped-away portion had grown anew and the pillar was as thick as before. They are still at it today.

THE KUPE-DYEB ("Alien Bat-tribe") (Apinaye)

In the sertao of Sao Vicente, which lies toward the Araguaya, there is the Bat mountain. In it is a big cave with an entrance from below, while high above there is a kind of window. There in ancient times dwelt the Kupe-dyeb, beings of human shape but with bat wings.

An Apinaye had shot a deer near the Bat rock and camped there overnight because it was already late. But while he slept, the Kupe-dyeb came flying and crushed his skull with their anchor axes. When he remained away too long, his relatives followed his tracks and found his corpse. Round it they also saw many tracks, but no traces of the arrival or departure of the malefactors.

[1] Ki—Hair, Kambleg—Red.

Consequently for a long time the Apinaye avoided spending the night in that region till one day two hunters and a boy decided to camp at the foot of Bat rock. After nightfall they heard singing from inside the mountain. Then the boy got frightened and hid in the bush away from the two men's camp. Soon after, the Bats came flying and killed the two hunters, while the boy escaped and reported the occurrence in the village.

Then the Apinaye warriors of all the four villages jointly marched out to destroy the Kupe-dyeb. When they got to the Bat rock, they immediately occupied the entrance to the cave, where they heaped up fuel. Meanwhile others tried to make a detour to the window of the cave. But this was harder than they had supposed, and they had not yet accomplished their end when those occupying the entrance set fire to the pile. So the Kupe-dyeb in a throng flew out of the upper opening without being injured by the Apinaye arrows. They flew south and are said to be still living somewhere there.

When the smoke had cleared, the Apinaye warriors penetrated into the cave, finding quantities of anchor axes left behind by the Kupe-dyeb in their flight. Far in the rear, hidden by a stone slab and stupefied by the smoke, they discovered a boy about six years of age. At first they wanted to kill him, but one Indian decided to bring him up, and took him along.

When the Apinaye on their journey made their bedding of palm leaves on the ground, they also assigned a sleeping place to the little Kupe-dyeb, but he would not remain lying, but wept and constantly looked skyward. When he would not lie still at all, his master suddenly had an idea. He remembered that the dwelling of the Kupe-dyeb lacked bedding on the ground as well as posts for fastening hammocks, but had many horizontal poles. He brought a pole and laid it horizontally into the forks of the branches of two little neighboring trees. Hardly had the boy seen this than he climbed up one of the trees so as to hang from the pole by his knees, head downward. He drew in his head, covered his face with crossed arms, and now slept quietly in this position.

This boy lived only a short time among the Apinaye, for he soon died. One day they observed him lying down singing, "U-ua! Kluna klocire! Klud pecetire!" Then he snatched up the kernels with his hands. When the Apinaye asked him about this, he said his tribesmen had danced this way. The Apinaye still sing this Kupe-dyeb song.

XXVIII. TAO—THE WAY

THE WAY: FATHER TO SON (*Aztec*)

My son, my jewel, my quetzal plumes beyond value:
You have come into life, you have been born,
the Master and Ruler of Creation has brought you into
the world.
He created you, He formed you, He gave you birth,
He for whom everything lives.
And your parents, your aunts, your uncles, all your
relatives, have seen your face and head,
they have studied your face and the nape of your neck
and they have wept and been filled with feeling
because you have come to life,
because you have been born on the earth.
Very well: for a short time you have come to contemplate
the world,
you have come evolving,
you have come to grow, to thrive.

The bird finally breaks through its shell;
as if you were breaking out of your confinement,
clothing yourself in feathers,
wings and tail sprouting forth.
Now you begin to move your hands and feet and head;
you begin to ready yourself to fly.
And what will be the design, the plan of your life?
You are lent a day or two as if they were jewels
or a crest of magnificent feathers,
lent to you by the goodness of Love.
So will you succeed? Will you live on the earth?
May you grow and prosper in inner peace and calm!
May you never be vain or frustrated.
May you for as ever a brief time as you have
stay by our side and under the support of our Love,
and may you always be kind.
He makes you see, He raises and measures you.
Our God of the large arms and shoulders is King.
God is your mother and father,
and neither your father nor your mother can ever love you
the way He loves you.
Of course;
He has determined and decreed your existence,
He has given you life,
He has brought about your birth . . .

If you act badly, if you lie and are false,
nothing of God will remain in your face and heart,
you will pervert your own inner being and
will fall into the vices of drunkenness and drugs.
You will drink maguey-wine and eat poisonous mushrooms
and with these you will so lower yourself that
you will forget who you are,
you will throw yourself into flames,
into the fire of burning stakes,

into the corner of the furnace,
over cliffs and into floods.
You will cast yourself into traps and nets and
nothing more will await you but
stakes and rocks and
you will fall into the trashpit or dunghill . . .
Unhappy you shall be if you do not grasp to you
the teachings your mother and father give you,
if you do not grasp to you what must be the sustenance
and guide of your life . . .
You will fall far from here,
you will fall into the claws of the tiger and coyote,
you will be insensitive to your own faults,
always behind, always in conflict,
if you do not receive the teaching, the bitterness
and even the cries of your elders,
as you should . . .
If you live well, if you live as you have been shown to live,
you will be loved and your life will serve as an example
to others . . .

THE WAY: THE KING TO HIS SONS (*Aztec*)

Come here, my sons, and listen to me.
I am your father and mother and you are my sons.
For a very brief time, for a very short time
I hold the royal power
making blunder and mistakes,
and whatever I do deserves scorn
and contempt
before God who has given me my power
and put me in the seat of His glory.
And now you are here,
the oldest, the firstborn,

285

you who follow me,
and you, the youngest of all.
And I weep and am saddened when I think
Who will be my dead hand?
Who will be my dry mouth?
Who shall be worthy?
Who shall be pious before the Lord?
Is there anyone among you who deserves to
sit on this throne,
who can carry the weight of this power?
Or is there no one to take my place?
Will the line of kings end with me?
With me will everything come to an end . . . ?
Listen to me, learn how to live on the earth
and be worthy of the divine piety of He who rules
the entire world.
What is needed is a man who cries,
who carries his feelings to God,
who never allows himself to be dominated by laziness.
He must always be watchful, ready to do the will of God,
to perform the rites of religion: to wash, to clean, to
cast out waste and filth.
And at the center of all ritual is the ritual of fire,
the offering of incense.
With the ritual of fire you stand at the side of God . . .
you become the mother and father of the Sun . . .
you stand on the left and wear the obsidian sandals of
the Father of the gods, the Mother of the gods,
He who lives in the center of the earth,
who is enclosed in turquoise
and lives in the waters of the blue pond,
the Ancient God of the Region of the Mists of Death,
the God of Time . . .
And what must you do on the earth?
You have come into this world, thanks to others,

in you your ancestors are reborn,
those who have come before you,
the kings and lords of the past . . .
Listen to me, this is your function:
attend to the song and the dance,
with the song and the dance you will awaken the people
and give pleasure to the Lord of the Universe . . .
this is the way to seek God's favor,
the way to follow the Lord.
Attend to the cultivation of the arts,
the art of feathers and the art of woodworking,
this is the cure of poverty and indigence,
this defends and supports the people,
this is how to obtain food and drink.
Attend to agriculture,
at the time of sowing, sow and work,
should not the corn you are to eat
have been cultivated with your own hands?
This is the tradition that has been left by our ancestors,
by those who have come before us.
They were fanatically dedicated to everything
concerned with planting and irrigation.
If you only occupy yourselves with the tasks of nobility,
who shall feed your people,
how shall you feed yourself . . . ?
First, seek refuge in the Lord of the World,
the Lord of All Things,
Night and Wind.
Give yourself to Him totally,
heart and body.
Never stray, never speak against Him in your heart;
He can see through wood and stone.
Lord of all, nothing stops Him,
He shall do what He wills with you,
freely and in His own way.

Second, live in peace and quietude,
be neither blind nor restless.
Be contemptuous of no one and no one will oppose you.
Let God have the final word;
be humble and let those who talk against you
say what they say . . .
Live in peace and you will have the gift of quietude . . .
Third, never be lazy and profitless,
never live even a day or a night
in vain.
Seek first what we need, the food
we need to maintain flesh and bone.
Busy yourself with your clothes,
ask for them from the Lord
and day and night never cease from
making them.
And so I've told you all you need to know to
fulfill the needs of your "office."
If you make fun of what I've said, cast it aside like garbage,
that is your business; for my part, I've done what I've
had to do . . .
Take what I've said to heart and you will benefit all
and live happily in this world.

THE OLD RELIGION AND THE OLD TIMES
(*Maya*)

They did not wish to join with the foreigners; they did not
desire Christianity. They did not wish to pay tribute, did those
whose emblems were the bird, the precious stone, the flat pre-
cious stone, and the jaguar, those with the three magic em-
blems. Four four-hundreds of years and fifteen score years
was the end of their lives; then came the end of their lives be-
cause they knew the measure of their days. Complete was the
month; complete, the year; complete, the day; complete, the

night; complete, the breath of life as it passed also; complete, the blood, when they arrived at their beds, their mats, their thrones. In due measure did they recite the good prayers; in due measure they sought the lucky days, until they saw the good stars enter into their reign; then they kept watch while the reign of the good stars began. Then everything was good.

Then they adhered to the dictates of their reason. There was no sin; in the holy faith their lives were passed. There was then no sickness; they had then no aching bones; they had then no high fever; they had then no smallpox; they had then no burning chest; they had then no abdominal pains; they had then no consumption; they had then no headache. At that time the course of humanity was orderly. The foreigners made it otherwise when they arrived here. They brought shameful things when they came. They lost their innocence in carnal sin; they lost their innocence in the carnal sin of Nacxit Xuchit,[1] in the carnal sin of his companions. There were no more lucky days for us; we had no sound judgment. At the end of our loss of vision, and of our shame, everything shall be revealed. There was no great teacher, no great speaker, no supreme priest, when the change of rulers occurred at their arrival. Lewd were the priests, when they came to be established here by the foreigners. Furthermore, they left their descendants here at Mayapan. These then received the misfortunes, after the affliction of these foreigners.

THE CALLAHUAYAS' MORAL CODE (Aymara)

—One should always fear spirits, gods and ancestors, but never the living.
—A man should be respected for his wealth and feared for his cunning.
—Robbing the rich is applying justice for the benefit of the poor.

[1] Nacxit—One of the names of Quetzalcoatl. In the context of South American titan myths the "sin" referred to here might be homosexuality; it most certainly refers to some aspect of Quetzalcoatl eroticism.

—Never lie, but prudently hide the truth. If you can make someone happy lying, though, then lie . . .

—The secret of life is to neither deceive nor be deceived.

—The best words are those used to hide the truth.

—One should always know everyone else's fears but keep his own fears secret. This is how to appear brave.

—Always be secretive; that is the only way to make yourself visible.

—The road of life is long and there's no sense stumbling over your own feet. The greatest of all stupidities is to be ashamed.

—Just as bodily decency lies in covering oneself, so spiritual decency lies in humility.

—In order to be happy, hide what you do just like you hide your old clothes, your hair that's been cut off, and your cut-off fingernails.

—Never try to "talk yourself superior." Real superiority lies in what you do, not say.

—Always learn, but never teach.

—The purpose of courtesy is to fool fools and the haughty. The Callahuaya should spend a lot on courtesy in order to change it into money.

—Men and women should be like plates that reproduce without any pleasure.

—If a man's afraid of spirits, he should be even more afraid of women who create both men and spirits.

—Only drunkards sing and talk in a loud voice. Decent men should always talk quietly . . .

—It's okay to insult a man, but never in front of his wife or his enemies.

—Always show respect for the old and for authorities, offering them the best places at the table and at parties.

—How you respect others gains the same kind of respect for yourself.

—Act how others want you to act, but never try to make
    them act the way you want them to act.
—Good lies in following good customs . . .
—Public punishment is not only to punish the guilty but also
    to punish those who carry grave sins secretly in their
    hearts.
—It takes great skill to escape the laws, but any fool can fall
    right into the middle of them.

THE PUNISHMENT OF THE GREEDY CALLAHUAYA (*Aymara*)

There was a Callahuaya Indian so greedy that he used to count
his money in the dark because he was afraid that even his
shadow might rob him if he counted it in the light. He was
fat, red-faced, and greasy-looking. One day a fox got it into
his head that he'd like to eat Callahuaya meat for a change and
he decided to trap the greedy Callahuaya with this little bit of
information:

"You can be the richest man in the world. Up on top of
Illampu I've seen some outcroppings of gold and you can have
the whole thing to yourself."

"And what do I have to do for it?" asked the Callahuaya.

"Nothing," answered the fox. "Follow me and I'll show you
where the gold is."

In spite of his great greed, the Callahuaya had some misgivings.

"You know, Fox," he said, "I understand plants but I'm not
a miner. I don't know anything about mining gold."

"You don't have to mine anything," said the fox. "The gold
is right on the surface, you can just take it in your hands. Before you know it you'll have a sackful of gold nuggets the size
of potatoes."

So finally they started out. The Callahuaya was determined
to turn himself from a pauper into a millionaire, and the fox

couldn't have been happier because he was going to get himself a good meal out of the fat, greasy, red-faced Indian.

They climbed up the mountain all day, reached heights where no one had ever set before, and that night they slept in a cave.

"How much further is it?" the Callahuaya asked the fox. "Is it much further till we get to the goldfields?"

"No," answered the fox. "We'll get there this afternoon."

The Callahuaya had found an armadillo in the cave, and still having some misgivings about the fox's plans, he told the armadillo, "Listen, I'm beginning to see myself as the victim of my own greed. In fact, I suspect that the moment it looks good for him, the fox is going to eat me. He has a whole bunch of pepper in his sack, dear Armadillo. Do me a favor and tell the rabbit what's happening and save me from the teeth of the fox. I'm sure of it, HE'S GOING TO KILL ME . . ."

The next day the fox and the Callahuaya continued up the mountain, over crevices and along precipitous ledges. Meanwhile the armadillo had gotten out of his cave, met up with the rabbit, and gave him the Callahuaya's message. The rabbit ran and found the vicuna and told him the message while way up above them the Callahuaya and the fox continued to climb.

It was getting harder and harder, the fox agile and optimistic, the Callahuaya every moment finding it a little more difficult to breathe. The fox's plan was to tire the Callahuaya out, kind of "maturing" him, "ripening" him for death, and then eating him while he slept.

At last the moment of truth arrived.

"I'm not going any further," protested the Callahuaya. "You're tricking me and I know it . . ."

"Dear friend," protested the fox, "you're mistaken. Fatigue is causing you to imagine things. Sleep, rest, tomorrow at dawn you'll be able to see the gold . . ."

The fox thought that at last the moment had arrived for him to satisfy his hunger, but when he got his pepper in hand and his teeth were all aching to bite into the Indian, suddenly a condor descended, grabbed the fox in his beak, carried him down to the valley, and dropped him in the middle of a road.

"Th . . . th . . . th . . . thanks, Condor," the Callahuaya managed to stammer out. "You've saved me, the fox was about to eat me."

"Don't thank me. Flying's my job. Who you should really thank is the vicuna, who galloped all night in order to get to my nest in time . . ."

The Callahuaya arrived home happy, and from that day forward he never counted his money in the dark again.

XXIX. SACRED LYRICISM

SONG AT THE BEGINNING (Nahuatl)

Where can I gather sweet flowers?
Who can I ask?
The bright hummingbird, the yellow butterfly
know where the sweet flowers are,
in the laurel tzinitzcan bird
or the flower tlauquechol bird
forests,
dew-fresh,
perfect.
I'll carry them folded in the folds of
my clothes,

green children with them
and gladden the hearts of nobles.

The rocks answer the flowers,
the bird-green fountain sings
in time to the mockingbird
and the answering coyal.
They scatter their song,
pour their song out,
blessing the earth.

May the hummingbirds come soon;
who are you looking for,
noble poet?
Flowers to cheer the lives of
the nobles,
song to cheer the lives of
my fellow nobles.

I was led to a spot filled
with glistening flowers,
and I was told to pick
the flowers and give them to my friends,
to lighten their days.

So I gathered the flowers in the folds of my clothes,
and I wanted everyone else to come
into this flower world,
to enjoy the flowers of the earth,
my noble friends,
flowers in the midst of their
nobility and dignity.

I picked the flowers
to clothe the nobles in them,
put them in their hands,
I glorified the nobles
before God,
where there is no slavery.

Here on earth I can only obtain the flower world
submitting myself to the Cause of All;
when I remember the flower world I saw
I am filled with sadness.
There is no flower spot on earth,
somewhere else there is,
but not here.
What good is there on earth?
Surely there must be another life
after this,
a flower-, bird-world,
flowers to get drunk on
alone,
to get drunk on and
lose myself in them
altogether.

OTOMI SPRING SONG (*Nahuatl*)

How many gardens have I lived in,
filled with flowers and birds rejoicing
in the Cause of All,
Ohuaya! Ohuaya!

The essence of song is in the
Beyond,
not here on earth,
here no poetry is born.
In the Beyond the coyal, quechol,
and zacuan birds sing together
in praise of the Cause of All,
Ohuaya! Ohuaya!

I try to remember
the songs, I want to go on the
wind to the yellow hummingbird

Beyond, where it sings
Ohuaya! Ohuaya!

Only here no bird sings,
the world of the Cause of All
fades,
I can't penetrate into the
Beyond,
see the Beyond,
listen to the birds sing
to the face of the Cause of All.
This is the world of lamentations
and I've lived here in illusion;
we die and it all ends here.
I want to sing to the Cause of All.
there in the mansion Beyond,
close to Thee, with Thee,
from whom we have our being.
Ohuaya! Ohuaya!

Listen to my song and the song of
the flower-covered drum
that kept pace with my singing.
I want to lighten the hearts of the nobles,
my songs are flowers,
they grow in glory before the face of the
Cause of All.
Ohuaya! Ohuaya!

A FLOWER SONG (*Nahuatl*)

Singer, place thy drum
amid feathers,
amid golden flowers.

Rejoice in the grandeur of
the nobles and the
young.

Song descends on the drum
and looses its feathers,
spreads its songs of the Life-Giver,
as the coyal bird answers,
spreads its song open,
offers its flower songs to
God.

The Life-Giver answers and the
coyal bird spreads out its
song flowers,
Songs are gemstones and feathers;
they are the food of the Giver of Life.

The nobles live in beauty, honor,
and pleasure,
pleasing the one God,
although no one knows where He lives,
whether He lives here or not.

May I have still more time to be
with these youths,
may I weave wreaths for their nobility,
may I still have time to wind more
songs around the drum.

I am a guest among the rulers of Huexotzinco;
I sing of gemstones, emeralds,
I choose the best among the young and
wreathe them with flowers.

A good flower song descends
which will end your sorrow.
Chief of the Chichimecs, be glad
and rejoice.

Friendship spirals down scarlet-winged,
flowering; the warriors hold the xilo flowers
in their hands and smell their sweet odors.

The yellow coyal bird
lifts its songlike flowers,
flowers in your hand,
and you talk, then
answer its song with your own.

You are a quechol bird
waiting for dawn
to sing,
the herald of the Life-Giver,
the herald of God.

Would that the Life-Giver
would shield you with flowers,
but even if you die,
your life still has meaning.

Your fame and deeds are
flowers
that decay,
but still you have not
lived in vain.

Be here, be now,
here and now on this flower-earth;
may our songs and flowers never end,
but may we go on in the Beyond
in the Mansion of the Life-Giver.

A short while and we'll all be gone.
What use is friendship when we have been
forgotten on earth.

Which is why my song is heavy,
beautiful though it may be,
played in the midst of the nobles.

In the house of flowers, the Lord of Waters,
the Lord of the Gate of Waters

answers thee,
has answered thee.

Sometimes the Life-Giver sends
pain into your life;
but I will gladden you with my songs,
in the place of pain,
the place of sorrow.

I will lighten thy heart
with the spring flowers
in spring's painted house.

O, you there in Tlaxcala,
you have played like bells,
like flowers
on your drums.
Xicontectal, Lord of Tizatlan,
the rose-mouthed
sing,
listened to the words of the
one and only God.

Thy house, Life-Giver,
is everywhere,
its mats are spun with
flowers
where thy children pray to thee.
A rain of flowers falls
on the drum,
wreaths of flowers entwine around it,
flowers pour down on it from
above.

The coyal bird answers the
songs of the nobles,
rejoices in their
strength and power.

My drum scatters flowers,
I anticipate your needs.

My song reaches God,
seeks him in the heavens,
and the blessed answer
on their flutes.

But I am still sad in the
forest of this world.

XXX.   TWINS AND HEROES

THE ROAD TO PERFECTION, TWO HEROES: KUARACHY ETE AND KARAI RU ETE MIRI (*Guarani*)

Kuarachy Ete let Chiku into the House of Prayers and Chiku dedicated himself to obtaining divine grace. He sang, he danced, he prayed, he begged for immortality. He lived on nothing else but cornmeal, and at the end of three months Kuarachy Ete told him:

"Put out your hand, Chiku, I want to see it."

Chiku put out his hand, and it was covered with dew.

"You are on the edge of acquiring fortitude; stick it out a little longer and you'll make it."

Chiku returned to the House of Prayers with his wife, Kuarachy Ete's daughter. After a while Kuarachy Ete came back again. "Show me your hand."

But this time it was dry; there was no dew as there had been the first time. And so Kuarachy Ete threw him out of the Prayer House and told him to be on his way.

Later Kuarachy Ete tested Chiku again, sticking him in the top of a tree hanging by his head. Kuarachy Ete's daughter told him, "Don't be afraid; it's my father playing tricks on us."

"As luminously learned as I am, and here I am tossed into the top of a tree. What can I do? What can I do?"

Once he had said the words, suddenly he was down on the ground again. Then the two of them left and built a house and continued to dedicate themselves to the business of sanctity. But when a child was born to Chiku and his wife and it reached the age of reason, Kuarachy Ete inserted a jaguar's soul in its body and so it ran away and disappeared into the jungle. Chiku's wife ran after her son praying prayers to Tupá.

"Don't be afraid," she told Chiku, "and don't kill the boy; it's my father again, 'testing' us."

Tupá himself finally came and gave the mother a grain of hail, advising her, "Throw it against his forehead!"

She threw the grain of hail against his forehead, killed him, and the soul of the jaguar escaped, the child was resurrected, and his own soul restored to him.

Chiku came to Asuncion and mingled with all kinds of strangers; he never stopped praying, and when they saw him praying they asked:

"Why does he act that way? Let's kill him."

And they grabbed him with the intention of killing him, and threw him shackled into jail. Only the Tupá rescued him and returned him to the jungle and Chiku alone obtained perfection, flames grew out of the palms of his hands, his heart glowed with knowledge, his body was turned into dew, his feathered headdress was covered with dew, his flowered crown was made out of flames and dew.

THE ADVENTURES OF HUN-CAMÉ AND VUCUB-CAMÉ WITH THE LORDS OF XIBALBA (Maya)

CHAPTER II

They were taken over the road to Xibalba and when they arrived at the council room of the Lords of Xibalba, they had already lost the match.

Well, the first ones who were seated there were only figures of wood, arranged by the men of Xibalba. These they greeted first:

"How are you, Hun-Camé?" they said to the wooden man. "How are you, Vucub-Camé?" they said to the other wooden man. But they did not answer. Instantly the Lords of Xibalba burst into laughter, and all the other lords began to laugh loudly because they already took for granted the downfall and defeat of Hun-Hunahpú and Vucub-Hunahpú. And they continued to laugh.

Then Hun-Camé and Vucub-Camé spoke: "Very well," they said. "You have come. Tomorrow you shall prepare the mask, your rings, and your gloves," they said.

"Come and sit down on our bench," they said. But the bench which they offered them was of hot stone, and when they sat down they were burned. They began to squirm around on the bench, and if they had not stood up they would have burned their seats.

The Lords of Xibalba burst out laughing again; they were dying of laughter; they writhed from pain in their stomach, in their blood, and in their bones, caused by their laughter, all the Lords of Xibalba laughed.

"Go now to that house," they said. "There you will get your sticks of fat pine and your cigar, and there you shall sleep."

Immediately they arrived at the House of Gloom. There was only darkness within the house. Meanwhile the Lords of Xibalba discussed what they should do.

"Let us sacrifice them tomorrow, let them die quickly, quickly, so that we can have their playing gear to use in play," said the Lords of Xibalba to each other.

Well, their fat pine sticks were round and were called zaquitoc, which is the pine of Xibalba. Their fat pine sticks were pointed and filed and were as bright as bone; the pine of Xibalba was very hard.

Hun-Hunahpú and Vucub-Hunahpú entered the House of Gloom. There they were given their fat pine sticks, a single lighted stick which Hun-Camé and Vucub-Camé sent them, together with a lighted cigar for each of them which the lords had sent. They went to give them to Hun-Hunahpú and Vucub-Hunahpú.

They found them crouching in the darkness when the porters arrived with the fat pine sticks and the cigars. As they entered, the pine sticks lighted the place brightly.

"Each of you light your pine sticks and your cigars; come and bring them back at dawn, you must not burn them up, but you must return them whole; this is what the lords told us to say."

So they said. And so they were defeated. They burned up the pine sticks, and they also finished the cigars which had been given to them.

There were many punishments in Xibalba; the punishments were of many kinds. The first was the House of Gloom, Quequma-ha, in which there was only darkness. The second was Xuxulim-ha, the house where everybody shivered, in which it was very cold. A cold, unbearable wind blew within. The third was the House of Jaguars; Balami-ha, it was called, in which there were nothing but jaguars which stalked about, jumped around, roared, and made fun. The jaguars were shut up in the house.

Zotzi-há, the House of Bats, the fourth place of punishment was called. Within this house there were nothing but bats which squeaked and cried and flew around and around. The bats were shut in and could not get out.

The fifth was called Chayim-há, the House of Knives, in which there were only sharp, pointed knives, silent or grating against each other in the house.

There were many places of torture in Xibalba, but Hun-Hunahpú and Vucub-Hunahpú did not enter them. We only mention the names of these houses of punishment. When Hun-Hunahpú and Vucub-Hunahpú came before Hun-Camé and Vucub-Camé, they said: "Where are my cigars? Where are my sticks of fat pine which I gave you last night?"

"They are all gone, sir."

"Well. Today shall be the end of your days. Now you shall die. You shall be destroyed; we will break you into pieces and here your faces will stay hidden. You shall be sacrificed," said Hun-Camé and Vucub-Camé.

They sacrificed them immediately and buried them in the Pucbal-Chah, as it was called. Before burying them, they cut off the head of Hun-Hunahpú and buried the older brother together with the younger brother.

"Take the head and put it in that tree which is planted on the road," said Hun-Camé and Vucub-Camé. And having put the head in the tree, instantly the tree, which had never borne fruit before the head of Hun-Hunahpú was placed among its branches, was covered with fruit. And this calabash tree, it is said, is the one which we now call the head of Hun-Hunahpú.

Hun-Camé and Vucub-Camé looked in amazement at the fruit on the tree. The round fruit was everywhere; but they did not recognize the head of Hun-Hunahpú; it was exactly like the other fruit of the calabash tree. So it seemed to all of the people of Xibalba when they came to look at it.

According to their judgment, the tree was miraculous because of what had instantly occurred when they put Hun-Hunahpú's head among its branches. And the Lords of Xibalba said: "Let no one come to pick this fruit. Let no one come and sit under this tree!" they said, and so the Lords of Xibalba resolved to keep everybody away.

The head of Hun-Hunahpú did not appear again because it had become one and the same as the fruit of the gourd tree. Nevertheless, a girl heard the wonderful story. Now we shall tell about her arrival.

CHAPTER III

This is the story of a maiden, the daughter of a lord named Cuchumaquic.

A maiden, then, daughter of a lord, heard this story. The name of the father was Cuchumaquic, and that of the maiden was Xquic. Whe she heard the story of the fruit of the tree which her father told, she was amazed to hear it.

"Why can I not go to see this tree which they tell about?" the girl exclaimed. "Surely the fruit of which I hear tell must be very good." Finally she went alone and arrived at the foot of the tree which was planted in Pucbal-Chah.

"Ah!" she exclaimed. "What fruit is this which this tree bears? Is it not wonderful to see how it is covered with fruit? Must I die, shall I be lost, if I pick one of these fruits?" said the maiden.

Then the skull which was among the branches of the tree spoke up and said: "What is it you wish? Those round objects which cover the branches of the tree are nothing but skulls." So spoke the head of Hun-Hunahpú, turning to the maiden. "Do you, perchance, want them?" it added.

"Yes, I want them," the maiden answered.

"Very well," said the skull. "Stretch your right hand up here."

"Very well," said the maiden, and with her right hand reached toward the skull. In that instant the skull let a few drops of spittle fall directly into the maiden's palm. She looked quickly and intently at the palm of her hand, but the spittle of the skull was not there.

"In my saliva and spittle I have given you my descendants," said the voice in the tree. "Now my head has nothing on it any more, it is nothing but a skull without flesh. So are the heads of the great princes, the flesh is all which gives them a handsome appearance. And when they die, men are frightened by their bones. So, too, is the nature of the sons, which are like saliva and spittle; they may be sons of a lord, of a wise man, or of an orator. They do not lose their substance when they go, but they bequeath it; the image of the lord, of the wise man, or of the orator does not disappear, nor is it lost, but he leaves it to the daughters and to the sons which he begets. I have done the same with you. Go up, then, to the surface of the earth, that you may not die. Believe in my words that it will

305

be so," said the head of Hun-Hunahpú and of Vucub-Hunahpú.

And all that they did together was by order of Huracán, Chipi-Caculhá, and Raxa-Caculhá. After all of the above talking, the maiden returned directly to her home, having immediately conceived the sons in her belly by virtue of the spittle only. And thus Hunahpú and Xbalanqué were begotten.

And so the girl returned home, and after six months had passed, her father, who was called Cuchumaquic, noticed her condition. At once the maiden's secret was discovered by her father when he observed that she was pregnant.

Then the lords, Hun-Camé and Vucub-Camé, held council with Cuchumaquic.

"My daughter is pregnant, sirs; she has been disgraced," exclaimed Cuchumaquic when he appeared before the lords.

"Very well," they said. "Command her to tell the truth, and if she refuses to speak, punish her; let her be taken far from here and sacrifice her."

"Very well, honorable Lords," he answered. Then he questioned his daughter:

"Whose are the children that you carry, my daughter?" And she answered, "I have no child, my father, for I have not yet known a youth."

"Very well," he replied. "You are really a whore. Take her and sacrifice her, Ahpop Achih; bring me her heart in a gourd and return this very day before the lords," he said to the two owls.

The four messengers took the gourd and set out carrying the young girl in their arms and also taking the knife of flint with which to sacrifice her.

And she said to them: "It cannot be that you will kill me, oh messengers, because what I bear in my belly is no disgrace, but was begotten when I went to marvel at the head of Hun-Hunahpú which was in Pucbal-Chah. So, then, you must not sacrifice me, oh messengers!" said the young girl, turning to them.

"And what shall we put in place of your heart? Your father told us: 'Bring the heart, return before the lords, do your duty, all working together, bring it in the gourd quickly, and put the heart in the bottom of the gourd.' Perchance, did he not speak to us so? What shall we put in the gourd? We wish, too, that you should not die," said the messengers.

"Very well, but my heart does not belong to them. Neither is your home here, nor must you let them force you to kill men. Later, in truth, the real criminals will be at your mercy and I will overcome Hun-Camé and Vucub-Camé. So, then, the blood and only the blood shall be theirs and shall be given to them. Neither shall my heart be burned before them. Gather the product of this tree," said the maiden.

The red sap gushing forth from the tree fell in the gourd and with it they made a ball which glistened and took the shape of a heart. The tree gave forth sap similar to blood, with the appearance of real blood. Then the blood, or that is to say the sap of the red tree, clotted, and formed a very bright coating inside the gourd, like clotted blood; meanwhile the tree glowed at the work of the maiden. It was called the "red tree of cochineal," but [since then] it has taken the name of blood tree because its sap is called blood.

"There on earth you shall be beloved and you shall have all that belongs to you," said the maiden to the owls.

"Very well, girl. We shall go there, we go up to serve you; you, continue on your way, while we go to present the sap, instead of your heart, to the lords," said the messengers.

When they arrived in the presence of the lords, all were waiting.

"You have finished?" asked Hun-Camé.

"All is finished, my lords. Here in the bottom of the gourd is the heart."

"Very well. Let us see," exclaimed Hun-Camé. And grasping it with his fingers he raised it, the shell broke and the blood flowed bright red in color.

"Stir up the fire and put it on the coals," said Hun-Camé.

As soon as they threw it on the fire, the men of Xibalba began to sniff and, drawing near to it, they found the fragrance of the heart very sweet. And as they sat deep in thought, the owls, the maiden's servants, left, and flew like a

flock of birds from the abyss toward earth, and the four be-
came her servants.

In this manner, the Lords of Xibalba were defeated. All
were tricked by the maiden.

CHAPTER IV

Well, then, Hunbatz and Hunchouén were with their mother
when the woman called Xquic arrived.

When the woman Xquic came before the mother of Hun-
batz and Hunchouén, she carried her sons in her belly, and it
was not long before Hunahpú and Xbalanqué, as they were
called, were to be born.

When the woman came to the old lady, she said to her: "I
have come, Mother; I am your daughter-in-law and your
daughter, Mother." She said this when she entered the grand-
mother's house.

"Where did you come from? Where are my sons? Did they,
perchance, not die in Xibalba? Do you not see these two who
remain, their descendants and blood, and are called Hunbatz
and Hunchouén? Go from here! Get out!" the old lady
screamed at the girl.

"Nevertheless, it is true that I am your daughter-in-law; I
have been for a long time. I belong to Hun-Hunahpú. They
live in what I carry, Hun-Hunahpú and Vucub-Hunahpú are
not dead; they will return to show themselves clearly, my
mother-in-law. And you shall soon see their image in what I
bring to you," she said to the old woman.

Then Hunbatz and Hunchouén became angry. They did
nothing but play the flute and sing, paint, and sculpt all day
long and were the consolation of the old woman.

Then the old woman said: "I do not wish you to be my
daughter-in-law because what you bear in your womb is fruit
of your disgrace. Furthermore, you are an imposter; my sons
of whom you speak are already dead."

Presently, the grandmother added: "This that I tell you is
the truth; but, well, it is all right, you are my daughter-in-law,
according to what I have heard. Go, then, bring the food for
those who must be fed. Go and gather a large net [full of

corn] and return at once, since you are my daughter-in-law, according to what I hear," she said to the girl.

"Very well," the girl replied, and she went at once to the cornfield which Hunbatz and Hunchouén had planted. They had opened the road and the girl took it and so came to the cornfield; but she found only one stalk of corn; there were not two or three; and when she saw that there was only one stalk with an ear on it, the girl became very anxious.

"Ah, sinner that I am, unfortunate me! Where must I go to get a net full of corn as she told me to do?" she exclaimed. Immediately, she began to beg Chahal for the food which she had to get and must take back.

"Xtoh, Xcanil, Xcacau, you who cook the corn; and you, Chahal, guardian of the food of Hunbatz and Hunchouén!" said the girl. And then she seized the beards, the red silk of the ears of corn and pulled them off without picking the ear. Then she arranged the silk in the net like ears of corn and the large net was completely filled.

The girl returned immediately; the animals of the field went along carrying the net, and when they arrived, they went to put the load in a corner of the house, as though she might have carried it. The old woman came and when she saw the corn in the large net she exclaimed: "Where have you brought all this corn from? Did you, perchance, take all the corn in our field and bring it all in? I shall go at once to see," said the old woman, and she set out on the road to the cornfield. But the one stalk of corn was still standing there, and she saw too where the net had been at the foot of the stalk. The old woman quickly returned to her house and said to the girl: "This is proof enough that you are really my daughter-in-law. I shall now see your little ones, those whom you carry and who also are to be soothsayers," she said to the girl.

CHAPTER V

Now we shall tell of the birth of Hunahpú and Xbalanqué. Here, then, we shall tell about their birth.

When the day of their birth arrived, the girl named Xquic gave birth; but the grandmother did not see them when they were born. Instantly, the two boys called Hunahpú and Xbalanqué were born. There in the wood they were born.

Then they came to the house, but they could not sleep.

"Go throw them out!" said the old woman, "because truly they cry very much." Then they went and put them on an anthill. There they slept peacefully. Then they took them from the anthill and laid them on thistles.

Now, what Hunbatz and Hunchouén wished was that they [Hunahpú and Xbalanqué] would die there on the anthill, or on the thistles. They wished this because of the hatred and envy Hunbatz and Hunchouén felt for them. At first they refused to receive their younger brothers in the house; they would not recognize them and so they were brought up in the fields.

Hunbatz and Hunchouén were great musicians and singers; they had grown up in the midst of trials and want and they had had much trouble, but they became very wise. They were flautists, singers, painters, and carvers; all of this they knew how to do.

They had heard about their birth and knew also that they were the successors of their parents, those who went to Xibalba and died there. Hunbatz and Hunchouén were diviners, and in their hearts they knew everything concerning the birth of their two younger brothers. Nevertheless, because they were envious, they did not show their wisdom, and their hearts were filled with bad will for them, although Hunahpú and Xbalanqué had not offended them in any way.

These two last did nothing all day long but shoot their blowguns; they were not loved by their grandmother, nor by Hunbatz, nor by Hunchouén; they were given nothing to eat; only when the meal was ended and Hunbatz and Hunchouén had already eaten, then the younger brothers came to eat. But they did not become angry, nor did they become vexed, but suffered silently because they knew their rank, and they understood everything clearly. They brought their birds when they came, and Hunbatz and Hunchouén ate them without giving anything to either of the two, Hunahpú and Xbalanqué.

The only thing that Hunbatz and Hunchouén did was to

play the flute and sing. And once when Hunahpú and Xbalan-
qué came without bringing any bird at all, they went into the
house and their grandmother became furious.

"Why did you bring no birds?" she said to Hunahpú and
Xbalanqué. And they answered:

"What happened, Grandmother, is that our birds were
caught in the tree and we could not climb up to get them,
dear Grandmother. If our elder brothers so wish, let them
come with us to bring the birds down," they said.

"Very well," the older brothers answered, "we shall go with
you at dawn."

The two younger brothers then discussed the way to over-
come Hunbatz and Hunchouén.

"We shall only change their nature, their appearance; and so
let our word be fulfilled, for all the suffering that they have
caused us. They wanted us to die, that we might be lost, we,
their younger brothers. In their hearts they really believe that
we have come to be their servants. For these reasons we shall
overcome them and teach them a lesson." Thus, they spoke.

Then they went toward the foot of the tree called Canté.
They were accompanied by their two elder brothers and they
were shooting their blowguns. It was not possible to count the
birds which sang in the tree, and their elder brothers marveled
to see so many birds. There were birds, but not one fell at the
foot of the tree.

"Our birds do not fall to the ground. Go and fetch them
down," they said to their elder brothers.

"Very well," the latter answered. And then they climbed
the tree; but the tree became larger and the trunk swelled.
Then Hunbatz and Hunchouén wanted to come down, but
they could not come down from the top of the tree.

Then they called from the treetop: "What has happened to
us, our brothers? Unfortunate we. This tree frightens us only
to look at it. Oh, our brothers!" they called from the treetop.
And Hunahpú and Xbalanqué answered: "Loosen your
breechclouts; tie them below your stomach, leaving the long
ends hanging and pull these from behind, and in this way you
can walk easily." Thus, said the younger brothers.

"Very well," they answered, pulling the ends of their belts

back, but instantly these were changed into tails and they took on the appearance of monkeys. Then they hopped over the branches of the trees, among the great woods and little woods, and they buried themselves in the forest, making faces and swinging in the branches of the trees.

In this way Hunbatz and Hunchouén were overcome by Hunahpú and Xbalanqué; and only because of their magic could they have done it.

Then they returned to their home, and when they arrived they spoke to their grandmother and their mother, and said to them: "What could it be, Grandmother, that has happened to our elder brothers, that suddenly their faces turned into the faces of animals?" So they said.

"If you have done any harm to your elder brothers, you have hurt me and have filled me with sadness. Do not do such a thing to your brothers, oh, my children," said the old woman to Hunahpú and Xbalanqué.

And they replied to their grandmother: "Do not grieve, Grandmother. You shall see our brothers' faces again; they shall return, but it will be a difficult trial for you, Grandmother. Be careful that you do not laugh at them. And now, let us cast our lot," they said.

Immediately they began to play their flutes, playing the song of Hunahpú-Qoy. Then they sang, playing the flute and drum, picking up their flutes and their drum. Afterward they sat down close to their grandmother and continued playing and calling back their brothers with music and song, intoning the song, called Hunahpú-Qoy.

At last, Hunbatz and Hunchouén came and began to dance; but when the old woman saw their ugly faces, she began to laugh, unable to control her laughter, and they went away at once and she did not see their faces again.

"Now you see, Grandmother! They have gone to the forest. What have you done, Grandmother of ours? We may make this trial but four times, and only three are left. Let us call them back again with flute and with song, but you, try to control your laughter. Let the trial begin!" said Hunahpú and Xbalanqué.

Immediately they began again to play. Hunbatz and Hunchouén returned dancing, and came as far as the center of the court of the house grimacing and provoking their grandmother to laughter, until finally she broke into loud laughter. They were really very amusing with their monkey-faces, their broad bottoms, their narrow tails, and the hole of their stomach, all of which made the old woman laugh.

Again the elder brothers went back to the woods. And Hunahpú and Xbalanqué said: "And now what shall we do, little Grandmother? We shall try once again, this third time."

They played the flute again, and the monkeys returned dancing. The grandmother contained her laughter. Then they went up over the kitchen; their eyes gave off a red light; they drew away and scrubbed their noses and frightened each other with the faces they made.

And as the grandmother saw all of this, she burst into violent laughter; and they did not see the faces of the elder brothers again because of the old woman's laughter.

"Only once more shall we call them, Grandmother, so that they shall come for the fourth time," said the boys. They began again, then, to play the flute, but their brothers did not return the fourth time; instead, they fled into the forest as quickly as they could.

The boys said to their grandmother: "We have done everything possible, dear Grandmother; they came once, then we tried to call them again. But do not grieve; here we are, your grandchildren; you must look to us, oh, our mother! Oh, our grandmother! to remind you of our elder brothers, those who were called and have the names of Hunbatz and Hunchouén," said Hunahpú and Xbalanqué.

They were invoked by the musicians and singers, and by the old people. The painters and craftsmen also invoked them in days gone by. But they were changed into animals and became monkeys because they became arrogant and abused their brothers.

In this way, they were disgraced; this was their loss; in this way Hunbatz and Hunchouén were overcome and became animals. They had always lived in their home; they were musicians and singers and also did great things when they lived with their grandmother and with their mother.

CHAPTER VI

Then they, Hunahpú and Xbalanqué, began to work, in order to be well thought of by their grandmother and their mother. The first thing they made was the cornfield.

"We are going to plant the cornfield, Grandmother and Mother," they said. "Do not grieve; here we are, your grandchildren, we who shall take the place of our brothers," said Hunahpú and Xbalanqué.

At once they took their axes, their picks, and their wooden hoes and went, each carrying his blowgun on his shoulder. As they left the house, they asked their grandmother to bring them their midday meal.

"At midday, come and bring our food, Grandmother," they said.

"Very well, my grandsons," the old woman replied.

Soon they came to the field. And as they plunged the pick into the earth, it worked the earth; it did the work alone. In the same way, they put the ax in the trunks of the trees and in the branches, and instantly they fell and all the trees and vines were lying on the ground. The trees fell quickly, with only one stroke of the ax.

The pick also dug a great deal. One could not count the thistles and brambles which had been felled with one blow of the pick. Neither was it possible to tell what it had dug and broken up, in all the large and small woods.

And, having taught an animal, called Xmucur,[1] they had it climb to the top of a large tree and Hunahpú and Xbalanqué said to it: "Watch for our grandmother to come with our food, and as soon as she comes, begin at once to sing, and we shall seize the pick and the ax."

"Very well," Xmucur answered.

And they began to shoot with their blowguns; certainly they did none of the work of clearing and cultivating. A little later, the dove sang, and they ran quickly, grabbing the pick

[1] Xmucur—Turtledove.

and ax. And one of them covered his head and also deliberately covered his hands with earth and in the same way smeared his face to look like a real laborer, and the other purposely threw splinters of wood over his head as though he really had been cutting the trees.

Thus, their grandmother saw them. They ate at once, but they had not really done the work of tilling the soil, and without deserving it they were given their midday meal. After a while, they went home.

"We are really tired, Grandmother," they said upon arriving, stretching their legs and arms before her, but without reason.

They returned the following day, and upon arriving at the field, they found that all the trees and vines were standing again and that the brambles and thistles had become entangled again.

"Who has played this trick on us?" they said. "No doubt all the small and large animals did it, the puma, the jaguar, the deer, the rabbit, the mountain cat, the coyote, the wild boar, the coati, the small birds, the large birds; they, it was who did it; in a single night, they did it."

They began again to prepare the field and to prepare the soil and cut the trees. They talked over what they would have to do with the trees which they had cut, and the weeds which they had pulled up.

"Now we shall watch over our cornfield; perhaps we can surprise those who come to do all of this damage," they said, talking it over together. And later they returned home.

"What do you think of it, Grandmother? They have made fun of us. Our field, which we had worked, has been turned into a field of stubble and a thick woods. Thus, we found it, when we got there, a little while ago, Grandmother," they said to her and to their mother. "But we shall return there and watch over it, because it is not right that they do such things to us," they said.

Then they dressed and returned at once to their field of cut trees, and there they hid themselves, stealthily, in darkness. Then all the animals gathered again; one of each kind came

315

with the other small and large animals. It was just midnight when they came, all talking as they came, saying in their own language: "Rise up, trees! Rise up, vines!"

So they spoke when they came and gathered under the trees, under the vines, and they came closer until they appeared before the eyes of Hunahpú and Xbalanqué. The puma and the jaguar were the first, and Hunahpú and Xbalanqué wanted to seize them, but the animals did not let them. Then the deer and the rabbit came close, and the only parts of them which they could seize were their tails, only these they pulled out. The tail of the deer remained in their hands, and for this reason the deer and the rabbit have short tails.

Neither the mountain cat, the coyote, the wild boar, nor the coati fell into their hands. All the animals passed before Hunahpú and Xbalanqué, who were furious because they could not catch them.

But, finally, another animal came hopping along, and this one, which was the rat, they seized instantly and wrapped him in a cloth. Then when they had caught him, they squeezed his head and tried to choke him, and they burned his tail in the fire, and for that reason the rat's tail has no hair. So, too, the boys, Hanahpú and Xbalanqué, tried to poke at his eyes.

The rat said: "I must not die at your hands. And neither is it your business to plant the cornfield."

"What are you telling us now?" the boys asked the rat.

"Loosen me a little, for I have something which I wish to tell you, and I shall tell you immediately, but first give me something to eat," said the rat.

"We will give you food afterward, but first speak," they answered.

"Very well. Do you know, then, that the property of your parents Hun-Hunahpú and Vucub-Hunahpú, as they were called, those who died in Xibalba, or rather the gear with which they played ball, has remained and is hanging from the roof of the house: the ring, the gloves, and the ball? Nevertheless, your grandmother does not want to show them to you, for it was on account of these things that your parents died."

"Are you sure of that?" said the boys to the rat. And they

were very happy when they heard about the rubber ball. And as the rat had now talked, they showed the rat what his food would be.

"This shall be your food: corn, chili seeds, beans, pataxte, cacao; all this belongs to you, and should there be anything stored away or forgotten, it shall be yours also. Eat it," Hunahpú and Xbalanqué said to the rat.

"Wonderful, boys," he said, "but what shall I tell your grandmother if she sees me?"

"Do not worry, because we are here and shall know what to say to our grandmother. Let us go! We shall go quickly to the corner of the house, go at once to where the things hang; we shall be looking at the garret of the house and paying attention to our food," they said to the rat.

And having arranged it thus, during the night after talking together, Hunahpú and Xbalanqué arrived at midday. When they arrived, they brought the rat with them, but they did not show it; one of them went directly into the house, and the other went to the corner and there let the rat climb up quickly.

Immediately they asked their grandmother for food. "Prepare our food. We wish a chili sauce, Grandmother," they said. And at once the food was prepared for them and a plate of broth was put before them.

But this was only to deceive their grandmother and their mother. And having dried up the water which was in the water jar, they said, "We are really dying of thirst; go and bring us a drink," they said to their grandmother.

"Good," she said and went. Then they began to eat, but they were not really hungry; it was only a trick. They saw then, by means of their plate of chili, how the rat went rapidly toward the ball which was suspended from the roof of the house. On seeing this in their chili sauce, they sent to the river a certain xan, an animal called xan, which is like a mosquito, to puncture the side of their grandmother's water jar, and although she tried to stop the water which ran out, she could not close the hole made in the jar.

"What is the matter with our grandmother? Our mouths are

dry with thirst, we are dying of thirst," they said to their mother and they sent her out. Immediately the rat went to cut the cord which held the ball and it fell from the garret of the house together with the ring and the gloves and the leather pads. The boys seized them and ran quickly to hide them on the road which led to the ball court.

After this they went to the river to join their grandmother and their mother, who were busily trying to stop the hole in the water jar. And arriving with their blowgun, they said when they came to the river: "What are you doing? We got tired of waiting and we came," they said.

"Look at the hole in my jar which I cannot stop," said the grandmother. Instantly, they stopped it, and together they returned, the two walking before their grandmother.

And in this way the ball was found.

CHAPTER VII

The boys returned happily to the ball court to play; they were playing alone a long time and cleared the court where their parents had played.

And the Lords of Xibalba, hearing them, said: "Who are they who play again over our heads and disturb us with the noise they make? Perchance Hun-Hunahpú and Vucub-Hunahpú did not die, those who wished to exalt themselves before us? Go at once and call them!"

So said Hun-Camé, Vucub-Camé, and all the lords. And sending the messengers to call them, they said to them: "Go and tell them when you get there: 'Let them come, the lords have said'; we wish to play ball with them here, within seven days we wish to play; tell them so when you arrive," thus said the lords. This was the command which they gave to the messengers. And they came then by the wide road which the boys had made that led directly to their house; by it the messengers arrived directly before the boys' grandmother. They were eating when the messengers from Xibalba arrived.

"Tell them to come, without fail, the lords commanded," said the messengers of Xibalba. And the messengers of Xibalba indicated the day: "Within seven days they will await them," they said to Xmucané.

"It is well, messengers; they will go," the old woman answered. And the messengers set out on their return.

Then the old woman's heart was filled with anxiety. "Whom shall I send to call my grandchildren? Was it not this same way that the messengers of Xibalba came before, when they came to take the boys' parents?" said the grandmother, entering her house, alone and grieving.

And immediately a louse fell into her lap. She seized it and put it in the palm of her hand, and the louse wriggled and began to walk.

"My child, would you like that I send you away to call my grandchildren from the ball court?" she said to the louse. "Messengers have come to your grandmother, tell them; 'come within seven days, tell them to come,' said the messengers of Xibalba; thus your grandmother told me to say," thus she told the louse.

At once the louse swaggered off. Sitting on the road was a boy called Tamazul, or the toad.

"Where are you going?" the toad said to the louse.

"I am carrying a message in my stomach; I go to find the boys," said the louse to Tamazul.

"Very well, but I see that you do not go quickly," said the toad to the louse. "Do you not want me to swallow you? You shall see how I run, and so we shall arrive quickly."

"Very well," the louse said to the toad. Immediately the toad swallowed him. And the toad walked a long time, but without hurrying. Soon he met a large snake, called Zaquicaz.

"Where are you going, young Tamazul?" said Zaquicaz to the toad.

"I go as a messenger; I carry a message in my stomach," said the toad to the snake.

"I see that you do not walk quickly. Would I not arrive sooner?" the snake said to the toad. "Come here," he said. At once Zaquicaz swallowed the toad. And from then on this was the food of snakes, who still today swallow toads.

The snake went quickly and, having met Vac, which is a very large bird, the hawk, the latter instantly swallowed the snake. Shortly afterward it arrived at the ball court. From that time, this has been the food of hawks, who devour snakes in the fields.

And upon arrival, the hawk perched upon the cornice of the ball court where Hunahpú and Xbalanqué were amusing themselves playing ball. Upon arriving, the hawk began to cry: "Vaccó! Vac-có!" it said, cawing, "Here is the hawk! Here is the hawk!"

"Who is screaming? Bring our blowguns!" the boys exclaimed. And shooting at the hawk, they aimed a pellet at the pupil of the eye and the hawk spiraled to the ground. They ran to seize it and asked: "What do you come to do here?" they asked the hawk.

"I bring a message in my stomach. First cure my eye and afterward I shall tell you," the hawk answered.

"Very well," they said, and taking a bit of the rubber of the ball with which they were playing, they put it in the hawk's eye. "Lotzquic," they called it, and instantly the hawk's eye was perfectly healed.

"Speak, then," they said to the hawk. And immediately it vomited a large snake.

"Speak, thou," they said to the snake.

"Good," the snake said and vomited the toad.

"Where is the message that you bring?" they asked the toad.

"Here in my stomach is the message," answered the toad. And immediately he tried, but could not vomit; his mouth only filled with spittle but he did not vomit. The boys wanted to hit him then.

"You are a liar," they said, kicking him in the rump, and the bone of the haunches gave way. He tried again, but his mouth only filled with spittle. Then the boys opened the toad's mouth, and once open, they looked inside of it. The louse was stuck to the toad's teeth; it had stayed in its mouth and had not been swallowed, but only pretended to be swallowed. Thus the toad was tricked, and the kind of food to give it is not known. It cannot run; and it became the food of the snakes.

"Speak," they said to the louse, and then it gave its message. "Your grandmother has said, boys: 'Go call them; the messen-

320

gers of Hun-Camé and Vucub-Camé have come to tell them to go to Xibalba, saying: "They must come here within seven days to play ball with us, and they must also bring their playing gear, the ball, the rings, the gloves, the leather pads, in order that they may amuse themselves here," said the lords. They have really come,' said your grandmother. That is why I have come. For truly your grandmother said this and she cries and grieves, for this reason I come."

"Is it true?" the boys asked themselves when they heard this. And running quickly they arrived at their grandmother's side; they went only to take their leave of her.

"We are going, Grandmother, we came only to say goodbye. But here will be the sign which we shall leave of our fate: each of us shall plant a reed, in the middle of the house we shall plant it; if it dries, this shall be the sign of our death. 'They are dead!' you shall say, if it begins to dry up. But if it sprouts again: 'They are living!' you shall say, oh, our Grandmother. And you, Mother, do not weep, for here we leave the sign of our fate," thus they said.

And before going, Hunahpú planted one reed and Xbalanqué planted another; they planted them in the house and not in the field, nor did they plant them in moist soil, but in dry soil; in the middle of their house, they left them planted.

CHAPTER VIII

Then they went, each one carrying his blowgun, and went down in the direction of Xibalba. They descended the steps quickly and passed between several streams and ravines. They passed among some birds, and these birds were called Molay.

They also passed over a river of corruption, and over a river of blood, where they would be destroyed, so the people of Xibalba thought; but they did not touch it with their feet; instead, they crossed it on their blowguns.

They went on from there, and came to a crossway of four roads. They knew very well which were the roads to Xibalba: the black road, the white road, the red road, and the green road. So then they sent an animal called Xan.[2] It was to go to

2 Xan—Mosquito.

gather information which they wanted. "Sting them, one by one; first sting the one seated in the first place, and then sting all of them, since this is the part you must play: to suck the blood of the men on the roads," they said to the mosquito.

"Very well," answered the mosquito. And immediately it flew on to the dark road and went directly toward the wooden men which were seated first and covered with ornaments. It stung the first, but this one said nothing; then it stung the next one, it stung the second, who was seated, but this one said nothing, either.

After that, it stung the third; the third of those seated was Hun-Camé. "Ah!" he exclaimed when it stung him. "What is this, Hun-Camé? What is it that has stung you? Do you not know who has stung you?" said the fourth one of the lords, who were seated.

"What is the matter, Vucub-Camé? What has stung you?" said the fifth.

"Ah! Ah!" then said Xiquiripat. And Vucub-Camé asked him, "What has stung you?" and when it stung the sixth who was seated he cried, "Ah!"

"What is this, Cuchumaquic?" asked Xiquiripat. "What is it that has stung you?" And the seventh one seated said, "Ah" when he was stung.

"What is the matter, Ahalpuh?" said Cuchumaquic. "What has stung you?" And when it stung him, the eighth of those seated said, "Ah!"

"What is the matter, Ahalcaná?" said Ahalpuh. "What has stung you?" And when he was stung, the ninth of those seated said, "Ah!"

"What is this, Chamiabac?" said Ahalcaná. "What has stung you?" And when the tenth of those seated was stung, he said, "Ah!"

"What is the matter, Chamiaholom?" said Chamiabac. "What has stung you?" And when the eleventh of those seated was stung he said, "Ah!"

"What happened?" said Chamiaholom. "What has stung you?" And when the twelfth of those seated was stung, he said, "Alas!"

"What is this, Patán?" they said. "What has stung you?" And the thirteenth of those seated said, "Alas!" when he was stung.

"What is the matter, Quicxic?" said Patán. "What has stung you?" And the fourteenth of those seated when he was stung said, "Alas!"

"What has stung you, Quicrixcac?" said Quicré.

In this way, they told their names, as they all said them one to the other. So they made themselves known by telling their names, calling each chief, one by one. And in this manner, each of those seated in his corner told his name.

Not a single one of the names was missed. All told their names when Hunahpú pulled out a hair of his leg, which was what had stung them. It was really not a mosquito which stung them, which went for Hunahpú and Xbalanqué to hear the names of all of them.

They, the youths, continued on their way and arrived where the Lords of Xibalba were.

"Greet the lord, the one who is seated," said one in order to deceive them.

"That is not a lord. It is nothing more than a wooden figure," they said, and went on. Immediately, they began to greet them: "Hail, Hun-Camé! Hail, Vucub-Camé! Hail, Xiquiripat! Hail, Cuchumaquic! Hail, Ahalpuh! Hail, Ahalcaná! Hail, Chamiabac! Hail, Chamiaholom! Hail, Quicxic! Hail, Patán! Hail, Quicré! Hail, Quicrixcac!" they said coming before them. And looking in their faces, they spoke the name of all, without missing the name of a single one of them.

But what the lords wished was that they should not discover their names.

"Sit here," they said, hoping that they would sit in the seat which they indicated.

"That is not a seat for us; it is only a hot stone," said Hunahpú and Xbalanqué, and they [the Lords of Xibalba] could not overcome them.

"Very well, go to that house," the lords said. And they [the youths] went on and entered the House of Gloom. And neither there were they overcome.

CHAPTER IX

This was the first test of Xibalba. The Lords of Xibalba thought that the boys' entrance there would be the beginning of their downfall. After a while, the boys entered the House of Gloom; immediately lighted sticks of fat pine were given them, and the messengers of Hun-Camé also took a cigar to each one.

" 'These are their pine sticks,' said the lord; 'they must return them at dawn, tomorrow, together with the cigars, and you must bring them back whole,' said the lord." So said the messengers when they arrived.

"Very well," the boys replied. But they really did not light the sticks of pine; instead, they put a red-colored thing in place of them, or some feathers from the tail of the macaw, which to the night watches looked like lighted pine sticks. And as for the cigars, they attached fireflies to their end.

All night everybody thought they were defeated. "They are lost," said the night watchmen. But the pine sticks had not been burned and looked the same, and the cigars had not been lighted and looked the same as before.

They went to tell the lords.

"How is this? Whence have they come? Who conceived them? Who gave birth to them? This really troubles us because it is not well what they do. Their faces are strange, and strange is their conduct," they said to each other.

Soon all the lords summoned the boys.

"Eh! Let us play ball, boys!" they said. At the same time they were questioned by Hun-Camé and Vucub-Camé:

"Where did you come from? Tell us, boys!" said the Lords of Xibalba.

"Who knows whence we came! We do not know," they said, and nothing more.

"Very well. Let us play ball, boys," said the Lords of Xibalba.

"Good," they replied.

"We shall use our ball," said the Lords of Xibalba.

"By no means shall you use your ball, but ours," the boys answered.

"Not that one, but ours we shall use," insisted the Lords of Xibalba.

"Very well," said the boys.

"Let us play for a worm, the chil,"[3] said the Lords of Xibalba.

"No, but instead, the head of the puma shall speak," said the boys.

"Not that," said those of Xibalba.

"Very well," said Hunahpú.

Then the Lords of Xibalba seized the ball; they threw it directly at the ring of Hunahpú. Immediately, while those of Xibalba grasped the handle of the knife of flint, the ball rebounded and bounced all around the floor of the ball court.

"What is this?" exclaimed Hunahpú and Xbalanqué. "You wish to kill us? Perchance you did not send to call us? And your own messengers did not come? In truth, unfortunate are we! We shall leave at once," the boys said to them.

This was exactly what those of Xibalba wanted to have happen to the boys, that they would die immediately, right there in the ball court, and thus they would be overcome. But it did not happen thus, and it was the Lords of Xibalba who were defeated by the boys.

"Do not leave, boys, let us go on playing ball, but we shall use your ball," they said to the boys.

"Very well," the boys answered, and then they drove their ball through the ring of Xibalba, and with this the game ended.

And offended by their defeat, the men of Xibalba immediately said: "What shall we do in order to overcome them?" And turning to the boys they said to them: "Go gather and bring us, early tomorrow morning, four gourds of flowers." So said the men of Xibalba to the boys.

"Very well. And what kind of flowers?" they asked the men of Xibalba.

"A branch of red chipilín, a branch of white chipilín, a

[3] Chil—An obscure word. Either a caterpillar or a centipede may be meant.

325

branch of yellow chipilín, and a branch of carinimac," said the men of Xibalba.

"Very well," replied the boys.

Thus the talk ended; equally strong and vigorous were the words of the boys. And their hearts were calm when they gave themselves up to be overcome.

The Lords of Xibalba were happy, thinking that they had already defeated them.

"This has turned out well for us. First they must cut them the flowers," said the Lords of Xibalba. "Where shall they go to get the flowers?" they said to themselves.

"Surely you will give us our flowers tomorrow early. Go, then, to cut them," the Lords of Xibalba said to Hunahpú and Xbalanqué.

"Very well," they replied. "At dawn we shall play ball again," they said upon leaving.

And immediately the boys entered the House of Knives, the second place of torture in Xibalba. And what the lords wanted was that they would be cut to pieces by the knives, and would be quickly killed; that is what they wished in their hearts.

But the boys did not die. They spoke at once to the knives and said to them: "Yours shall be the flesh of all the animals," they said to the knives. And they did not move again, but all the knives were quiet.

Thus they passed the night in the House of Knives, and calling all the ants, they said to them: "Come, cutting ants, come, zompopos, and all of you go at once, go and bring all the kinds of flowers that we must cut for the lords."

"Very well," they said, and all the ants went to bring the flowers from the gardens of Hun-Camé and Vucub-Camé.

Previously the lords had warned the guards of the flowers of Xibalba: "Take care of our flowers, do not let them be taken by the boys who shall come to cut them. But how could the boys see and cut the flowers? Not at all. Watch, then, all night!"

"Very well," they answered. But the guards of the garden heard nothing. Needlessly, they shouted up into the branches

326

of the trees in the garden. There they were all night, repeating their same shouts and songs.

Puhuyú was the name of the two who watched the garden of Hun-Camé and Vucub-Camé. But they did not notice the ants who were robbing them of what they were guarding, turning around and moving here and there, cutting the flowers, climbing the trees to cut the flowers, and gathering them from the ground at the foot of the trees.

Meanwhile the guards went on crying, and they did not feel the teeth which were cutting their tails and their wings.

And thus the ants carried, between their teeth, the flowers which they took down, and gathering them from the ground, they went on carrying them with their teeth.

Quickly they filled the four gourds with flowers, which were moist with dew when it dawned. Immediately, the messengers arrived to get them. " 'Tell them to come,' the lord has said, 'and bring here instantly what they have cut,'" they said to the boys.

"Very well," the boys answered. And carrying the flowers in the four gourds, they went, and when they arrived before the Lords of Xibalba, it was lovely to see the flowers they had brought. And in this way the Lords of Xibalba were overcome.

The boys had only sent the ants to cut the flowers, and in a night the ants cut them and put them in the gourds.

Instantly the Lords of Xibalba paled and their faces became livid because of the flowers. They sent at once for the guardians of the flowers: "Why did you permit them to steal our flowers? These which we see here are our flowers," they said to the guardians.

"We noticed nothing, my lord. Our tails also suffered," they answered. And then the lords tore at their mouths as a punishment for having let that which was under their care be stolen.

Thus were Hun-Camé and Vucub-Camé defeated by Hunahpú and Xbalanqué. And this was the beginning of their deeds. From that time the mouth of the owl is divided, cleft as it is today.

Immediately, they went down to play ball, and also they played several tie matches. Then they finished playing and agreed to play again the following day at dawn. So said the Lords of Xibalba.

"It is well," said the boys upon finishing.

CHAPTER X

Afterward, they entered the House of Cold. It is impossible to describe how cold it was. The house was full of hail; it was the mansion of cold. Soon, however, the cold was ended because with a fire of old logs the boys made the cold disappear.

That is why they did not die; they were still alive when it dawned. Surely what the Lords of Xibalba wanted was that they would die; but it was not thus, and when it dawned, they were still full of health, and they went out again when the messengers came to get them.

"How is this? They are not dead yet?" said the Lords of Xibalba. They were amazed to see the deeds of Hunahpú and Xbalanqué.

Presently the boys entered the House of Jaguars. The house was full of jaguars. "Do not bite us! Here is what belongs to you," the boys said to the jaguars. And quickly they threw some bones to the animals, which pounced upon the bones.

"Now surely they are finished. Now already they have eaten their own entrails. At last they have given themselves up. Now their bones have been broken," so said the guards, all happy because of this.

But they [the boys] did not die. As usual, well and healthy, they came out of the House of Jaguars.

"What kind of people are they? Where did they come from?" said all the Lords of Xibalba.

Presently, they [the boys] entered into the midst of fire in the House of Fire, inside which there was only fire; but they were not burned. Only the coals and the wood burned. And, as usual, they were well when it dawned. But what they [the Lords of Xibalba] wished was that the boys would die rapidly, where they had been. Nevertheless, it did not happen thus, which disheartened the Lords of Xibalba.

Then they put them into the House of Bats. There was nothing but bats inside this house, the house of Camazotz,[4] a large animal, whose weapons for killing were like a dry point, and instantly those who came into their presence perished.

They [the boys] were in there, then, but they slept inside their blowguns. And they were not bitten by those who were in the house. Nevertheless, one of them had to give up because of another Camazotz that came from the sky, and made him come into sight.

The bats were assembled in council all night, and flew about. "Quilitz, quilitz," they said. So they were saying all night. They stopped for a little while, however, and they did not move and were pressed against the end of one of the blow-guns.

Then Xbalanqué said to Hunahpú: "Look you, has it begun already to get light?"

"Maybe so. I am going to see," Hunahpú answered.

And as he wished very much to look out of the mouth of the blowgun, and wished to see if it had dawned, instantly Camazotz cut off his head and the body of Hunahpú was de-capitated.

Xbalanqué asked again: "Has it not yet dawned?" But Hunahpú did not move. "Where have you gone, Hunahpú? What have you done?" But he did not move and remained si-lent.

The Xbalanqué felt concerned and exclaimed: "Unfortunate are we. We are completely undone."

They went immediately to hang the head of Hunahpú in the ball court by special order of Hun-Camé and Vucub-Camé, and all the people of Xibalba rejoiced for what had happened to the head of Hunahpú.

CHAPTER XI

Immediately, he [Xbalanqué] called all the animals, the coati, the wild boar, all the animals small and large, during the night, and at dawn he asked them what their food was.

"What does each of you eat? For I have called you so that you may choose your food," said Xbalanqué to them.

4 Camazotz—Bat.

329

"Very well," they answered. And immediately each went to take his own food and they all went together. Some went to take rotten things; others went to take grasses; others went to get stones. Others went to gather earth. Varied was the food of the small animals and of the large animals.

Behind them the turtle was lingering, it came waddling along to take its food. And reaching at the end of Hunahpú's body, it assumed the form of the head of Hunahpú, and instantly the eyes were fashioned.

Many soothsayers came then from heaven. The Heart of Heaven, Huracán, came to soar over the House of Bats.

It was not easy to finish making the face, but it turned out very well; the hair had a handsome appearance and the head could also speak.

But as it was about to dawn and the horizon reddened: "Make it dark again, old one!" the buzzard was told.

"Very well," said the old one, and instantly the old one darkened the sky. "Now the buzzard has darkened it," the people say nowadays.

And so, during the cool of dawn, the Hunahpú began his existence.

"Will it be good?" they said. "Will it turn out to look like Hunahpú?"

"It is very good," they answered. And really it seemed that the skull had changed itself back into a real head.

Then they [the two boys] talked among themselves and agreed. "Do not play ball; only pretend to play; I shall do everything alone," said Xbalanqué.

At once, he gave his orders to a rabbit. "Go and take your place over the ball court; stay there within the oak grove," the rabbit was told by Xbalanqué. "When the ball comes to you, run out immediately, and I shall do the rest," the rabbit was told, when they gave him these instructions during the night.

Presently, day broke and the two boys were well and healthy. Then they went down to play ball. The head of Hunahpú was suspended over the ball court.

"We have triumphed!" said the Lords of Xibalba. "You worked your own destruction, you have delivered yourselves," they said. In this way, they annoyed Hunahpú.

"Hit his head with the ball," they said. But they did not bother him with it; he paid no attention to it.

Then the Lords of Xibalba threw out the ball. Xbalanqué went out to get it; the ball was going straight to the ring, but it stopped, bounced, and passed quickly over the ball court and with a jump went toward the oak grove.

Instantly, the rabbit ran out and went hopping, and the Lords of Xibalba ran after it. They went, making noise and shouting after the rabbit. It ended with all of the Lords of Xibalba going.

At once, Xbalanqué took possession of the head of Hunahpú; and taking the turtle he went to suspend it over the ball court. And that head was actually the head of Hunahpú, and the two boys were very happy.

Those of Xibalba ran then to find the ball, and having found it between the oaks, called them, saying: "Come here. Here is the ball. We found it," they said, and they brought it.

When the Lords of Xibalba returned, they exclaimed, "What is this we see?"

Then they began to play again. Both of them tied.

Presently, Xbalanqué threw a stone at the turtle, which came to the ground and fell in the ball court, breaking into a thousand pieces like seeds, before the lords.

"Who of you shall go to find it? Where is the one who shall go to bring it?" said the Lords of Xibalba.

And so were the Lords of Xibalba overcome by Hunahpú and Xbalanqué. These two suffered great hardships, but they did not die despite all that was done to them.

CHAPTER XII

Here is the account of the death of Hunahpú and Xbalanqué. Now we shall tell of the way they died.

Having been forewarned of all the suffering which the Lords of Xibalba wished to impose upon them, they did not die of the tortures of Xibalba, nor were they overcome by all the fierce animals which were in Xibalba.

Afterward, they sent for two soothsayers who were like prophets; they were called Xulú and Pacam and were diviners, and they said unto them: "You shall be questioned by the

Lords of Xibalba about our deaths, for which they are planning and preparing because of the fact that we have not died, nor have they been able to overcome us, nor have we perished under their torments, nor have the animals attacked us. We have the presentiment in our hearts that they shall kill us by burning us. All the people of Xibalba have assembled, but the truth is, that we shall not die. Here, then, you have our instructions as to what you must say:

"If they should come to consult you about our death and that we may be sacrificed, what shall you say then, Xulú and Pacam? If they ask you: 'Will it not be good to throw their bones into the ravine?' 'No, it would not be well,' tell them, 'because they would be brought to life again afterward!' If they ask you: 'Would it not be good to hang them from the trees?' you shall answer: 'By no means would it be well, because then you shall see their faces again.' And when for the third time they ask you: 'Would it be good to throw their bones into the river?' If you were asked all the above by them, you should answer: 'It would be well if they were to die that way; then it would be well to crush their bones on a grinding stone, as cornmeal is ground; let each one be ground separately; throw them into the river immediately, there where the spring gushes forth, in order that they may be carried away among all the small and large hills.' Thus you shall answer them when the plan which we have advised you is put into practice," said Hunahpú and Xbalanqué. And when they [the boys] took leave of them, they already knew about their approaching death.

They made then a great bonfire, a kind of oven; the men of Xibalba made it and filled it with thick branches.

Shortly afterward, the messengers arrived who had to accompany the boys, the messengers of Hun-Camé and Vucub-Camé.

" 'Tell them to come. Go and get the boys; go there so that they may know we are going to burn them.' This the lords said, oh boys!" the messengers exclaimed.

"It is well," they answered. And setting out quickly, they arrived near the bonfire. There the Lords of Xibalba wanted to force the boys to play a mocking game with them.

"Let us drink our chicha[5] and fly four times, each one, over the bonfire, boys!" was said to them by Hun-Camé.

"Do not try to deceive us," the boys answered. "Perchance, we do not know about our death, oh lords, and that this is what awaits us here?" And embracing each other, face to face, they both stretched out their arms, bent toward the ground and jumped into the bonfire, and thus the two died together.

All those of Xibalba were filled with joy; shouting and whistling, they exclaimed: "Now we have overcome them. At last they have given themselves up."

Immediately, they called Xulú and Pacam, to whom they [the boys] had given their instructions, and asked them what they must do with their bones, as they [the boys] had foretold. Those of Xibalba then ground their bones and went to cast them into the river. But the bones did not go very far, for settling themselves down at once on the bottom of the river, they were changed back into handsome boys. And when again they showed themselves, they really had their same old faces.

CHAPTER XIII

On the fifth day, they appeared again and were seen in the water by the people. Both had the appearance of fishmen when those of Xibalba saw them, after having hunted them all over the river.

And the following day, two poor men presented themselves with very old-looking faces and of miserable appearance, and ragged clothes, whose countenances did not commend them. So they were seen by all those of Xibalba.

And what they did was very little. They only performed the dance of the owl, the dance of the weasel, and the dance of the armadillo, and they also danced the centipede and the stilt dance.

Furthermore, they worked many miracles. They burned houses as though they were really burning, and instantly they were as they had been before. Many of those of Xibalba watched them in wonder.

Presently, they cut themselves into bits; they killed each

[5] Chicha—Corn liquor.

333

other; the first one whom they had killed stretched out as though he were dead, and instantly the other brought him back to life. Those of Xibalba looked on in amazement at all they did, and they performed it, as the beginning of their triumph over those of Xibalba.

Presently, word of their dances came to the ears of the lords Hun-Camé and Vucub-Camé. Upon hearing it, they exclaimed: "Who are these two orphans? Do they really give you so much pleasure?"

"Surely their dances are very beautiful, and all that they do," answered he who had brought the news to the lords.

Happy to hear this, the lords then sent their messengers to call the boys with flattery. "Tell them to come here, tell them to come so that we may see what they do, that we may admire them and regard them with wonder," this the lords said. "So you shall say unto them." This was told to the messengers.

They arrived at once before the dancers and gave them the message of the lords.

"We do not wish to," the boys answered, "because, frankly, we are ashamed. How could we not but be ashamed to appear in the house of the lords with our ugly countenances, our eyes which are so big, and our poor appearance? Do you not see that we are nothing more than some poor dancers? What shall we tell our companions in poverty who have come with us and wish to see our dances and be entertained by them? How could we do our dances before the lords? For that reason, then, we do not want to go, oh messengers," said Hunahpú and Xbalanqué.

Finally, with downcast faces and with reluctance and sorrow they went; but for a while they did not wish to walk, and the messengers had to beat them in the face many times when they led them to the house of the lords.

They arrived then before the lords, timid and with heads bowed; they came prostrating themselves, making reverences and humiliating themselves. They looked feeble, ragged, and their appearance was really that of vagabonds when they arrived.

They were questioned immediately about their country and

their people; they also asked them about their mother and father.

"Where do you come from?" the lords said.

"We do not know, sirs. We do not know the faces of our mother and father; we were small when they died," they answered, and did not say another word.

"All right. Now do your dances so that we may admire you. What do you want? We shall give you pay," they told them.

"We do not want anything; but really we are very much afraid," they said to the lord.

"Do not grieve, do not be afraid. Dance! And do first the part in which you kill yourselves; burn my house, do all that you know how to do. We shall marvel at you, for that is what our hearts desire. And afterward, poor things, we shall give help for your journey," they told them.

Then they began to sing and dance. All the people of Xibalba arrived and gathered together in order to see them. Then they performed the dance of the weasel, they danced the owl, and they danced the armadillo.

And the lord said to them: "Cut my dog into pieces and let him be brought back to life by you," he said to them.

"Very well," they answered, and cut the dog into bits. Instantly, they brought him back to life. The dog was truly full of joy when he was brought back to life, and wagged his tail when they revived him.

The lord said to them then: "Burn my house now!" Thus he said to them. Instantly they put fire to the lord's house, and although all the lords were assembled together within the house, they were not burned. Quickly it was whole again, and not for one instant was the house of Hun-Camé destroyed.

All of the lords were amazed, and in the same way the boys' dances gave them much pleasure.

Then they were told by the lord: "Now kill a man, sacrifice him, but do not let him die," he told them.

"Very well," they answered. And seizing a man, they quickly sacrificed him, and raising his heart on high, they held it so that all the lords could see it.

Again Hun-Camé and Vucub-Camé were amazed. A moment afterward, the man was brought back to life by them [the boys], and his heart was filled with joy when he was revived.

The lords were astounded. "Sacrifice yourselves now, let us see it! We really like your dances!" said the lords. "Very well, sirs," they answered. And they proceeded to sacrifice each other. Hunahpú was sacrificed by Xbalanqué; one by one his arms and his legs were sliced off; his head was cut from his body and carried away; his heart was torn from his breast and thrown onto the grass. All the Lords of Xibalba were fascinated. They looked on in wonder, but really it was only the dance of one man; it was Xbalanqué.

"Get up!" he said, and instantly Hunahpú returned to life. They [the boys] were very happy and the lords were also happy. In truth, what they did gladdened the hearts of Hun-Camé and Vucub-Camé, and the latter felt as though they themselves were dancing.

Then their hearts were filled with desire and longing by the dances of Hunahpú and Xbalanqué; and Hun-Camé and Vucub-Camé gave their commands.

"Do the same with us! Sacrifice us!" they said. "Cut us into pieces, one by one!" Hun-Camé and Vucub-Camé said to Hunahpú and Xbalanqué.

"Very well; afterward you will come back to life again. Perchance, did you not bring us here in order that we should entertain you, the lords, and your sons, and vassals?" they said to the lords.

And so it happened that they first sacrificed the one who was the chief and Lord of Xibalba, the one called Hun-Camé, king of Xibalba.

And when Hun-Camé was dead, they overpowered Vucub-Camé, and they did not bring either of them back to life.

The people of Xibalba fled as soon as they saw that their lords were dead and sacrificed. In an instant both were sacrificed. And this they [the boys] did in order to chastise them. Quickly, the principal lord was killed. And they did not bring him back to life.

And another lord humbled himself then, and presented himself before the dancers. They had not discovered him, nor had they found him. "Have mercy on me!" he said when they found him.

All the sons and vassals of Xibalba fled to a great ravine, and all of them were crowded into this narrow, deep place. There they were crowded together and hordes of ants came and found them and dislodged them from the ravine. In this way [the ants] drove them to the road, and when they arrived the people prostrated themselves and gave themselves up; they humbled themselves and arrived, grieving.

In this way, the Lords of Xibalba were overcome. Only by a miracle and by their own transformation could the boys have done it.

CHAPTER XIV

Immediately, the boys told their names and they extolled themselves before all the people of Xibalba.

"Hear our names. We shall also tell you the names of our fathers. We are Hunahpú and Xbalanqué; those are our names. And our fathers are those whom you killed and who were called Hun-Hunahpú and Vucub-Hunahpú. We, those whom you see here, are, then, the avengers of the torments and suffering of our fathers. That is the reason why we resent all the evil you have done to them. Therefore, we shall put an end to all of you, we shall kill you, and not one of you shall escape," they said.

Instantly, all the people of Xibalba fell to their knees, crying.

"Have mercy on us, Hunahpú and Xbalanqué! It is true that we sinned against your fathers as you said, and that they are buried in Pucbal-Chah," they said.

"Very well. This is our sentence, that we are going to tell you. Hear it, all you of Xibalba:

"Since neither your great power nor your race any longer exist, and since neither do you deserve mercy, your rank shall be lowered. Not for you shall be the ball game. You shall spend your time making earthen pots and tubs and stones to

337

grind corn. Only the children of the thickets and desert shall speak with you. The noble sons, the civilized vassals shall not consort with you, and they will forsake your presence. The sinners, the evil ones, the sad ones, the unfortunate ones, those who give themselves up to vice, these are the ones who will welcome you. No longer will you seize men suddenly for sacrifice, remember your rank has been lowered."

Thus they spoke to all the people of Xibalba.

In this way, their destruction and their lamentations began. Their power in the olden days was not much. They only liked to do evil to men in those times. In truth, in those days, they did not have the category of gods. Furthermore, their horrible faces frightened people. They were the enemies, the owls. They incited to evil, to sin, and to discord.

They were also false in their hearts, black and white at the same time, envious and tyrannical, according to what was said of them. Furthermore, they painted and greased their faces.

In this way, then, occurred the loss of their grandeur and the decadence of their empire.

And this was what Hunahpú and Xbalanqué did.

Meanwhile, the grandmother was crying and lamenting before the reeds which they had left planted. The reeds sprouted, then they dried up when the boys were consumed in the bonfire; afterward the reeds sprouted again. Then the grandmother lighted the fire and burned incense before the reeds in memory of her grandchildren. And the grandmother's heart filled with joy when, for the second time, the reeds sprouted. Then they were worshiped by the grandmother, and she called them the Center of the House; Nicah, the center, they were called.

"Green reeds growing in the plains," Cazam Ah Chatam Uleu was their name. And they were called the Center of the House and the Center, because in the middle of the house they planted the reeds. And the reeds, which were planted, were called the plains, green reeds growing on the plains. They also were called green reeds because they had resprouted. This name was given them by Xmucané, given to those [reeds] which Hunahpú and Xbalanqué left planted in order that they should be remembered by their grandmother.

Well, now, their fathers, those who died long ago, were Hun-Hunahpú and Vucub-Hunahpú. They also saw the faces of their fathers there in Xibalba, and their fathers talked with their descendants, that is, the ones who overthrew those of Xibalba.

And here is how their fathers were honored by them. They honored Vucub-Hunahpú; they went to honor him at the place of sacrifice of the ball court. And at the same time they wanted to make Vucub-Hunahpú's face. They hunted there for his entire body, his mouth, his nose, his eyes. They found his body, but it could do very little. It could not pronounce his name, this Hunahpú. Neither could his mouth say it.

And here is how they extolled the memory of their fathers, whom they had left there in the place of sacrifice at the ball court. "You shall be invoked," their sons said to them, when they fortified their heart. "You shall be the first to arise, and you shall be the first to be worshiped by the sons of the noblemen, by the civilized vassals. Your names shall not be lost. So it shall be!" they told their fathers and thus consoled themselves. "We are the avengers of your death, of the pains and sorrows which they caused you."

Thus was their leave-taking, when they had already overcome all the people of Xibalba.

Then they rose up in the midst of the light, and instantly they were lifted into the sky. One was given the sun, the other the moon. Then the arch of heaven and the face of the earth were lighted. And they dwelt in heaven.

Then the four hundred boys whom Zipacná had killed also ascended, and so they again became the companions of the boys and were changed into stars in the sky.

XXXI. DRAMA

OLLANTAY (Inca)

In Cuzco and its environs and Ollantay-tampu

DRAMATIS PERSONAE

Apu Ollantay—General of Anti-suyu, the eastern province of the empire. A young chief, but not of the blood-royal. His rank was that of a Tucuyricuo or Viceroy. The name occurs among the witnesses examined by order of the Viceroy Toledo, being one of the six of the Antasayac ayllu.

Pachacuti—The Sovereign Inca.

Tupac Yupanqui—Sovereign Inca, son and heir of Pachacuti.

Rumi-naui—A great chief, General of Colla-suyu. The word means "Stone-eye."

Uillac Uma—High Priest of the Sun. The word "Uma" means head, and "Uillac," a councillor and diviner.

Urco Huaranca—A chief. The words mean "Mountain Chief." The word "huaranca" means 1,000; hence Chief of a Thousand.

Hanco Huayllu Auqui—An old officer, of the blood-royal.

Piqui Chaqui—Page to Ollantay. The words mean "fleet-footed."

Anahuarqui—The Ccoya or Queen, wife of Pachacuti.

Cusi Coyllur Nusta—A Princess, daughter of Pachacuti. The words mean "the joyful star."

Yma Sumac—Daughter of Cusi Coyllur. The words mean "how beautiful."

Pitu Salla—A girl, companion of Yma Sumac.

Mama Ccacca—A matron of Virgins of the Sun. Jailer of Cusi Coyllur.

Nobles, captains, soldiers, boys and girls dancing, singers, attendants, messengers or Chasquis.

ACT I

*An open space near the junction of the two torrents of Cuzco,
the Huatanay and Tullumayu or Rodalero, called Pumap
Chupan, just outside the gardens of the Sun. The Temple of
the Sun beyond the gardens, and the Sacsahuaman hill sur-
mounted by the fortress, rising in the distance. The palace of
Colcampata on the hillside.*

> (*Enter* OLLANTAY L. [*in a gilded tunic, breeches of llama
> sinews, usutas or shoes of llama hide, a red mantle of ccompi
> or fine cloth, and the chucu or headdress of his rank, hold-
> ing a battle-ax* (*champi*) *and club* (*macana*)] *and* PIQUI
> CHAQUI *coming up from the back R.* [*in a coarse brown
> tunic of auasca or llama cloth, girdle used as a sling, and
> chucu or headdress of a Cuz queno*].)

OLLANTAY: Where, young fleet-foot, hast thou been?
Hast thou the starry Nusta seen?

PIQUI CHAQUI: The Sun forbids such sacrilege;
'Tis not for me to see the star.
Dost thou, my master, fear no ill,
Thine eyes upon the Inca's child?

OLLANTAY: In spite of all I swear to love
That tender dove, that lovely star;
My heart is as a lamb with her,
And ever will her presence seek.

PIQUI CHAQUI: Such thoughts are prompted by Supay;[1]
That evil being possesses thee.
All round are beauteous girls to choose
Before old age and weakness come.
If the great Inca knew thy plot
And what thou seekest to attain,
Thy head would fall by his command,
Thy body would be quickly burnt.

---

[1] Supay—An evil spirit.

OLLANTAY: Boy, do not dare to cross me thus.
One more such word and thou shalt die.
These hands will tear thee limb from limb,
If still thy councils are so base.

PIQUI CHAQUI: Well! treat thy servant as a dog,
But do not night and day repeat,
"Piqui Chaqui! swift of foot!
Go once more to seek the star."

OLLANTAY: Have I not already said
That e'en if death's fell scythe was here,
If mountains should oppose my path
Like two fierce foes who block the way,
Yet will I fight all these combined
And risk all else to gain my end,
And whether it be life or death
I'll cast myself at Coyllur's feet.

PIQUI CHAQUI: But if Supay himself should come?

OLLANTAY: I'd strike the evil spirit down.

PIQUI CHAQUI: If thou shouldst only see his nose,
Thou wouldst not speak as thou dost now.

OLLANTAY: Now, Piqui Chaqui, speak the truth,
Seek not evasion or deceit.
Dost thou not already know,
Of all the flowers in the field,
Not one can equal my Princess?

PIQUI CHAQUI: Still, my master, thou dost rave.
I think I never saw thy love.
Stay! Was it her who yesterday
Came forth with slow and faltering steps
And sought a solitary path?
If so, 'tis true she's like the Sun,
The Moon less beauteous than her face.

342

OLLANTAY: It surely was my dearest love.
How beautiful, how bright is she!
This very moment thou must go
And take my message to the Star.

PIQUI CHAQUI: I dare not, master; in the day,
I fear to pass the palace gate.
With all the splendor of the court,
I could not tell her from the rest.

OLLANTAY: Didst thou not say thou sawest her?

PIQUI CHAQUI: I said so, but it was not sense.
A star can only shine at night;
Only at night could I be sure.

OLLANTAY: Be gone, thou lazy good-for-nought.
The joyful star that I adore,
If placed in presence of the Sun,
Would shine as brightly as before.

PIQUI CHAQUI: Lo! some person hither comes,
Perhaps an old crone seeking alms;
Yes! Look! He quite resembles one.
Let him the dangerous message take.
Send it by him, O noble Chief!
From me they would not hear the tale;
Thy page is but a humble lad.

(*Enter the* UILLAC UMA, *or High Priest of the Sun, at the
back, arms raised to the Sun. In a gray tunic and black man-
tle from the shoulders to the ground, a long knife in his belt,
the undress chucu on his head.*)

UILLAC UMA: O giver of all warmth and light!
O Sun! I fall and worship thee.
For thee the victims are prepared,
A thousand llamas and their lambs
Are ready for thy festal day.

343

The sacred fire'll lap their blood,
In thy dread presence, mighty one,
After long fasting thy victims fall.

OLLANTAY: Who comes hither, Piqui Chaqui?
Yes, 'tis the holy Uillac Uma;
He brings his tools of augury.
No puma more astute and wise—
I hate that ancient conjurer
Who prophesies of evil things,
I feel the evils he foretells;
'Tis he who ever brings ill luck.

PIQUI CHAQUI: Silence, master, do not speak,
The old man doubly is informed;
Foreknowing every word you say,
Already he has guessed it all.

(*He lies down on a bank.*)

OLLANTAY (*aside*):   He sees me. I must speak to him.

(*The* UILLAC UMA *comes forward.*)

O Uillac Uma Great High Priest,
I bow before thee with respect;
May the skies be clear for thee,
And brightest sunshine meet thine eyes.

UILLAC UMA: Brave Ollantay! Princely one!
May all the teeming land be thine;
May thy far-reaching arm of might
Reduce the widespread universe.

OLLANTAY: Old man! thine aspect causes fear,
Thy presence here some ill forebodes;
All round thee dead men's bones appear,
Baskets, flowers, sacrifice.
All men when they see thy face
Are filled with terror and alarm.

344

What means it all? Why comest thou?
It wants some months before the feast.
Is it that the Inca is ill?
Perchance hast thou some thought divined
Which soon will turn to flowing blood.
Why comest thou? The Sun's great day,
The Moon's libations, are not yet,
The Moon has not yet nearly reached
The solemn time for sacrifice.

UILLAC UMA: Why dost thou these questions put,
In tones of anger and reproach?
Am I, forsooth, thy humble slave?
That I know all I'll quickly prove.

OLLANTAY: My beating heart is filled with dread,
Beholding thee so suddenly;
Perchance thy coming is a sign
Of evils overtaking me.

UILLAC UMA: Fear not, Ollantay! Not for that
The High Priest comes to thee this day.
It is perhaps for love of thee
That, as a straw is blown by wind,
A friend, this day, encounters thee.
Speak to me as to a friend,
Hide nothing from my scrutiny.
This day I come to offer thee
A last and most momentous choice—
'Tis nothing less than life or death.

OLLANTAY: Then make thy words more clear to me,
That I may understand the choice;
Till now 'tis but a tangled skein,
Unravel it that I may know.

UILLAC UMA: 'Tis well. Now listen, warlike Chief:
My science has enabled me
To learn and see all hidden things

345

Unknown to other mortal men.
My power will enable me
To make of thee a greater prince.
I brought thee up from tender years,
And cherished thee with love and care;
I now would guide thee in the right,
And ward off all that threatens thee
As chief of Anti-suyu[2] now,
The people venerate thy name;
Thy Sovereign trusts and honors thee,
E'en to sharing half his realm.
From all the rest he chose thee out
And placed all power in thy hands;
He made thy armies great and strong,
And strengthened thee against thy foes;
How numerous soe'er they be,
They have been hunted down by thee.
Are these good reasons for thy wish
To wound thy Sovereign to the heart?
His daughter is beloved by thee;
Thy passion thou wouldst fain indulge,
Lawless and forbidden though it be.
I call upon thee, stop in time,
Tear this folly from thy heart.
If thy passion is immense,
Still let honor hold its place.
You reel, you stagger on the brink—
I'd snatch thee from the very edge.
Thou knowest well it cannot be,
The Inca never would consent.
If thou didst e'en propose it now,
He would be overcome with rage;
From favored prince and trusted chief,
Thou wouldst descend to lowest rank.

[2] Anti-suyu—Northern (montana) provinces of Inca empire.

346

OLLANTAY: How is it that thou canst surely know
What still is hidden in my heart?
Her mother only knows my love,
Yet thou revealest all to me.

UILLAC UMA: I read thy secret on the Moon,
As if upon the Quipu³ knots;
And what thou wouldst most surely hide
Is plain to me as all the rest.

OLLANTAY: In my heart I had divined
That thou wouldst search me through and through;
Thou knowest all, O Councillor,
And wilt thou now desert thy son?

UILLAC UMA: How oft we mortals heedless drink,
A certain death from golden cup;
Recall to mind how ills befall,
And that a stubborn heart's the cause.

OLLANTAY (*kneeling*):   Plunge that dagger in my breast,
Thou holdst it ready in thy belt;
Cut out my sad and broken heart—
I ask the favor at thy feet.

(PIQUI CHAQUI *gives him a withered flower and lies down
again, pretending to sleep.*)

(*To* OLLANTAY):   Behold, it is quite dead and dry.
Once more behold! E'en now it weeps,
It weeps. The water flows from it.

(*Water flows out of the flower.*)

OLLANTAY: More easy for the barren rocks
Or for sand to send forth water
Than that I should cease to love
The fair princess, the joyful star.

UILLAC UMA: Put a seed into the ground,
It multiplies a hundredfold;

³ Quipu—Inca knotted-cord information system.

347

The more thy crime shall grow and swell,
The greater far thy sudden fall.

OLLANTAY: Once for all, I now confess
To thee, O great and mighty Priest;
Now learn my fault. To thee I speak,
Since thou hast torn it from my heart.
The lasso to tie me is long,
'Tis ready to twist round my throat;
Yet its threads are woven with gold,
It avenges a brilliant crime.
Cusi Coyllur e'en now is my wife,
Already we're bound and are one;
My blood now runs in her veins,
E'en now I am noble as she.
Her mother has knowledge of all,
The Queen can attest what I say;
Let me tell all this to the King,
I pray for thy help and advice.
I will speak without fear and with force,
He may perhaps give way to his rage;
Yet he may consider my youth,
May remember the battles I've fought;
The record is carved on my club.

(*Holds up his macana.*)

He may think of his enemies crushed,
The thousands I've thrown at his feet.

UILLAC UMA: Young Prince! thy words are too bold,
Thou hast twisted the thread of thy fate—
Beware, before 'tis too late;
Disentangle and weave it afresh,
Go alone to speak to the King,
Alone bear the blow that you seek;
Above all, let thy words be but few,
And say them with deepest respect;

Be it life, be it death that you find,
I will never forget thee, my son.

(*Walks up and exit.*)

OLLANTAY: Ollantay, thou art a man,
No place in thy heart for fear;
Cusi Coyllur, surround me with light.
Piqui Chaqui, where art thou?

PIQUI CHAQUI (*jumping up*):   I was asleep, my master,
And dreaming of evil things.

OLLANTAY: Of what?

PIQUI CHAQUI: Of a fox[4] with a rope round its neck.

OLLANTAY: Sure enough, thou art the fox.

PIQUI CHAQUI: It is true that my nose is growing finer,
And my ears a good deal longer.

OLLANTAY: Come, lead me to the Coyllur.

PIQUI CHAQUI: It is still daylight.

(*Exeunt.*)

SCENE 2

*A great hall in the Colcampata, then the palace of the Queen
or Ccoya Anahuarqui. In the center of the back scene a door-
way, and seen through it gardens with the snowy peak of Vil-
canota in the distance. Walls covered with golden slabs. On ei-
ther side of the doorway three recesses, with household gods
in the shape of maize cobs and llamas, and gold vases in them.
On R. a golden tiana or throne. On L. two lower seats covered
with cushions of fine woolen cloth.*

(ANAHUARQUI, *the Queen or Ccoya* [*in blue chucu, white
cotton bodice, and red mantle secured by a golden topu or
pin, set with emeralds, and a blue skirt*], *and the princess*
CUSI COYLLUR [*in a chucu, with feathers of the tunqui, white*

4 In the original, the animal is a puma.

349

bodice and skirt, and gray mantle with topu, set with pearls]
discovered seated.)

ANAHUARQUI: Since when art thou feeling so sad,
Cusi Coyllur! The apple of the Sun-King's eye.
Since when hast thou lost all thy joy,
Thy smile and thy once merry laugh?
Tears of grief now pour down my face
As I watch and mourn over my child;
Thy grief makes me ready to die.
Thy union filled thee with joy,
Already you're really his wife.
Is he not the man of thy choice?
O daughter, devotedly loved,
Why plunged in such terrible grief?

(CUSI COYLLUR *has had her face hidden in the pillows. She
now rises to her feet, throwing up her arms.*)

CUSI COYLLUR: O my mother! O most gracious Queen!
How can my tears e'er cease to flow,
How can my bitter sighs surcease
While the valiant Chief I worship
For many days and sleepless nights,
All heedless of my tender years,
Seems quite to have forgotten me?
He has turned his regard from his wife
And no longer seeks for his love.
O my mother! O most gracious Queen!
O my husband so beloved!
Since the day when I last saw my love
The Moon has been hidden from view;
The Sun shines no more as of old,
In rising it rolls among mist;
At night the stars are all dim,
All nature seems sad and distressed;
The comet with fiery tail,

350

Announces my sorrow and grief;
Surrounded by darkness and tears,
Evil auguries fill me with fears.
O my mother! O most gracious Queen!
O my husband so beloved!

ANAHUARQUI: Compose thyself and dry thine eyes,
The King, thy father, has arrived.
Thou lovest Ollantay, my child?

> (*Enter the* INCA PACHACUTI. *On his head the mascapaycha,
> with the llautu or imperial fringe. A tunic of cotton
> embroidered with gold; on his breast the golden breastplate
> representing the Sun, surrounded by the calendar of months.
> Round his waist the fourfold belt of tocapu. A crimson
> mantle of fine vicuna wool, fastened on his shoulders by
> golden puma's heads. Shoes of cloth of gold. He sits down
> on the golden tiana.*)

INCA PACHACUTI: Cusi Coyllur! Star of joy,
Most lovely of my progeny!
Thou symbol of parental love—
Thy lips are like the huayruru.
Rest upon thy father's breast,
Repose, my child, within mine arms.

> (CUSI COYLLUR *comes across. They embrace.*)

Unwind thyself, my precious one,
A thread of gold within the woo.
All my happiness rests upon thee,
Thou art my greatest delight.
Thine eyes are lovely and bright,
As the rays of my father the Sun.
When thy lips are moving to speak,
When thine eyelids are raised with a smile,
The wide world is fairly entranced.
Thy breathing embalms the fresh air;
Without thee thy father would pine,

351

Life to him would be dreary and waste.
He seeks for thy happiness, child,
Thy welfare is ever his care.

(CUSI COYLLUR *throws herself at his feet.*)

CUSI COYLLUR: O father, thy kindness to me
I feel; and embracing thy knees
All the grief of thy daughter will cease,
At peace when protected by thee.

PACHACUTI: How is this! my daughter before me
On knees at my feet, and in tears?
I fear some evil is near—
Such emotion must needs be explained.

CUSI COYLLUR: The star does weep before Inti,
The limpid tears wash grief away.

PACHACUTI: Rise, my beloved, my star,
Thy place is on thy dear father's knee.

(CUSI COYLLUR *rises and sits on a stool by her father. An attendant approaches.*)

ATTENDANT: O King! thy servants come to please thee.

PACHACUTI: Let them all enter.

(*Boys and girls enter dancing. After the dance they sing a harvest song.*)

> Thou must not feed,
>   O Tuyallay,[5]
> In Nusta's field,
>   O Tuyallay.
> Thou must not rob,
>   O Tuyallay,
> The harvest maize,
>   O Tuyallay.

[5] More or less "my little inch."

352

The grains are white,
        O Tuyallay,
So sweet for food,
        O Tuyallay.
The fruit is sweet,
        O Tuyallay,
The leaves are green
        O Tuyallay;
But the trap is set,
        O Tuyallay.
The lime is there,
        O Tuyallay.
We'll cut thy claws,
        O Tuyallay,
To seize thee quick,
        O Tuyallay.
Ask Piscaca,[6]
        O Tuyallay,
Nailed on a branch,
        O Tuyallay.
Where is her heart,
        O Tuyallay?
Where her plumes,
        O Tuyallay?
She is cut up,
        O Tuyallay,
For stealing grain,
        O Tuyallay.
See the fate,
        O Tuyallay,
Of robber birds,
        O Tuyallay.

[6] Piscaca—Black bird with white breast, killed and used as a "scare-crow."

PACHACUTI: Cusi Coyllur, remain thou here,
Thy mother's palace is thy home;
Fail not to amuse thyself,
Surrounded by thy maiden friends.

(*Exeunt the* INCA PACHACUTI, *the* CCOYA ANAHUARQUI, *and attendants.*)

CUSI COYLLUR: I should better like a sadder song.
My dearest friends, the last you sang
To me foreshadowed evil things;
You who sang it leave me now.

(*Exeunt boys and girls, except one girl who sings.*)

Two loving birds are in despair,
They moan, they weep, they sigh;
For snow has fallen on the pair,
To hollow tree they fly.

But lo! one dove is left alone
And mourns her cruel fate;
She makes a sad and piteous moan,
Alone without a mate.

She fears her friend is dead and gone—
Confirmed in her belief,
Her sorrow finds relief in song,
And thus she tells her grief.

"Sweet mate! Alas, where art thou now?
I miss thine eyes so bright,
Thy feet upon the tender bough,
Thy breast so pure and bright."
She wanders forth from stone to stone
She seeks her mate in vain;
"My love! my love!" she makes her moan,
She falls, she dies in pain.

354

CUSI COYLLUR: That song is too sad,
Leave me alone.

(*Exit the girl who sang the yarahui.*)

Now my tears can freely flow.

Great hall in the palace of PACHACUTI. *The* INCA, *as before, discovered seated on a golden tiana L. Enter to him R.* OLLANTAY *and* RUMI-NAUI.

PACHACUTI: The time has arrived, O great Chiefs,
To decide on the coming campaign.
The spring is approaching us now,
And our army must start for the war.
To the province of Colla[7] we march—
There is news of Chayanta's advance.
The enemies muster in strength,
They sharpen their arrows and spears.

OLLANTAY: O King, that wild rabble untaught
Can never resist thine array;
Cuzco alone with its height
Is a barrier that cannot be stormed.
Twenty-four thousand of mine
With their battle-axes selected with care,
Impatiently wait for the sign,
The sound of the beat of my drums,
The strains of my clarion and fife.

PACHACUTI: Strive then to stir them to fight,
Arouse them to join in the fray,
Lest some should desire to yield,
To escape the effusion of blood.

RUMI-NAUI: The enemies gather in force,
The Yuncas are called to their aid;

[7] Colla—Area near Lake Titicaca.

355

They have put on their garbs for the war,
And have stopped up the principal roads.
All this is to hide their defects—
The men of Chayanta are base.
We hear they're destroying the roads,
But we can force open the way;
Our llamas are laden with food—
We are ready to traverse the wilds.

PACHACUTI: Are you ready to start
To punish those angry snakes?
But first you must give them a chance
To surrender, retiring in peace,
So that blood may not flow without cause,
That no deaths of my soldiers befall.

OLLANTAY: I am ready to march with my men,
Every detail prepared and in place,
But alas! I am heavy with care,
Almost mad with anxious suspense.

PACHACUTI: Speak, Ollantay. Tell thy wish—
'Tis granted, e'en my royal fringe.

OLLANTAY: Hear me in secret, O King.

PACHACUTI (*to* RUMI-NAUI):   Noble Chief of Colla, retire;
Seek repose in thy house for a time;
I will call thee before very long,
Having need of thy valor and skill.

RUMI-NAUI: With respect I obey thy command.

(*Exit* RUMI-NAUI.)

OLLANTAY: Thou knowest, O most gracious Lord,
That I have served thee from a youth,
Have worked with fortitude and truth,
Thy treasured praise was my reward.

All dangers I have gladly met,
For thee I always watched by night,

356

For thee was forward in the fight,
My forehead ever bathed in sweat.

For thee I've been a savage foe,
Urging my Antis not to spare,
But kill and fill the land with fear,
And make the blood of conquered flow.

My name is as a dreaded noose
I've made the hardy Yuncas[8] yield,
By me the fate of Chancas[9] sealed,
They are thy thralls without a hope.

'Twas I who struck the fatal blow
When warlike Huancavilca[10] rose,
Disturbing thy august repose
And laid the mighty traitor low.

Ollantay ever led the van,
Wherever men were doomed to die;
When stubborn foes were forced to fly,
Ollantay ever was the man.

Now every tribe bows down to thee—
Some nations peacefully were led,
Those that resist their blood is shed—
But all, O King, was due to me.

O Sovereign Inca, great and brave
Rewards I know were also mine,
My gratitude and thanks are thine,
To me the golden ax you gave.

Inca! thou gavest me command
And rule o'er all the Anti race,
To me they ever yield with grace,
And thine, great King, is all their land.

[8] Yuncas—Tribes of the Montana.
[9] Chancas—Tribe from the Valley of Anda-Luaylas.
[10] Huancavilca—Chief of the Chancas.

My deeds, my merits are thine own,
To thee alone my work is due.
For one more favor I would sue,
My faithful service—thy renown.

(OLLANTAY *kneels before the Inca.*)

Thy thrall: I bow to thy behest,
Thy fiat now will seal my fate.
O King, my services are great,
I pray thee grant one last request.

I ask for Cusi Coyllur's hand
If the Nusta's[11] love I've won.
O King! you'll have a faithful son,
Fearless, well tried, at thy command.

PACHACUTI: Ollantay, thou dost now presume.
Thou art a subject, nothing more.
Remember, bold one, who thou art,
And learn to keep thy proper place.

OLLANTAY: Strike me to the heart.

PACHACUTI: 'Tis for me to see to that,
And not for thee to choose.
Thy presumption is absurd.
Be gone!

(OLLANTAY *rises and exit R.*)

SCENE 4

A rocky height above Cuzco to the NE. Distant view of the city of Cuzco and of the Sacsahuaman hill, crowned by the fortress.

(*Enter* OLLANTAY *armed.*)

OLLANTAY: Alas, Ollantay! Ollantay!
Thou master of so many lands,

11 Nusta—Princess.

358

Insulted by him thou servedst well.
O my thrice-beloved Coyllur,
Thee too I shall lose forever.
O the void within my heart,
O my princess! O precious dove!
Cuzco! O thou beautiful city!
Henceforth behold thine enemy.
I'll bare thy breast to stab thy heart,
And throw it as food for condors;
Thy cruel Inca I will slay.
I will call my men in thousands,
The Antis will be assembled,
Collected as with a lasso.
All will be trained, all fully armed,
I will guide them to Sacsahuaman.
They will be as a cloud of curses
When flames rise to the heavens.
Cuzco shall sleep on a bloody couch,
The King shall perish in its fall;
Then shall my insulter see
How numerous are my followers.
When thou, proud King, art at my feet,
We then shall see if thou wilt say,
"Thou art too base for Coyllur's hand."
Not then will I bow down and ask,
For I, not thou, will be the King—
Yet, until then, let prudence rule.

(*Enter* PIQUI CHAQUI *from back, R.*)

Piqui Chaqui, go back with speed,
Tell the Princess I come tonight.

PIQUI CHAQUI: I have only just come from there—
The palace was deserted quite,
No soul to tell me what had passed,
Not even a dog was there.

All the doors were closed and fastened,
Except the principal doorway,
And that was left without a guard.

OLLANTAY: And the servants?

PIQUI CHAQUI: Even the mice had fled and gone,
For nothing had been left to eat.
Only an owl was brooding there,
Uttering its cry of evil omen.

OLLANTAY: Perhaps then her father has taken her,
To hide her in his palace bounds.

PIQUI CHAQUI: The Inca may have strangled her;
Her mother too has disappeared.

OLLANTAY: Did no one ask for me
Before you went away?

PIQUI CHAQUI: Near a thousand men are seeking
For you, and all are enemies,
Armed with their miserable clubs.

OLLANTAY: If they all arose against me,
With this arm I'd fight them all;
No one yet has beat this hand,
Wielding the champi sharp and true.

PIQUI CHAQUI: I too would like to give a stroke—
At least, if my enemy was unarmed.

OLLANTAY: To whom?

PIQUI CHAQUI: I mean that Urco Huaranca chief,
Who lately was in search of thee.

OLLANTAY: Perhaps the Inca sends him here;
If so my anger is aroused.

PIQUI CHAQUI: Not from the King, I am assured,
He cometh of his own accord;
And yet he is an ignoble man.

OLLANTAY: He has left Cuzco, I believe;
My own heart tells me it is so—
I'm sure that owl announces it.
We'll take to the hills at once.

PIQUI CHAQUI: But wilt thou abandon the Star?

OLLANTAY: What can I do, alas!
Since she has disappeared?
Alas, my dove! my sweet princess.

(*Music heard among the rocks.*)

PIQUI CHAQUI: Listen to that yarahui,
The sound comes from somewhere near.

(*They sit on rocks.*)

Song

In a moment I lost my beloved,
    She was gone, and I never knew where;
I sought her in fields and in woods,
    Asking all if they'd seen the Coyllur.

Her face was so lovely and fair,
    They called her the beautiful Star.
No one else can be taken for her,
    With her beauty no girl can compare.

Both the sun and the moon seem to shine,
    Resplendent they shine from a height,
Their rays to her beauty resign
    Their brilliant light with delight.

Her hair is a soft raven black,
    Her tresses are bound with gold thread,
They fall in long folds down her back,
    And add charm to her beautiful head.

361

Her eyelashes brighten her face,
    Two rainbows less brilliant and fair,
Her eyes full of mercy and grace,
    With nought but two suns can compare.

The eyelids with arrows concealed,
    Gaily shoot their rays into the heart;
They open, lo! beauty revealed,
    Pierces through like a glittering dart.

Her cheeks Achacara[12] on snow,
    Her face more fair than the dawn,
From her mouth the laughter doth flow,
    Between pearls as bright as the morn.

Smooth as crystal and spotlessly clear
    Is her throat, like the corn in a sheaf;
Her bosoms, which scarcely appear,
    Like flowers concealed by a leaf.

Her beautiful hand is a sight,
    As it rests from all dangers secure,
Her fingers transparently white,
    Like icicles spotless and pure.

OLLANTAY (*rising*):   That singer, unseen and unknown,
Has declared Coyllur's beauty and grace;
He should fly hence, where grief overwhelms.
O Princess! O loveliest Star,
I alone am the cause of thy death,
I also should die with my love.

PIQUI CHAQUI: Perhaps thy Star has passed away,
For the heavens are somber and gray.

OLLANTAY: When they know that their Chief has fled,
My people will rise at my call,
They will leave the tyrant in crowds
And he will be nearly alone.

[12] Achacara—Begonia.

362

PIQUI CHAQUI: Thou hast love and affection from men,
For thy kindness endears thee to all,
For thy hand's always open with gifts,
And is closely shut only to me.

OLLANTAY: Of what hast thou need?

PIQUI CHAQUI: What? the means to get this and that,
To offer a gift to my girl,
To let others see what I have,
So that I may be held in esteem.

OLLANTAY: Be as brave as thou art covetous,
And all the world will fear thee.

PIQUI CHAQUI: My face is not suited for that;
Always gay and ready to laugh,
My features are not shaped that way.
To look brave! not becoming to me.
What clarions sound on the hills?
It quickly cometh near to us.

   (*Both look out at different sides.*)

OLLANTAY: I doubt not those who seek me—come,
Let us depart and quickly march.

PIQUI CHAQUI: When flight is the word, I am here.

                                        (*Exeunt.*)

                   SCENE 5

The great hall of the palace of PACHACUTI. *The* INCA, *as before,
seated on the tiana. Enter to him* RUMI-NAUI.

PACHACUTI: I ordered a search to be made,
But Ollantay was not to be found.
My rage I can scarcely control—
Hast thou found this infamous wretch?

RUMI-NAUI: His fear makes him hide from thy wrath,

PACHACUTI: Take a thousand men fully armed,
And at once commence the pursuit.

                   363

RUMI-NAUI: Who can tell what direction to take?
Three days have gone by since his flight,
Perchance he's concealed in some house,
And till now he is there, safely hid.

(*Enter a chasqui or messenger with quipus.*)

Behold, O King, a messenger;
From Urubamba he has come.

CHASQUI: I was ordered to come to my King,
Swift as the wind, and behold me.

PACHACUTI: What news bringest thou?

CHASQUI: This quipu will tell thee, O King.

PACHACUTI: Examine it, O Rumi-naui.

RUMI-NAUI: Behold the llanta,[13] and the knots
Announce the number of his men.

PACHACUTI (*to* CHASQUI):   And thou, what hast thou seen?

CHASQUI: 'Tis said that all the Anti host
Received Ollantay with acclaim;
Many have seen, and they recount,
Ollantay wears the royal fringe.

RUMI-NAUI: The quipu record says the same.

PACHACUTI: Scarcely can I restrain my rage!
Brave chief, commence thy march at once,
Before the traitor gathers strength.
If thy force is not enough,
Add fifty thousand men of mine.
Advance at once with lightning speed,
And halt not till the foe is reached.

RUMI-NAUI: Tomorrow sees me on the route,
I go to call the troops at once;
The rebels on the Colla road,
I drive them flying down the rocks.

[13] Llanta—Main cord of Quipul.

364

Thine enemy I bring to thee,
Dead or alive, Ollantay falls.
Meanwhile, O Inca mighty Lord,
Rest and rely upon thy thrall.

(Exeunt.)

End of Act I

ACT II

SCENE I

Ollantay-tampu Hall of the fortress palace. Back scene seven immense stone slabs, resting on them a monolith right across. Above masonry. At sides masonry with recesses; in the R. center a great doorway. A golden tiana against the central slab.

(*Enter* OLLANTAY *and* URCO HUARANCA, *both fully armed.*)

URCO HUARANCA: Ollantay, thou hast been proclaimed
By all the Antis as their Lord.
The women weep, as you will see—
They lose their husbands and their sons,
Ordered to the Chayanta war.
When will there be a final stop
To distant wars? Year after year
They send us all to far-off lands,
Where blood is made to flow like rain.
The King himself is well supplied
With coca[1] and all kinds of food.
What cares he that his people starve?
Crossing the wilds our llamas die,
Our feet are wounded by the thorns,
And if we would not die of thirst
We carry water on our backs.

---

[1] Coca—Cocaine leaves commonly chewed in Andes.

365

OLLANTAY: Gallant friends! Ye hear those words,
Ye listen to the mountain chief.
Filled with compassion for my men,
I thus, with sore and heavy heart,
Have spoken to the cruel King:
"The Anti-suyu must have rest;
All her best men shan't die for thee,
By battle, fire, and disease—
They die in numbers terrible.
How many men have ne'er returned,
How many chiefs have met their death
For enterprises far away?"
For this I left the Inca's court,
Saying that we must rest in peace;
Let none of us forsake our hearths,
And if the Inca still persists,
Proclaim with him a mortal feud.

(*Enter* HANCO HUAYLLU, *several chiefs, and a great crowd
of soldiers and people.*)

PEOPLE: Long live our king, Ollantay!
Bring forth the standard and the fringe,
Invest him with the crimson fringe;
In Tampu now the Inca reigns,
He rises like the star of day.

(*The chiefs, soldiers, and people range themselves round.*
OLLANTAY *is seated on the tiana by* HANCO HUAYLLU, *an aged
Auqui or Prince.*)

HANCO HUAYLLU: Receive from the royal fringe,
'Tis given by the people's will.
Uilcanota[2] is a distant land,
Yet, even now, her people come
To range themselves beneath thy law.

(OLLANTAY *is invested with the fringe. He rises.*)

2 Uilcanota—Mountain near Cuzco.

OLLANTAY: Urco Huaranca, thee I name
Of Anti-suyu Chief and Lord;
Receive the arrows and the plume,

(*Gives them.*)

Henceforth thou art our general.

PEOPLE: Long life to the Mountain Chief.

OLLANTAY: Hanco Huayllu, of all my lords
Thou art most venerable and wise,
Being kin to the august High Priest,
It is my wish that thou shouldst give
The ring unto the Mountain Chief.

(URCO HUARANCA *kneels, and* HANCO HUAYLLU *addresses him.*)

HANCO HUAYLLU: This ring around thy finger's placed
That thou mayst feel, and ne'er forget,
That when in fight thou art engaged,
Clemency becomes a hero chief.

URCO HUARANCA: A thousand times, illustrious king,
I bless thee for thy trust in me.

HANCO HUAYLLU: Behold the valiant Mountain Chief.
Now fully armed and bristling from head to foot,
Accoutred as becomes a knight.

(*Turning to* URCO HUARANCA.)

Ne'er let thine enemies take thee in rear;
Man of the Puna,[3] it ne'er can be said
You fled or trembled as a reed.

URCO HUARANCA: Hear me, warriors of the Andes!
Already we have a valiant king,
It might be he will be attacked;
'Tis said th'old Inca sends a force,
The men of Cuzco now advance.

[3] Puna-Altiplano—The high Andes.

367

We have not a single day to lose;
Call from the heights our Puna men,
Prepare their arms without delay,
Make Tampu strong with rampart walls,
No outlet leave without a guard;
On hill slopes gather pois'nous herbs
To shoot our arrows, carrying death.
OLLANTAY (*to* URCO HUARANCA):   Select the chiefs!
Fix all the posts for different tribes;
Our foes keep marching without sleep—
Contrive to check them by surprise.
URCO HUARANCA: Thirty thousand brave Antis are here.
Amongst them no weakling is found;
Apu Maruti, the mighty in war,
From high Uilcapampa will come,
On steep Tinquiqueru he'll stand
To march when the signal appears;
On the opposite side of the stream
Prince Chara has mustered his force;
In the gorge Charamuni post
Ten thousand armed Antis on watch;
Another such force is in wait
On the left, in the vale of Pachar.
We are ready to meet our foes,
We await them with resolute calm;
They will march in their confident pride
Until their retreat is cut off,
Then the trumpet of war shall resound,
From the mountains the stones shall pour down,
Great blocks will be hurled from above.
The Huancas[4] are crushed or dispersed,
Then the knife shall do its fell work,
All will perish by blows from our hands,
Our arrows will follow their flight.

[4] Huancas—Allies of the Incas. The other names mentioned here refer to Ollantay's allies and forces.

PEOPLE *and* SOLDIERS: It is well! It is very well!

(*Cheers and martial music.*)   (*Exeunt.*)

SCENE 2

*A wild place in the mountains. Distant view of Ollantay-
tampu.*

(*Enter* RUMI-NAUI, *torn and ragged, and covered with
blood, with two attendants.*)

RUMI-NAUI: Ah! Rumi-naui—Rumi-naui,
Thou art a fated rolling stone,
Escaped indeed, but quite alone,
And this is now thy yarahui.

Ollantay posted on the height,
Thou couldst not either fight or see,
Thy men did quickly fall or flee;
No room was there to move or fight.

Thou knowest now thy heart did beat
And flutter like a butterfly;
Thy skill thou couldst not then apply,
No course was left thee but retreat.

They had recourse to a surprise,
Our warriors immolated quite.
Ah! that alone could turn thee white—
From shame like that, canst e'er arise?

By thousands did thy warriors fall,
I hardly could alone escape,
With open mouth fell death did gape,
A great disaster did befall.

Holding that traitor to be brave,
I sought to meet him face to face—
Rushing to seek him with my mace,
I nearly found a warrior's grave.

369

My army then was near the hill,
When suddenly the massive stones
Came crashing down, with cries and moans,
While clarions sounded loud and shrill.

A rain of stones both great and small
Down on the crowd of warriors crashed,
On every side destruction flashed,
Thy heart the slaughter did appal.

Like a strong flood the blood did flow,
Inundating the ravine;
So sad a sight thou ne'er hast seen—
No man survived to strike a blow.

O thou who art by this disgraced,
What figure canst thou ever show
Before the King, who seeks to know
The truth, which must be faced?

'Tis better far myself to kill,
Or losing every scrap of hope,
To hang my body with this rope.

(*Takes a sling off his cap—going.*)

Yet may it not be useful still?

(*Turns again.*)

When bold Ollantay's end has come.

(*Exit.*)

SCENE 3

A garden in the house of the Virgins of the Sun. Chilca shrubs and mulli trees (Schinus Molle) *with panicles of red berries. The walls of the house at the back, with a door. A gate* (L.) *opening on the street.*

(YMA SUMAC *discovered at the gate looking out. To her enters* [R.] PITU SALLA. *Both dressed in white with golden belts.*)

PITU SALLA: Yma Sumac, do not approach
So near that gate, and so often;
It might arouse the Mother's wrath.
Thy name, which is so dear to me,
Will surely pass from mouth to mouth.
Honor shall be shown to chosen ones
Who wish to close the outer gate.
Amuse thyself within the walls,
And no one then can say a word.
Think well what you can find within—
It gives you all you can desire,
Of dresses, gold, and dainty food.
Thou art beloved by everyone,
E'en Virgins of the royal blood.
The mothers love to carry thee,
They give thee kisses and caress—
You they prefer to all the rest.
What more could any one desire,
Than always to remain with them,
Destined to be servant of the Sun?
In contemplating Him there's peace.

YMA SUMAC: Pitu Salla, ever you repeat
The same thing and the same advice;
I will open to thee my whole heart,
And say exactly what I think
Know that to me this court and house
Are insupportable—no less;
The place oppresses—frightens me—
Each day I curse my destiny.
The faces of all the Mama Cuna
Fill me with hatred and disgust,

And from the place they make me sit,
Nothing else is visible.
Around me there is nothing bright,
All are weeping and ne'er cease;
If I could ever have my way,
No person should remain within.
I see the people pass outside,
Laughing as they walk along.
The reason it is plain to see—
They are not mewed and cloistered here.
Is it because I have no mother,
That I am kept a prisoner?
Or is it I'm a rich novice?
Then from today I would be poor.
Last night I could not get to sleep,
I wandered down a garden walk;
In the dead silence of the night,
I heard one mourn. A better cry,
As one who sought and prayed for death.
On every side I looked about,
My hair almost on end with fright,
Trembling, I cried, "Who canst thou be?"
Then the voice murmured these sad words:
"O Sun, release me from this place!"
And this amidst such sighs and groans!
I searched about, but nothing found—
The grass was rustling in the wind.
I joined my tears to that sad sound,
My heart was torn with trembling fear.
When now the recollection comes,
I'm filled with sorrow and with dread.
You know now why I hate this place.
Speak no more, my dearest friend,
Of reasons for remaining here.

PITU SALLA: At least go in. The mother may appear.

YMA SUMAC: But pleasant is the light of the day.

(*Exit, R.*)

(*Enter* MAMA CCACCA, *L. in gray with black edges and belt.*)

MAMA CCACCA: Pitu Salla, hast thou spoken
All I told thee to that child?

PITU SALLA: I have said all to her.

MAMA CCACCA: And she, does she answer freely?

PITU SALLA: She has wept and asked for pity,
Refusing to comply at all.
She will not take the virgin's oath.

MAMA CCACCA: And this in spite of thy advice?

PITU SALLA: I showed her the dress she will wear,
Telling her misfortune would befall
If she refused to be a chosen one—
That she would ever be an outcast,
And for us a child accursed.

MAMA CCACCA: What can she imagine,
Wretched child of an unknown father,
A maid without a mother,
Just a fluttering butterfly?
Tell her plainly, very plainly,
That these walls offer her a home,
Suited for outcasts such as she,
And here no light is seen.

(*Exit, L.*)

PITU SALLA: Ay, my Sumac! Yma Suma!
These walls will be cruel indeed
To hide thy surpassing beauty.

(*Glancing to where* MAMA CCACCA *went out.*)

What a serpent! What a puma!

ACT III

SCENE I

The Pampa Moroni, a street in Cuzco. Enter RUMI-NAUI *(L.)*
in a long black cloak with a train, and PIQUI CHAQUI *(R.),*
meeting each other.

RUMI-NAUI: Whence, Piqui Chaqui, comest thou?
Dost thou here seek Ollantay's fate?

PIQUI CHAQUI: Cuzco, great lord, is my birthplace;
I hasten back unto my home.
I care not more to pass my days
In dismal and profound ravines.

RUMI-NAUI: Tell me, Ollantay—what does he?

PIQUI CHAQUI: He is busy now entangling
An already entangled skein.

RUMI-NAUI: What skein?

PIQUI CHAQUI: Should you not give me some present
If you want me to talk to you.

RUMI-NAUI: With a stick will I give thee blows,
With a rope I will hang thee.

PIQUI CHAQUI: O, do not frighten me!

RUMI-NAUI: Speak then.

PIQUI CHAQUI: Ollantay. Is it Ollantay?
I can remember no more.

RUMI-NAUI: Piqui Chaqui! Take care!

PIQUI CHAQUI: But you will not listen!
I am turning blind,
My ears are getting deaf,
My grandmother is dead,
My mother is left alone.

RUMI-NAUI: Where is Ollantay? Tell me.

374

PIQUI CHAQUI: I am in want of bread,
And the Paccays are not ripe.
I have a long journey today—
The desert is very far off.

RUMI-NAUI: If you continue to vex me
I will take your life.

PIQUI CHAQUI: Ollantay, is it? He is at work.
Ollantay! He is building a wall,
With very small stones indeed;
They are brought by little dwarfs—
So small that to be a man's size
They have to climb on each other's backs
But tell me, O friend of the King,
Why art thou in such long clothes,
Trailing like the wings of a sick bird—
As they are black it is better.

RUMI-NAUI: Hast thou not seen already
That Cuzco is plunged in grief?
The great Inca Pachacuti is dead,
All the people are in mourning,
Every soul is shedding tears.

PIQUI CHAQUI: Who, then, succeeds to the place
Which Pachacuti has left vacant?
If Tupac Yupanqui succeeds,
That Prince is the youngest;
There are some others older.

RUMI-NAUI: All Cuzco has elected him,
For the late King chose him,
Giving him the royal fringe;
We could elect no other.

PIQUI CHAQUI: I hasten to bring my bed here.

(*Exit running.*)

Great hall of the palace of TUPAC YUPANQUI. *The* INCA *seated on golden tiana* (C.).

(*Enter the* HIGH PRIEST *or* UILLAC UMA, *with priests and chosen Virgins of the Sun. The* INCA *dressed as his father.* UILLAC UMA *in full dress, wearing the huampar chucu. Virgins in white with gold belts and diadems. They range themselves by the throne* [L.]. *Then enter* RUMI-NAUI *and a crowd of chiefs, all in full dress, ranging themselves by the throne* [R.].)

TUPAC YUPANQUI: This day, O Councillors and Chiefs,
Let all receive my benison;
You Holy Virgins of the Sun
Receive our father's tenderest care.
The realm, rejoicing, hails me King;
From deep recesses of my heart
I swear to seek the good of all.

UILLAC UMA: Today the smoke of many beasts
Ascends on high towards the Sun,
The Deity with joy accepts
The sacrifice of prayer and praise.
We found in ashes of the birds
Our only Inca, King, and Lord,
In the great llama sacrifice;
All there beheld an eagle's form,
We opened it for augury,
But lo! the heart and entrails gone.
The eagle Anti-suyu means—
To thy allegiance they return.

(*Bowing to the* INCA.)

Thus I, thy augur, prophesy.

(*Acclamation.*) (*Exeunt all but* UILLAC UMA *and* RUMI-NAUI.)

TUPAC YUPANQUI (*turning to* RUMI-NAUI): Behold the
Hanan-suyu Chief
Who let the enemy escape,
Who led to almost certain death
So many thousands of my men.

RUMI-NAUI: Before his death thy father knew
Disaster had befallen me;
'Tis true, O King, it was my fault,
Like a stone I gave my orders,
And volleying stones soon beat me down;
It was with stones I had to fight,
And in the end they crushed my men.
Oh! grant me, Lord, a single chance,
Give perfect freedom to my plans,
Myself will to the fortress march,
And I will leave it desolate.

TUPAC YUPANQUI: For thee to strive with all thy might,
For thee thine honor to regain,
For thou shalt ne'er command my men
Unless thy worthiness is proved.

UILLAC UMA: Not many days shall pass, O King,
E'er all the Antis are subdued.
I've seen it in the quipu roll,
Haste! Haste! thou Rumi Tunqui.

(*Exeunt.*)

SCENE 3

*The great terrace entrance to Ollantay-tampu. On R. a long
masonry wall with recesses at intervals. At back a great en-
trance doorway. On L. terraces descend, with view of val-
ley and mountains.*

(*Guards discovered at entrance doorway. To them enter
RUMI-NAUI in rags, his face cut and slashed with wounds,
and covered with blood.*)

377

RUMI-NAUI: Will no one here have pity on me?

ONE OF THE GUARDS: Who art thou, man?
Who has ill-treated thee?
Thou comest in a frightful state,
Covered with blood and gaping wounds.

RUMI-NAUI: Go quickly to thy King and say
That one he loves has come to him.

ONE OF THE GUARDS: Thy name?

RUMI-NAUI: There is no need to give a name.

ONE OF THE GUARDS: Wait here.

(*Exit one of the guards.*)

(*Enter* OLLANTAY *with guards, R. front.*)

RUMI-NAUI: A thousand times I thee salute,
Ollantay, great and puissant King!
Have pity on a fugitive
Who seeks a refuge here with thee.

OLLANTAY: Who art thou, man? Approach nearer.
Who has thus ill-treated thee?
Were such deep and fearful wounds
Caused by a fall, or what mishap?

RUMI-NAUI: Thou knowest me, O mighty Chief.
I am that stone that fell down once,
But now I fall before thy feet;
O Inca! mercy! Raise me up!

(*Kneels.*)

OLLANTAY: Art thou the noble Rumi-naui,
Great Chief and Lord of Hanan-suyu?

RUMI-NAUI: Yes, I was that well-known Chief—
A bleeding fugitive today.

OLLANTAY: Rise, comrade mine. Let us embrace.

(Rises.)

Who has dared to treat thee thus,
And who has brought thee here to me
Within my fortress, on my hearth?

(To attendant.)

Bring new clothes for my oldest friend.

(Exit an attendant.)

How is it that thou art alone?
Camest thou not fearing death?

RUMI-NAUI: A new King reigns in Cuzco now—
Tupac Yupanqui is installed.
Against the universal wish,
He rose upon a wave of blood;
Safety he sees in headless trunks,
The sunchu and the nucchu[1] red
Are sent to all he would destroy.
Doubtless you have not forgot
That I was Hanan-suyu's Chief.
Yupanqui ordered me to come;
Arrived, I came before the King,
And as he has a cruel heart,
He had me wounded as you see;
And now thou knowest, King and friend,
How this new Inca treated me.

OLLANTAY: Grieve not, old friend Rumi-naui,
Thy wounds before all must be cured;
I see in thee th' avenging knife,
To use against the tyrant's heart.
At Tampu now we celebrate
The Sun's great Raymi[2] festival,

[1] Sunchu and Nucchu—Flower symbolism seems implied here.
[2] Raymi—Winter Solstice Sun Festival.

On that day all who love my name,
Throughout my realms hold festival.

RUMI-NAUI: Those three days of festival
To me will be a time of joy,
Perhaps I may be healed by then,
So that my heart may pleasure seek.

OLLANTAY: It will be so. For three whole nights
We drink and feast, to praise the Sun,
The better to cast all care aside
We shall be shut in Tampu fort.

RUMI-NAUI: The youths, as is their wont, will find
Their great delight in those three nights,
Then will they rest from all their toils,
And carry off the willing girls.

SCENE 4

A corridor in the palace of Chosen Virgins.

(*Enter* YMA SUMAC *and* PITU SALLA.)

YMA SUMAC: Pitu Salla, beloved friend,
How long wilt thou conceal from me
The secret that I long to know?
Think, dearest, of my anxious heart,
How I shall be in constant grief
Until you tell the truth to me.
Within these hard and cruel bounds
Does someone suffer for my sins?
My sweet companion, do not hide
From me, who 'tis that mourns and weeps
Somewhere within the garden walls.
How is it she is so concealed
That I can never find the place?

PITU SALLA: My Sumac, now I'll tell thee all—
Only concerning what you hear,

380

And still more surely what you see,
You must be dumb as any stone;
And you too must be well prepared
For a most sad heart-rending sight—
'Twill make thee weep for many days.

YMA SUMAC: I will not tell a living soul
What you divulge. But tell me all,
I'll shut it closely in my heart.

SCENE 5

A secluded part of the gardens of the Virgins, (L.) flowers, (R.) thicket concealing a stone door.

(PITU SALLA *and* YMA SUMAC.)

PITU SALLA: In this garden is a door of stone,
But wait until the mothers sleep,
The night comes on. Wait here for me.

(*Exit.*)

(YMA SUMAC *reclines on a bank and sleeps. Night comes on,* YMA SUMAC *awakes.*)

YMA SUMAC: A thousand strange presentiments
Crowd on me now, I scarce know what—
Perhaps I shall see that mournful one
Whose fate already breaks my heart.

(PITU SALLA *returns with a cup of water, a small covered vase containing food, and a torch which she gives to* YMA SUMAC. *She leads* YMA SUMAC *through bushes to the stone door, fixes the torch, presses something, and the door swings round.*)

(CUSI COYLLUR *is discovered senseless, extended on the ground, a snake twining itself round her waist.*)

PITU SALLA: Behold the princess for whom you seek.
Well! is thy heart now satisfied?

381

YMA SUMAC: Oh, my friend, what do I behold?
Is it a corpse that I must see?
Oh, horror! A dungeon for the dead!

   (*She faints.*)

PITU SALLA: What misfortune has now arrived?
O my Sumac, my dearest love,
O come to thyself without delay!
Arouse thee. Arise, my lovely flower.

   (YMA SUMAC *revives.*)

Fear not, my dove, my lovely friend,
'Tis not a corpse. The princess lives,
Unhappy, forlorn, she lingers here.

YMA SUMAC: Is she, then, still a living being?

PITU SALLA: Approach nearer, and you can help.
She lives indeed. Look. Watch her now.
Give me the water and the food.

   (*To* CUSI COYLLUR, *while helping her to sit up.*)

O fair princess, I bring thee food
And cooling water to refresh.
Try to sit up. I come with help.

YMA SUMAC: Who art thou, my sweetest dove?
Why art thou shut in such a place?

PITU SALLA: Take a little food, we pray.
Perchance without it you may die.

CUSI COYLLUR: How happy am I now to see,
After these long and dismal years,
The new and lovely face of one
Who comes with thee and gives me joy.

YMA SUMAC: O my princess, my sister dear,
Sweet bird, with bosom of pure gold,
What crime can they accuse thee of,

That they can make thee suffer thus?
What cruel fate has placed thee here
With death on watch in serpent's form?

CUSI COYLLUR: O charming child, the seed of love,
Sweet flower for my broken heart,
I have been thrust in this abyss.
I once was joined to a man
As pupil is part of the eye;
But alas! has he forgotten me?
The King knew not that we were joined
By such indissoluble bonds.
And when he came to ask my hand,
That King dismissed him in a rage,
And cruelly confined me here.
Many years have passed since then,
Yet, as you see, I'm still alive;
No single soul have I beheld
For all those sad and dismal years,
Nor have I found relief nor hope.
But who art thou, my dear, my love,
So young, so fresh, so pitiful?

YMA SUMAC: I too, like thee, am full of grief,
For long I've wished to see and love,
My poor forlorn and sad princess.
No father, no mother are mine.
And there are none to care for me.

CUSI COYLLUR: What age art thou?

YMA SUMAC: I ought to number many years,
For I detest this dreadful house,
And as it is a dreary place,
The time in it seems very long.

PITU SALLA: She ought to number just ten years
According to the account I've kept.

CUSI COYLLUR: And what is thy name?

YMA SUMAC: They call me Yma Sumac now,
But to give it me is a mistake.

CUSI COYLLUR: O my daughter! O my lost love,
Come to thy mother's yearning heart.

(*Embraces* YMA SUMAC.)

Thou art all my happiness,
My daughter, come, O come to me;
This joy quite inundates my soul,
It is the name I gave to thee.

YMA SUMAC: O my mother, to find thee thus!
We must be parted never more.
Do not abandon me in grief.
To whom can I turn to free thee,
To whom can I appeal for right?

PITU SALLA: Make no noise, my dearest friend;
To find us thus would ruin me.
Let us go. I fear the mothers.

YMA SUMAC (*to* CUSI COYLLUR):   Suffer a short time
longer here,
Until I come to take thee hence,
Patience for a few more days.
Alas! my mother dear! I go,
But full of love, to seek for help.

(*Exeunt closing the stone door, all but* CUSI COYLLUR.
They extinguish the torch.)

SCENE 6

Great hall in the palace of TUPAC YUPANQUI.

(*The* INCA *discovered seated on the tiana. To him enter
the* UILLAC UMA, *in full dress.*)

TUPAC YUPANQUI: I greet thee, great and noble Priest!
Hast thou no news of Rumi-naui.

384

UILLAC UMA: Last night, with guards, I wandered out
On heights towards Uilcanuta.
Far off I saw a crowd in chains,
No doubt the Anti prisoners,
For they are all defeated quite.
The cacti on the mountains smoke,
E'en now the fortress is in flames.

TUPAC YUPANQUI: And Ollantay, is he taken?
Perhaps—I hope his life is saved.

UILLAC UMA: Ollantay was among the flames,
'Tis said that no one has escaped.

TUPAC YUPANQUI: The Sun, my Father, is my shield,
I am my father's chosen child.
We must subdue the rebel host,
For that I am appointed here.

(*Enter a* CHASQUI *with a quipu in his hand.*)

THE CHASQUI: This morning at the dawn of day,
Rumi-naui despatched this quipu.

TUPAC YUPANQUI (*to the* UILLAC UMA):   See what it says.

UILLAC UMA: This knot, colored burnt ahuarancu,
Tells us that Tampu too is burnt;
This triple knot to which is hung
Another which is quintuple,
In all of quintuples are three,
Denotes that Anti-suyu's thine,
Its ruler prisoner of war.

TUPAC YUPANQUI (*to the* CHASQUI): And thou. Where
were thou?

THE CHASQUI: Sole King and Lord! Child of the Sun!
I am the first to bring the news,
That thou mayst trample on the foe,
And in thine anger drink their blood.

385

TUPAC YUPANQUI: Did I not reiterate commands
To spare and not to shed their blood—
Not anger but pity is my rule.

THE CHASQUI: O Lord, we have not shed their blood;
They were all captured in the night,
Unable to resist our force.

TUPAC YUPANQUI: Recount to me in full detail
The circumstances of the war.

THE CHASQUI: For a signal thy warriors wait,
The nights passed at Tinquiqueru,
Concealed in the cavern below,
Yanahuara men joining us late.

We waited within the large cave,
Thy men always ready to fight,
Behind foliage well out of sight,
Thy warriors patient and brave,

But for three long days and dark nights,
No food for the zealous and bold;
Feeling hungry, thirsty, and cold,
We waited and watched for the lights.

Rumi-naui sent orders at length,
When the Raymi[3] they carelessly keep,
And all of them drunk or asleep,
We were then to rush on with our strength.

Word came to surprise our foes,
Rumi-naui had opened the gate,
As cautious and silent as fate—
We were masters with none to oppose.

Those rebels fell into the trap,
The arrows came on them like rain,

---

[3] Raymi—Literally *December*. The *Inti Raymi*, Winter Solstice Ceremony is referred to.

Most died in their sleep without pain,
Not knowing their fatal mishap.

Ollantay, still trusting, was ta'en,
The same Urco Huaranca befell;
Hanco Huayllu is captive as well,
We thy rebels in fetters detain.

The Antis by thousands are slain,
A fearful example is made,
They are beaten, crushed, and betrayed,
Their women in sorrow and pain.

TUPAC YUPANQUI: As witness of what has occurred,
On Vilcamayu's storied banks,
No doubt thou hast told me the truth.
It was a well-designed attack.

(*Enter* RUMI-NAUI *followed by several chiefs.*)

RUMI-NAUI: Great Inca, I kneel at thy feet,
This time you will hear my report,
I beseech thee to deign to restore
The trust that I forfeited once.

(*Kneels.*)

TUPAC YUPANQUI: Rise, great Chief, receive my regard,
I accept thy great service with joy;
Thou didst cast o'er the waters thy net,
And hast captured a marvelous fish.

RUMI-NAUI: Our enemies perished in crowds,
Their chiefs were captured and bound,
Overwhelmed by my terrible force,
Like a rock detached from the heights.

TUPAC YUPANQUI: Was much blood shed in the assault?

RUMI-NAUI: No, Lord, not a drop has been shed,
To thine orders I strictly adhered.

Those Antis were strangled in sleep,
But the fort is entirely razed.

TUPAC YUPANQUI: Where are the rebels?

RUMI-NAUI: They are waiting with agonized fear,
For their fate, to perish by cords.
The people are sending up cries,
Demanding their deaths without fail.
Their women are now in their midst,
The children raise hideous cries;
It is well that thine order should pass
To finish their traitorous lives.

TUPAC YUPANQUI: It must be so without any doubt,
That the orphans may not be alone,
Let all perish, not sparing one,
Thus Cuzco recovers her peace,
Let the traitors be brought before me.
In my presence the sentence they'll hear.

(*Exit* RUMI-NAUI *and re-enter followed by guards in charge
of* OLLANTAY, URCO HUARANCA, *and* HANCO HUAYLLU,
bound and blindfolded, followed by the guards with PIQUI
CHAQUI *bound.*)

TUPAC YUPANQUI: Take the bands off the eyes of those
men.
And now, Ollantay, where art thou?
And where art thou, O Mountain Chief?
Soon thou wilt roll down from the heights.

(*To the soldiers who bring in* PIQUI CHAQUI.)

Whom have we here?

PIQUI CHAQUI: Many fleas in the Funcas abound,
And torment the people full sore,
With boiling water they are killed,
And I, poor flea, must also die.

TUPAC YUPANQUI: Tell me, Hanco Huayllu, tell me,
Why art thou Ollantay's man?

388

Did not my father honor thee?
Did he not grant thy requests?
Did he ever have a secret from thee?
Speak also, you, the other rebels,
Ollantay and the Mountain Chief.

OLLANTAY: O father, we have nought to say,
Our crimes are overwhelming us.

TUPAC YUPANQUI (*to the* UILLAC UMA):   Pronounce
their sentence, great High Priest.

UILLAC UMA: The light that fills me from the Sun
Brings mercy and pardon to my heart.

TUPAC YUPANQUI: Now thy sentence, Rumi-naui.

RUMI-NAUI: For crimes enormous such as these
Death should ever be the doom;
It is the only way, O King!
To warn all others from such guilt.
To stout tocarpus they should be
Secured and bound with toughest rope,
Then should the warriors freely shoot
Their arrows until death is caused.

PIQUI CHAQUI: Must it be that evermore
The Antis must all perish thus?
Alas! then let the branches burn—
What pouring out of blood is here.

RUMI-NAUI: Silence, rash man, nor dare to speak,

   (*General lamentation outside.*)

Having been rolled just like a stone,
My heart has now become a stone.

TUPAC YUPANQUI: Know that tocarpus are prepared.
Remove those traitors from my sight,
Let them all perish, and at once.

RUMI-NAUI: Take these three men without delay
To the dreaded execution stakes;

Secure them with unyielding ropes,
And hurl them from the lofty rocks.

TUPAC YUPANQUI: Stop! Cast off their bonds.

(*The guards unbind them. They all kneel.*)

(*To* OLLANTAY, *kneeling.*) Rise from thy knees; come to my
side.

(*Rise.*)

Now thou hast seen death very near,
You that have shown ingratitude,
Learn how mercy flows from my heart;
I will raise thee higher than before.
Thou wert Chief of Anti-suyu,
Now see how far my love will go;
I make thee Chief in permanence,
Receive this plume as general,
This arrow emblem of command.

TUPAC YUPANQUI (*to the* UILLAC UMA):   Thou mighty
Pontiff of the Sun,
Robe him in the regal dress.
Raise up the others from their knees,
And free them from the doom of death.

(URCO HUARANCA, HANCO HUAYLLU, *and* PIQUI CHAQUI *rise,
the latter looking much relieved. The* UILLAC UMA *places the
robe on* OLLANTAY'*s shoulders.*)

UILLAC UMA: Ollantay, learn to recognize
Tupac Yupanqui's generous mind;
From this day forth be thou his friend,
And bless his magnanimity.
This ring contains my potent charm,
For this I place it on thy hand.

(*Gives him a ring, or bracelet.*)

This mace receive, 'tis from the King,

(*Gives him a mace* [champi].)

It is his gracious gift to thee.

OLLANTAY: With tears I shall nearly consume
That mace thus presented to me;
I am tenfold the great Inca's slave,
In this world no equal is found,
My heart's fibers his latchets shall be;
From this moment my body and soul
To his service alone shall belong.

TUPAC YUPANQUI: Now, Mountain Chief! come near
to me,
Ollantay is given the arrow and plume,
Though to me he gave fury and war.
Notwithstanding all that has passed
He continues the Andean Chief,
And will lead his rebels to peace;
Thee also I choose for the plume;
From this day thou art a great chief,
And never forget in thy thoughts,
I saved thee from death and disgrace.

URCO HUARANCA: Great King and most merciful Lord,
But now, expecting my death,
I am ever thy most faithful slave.

(UILLAC UMA *gives him the plume and arrow.*)

UILLAC UMA: O Urco, the Inca has made
A great and a powerful chief,
And grants thee with marvelous grace
The arrow and also the plume.

RUMI-NAUI: Illustrious King, I venture to ask,
Will Anti-suyu have two chiefs?

TUPAC YUPANQUI: There will not be two, O Rumi-naui:
The Mountain Chief will rule the Antis;
In Cuzco Ollantay will reign—

As Viceroy deputed by me
His duties will call him to act
As ruler throughout the whole realm.

OLLANTAY: O King! thou dost raise me too high,
A man without service or claim;
I am thy obedient slave—
Mayst thou live for a thousand years.

TUPAC YUPANQUI: The mascapycha now bring forth.
And to it the llautu attach.
Uillac Uma, adorn him with these,
And proclaim his state to the world.
Yes, Ollantay shall stand in my place,
Raised up like the star of the morn,
For Colla this month I shall start;
All preparations are made.
In Cuzco Ollantay will stay,
My Ranti and Viceroy and friend.

OLLANTAY: I would fain, O magnanimous King,
Follow them in the Chayanta war;
Thou knowest my love for such work.
Peaceful Cuzco is not to my taste,
I prefer to be thy Canari,
To march in the van of thy force,
And not to be left in the rear.

TUPAC YUPANQUI: Thou shouldst find the wife of thy choice,
And with her reign happily here
In Cuzco; repose without care;
Rest here while I'm absent in war.

OLLANTAY: Great King, thy sorrowful slave
Already had chosen a wife.

TUPAC YUPANQUI: How is it I know not of this?
It should be reported to me.
I will load her with suitable gifts;
Why was this concealed from my eyes?

392

OLLANTAY: In Cuzco itself disappeared
That sweet and adorable dove;
One day she did rest in my arms,
And the next no more to be seen.
In grief I made search far and near,
Earth seemed to have swallowed her up,
To have buried her far from my sight;
O such, mighty King, is my grief.

TUPAC YUPANQUI: Ollantay! afflict not thyself,
For now thou must take up thy place
Without turning thy eyes from thy work.

(*To* UILLAC UMA.)

High priest, obey my command.

(*The* UILLAC UMA *goes to the wings* (*R.*) *and addresses the people outside.*)

UILLAC UMA: O people, hear what I say:
The Inca, our King and our Lord,
Thus declares his imperial will:
Ollantay, shall reign in his place.

PEOPLE OUTSIDE: Ollantay Ranti! Ollantay Ranti!

(*Shouts and acclamations.*)

TUPAC YUPANQUI (*to* RUMI-NAUI *and other chiefs*):   You also render him homage.

RUMI-NAUI: Prince Ollantay! Incap Ranti!
Thy promotion gives me joy.
All the Antis now released,
Return rejoicing to their homes.

(*He and all the chiefs bow to* OLLANTAY.)

GUARDS WITHOUT: You cannot pass. Go back! go back!

VOICE WITHOUT: Why, is this a festive day?
Let me pass. I must see the King:

I pray you do not stop me,
Do not drive me from the door;
If you stop me I shall die.
Have a care. You will kill me.

TUPAC YUPANQUI: What noise is that without?

GUARD: It is a young girl who comes weeping
And insists upon seeing the King.

TUPAC YUPANQUI: Let her come in.

(*Enter* YMA SUMAC.)

YMA SUMAC: Which is the Inca, my lord,
That I may kneel down at his feet?

UILLAC UMA: Who art thou, charming maid?
Behold the King.

(YMA SUMAC *throws herself at the King's feet.*)

YMA SUMAC: O my King! be thou my father,
Snatch from evil thy poor servant,
Extend thy royal hand to me.
O merciful child of the Sun,
My mother is dying as this hour
In a foul and loathsome cave;
She is killed in cruel martyrdom—
Alas—she is bathed in her own blood.

TUPAC YUPANQUI: What inhumanity, poor child!
Ollantay, take this case in hand.

OLLANTAY: Young maiden, take me quickly there;
We will see who it is that suffers.

YMA SUMAC: No sir. Not so. It is the King himself
Should go with me.
Perhaps he may recognize her;

(*To* OLLANTAY.)

For you, I know not who you are.
O King, arise, do not delay,

I fear my mother breathes her last,
At least may be in mortal pain;
O Inca! Father! grant my prayer.

UILLAC UMA: Illustrious King, thou wilt consent;
Let us all seek this luckless one—
Thou canst release from cruel bonds.
Let us go, O King!

TUPAC YUPANQUI (*rising*):   Come all! Come all!
In midst of reconciliations
This young maid assaults my heart.

                                        (*Exeunt.*)

SCENE 7

*The garden in the palace of Virgins of the Sun (same scene as
Act III, Scene 5). Stone door more visible.*

(*Enter the* INCA TUPAC YUPANQUI *with* YMA SUMAC,
OLLANTAY, UILLAC UMA *and* RUMI-NAUI; URCO HUARANCA,
HANCO HUAYLLU, *and* PIQUI CHAQUI *in the background.*)

TUPAC YUPANQUI: But this is the Aclla Huasi;
My child, art thou not mistaken?
Where is thy imprisoned mother?

YMA SUMAC: In a dungeon within these bounds
My mother has suffered for years,
Perhaps even now she is dead.

(*She points to the stone door.*)

TUPAC YUPANQUI: What door is this?

(*Enter* MAMA CCACCA *and* PITU SALLA. MAMA CCACCA
kneels and kisses the INCA'S *hand.*)

MAMA CCACCA: Is it a dream or reality,
That I behold my sovereign?

TUPAC YUPANQUI: Open that door.

395

(MAMA CCACCA *opens the door.*)
(CUSI COYLLUR *discovered chained and fainting, with a puma and a snake, one on each side of her.*)

YMA SUMAC: O my mother, I feared to find
That you had already passed away;
Pitu Salla! Haste. Bring water.
Perhaps my dove may still revive.

(*Exit* PITU SALLA.)

TUPAC YUPANQUI: What horrid cavern do I see?
Who is this woman? what means it?
What cruel wretch thus tortures her?
Mama Ccacca, come near to me:
What means that chain bound around her?
What hast thou to say to this?
Is it the effect of malice
That this poor creature lingers here?

MAMA CCACCA: It was thy father's dread command;
A punishment for lawless love.

TUPAC YUPANQUI: Begone! begone! harder than rock!
Turn out that puma and the snake,
Break down that door of carved stone.
   (*To* MAMA CCACCA)   Let me not see thy face again.
A woman living as a bat;
This child has brought it all to light.

(*Enter* PITU SALLA *with water. She sprinkles it over* CUSI COYLLUR, *who revives.*)

CUSI COYLLUR: Where am I? Who are these people?
Yma Sumac, my beloved child,
Come to me, my most precious dove.
Who are all these men before me?

(*She begins to faint again and is restored by water.*)

YMA SUMAC: Fear not, my mother, 'tis the King;
The King himself comes to see you.

396

The great Yupanqui is now here.
Speak to him. Awake from thy trance.

TUPAC YUPANQUI: My heart is torn and sorrowful
At sight of so much misery.
Who art thou, my poor sufferer?
Child, tell me now thy mother's name?

YMA SUMAC: Father! Inca! Clement Prince!
Have those cruel bonds removed.

THE UILLAC UMA: It is for me to remove them,
And to relieve this sore distress.

(*Cuts the rope fastening* CUSI COYLLUR *to the wall.*)

OLLANTAY (*to* YMA SUMAC):   What is thy mother's
name?

YMA SUMAC: Her name was once Cusi Coyllur,
But it seems a mistake. Her joy
Was gone when she was prisoned here.

OLLANTAY: O renowned King, great Yupanqui,
In her you see my long lost wife.

(*Prostrates himself before the* INCA.)

TUPAC YUPANQUI: It all appears a dream to me.
The "Star"! my sister! and thy wife.
O sister! what newly found joy.
O Cusi Coyllur, my sister,
Come here to me, and embrace me,
Now thou art delivered from woe.

(*Music.*)

Thou hast found thy loving brother;
Joy calms the anguish of my heart.

(*Embraces* CUSI COYLLUR.)

CUSI COYLLUR: Alas! my brother, now you know
The cruel tortures I endured

During those years of agony;
Thy compassion now has saved me.

TUPAC YUPANQUI: Who are thou, dove, that hast
suffered?
For what sin were you prisoned here?
Thou mightest have lost thy reason.
Thy face is worn, thy beauty gone,
Thy looks as one risen from death.

OLLANTAY: Cusi Coyllur, I had lost thee,
Thou art brought again to life—
Thy father should have killed us both.
My whole heart is torn with sorrow.
Star of joy, where is now thy joy?
Where now thy beauty as a star?
Art thou under thy father's curse?

CUSI COYLLUR: Ollantay, for ten dreary years
That dungeon has kept us apart;
But now, united for new life,
Some happiness may yet be ours.
Yupanqui makes joy succeed grief,
He may well count for many years.

UILLAC UMA: Bring new robes to dress the princess.

(*They put on her royal robes. The* HIGH PRIEST *kisses her hand.*)

TUPAC YUPANQUI: Ollantay, behold thy royal wife,
Honor and cherish her henceforth.
And thou, Yma Sumac, come to me,
I enlace you in the thread of love;
Thou art the pure essence of Coyllur.

(*Embraces her.*)

OLLANTAY: Thou art our protector, great King,
Thy noble hands disperse our grief;

398

Thou art our faith and only hope—
Thou workest by virtue's force.

TUPAC YUPANQUI: Thy wife is now in thy arms;
All sorrow now should disappear,
Joy, newborn, shall take its place.

(*Acclamations from the* CHIEFS, *and* PIQUI CHAQUI. *Music:
huancars* [*drums*], *pincullus* [*flutes*], *and pututus* [*clar-
ions*].)

NOTES

THE CREATION OF THE WORLD (*Maya*)—*Yucatan*

Page 1

SOURCE: *The Book of Chilam Balam of Chumayel,* trans. Ralph L. Roys
          (Norman, Oklahoma, 1967).

In contemporary Guatemala among the Maya a priest is still called
Chiman (see Maud Oakes, *The Two Crosses of Todos Santos,* Bollin-
gen Foundation, New York, 1951). The colonial Yucatan name for priest
was Chilam, Balam means Jaguar, and so The Book of Chilam Balam is re-
ally The Book of the Jaguar Priest. This one comes from Chumayel in
Northern Yucatan. There were various Jaguar Priest books in post-
Conquest Yucatan, attempts of native priests to get down on paper (in
Maya, using European script) whatever they could of the old Maya
religion that was slowly being stamped out by Spanish Catholicism.
Even in the seventeenth century, though, a great deal of syncretic
blending had taken place, and the various books of the Jaguar Priests
are curious mixtures of the Maya religion and Catholicism.

The reference to "stones" in the first paragraph seems to be a met-
aphorical way of saying "truths" and probably refers back to Maya
stone hieroglyphics; the writer is writing on paper, but thinking in
terms of carving on stone. *Balché* in the first paragraph is Maya sacred/
sacramental wine. The Maya God "drank" the truths of religion like
wine.

The conflict in paragraph three is between the Oxlahun-ti-ku (the
Sky Gods of the thirteen Maya heavens) and the Bolon-ti-ku (the gods
of the nine underworlds, the Nine Lords of the Night). The Ah
Mucencab are the Bee Gods who carry out the work of blindfolding
the Sky Gods, who are then literally annihilated; the First Universe is
destroyed, allowing the establishment of the classic four quarters with
their four cosmic trees and the pillar of the sky in the middle. Then an-

other "katun" (twenty-year period) can be established, and in this katun
heaven (Divine Power) can be brought down to earth.

Thompson in his *Maya History and Religion* (Norman: University of
Oklahoma Press, 1970) very perceptively compares this heavenly battle
to the "war in which Saint Michael and the heavenly host overcame
and cast out the great dragon, Satan, and all the powers of evil and
darkness" (p. 281), although perhaps it is even more to the point to
compare this account with the war of the Greek Titans against the
Olympians, which in turn seems to be derived from an actual historical
war between the Aryans as they invaded India around 3,000 B.C. (or
earlier) and the aboriginal Indian population, the Dravidians. For the
Greek background, see J. Lindsay's *The Clashing Rocks* (London:
Chapman & Hall, 1965), especially Chapters 8–12. The Aryan-Dravidian
war is best described in Indian sources in *The Siva-Purana* (4 volumes,
Delhi: Motilal Banarsidass, 1970) and *The Markandeya Purana* (Delhi:
Indological Book House, 1969). One of the "Titans" is Prometheus, and
as Trickster he assumes a key role throughout American theology as the
link between indifferent "Heaven" and needy mankind.

Other Maya concepts/words that need explaining: *Bacabs*—The
"Atlases" who support the four corners of the world/the sky. The East
Indian theological concepts of (1) The Cosmic Tree and (2) The Re-
gents of the Directions are combined to form an idea of a central tree
and four trees at the four world-corners, each with a bird perched in it.

Lahun Chaan is the Regent of the West, the Maya version of the
Dravidian King of Nagas/Serpent who "rules" the West. *Chaan* in
Maya means both sky and serpent, *Lahun* means ten. In Tibetan Bud-
dhism, this King of Serpents who rules the West is known as
Virupaksha or Ja-mi-zan. (See L. Austine Waddell's *Tibetan Buddhism*
[New York: Dover Publications, 1972, p. 84].) Here he is the ruler of
the "tenth" heaven.

Ah Uuc Cheknal seems to be seen as "overlord" of this entire world,
and since the Amerindian-Dravidian world is the "underworld" of tradi-
tional Hinduism, probably Ah Uuc Cheknal is a variant form of Yama.
The name literally means "he who fertilizes the maize seven times."

Itzam-kab-ain—"The whale with the feet of a crocodile." This is a
Maya version of the general Dravidian fertility god, the Makara, pic-
tured in India as a crocodile, a fish, an elephant—in fact, in any combi-
nation or variation of general "water"/fertility god. The principle in-
volved here is that all fertility comes from the "underworld"; it is
always subterranean, submarine, cthonic.

DESANA CREATION MYTH *(Tukano/Desana)—Amazon*

Page 3

SOURCE: G. Reichel-Dolmatoff, *Amazonian Cosmos: The Sexual and
Religious Symbolism of the Tukano Indians* (University of
Chicago Press, 1971).

Pamurí-mahsë, the culture hero in Part IIff. of this myth, is a variant form of Masauwuh/Másaw (see Frank Waters, *Book of the Hopi*, New York: Ballantine Books, 1971, and J. W. Fewkes's "Tusayan Katcinas," 15th Annual Report of the Bureau of Ethnology, Washington: U. S. Government Printing Office, 1897), the Pueblo-Indian God of the Underworld. Mahsë-Másaw is as close as we can get in terms of actual etymological parallels in Amerindia, but both names are probably derived from the general Dravidian root MA—related to blackness, clouds, charcoal, etc., which in turn is related to MAGU—to ripen, MARUMAI—the next birth, the next world (see T. Burrow and M. B. Emeneau, *A Dravidian Etymological Dictionary*, Oxford: Clarendon Press, 1961, paragraphs 3,893, 3,903, 3,918, 3,925, 4,187). Mahsë/Másaw functionally, however, appears in a myriad of "masks" in the New and Old Worlds. He is Hermes, Trickster, Prometheus, Raven, Quetzalcoatl, the Plumed Serpent, Siva, and functions as the link between the indifferent sky gods and the earth (and underworld). Karl Kerenyi has an essay appended to Paul Radin's classic study, *The Trickster: A Study in American Indian Mythology* (New York: Schocken Books, 1973), in which he discusses the analogues between Trickster (Hermes) in ancient Greece and Trickster in the New World. In section III various avatars/forms of Mahsë/Másaw emerge, which is typical of the Amerindian-Dravidian multiplication of gods through the multiplication of functions. In section X, the Sun's daughter brings fire to earth instead of Vihó-mahsë—which is an interesting variation on Trickster's usual bringing of fire to earth. In section XII, though, Pamurí-mahsë drinks the first corn beer (*Chicha*), which links him to the traditionally Dionysian Trickster figure.

Some terms that need explaining are:

Vihó and Yajé—Hallucinogenic drugs analagous to Soma in traditional E. Indian ritual.

Maloca—Longhouse or lodge.

Chagra—(Spanish *Chacra*) Field.

Payés—Priest/Yoga.

Volumes could be written on this account, but suffice it to say that it is one of the most vividly written Amerindian accounts stressing the importance of Yoga, the ritual use of hallucinogenics, the whole cyclic principle of death/rebirth-initiation.

THE ORIGIN OF THE YAGUA (Yagua)—N.E. Peru

Page 16

SOURCE: Paul Fejos, *Ethnology of the Yagua* (New York: Viking Fund Publications in Anthropology, 1943).

Cf. "How the World Was Made," in James Mooney's *Myths of the Cherokee*, 19th Annual Report of the Bureau of American Ethnology

(Washington, D.C.: U. S. Government Printing Office, 1900), pp. 239–40. Also, Frank Waters' *Book of the Hopi*, p. 137ff. The actual "descent" from the sky may be a symbolic rendering of the trans-Pacific crossing in the third millennium B.C.–or earlier.

GUARANI CREATION MYTH–*Paraguay*

Page 18

SOURCE: *La Literatura de los Guaraniés* by Leon Cadogan (Mexico: Editorial Joaquín Mortiz, 1965).

The Maya sacred book, *Popol Vuh*, is very helpful in "explicating" the true nature of Namandu, the Creator, Hummingbird. The *Popol Vuh* begins with an account of "the Creator, the Maker, Tepeu, Gucumatz . . . in the water surrounded with light," and Gucumatz, it turns out, is a Feathered Serpent. So essentially, what we have here is the Feathered Serpent/Hummingbird as the original creator-figure. (See *Popol Vuh*, Recinos-Goetz-Morley, Norman: University of Oklahoma Press, 1969, p. 81.) I think we can project back to an archetypal creative *couple* akin to the Aztec Ometecuhtli-Omecíhuatl (see M. León-Portilla, *Aztec Thought and Culture*, (Norman: University of Oklahoma Press, 1963, pp. 82–84), analagous to the Hermopolitan (Egyptian) pair Nun-Naumet (see E. O. James, *Creation and Cosmology*, Leiden: E. J. Brill, 1969, p. 17), a bisexual reality that is later broken down to either a female or male "creator." The idea of a primordial serpent-creator, though, appears again and again throughout the Dravidian-influenced world. Vishnu, the Creator, is often pictured asleep on the Cosmic Serpent, Sesa (see A. Danielou, *Hindu Polytheism* (London: Bollingen Foundation, 1964, p. 162)–who is also called Ananta. Among the Aztecs, Coatlicue is often pictured as a Cosmic Creator God in the form of a serpent, Cihuacoatl; the Fire Goddess, is also a Snake Goddess. What we seem to have here is a need to unite sky (bird) and water-earth (serpent)–and so the plumed serpent emerges and remains a constant theme in Amerindian/Dravidian theology . . . always related to water, fertility, creation. Interestingly enough, the contemporary Dravidian NA- and NAN-related words still reflect this fertility-centered reality: NANTU–to increase; NAME–to become moist, damp; NANAI–to become wet; NANAI–to bud. (See Burrow, *op. cit.*, paragraphs 2,968, 2,969, 3,006, 3,007.)

At the same time, this entire, almost narcissistic, creation account is very similar to what became classical Hinduism. See *Hindu Polytheism*, p. 240ff.

The owl in section 1, VII, seems related to the Minoan-Mycenaean concept of the Great Goddess. See "The Divine Lady" in C. J. Bleeker's *The Sacred Bridge* (Leiden: E. J. Brill, 1963), p. 101. The idea of a world tree in the center of "paradise" connected with a serpent (section

3, I & II) belong to the same mythic substratum out of which developed both Dravidian and Semitic myth systems. See M. Eliade's *Patterns in Comparative Religion* (New York: Sheed and Ward, 1958), p. 273ff. and p. 380ff. The same also holds true for the Logo preceding "creation" (section 2, II). In the *Aitareya Upanishad*, for example, we read: "He thought: 'Now here are worlds. Let me create world guardians.' From the waters he drew forth and shaped a being. He hatched it. When it had been hatched, its mouth was separated, egglike; from the mouth came forth speech and from speech fire. The nostrils were separated; from the nostrils came forth the life breath; from breath the wind. The eyes were separated; from the eyes came forth sight; from sight the sun . . ." (See A. Danielou, *Hindu Polytheism*, p. 244.)

Part II, section 9 ("How there was Originally Fire on the New Earth") is a variation of the classic Trickster/Prometheus legend. As W. Crooke points out in *The Popular Religion and Folklore of Northern India* (Delhi: S. Chand & Co., 1968), "One of the earliest legends of the Hindu race is that recorded in the *Rig Veda*, where Agni, the god of fire, concealed himself in heaven, was brought down to earth by Matarisvan, and made over to the princely tribe of Bhrigu, in which we have the Oriental version of the myth of Prometheus."

WHAT THE WORLD USED TO BE LIKE (Chorti Maya)—Guatemala

Page 34

SOURCE: John G. and Sarah Fought, *Chorti (Mayan) Texts* (Philadelphia: University of Pennsylvania Press, 1972).

In this almost pathetically simplified account of the old myths, some rather interesting "fragment traces" still remain. There is the "remembrance" of the Dravidian cosmological structure of seven seas which come down into Buddhism as follows: milk, curds, butter, blood or sugarcane juice, poison or wine, fresh water, and salt water (see L. Austine Waddell's *Tibetan Buddhism*, p. 78). There is some hint of periodic cosmic cycles (". . . the sea, from time to time, rose up") similar to the Dravidian/Amerindian concept of Yugas or Suns (see León-Portilla's *Aztec Thought and Culture*, p. 37ff.). The people with horns can go back to such prototypical figures as the proto-Siva horned god of the Indus Valley Yama, the E. Indian Death God, or a number of other figures. What we are really confronting here is a buffalo or bull god, the consort of the Great Goddess (see Bleeker's "The Divine Lady," especially p. 91, where the Sumerian Great Goddess, Inanna, marries Dumuzi, the God of Herds). We are in the same archaic myth level in relation to the "four-eyed" people. The figure is, of course, the prototype of Kronos: "four eyes in front and behind . . . two of them wide awake . . . and two quietly closing." A. B. Cook, *Zeus: A Study in*

Ancient Religion (Cambridge: Cambridge University Press, 1925), II, p. 553. Cook associates Kronos with a Minoan sky god who was the object of cultic sacrifices—which he sees as the origin of the legend of Kronos' eating his own children (Ibid., II, p. 549). Which also neatly links in with the Chorti mention of cannibalism.

The idea of a four-eyed man still appears in popular folklore in India. Janua/Kronos appears in a northeast frontier tale in India as Tani. Perhaps there is even an etymological link. See Verrier Elwin's *Myths of the North-East Frontier of India* (Shillong: North-East Frontier Agency, 1968), p. 159.

TREN TREN AND KAI KAI (*Mapuche*)—*Chile*

Page 36

SOURCE: L. C. Faron, *Hawks of the Sun* (Pittsburgh: University of Pittsburgh Press, 1964), p. 76.

In the transference of Dravidian terminology from the Old to the New World in many instances names for "places" become the names of "gods." One notable example is the transformation of MANU (Egyptian for West—Land of the Dead) into MANA (Hopi—Underworld fertility spirits). This is, in turn, related to the Hindu god MANU, the Lawgiver. What seems to establish the variations here is a kind of loose function-association that interrelates Law/Order with the Underworld, the West, the Katchinas, and various avatars of the Mother Goddess (Mana). In this Mapuche creation myth, the Great Serpent Kai Kai is probably derived from Kailasa (see A. Danielou, p. 136), the home of Kubera and the Yaksas, the serpentine, underworld people in Hindu mythology who guard the world's treasures. Kubera has three legs; the Mapuche myth gives him three arms. In Hindu mythology, he is called Raksasendra, Lord of Demons, and the treasure he controls is guarded by a serpent/dragon. In the Mapuche version, Kubera himself becomes the serpent/dragon. Kubera is the prototype of Leprechauns (Lu—Old Irish for Small, and Chan/Kan—Dravidian-Amerindian for Snake) and throughout Dravidian Lord Kubera, the Yaksas, Raksas, Asuras, and Nagas are all associated with the underworld and serpents.

Ultimately, the Mapuche myth represents a curious inversion (under Christian influence) that transforms a protective deity into a malevolent deity. Dravidian languages still associate KAY/KAI with fertility, ripeness, warmth and water (see Burrow and Emeneau, *A Dravidian Etymological Dictionary*, already cited, paragraphs 1,219, 1,220, 1,224).

Tren Tren probably should be Ten Ten and related to the South (see Burrow-Emeneau, paragraph 2,839), which is the realm of Yama (in Hinduism), the God of the Dead and associated with justice and help for the dead (see Danielou, p. 131). There is an old Mongolian god TEN-gri (Heaven) that may also be related to Waddell's *Tibetan Bud-*

dhism (New York: Dover Books, 1972, p. 372, note 2), and in general the T-root in Dravidian-related languages refers to God and is the root that later—through Semitic and then Greek sources—serves as the basis for our God words, T-heology, T-heocentric, etc.

THE FLOOD (*Toba-Pilagá—Chaco, Argentina*)

Page 37

SOURCE: Alfred Métraux, *Myths of the Toba and Pilagá Indians of the Gran Chaco* (Philadelphia: American Folklore Society, 1946), pp. 29–30.

In the Dravidian-Amerindian mind there is a strong taboo associated with childbirth, pregnancy, and menstruation. As William Crooke and R. E. Enthoven point out in *Religion and Folklore of Northern India*, menstrual blood causes Evil Eye (p. 290) and women who die in childbirth, while pregnant, or while menstruating, become evil spirits called Churels (a form of predatory Dakini spirit) (pp. 194–95). Why? The associations that underlie this belief seem to be: (1) That women are rain-producers/minor, individual versions of the Great Fertility Goddess, (2) That female blood is especially fertile and rain-producing. Crooke and Enthoven cite one case of a tribe in India where "in times of drought [the] . . . women . . . go, unseen by the men, to some lonely place, throw back their head-dresses, gird their waists, and belabour one another, with thorny branches till blood begins to flow, which ensures a fall of rain" (p. 72).

The point of going "unseen by the men" is particularly applicable here because in all three Toba-Pilagá versions of the flood there is an explicit antagonism between Rainbow (the Siva-Naga-Rain-Dragon figure) and the woman who causes the flood. This male-female "tension" is an inherent characteristic of the Amerindian-Dravidian mind and Claude Lévi-Strauss in his *Structural Anthropology* (New York: Basic Books, 1963) discusses it at great length in terms of actual social structures in Brazil (Chapter VII)—relatively close to the Toba-Pilagá area. Certainly, the myth expresses male awe at the power of female fertility; female fertility is a positive blessing, but inherent in it is always the possibility of nature going wild, overstepping boundaries and breaking "laws." The etymological links between *measuring/menstruation* and *menstruation* aren't superficial, but rather deep-rooted in the notion that the female menstrual period, the lunar month, and cosmic "order" are all intimately interrelated.

THE DELUGE (*Apinaye*)—Brazil

Page 39

SOURCE: Curt Nimuendajú, *The Apinayé* (Oosterhout, The Netherlands, 1967), trans. R. H. Lowie.

To this day, there is a custom in rural India of watering a representation of Siva's lingam (penis) in order to bring rain. Siva is Lord of Nagas (snakes) and throughout the Dravidian/Amerindian world there is an association between phallicism, serpents and rain (see W. Crooke's *The Popular Religion and Folklore of Northern India*, Delhi: Munshiram Manoharlal, 1968, I, 76). During the Hopi March festival, Ankwanti, Palulukonti, the great Rain Serpent, appears on the scene (see J. W. Fewkes's "Hopi Katcinas," *Twenty-first Annual Report of the Bureau of American Ethnology*, Washington, D.C.: U. S. Government Printing Office, 1903, p. 86ff.), and this is typical of the snake-rain association throughout the world of the Great Tradition.

The name Kaṇẹ̄-rōti, of course, is derived from a fundamental Dravidian-Amerindian name for snake (and sky): KAN/KAAN. The association of the parrot with good luck savors of the traditional linking of parrots with Laksmi, the E. Indian Goddess of Good Fortune, an association that appears in, say, the Hopi association of the fertility rituals of Soyal and The Flute Ceremonies with parrots and/or The Parrot Clan. Parrots-fertility-luck. See Waters, *The Book of the Hopi*, already cited, pp. 196 and 260.

This whole complex of ideas is perhaps most succinctly summed up in a short tale from the northeast frontier area in India:

> There is a great snake whose name is Ka which lives sometimes in the water, sometimes in the ground. The rainbow comes from its head and climbs across the sky. When the snake is in the water, the rainbow is large and beautiful. When the snake is on the ground, the rainbow is small and you can hardly see it. (Verrier Elwin, *Myths of the North-East Frontier of India*, already cited, p. 89)

THE UNIVERSAL FLOOD (Guarao)—*Venezuela*

Page 40

SOURCE: Basilio M. de Barral, *Guarao Guarata: Lo que Cuentan los Indios Guaraos* (Caracas: no publisher cited, 1960).

Two very important motifs are simplified out of this Guarao version of the flood: (1) The motif of an angry avenging god, and (2) The motif of mankind having grown sinful and bringing down this avenging god's anger on their heads. See Eliade's *Patterns in Comparative Religion*, already cited, pp. 43–46, 88–89, 210–12.

THE STORY OF THE GREAT FLOOD (Yagua)—*Northeast Peru*

Page 41

SOURCE: Paul Fejos, *Ethnography of the Yagua* (already cited).

The simple flood story here is complicated by the appearance of a great shaman who kills the Noah prototype, Iwaoi, and takes over the "ark"/raft, which points up the essential Dravidian-Amerindian association between flood (rain) and enlightenment. "Fertility"/"Power" always is two-leveled: physical and psychic. Only a yoga, a shaman, can survive the flood, which implies that the original builder of the raft, Iwaoi, was "unenlightened," unfit.

This same death-resurrection theme ends the account: mankind had to be sacrificed for the survival of the "enlightened," just as the year (or for that matter, the day) goes through a regular death and resurrection renewal cycle.

THE GREAT DARK (Warao)—Venezuela

Page 43

SOURCE: Henry Osborn, "Textos Folkloricos Warao V," in *Antropologica* (Caracas–Los Angeles: Instituto Caribe de Antropologia y Sociologia, 1970).

The gourd trees here, of course, are women. Gourds, pots, water jars are basic Dravidian-Amerindian woman symbols, and there is a myth from India that makes this connection quite explicit. A man finds some gourds in the forest, takes them home and puts them in a corner. He lives alone, but every day when he comes home he finds all the housework done. So he hides, waits, and "after a little while, he saw a girl come out of one of the gourds and clean the house, fetch water and cook the food. When she had finished, and was about to return into the gourd . . . [he] came out of his hiding-place and caught her by the hair. She struggled to escape, but he held her tightly and at last broke the gourd and persuaded the girl to live with him as his wife." (Elwin, *Myths of the North-East Frontier of India*, already cited, p. 112.)

We have already discussed the association between women and rain/water (see notes on Toba-Pilagá "The Flood"), but it is rather interesting to see the myth of the "Fall" associated not with the Tree of Knowledge but the Gourd-Tree of woman, which may reflect an earlier totally matrilinear, matriarchal society in which the primary taboos centered around male violation of female social (and sexual) rights. Might the original "Fall" have been related to a male abuse of the equilibrium in the primal matriarchal world?

THE LONG NIGHT (Toba-Pilagá)—Gran Chaco, Argentina

Page 44

SOURCE: Alfred Métraux, *Myths of the Toba and Pilagá Indians of the Gran Chaco* (already cited).

"The Long Night" nicely illustrates the essentially cyclic nature of the Dravidian-Amerindian cosmic vision. To the Dravidian-Amerindian, both the day and the year were forms of cosmic death and resurrection.

Added to these were the "yugas," the longer death-resurrection time spans (see Danielou's *Hindu Polytheism,* already cited, p. 249). John Dowson gives a rather bloodlessly analytical account of the Yugas in his *A Classical Dictionary of Hindu Mythology* . . . (London: Routledge and Kegan Paul, 1950, pp. 381–83), but perhaps the fullest account that has come down to us is the Aztec version, "The Legend of the Four Suns." The Toba-Pilagá account describes the period of the First Sun (the Krta Yuga). The Aztec version reads: "Those who lived in this first Sun were eaten by ocelots. It was the time of the Sun 4-Tiger . . . Thus, they perished and all ended. At this time, the Sun was destroyed." (León-Portillo, *Aztec Thought and Culture,* already cited, p. 38.)

The idea of people turning into animals seems symbolic of moral/spiritual decay. In fact, the original Dravidian yuga-system is actually mathematical in its degree of progressive decay. Righteousness decreases by a fourth, a half, three fourths, then practically disappears altogether. Opening the eyes slowly in order to stay human, consequently, is probably a reference to slowly returning to spiritual "rightness." Those who repent remain human.

In order to understand the full importance of individual penance in relation to cosmic events, read Duran's account of Aztec penances/festivals preceding the feast of Huitzilopochtli (the sun) in his *Book of the Gods and Rites and the Ancient Calendar* (Norman: University of Oklahoma Press, 1971), p. 450ff. In Frank Waters' *Book of the Hopi* (already cited, p. 168ff.), you get an excellent feeling for the penitential atmosphere that precedes and surrounds the winter solstice.

THE FIRST INHABITANTS OF THE EARTH (Guarao)—Venezuela

Page 45

SOURCE: Basilio Maria de Barral, *Guarao Guarata: Lo que Cuentan los Indios Guaraos* (already cited), pp. 139–40.

On a symbolic level, this story confronts the problem of Yogic "enlightenment." What usually confuses the Western/occidental reader is that the "ascent" to "enlightenment" here isn't an ascent at all, but a descent: in the Amerindian-Dravidian mind there is a permanent structural ambiguity about the source of Yogic power. Within the parameters of the Earth-Mother/Earth-Power mystique, the real source of power is always *down*. See, for example, Thompson's *Maya History and Religion* (Norman: University of Oklahoma Press, 1970), pp. 294–97, 300–4, for an account of earth-oriented deities among the Maya. For an East Indian analogue, see Elwin's *Myths of the North-East Frontier of India,* already cited, pp. 15–16.

Another theme implicit in this myth is that of "necessary sacrifice," a theme that is much more obvious in the Iroquoian version (see J. N. B.

Hewitt, *Iroquoian Cosmology* in the *21st Annual Report of the U. S. Bureau of Ethnology*, Washington, D.C.: U. S. Government Printing Office, 1903, especially p. 178ff.). In a sense, a sacrifice has to be made, the old woman has to stay behind in the sky, or (in the Onondaga-Iroquoian version) a woman has to be cast *out of the sky* . . . for the sake of cosmic order. The Pleiades quite significantly play a key role in the Hopi Soyal (Winter Solstice) ceremonies (see Waters, *Book of the Hopi*, p. 193). The Guarao version speaks of the old woman "plugging up the opening into heaven." She—as Pleiades—serves as the year's pivot point. The ascent/descent into "enlightenment" parallels the year's pivoting back to spring/fertility—both based on the sacrifice of the old chief's wife.

WHEN IT WAS DECIDED TO MAKE MAN (Maya)—Meso-America

Page 46

SOURCE: *Popol Vuh: The Sacred Book of the Ancient Quiché Maya*, English translation by D. Goetz and S. G. Morley from Adrián Recinos' Spanish version (Norman: University of Oklahoma Press, 1969), pp. 165–73.

Written shortly after the Spanish Conquest by an anonymous Quiché Indian, the *Popol Vuh* is one of the largest sources of Amerindian-Dravidian lore that has survived.

One of the basic themes in the world of the Great Tradition is the inherent antagonism between the "gods" and "men," an antagonism concretized around the terms "Titans" and "Olympians" among the Greeks. The *Popol Vuh* throws some interesting light on this antagonism. The first men were completely "yogic": "when they looked, instantly they saw all around them, and they contemplated in turn the arch of heaven and the round face of the earth." The creators, the "Olympians," in order to avoid equality between them and their creation, change the visionary scope of mankind: "Let their sight reach only to that which is near." The image of the clouded mirror comes through here, "through a glass darkly," a much-used theme in Aztec mysticism (see, for example, C. A. Burland's *The Gods of Mexico*, London: Eyre and Spottiswoode, 1967, pp. 44, 64, 65, regarding the Aztec magic-centered mirror cult) and, in fact, throughout Amerindian yoga. I have seen various Meso-American mirror-cult objects showing a Yoga staring into a mirror which can be explained—in this overall crystal- and mirror-related Yoga—as a common practice in Tibetan Yoga: "During the mystic initiation, here called the mystic conferring of power, there is employed a mirror, symbolical of the Mirror of Karma, in which all good and evil deeds of the neophyte are said to be mystically reflected." (*Tibetan Yoga and Secret Doctrines*, ed. W. Y. Evans-Wentz, London: Oxford Press, 1958, p. 210ff.)

The prayer for "light" at the end of this selection is a prayer for "enlightenment," and specifies the Morning Star, the Great Star—which in Middle America refers specifically to Quetzalcoatl, the Great Yoga, and who appears under various names throughout the Great Tradition: Hermes, Siva, Prometheus, etc. In this context, the whole idea of "trickster" takes on a different light. The "trickster" is the one who attempts to return mankind to its primal state of enlightenment. The whole process of the bringing of "fire" ultimately refers to the bringing of "enlightenment."

EMERGENCE MYTH (Cubeo)—Northwest Amazon, mainly in Colombia

Page 52

SOURCE: I. Goldman's *The Cubeo* (Urbana: University of Illinois Press, Illinois Studies in Anthropology, No. 2, 1963), pp. 111–12.

This is an analogue to the Hopi migration-emergence myth (see Waters, *Book of the Hopi*, p. 37ff.), which in turn is analagous to the Peyote Pilgrimage of the Huichol Indians in Mexico (see Peter T. Furst, *Flesh of the Gods*, New York: Praeger, 1972, p. 136ff.). The "migration-emergence" is two-leveled, actual and symbolic. Take the section about the Milk Tree, for example. The Huichol analogue is the Water of Our Mothers (Furst, pp. 166–67). The milk here means "enlightenment" and the whole pilgrimage under the tutorship of the Ancients (*gurus*) is precisely for the tribe as a whole to "shed their anaconda skins"—in other words, be reborn.

One difficulty in this Cubeo version of this initiation/death-rebirth process is the problem of ellipsis or omission. Take the section about the milk-whirlpool and the dove turning into a rock. The full account (here in a Greek version dating from about 200 B.C.) is found in the story of the Argonauts in which the doves are let loose and they fly between clashing rocks which represent the passageway into "enlightenment":

After being delivered from the Harpies, Phineus revealed to the Argonauts their sailing course and advised them about the Symmplegades [rocks] which were in the sea. They were vastly high, and when swung together by the winds' force, they closed the sea-passage. A thick mist swept over them and the crash was severe; it was impossible even for birds to slip through. So, he told them to let a dove fly through the rocks, and if they saw it get through safe, to steer through with easy minds, but if they saw it perish, not to force a passage.

With this information, they put to sea, and on nearing the rocks, let a dove fly from the prow. As she flew in, the clash of the rocks nipped off the tip of her tail. So, they waited till the rocks slid open; then

411

with hard rowing and Hera's aid, they won through . . . (Jack Lindsay, *The Clashing Rocks*, London: Chapman and Hall, 1965, p. 34)

Compare this to the Cubeo version, which has merely: "They came to the place of rushing waters, a whirlpool of milk, to the rapids of the dove, where a dove dropped into the water and turned into a rock."

Space here doesn't allow, but in order to extract the full meaning of the Cubeo myth, what has to be done is to reconstitute the myth from Greek and other sources. The version that has come down to us in classical Hinduism centers around the churning of the ocean which produced SOMA—the Indian equivalent of Greek Ambrosia, the Huichol Peyote (see Danielou, *Hindu Polytheism*, p. 167).

For an analogue of the water-leaping (Bwü, the agouti), see Lindsay, p. 217. The leap represents ecstasy/initiation. The phallic-dwarf, Opómbibekü, is probably a Yaksa—an "underworld" water-, fertility-, vegetation-spirit. He might even be Varuna, the "owner of the magic power (*maya*)." He is the owner of Soma, ruler of the Yaksas and antigods, and is even the god of death/the underworld (see Danielou, *Hindu Polytheism*, p. 118ff. and Ananda K. *Coomaraswamy*, Yaksas, Part II, Washington: Smithsonian Institution, 1931, Miscellaneous Collections, Vol. 80, No. 6).

THE HOUSE OF THE CREATOR (Guarao)—Venezuela

Page 54

SOURCE: Barral's *Guarao Guarata: Lo que Cuentan los Indios Guaraos*, pp. 4–5.

There are echoes here of the Buddhist theory of the universe and the ocean around the central mountain, Mount Meru, which in turn *may* be actually based on the city of Tiahuanaco, lying on the shores of Lake Titicaca, the highest lake in the world (see Waddell's *Tibetan Buddhism*, already cited, pp. 77–78). At the same time, though, the account itself is similar in many ways to the common Amerindian account of the visit to the House of the Sun (see, for example, the Cherokee version in the *19th Annual Report of the Bureau of American Ethnology*, pp. 255–56, Washington, D.C.: U. S. Government Printing Office, 1900) *and* the account of life after death in *The Tibetan Book of the Dead*. It is almost as if the New World, the Andes, Titicaca, Tiahuanaco, the Rocky Mountains, the Grand Canyon, etc. somehow became transformed into the standard New and Old World symbols for Heaven and Hell.

This Guaraos account, then, may be merely a symbolic story of after-death and its trials in the under-/over-world, but having seen the procession of the Incas with their Condor-head emblems ("City of the Vultures") after the Devil's Dance (Diablada) in Bolivia, having been stung by a Bolivian hornet, having gone in a reed boat out into the waters of the "Upper Sea" (Lake Titicaca), having stood in front of the Gateway of the Sun . . . ("It's like a gate, a door . . ."), it is difficult not to imagine that in some remote age religious/ceremonial centers like Tiahuanaco became—for less "developed" tribes like those in Venezuela —something like what Mecca is for the contemporary Moslem; hence the association with "heaven," the holy.

THE GREAT FIRE (Toba-Pilagá)—Gran Chaco, Argentina

Page 56

SOURCE: Métraux's *Myths of the Toba and Pilagá Indians of the Gran Chaco* (already cited), pp. 33–34.

What we have here is an almost exact duplication of the section of the Aztec Legend of the Four Suns dealing with destruction by fire:

It rained fire upon them. They became turkeys.
This Sun was consumed by fire. All their homes burned . . .
They perished when it rained fire for a whole day . . .
They who perished were those who had become turkeys. (León-Portilla's *Aztec Thought and Culture*, pp. 38–39)

Although what we have here on one level is a retelling of a common myth, there are two other levels to be considered: (1) The myth as cosmological event (see, for example, Velikovsky's *Worlds in Collision, Ages in Chaos*, etc.) and (2) Myth as description of spiritual states. There is, after all, implicit in this whole structure of successive ages, the idea of moral decline and divine punishment.

FIRE (Apinaye)—Brazil

Page 57

SOURCE: *The Apinayé* by Curt Nimuendajú, trans. R. H. Lowie (Oosterhout: Anthropological Publications, 1967), pp. 154–58.

Here we have another variation on the Trickster Myth—which at the same time is a parable centering around "enlightenment," the second-level meaning of "fire." In Christian terms, there must be a "redeemer," an intermediary between Heaven (enlightenment) and Earth (yet-to-be-enlightened); the bringing down of fire is analogous to the descent of the Holy Spirit on Pentecost. There is an interesting variation here from the Aztec version of the fire-bringing myth, because among the Aztecs the fire-bringer is Xolotl, Quetzalcoatl in his form as Hound of Heaven, and elsewhere the fire-bringer is Raven (see Laurette Séjourné, *El Universo de Quetzalcoatl*, Mexico: Fondo de Cultura Economica, 1962, p. 70ff.). At the same time, though, Xolotl is sometimes (Ibid., p. 75) identified with the SUN. He is Siva-Hermes-Prometheus, the Hopi

413

Másaw, the Chief Yoga, Chief Ascetic, the link between the Under- and Over-Worlds. In this Apinaye version, the Fire-Bringer is not really the sun of the Sun-Jaguar. And it's the same situation with the Greek Titans:

> . . . the Titans were gods, the earlier gods, *próteroi theoi*. Gaia, the Earth, the Pristine Mother, had borne them by Urbanos, her firstborn son. As gods and sons of Heaven, they belonged to the divine-heavenly pole of the two-part cosmology. But, nearly all of them ended up under ground, in the deepest maw of the earth, under Tartaros. (C. Kerenyi, *Prometheus: Archetypal Image of Human Existence,* trans. R. Manheim, New York: Bollingen Books, 1963, p. 25)

See also Kerenyi's excellent essay at the back of P. Radin's *The Tricksters: A Study in American Indian Mythology* (already cited).

I also can't help but feel that the TITANOMACHIA, the War of the Titans, with their exile to the Greek Underworld (which, incidentally, is paralleled in the Hindu *Siva-Purana,* Vol. II, already cited) is really a description of the migrations of the Dravidians with their gods —the próteroi theoí—to the New World.

SUN AND MOON (Apinaye)—Brazil

Page 61

SOURCE: *The Apinayé,* pp. 158–65.

The Sun and Moon here represent the Twin Form of the primordial Trickster. The Twins (the Dioscuri), like the Titans, serve as intermediaries between Heaven and Earth, and there is a vast literature and tradition out of which this Brazilian version has emerged. See, for example, Rendel Harris' study of the twins, *Boanerges* (Cambridge: Cambridge University Press, 1913), especially Chapter I, and Donald Ward's *The Divine Twins: An Indo-European Myth in Germanic Tradition* (Berkeley–Los Angeles: University of California Press, 1968), especially the first two chapters. The Twins, here Sun and Moon, often represent the Morning and Evening Star; one is usually of divine/heavenly origin, the other has an earthly father—although they are twins and do have the same mother. One usually is "smooth," the other is "rough"; one is "celestial," the other "earthly." My own feeling is that this dichotomy is perhaps best explained in terms of the antagonism between the Powers of Day and the Powers of Night, something which comes out very explicitly in Egyptian myth, especially in the *Am-Tuat* (see E. A. W. Budge, *The Egyptian Heaven and Hell,* London: M. Hopkinson, 1925, pp. 3–40).

One other point needs some explanation: the nastiness of Sun/ Trickster here toward Moon, who almost seems to represent Mankind. Trickster tries to create imperfections and defects in things. He is both "redeemer" and at the same time "cause" of a "fall" from a paradisal condition, a fact that I feel may mirror an aristocratic-plebeian antagonism in Trickster's original nature. He serves as an intermediary between Heaven (the Ruling Class) and Mankind; but at the same time he leans heavily toward the aristocratic elements in his own background. I wonder, might not this antagonism mirror some historical-sociological tensions between King and People in prehistoric times when this "myth" was being formed?

THE SUN, THE SUN'S WIFE, SUN, MOON, AND STARS, and THE MOON'S DAUGHTERS (all Guarao)—Venezuela

Pages 67–69

SOURCE: *Guarao Guarata* (Barral), pp. 61–64, 66–67.

The least garbled, most straightforward version of these various sun and moon myths is in Alexander M. Stephen's "Hopi Tales," *The Journal of American Folklore*, (New York: American Folklore Society, January–March 1929), Vol. 42, No. 163. The "constants" in terms of the Great Tradition are: (1) A Sun-Father, (2) A Virgin Mother who gets pregnant through the agency of the sun's rays, (3) Twins, (4) The Twins seeking their father, (5) Their being tested by their father, (6) The Twins as Tricksters/Helpers of mankind. This whole complex story is perhaps best served by comparing it to its somewhat familiar Greek version where the Sun is Zeus, the mother of the Twins is the Earth-Mother, and the Twins themselves are the Dioscuri (see Arthur Bernard Cook's *Zeus: A Study in Ancient Religion*, Cambridge: Cambridge University Press, 1914, I, p. 776ff.). The whole relation of Siva and Parvati and their offspring Kama (Cupid) reflect yet another version of this same myth—perhaps retaining archaic elements such as Siva's and Parvati's (under the avatar of Kali) essential earth- (snake-) nature.

The Guaraos' sun myth "The Sun," of course, is an inversion of the Trickster/Prometheus/Quetzalcoatl myth whereby fire is brought to the earth and not vice versa. "The Sun's Wife," interestingly enough, shows the Great Goddess swallowing the Sun at night, which reflects back on the Egyptian concept of the sun's being "destroyed" every night, which I discussed in the notes on the Apinaye myth "Sun and Moon." "Sun, Moon, and Stars" is very close to its Greek analogues where the Great Goddess appears (under the names Selene, Io, Pasiphae, Europe, and Antiope) as Moon Goddess. "The Moon's Daughters" is an American version of the story of Cupid and Psyche (see M. Grant, *Myths of the Greeks and Romans*, New York: Mentor Books, 1962, p. 537ff.), which in turn seems to be a variation of the Orpheus theme (descent into Hades and reascent), which in turn is both a dramatization of the year cycle *and* Yogic initiation.

THE ADVENTURES OF THE SUN GOD (*Guaraní-Mybá*)—Paraguay

Page 70

SOURCE: Cadogan's *La Literatura de los Guaranies* (already cited), pp. 74–85.

Here, the "sky father" ("Zeus" for the sake of identification) assumes a bird form in order to seduce Mother Earth (here still a child), a very important tie-in between the Sky-, Rain-God and a whole host of Amerindian bird associations: Thunder birds, Creator birds, feather headdresses, feather *pahos* (votive "sticks"), etc. Zeus as rain, as rain of gold, as bird, etc. is all part of a general identification with Sky Father and Fertility. However, I think, the Sky Father more closely retains the original Dravidian symbolism of the Bird God as a vehicle of Yoga/Enlightenment (see Danielou, *Hindu Polytheism*, p. 160). The paradisal garden with its accompanying tree are also standard props in the story (see Eliade's *Patterns in Comparative Religion*, p. 100).

There are some important departures from the "standard" story here that bear noting. Usually, the grandmother helps the son of the Sun get to his Father, and it's usually the Father (the Sun) who "tests" his son (part of an initiation ritual). (See "Hopi Tales" gathered by A. M. Stephens, referred to in the notes on "The Sun," "The Sun's Wife," etc.) Also, the narrative is a bit confusing regarding the Twins. Instead of having Twins at first (the expected), the whole theme of twins/brothers comes in when the children with Our Grandmother suddenly becomes Pa'i's closest of companions and the brother/twin relationship is made even more implicit by the fact that one of these companions is "Future Moon."

The poignant theme of bringing back the dead to life here is another constant in the story (see Elwin's *Myths of the North-East Frontier of India*, p. 78), as is the theme of animals or plants appearing as the result of someone's death (see Ibid., pp. 214–15, 216–19), and both of these themes seem related to the need to be occult (and 100 per cent precise) about magic formulae and rituals and the need of sacrifice to ensure fertility. The fragment about Nande Ru Pa'i burning up and the ashes turning into flying insects is a variation on the Phoenix theme and ties in with Garuda, the Indian Phoenix, and the whole mechanism of psychic second birth.

There is one point here that may throw some light on Greek myth: the identity of the owl as Sky Father. Cook, III, p. 776ff., identifies Athena's owl as an avatar of Athena herself and then links (p. 837ff.) Athena and Gorgon with snake- as well as owl-avatars . . . which seems an unmistakable revelation of the original bird and/or snake nature of both Sky Father and Earth Mother . . . in other terms Siva, Lord Snake, and Kali, Lady Snake.

THE STORY OF THE MOON (Tukano)—Interior of Colombia bordering on Brazil

Page 76

SOURCE: Alfonso Torres Laborde's *Mito y Cultura entre los Barasana: Un Grupo Indigena Tukano del Vaupes* (Bogota: Universidad de Los Andes, 1969), pp. 31–44.

This posthumously published volume is both one of the most irritating and valuable records in this entire anthology. Much of the text is barely translated into Spanish and the translator is left to "guess" at many of the meanings of words. But, the discontinuous, "choppy," seemingly illogical flavor of the text is valuable because it captures the essential drug-based, hallucinogenic tone of the culture.

The theme, of course, is that of initiation—which is the meaning underlying all the multiple deaths and rebirths, and transformations into animals (tigers, eagles, etc.). In order to be "initiated" one must die, be annihilated, one's old self must be destroyed. Then—through magic, through suffering—one can be revived.

The initial story (Muyhu-Méneri-Ya) is explicitly recognizable as Cupid and Psyche, which is also related to initiation/death-rebirth. See, for example, Eric Neumann's *Amor (Cupid) and Psyche* (London: Routledge and Kegan Paul, 1952) and Mircea Eliade's extremely valuable *Shamanism—Archaic Techniques of Ecstasy* (New York: Bollingen Foundation, 1964). Eliade talks about the ritual death-rebirth (p. 43), the symbolism of tiger/bear gurus/initiates (p. 72), the marriage of initiate/guru with neophyte (pp. 72–73), etc. and has a great deal of information on aboriginal Indian "supernatural marriages" (p. 432ff.), which is the E. Indian equivalent of the Cupid and Psyche tale. See also C. Kerenyi's *Eleusis—Archetypal Image of Mother and Daughter* (New York: Bollingen Foundation, 1967) (especially p. 35ff. for the rape of Kore by Dionysos as Lord of the Underworld).

The symbolic "giveaway" in this whole tale is the section that begins, "There was a place there where there was a trap just like a pair of scissors . . ." This "scissors trap" is the already familiar pair of clashing rocks through which the neophyte must pass in the course of his initiation and which we've already discussed at some length in the notes for the Cubeo Emergence Myth. The important thing to keep in mind is that every death and/or transformation is an initiation process all aimed at eventual "guruhood"—tasting the "poison," dying, being reborn and in a sense killing "god," the Eagle who is sacrificed, for the collective tribal good, but spiritual and temporal.

THE STORY OF THE STARS (Tukano)—Interior of Colombia bordering on Brazil

Page 90

SOURCE: Same as previous selection.

Here we have an interesting variation on the Fire-Bringer/Fertility-Bringer theme. These South American star maidens are close relatives of the Karatgurk (Pleiades) in Australia who carried "fire at the end of their digging sticks." See Aldo Massola, Bunjil's Cave (Melbourne, 1968), p. 108. See also "The Star Husband" (a sex-reverse of The Story of the Stars) in Sith Thompson's Tales of the North American Indians (Bloomington–London: Indiana University Press, 1966), p. 128ff.

Mingao here seems to refer to manioc (a tuber cultivated by the Amazonian Indians). As already mentioned, it is a powerful ritual hallucinogenic.

EARTH, SKY, AND WATER (Maya)—Guatemala

Page 91

SOURCE: Chorti (Mayan) Texts, already cited, pp. 371–80.

Perhaps the best place to begin to understand this account of the Underworld is in the Odyssey (see Michael Grant's Myths of the Greeks and Romans, already cited, pp. 81–83) and/or in the New Hebrides myth of Malekula. The Sea of Tar (in Maya, Tar is Tzak-in) may be even etymologically related to Tartaros, both a name for Hades (see Kerényi's Prometheus, already cited, p. 112) and the name of the darkness that "filled the world before earth, air, and heaven appeared." (See J. Fontenrose, Python: The Study of Delphic Myth and Its Origins, Berkeley–Los Angeles: University of California Press, 1959, p. 223.) The "Underworld" Naga-Loka is classical Hinduism—the Snake World in both Greek and ancient East Indian myth—is "beyond ocean." It is the "netherworld" . . . the New World. Here in the Maya version, it is no longer "out there" but "under here." The New World is Hades, and Maya himself was a Dravidian chief who built cities for the Dravidians exiled to the New World. (See The Siva-Purana, already cited, II, 807.)

HYMN TO VIRACOCHA, INCA PRAYER FOR ENLIGHTENMENT, HYMN TO THE SUN, PRAYER FOR THE INCA, HYMN OF THE INCA RUKA, THE INCA WASKAR PRAYS TO THE WAK'AS (Inca)—Peru-Bolivia

Pages 97–101

SOURCE: J. Lara's La Literatura de los Quechuas (Cochabama: Bolivia Editorial Canelas, 1960) pp. 158, 159, 160–62, 166–67.

Viracocha is one of the most tantalizing god names in all of Indo-America. *Bir* or *Vira* is still a common god name in aboriginal India; KailuBIR/VIR, for example, is the father of all Nagas (snakes), and Narsingh-Bir/Vira is a name applied to Vishnu as Man-Lion. (See W. Crooke and R. E. Enthoven, *Religion and Folklore of Northern India*, New Delhi, 1925, pp. 200–1.) *Cocha* in Quechua means sea; *Mamacocha* is Mother Sea. So, perhaps *Viracocha* is the Vira (God) of the Sea or *from* the Sea—a Peruvian version of Quetzalcoatl.

In the "Hymn to the Sun," instead of using Lara's Spanish version, where he translates *Inka* as "Monarca," I've put in the original Inka to show the very essential identification between the Sun and the Sun King, the Inca.

Another interesting word link that ties the Incas to the North American tribes is WAKA. The WAKANDA are the gods to the Sioux; here they are the gods of the Incas, only here the negative, "evil" nature of the gods/"powers" is stressed. The Inca prays to the Powers, identifies them with Thieves, thereby tying them in with Hermes/Siva/Quetzal-coatl—Masau'u (Hopi)—who are also all Patrons of Thieves—and then shows a curious ambivalence of hatred . . . and total submissiveness. Nowhere else in this anthology is this typically Tibetan/East Indian ambivalence of the gods' nature shown as dramatically as here. See H. A. Tyler, *Pueblo Gods and Myths* (Norman: University of Oklahoma Press, 1964), especially Chapter I; also R. B. Ekvall's *Religious Observances in Tibet: Patterns and Function* (Chicago: University of Chicago Press, 1964), especially p. 21ff.

PRAYER TO THE MOTHER OF THE GODS (Aztec)—Mexico

Page 101

SOURCE: Angel M. Garibay K., *La Literatura de los Aztecas* (Mexico: Editorial Joaquín Mortiz, 1964), p. 74.

The symbolic core of this song centers around the idea of sacrifice and rebirth. The image of the Obsidian Butterfly, for example, couples the idea of the sacrificial knife (Obsidian) and that of the reborn soul (Butterfly). (See Durán's *Book of the Gods*, p. 32, for description of obsidian-knife washing to prepare reanimating drink for sacrificial victim.)

The Mother of the Gods (identified as Teteu Innan, Tlalli Yiollo, and Toci by Sahagún in his *General History of the Things of New Spain*, Sante Fe: Monographs of the School of American Research, 1950, II, p. 4) is also a Goddess of Healing ("removing stones or obsidian knives from the body") and Warriors—which helps to account for the reference to broken lances. Here, she seems to be especially a Goddess of Spring/Rebirth, and as such her symbolic content is derived from the ancient strata that in archaic Greece involved the Dancing Warriors

(Kouretez), the Murder and Rebirth of Dionysus by the Mud-Headed Titans, Mock Battles, Animal Sacrifice, etc. Perhaps the best account of this whole complex of associations is in J. Harrison's *Epilego-mena and Themis* (Hyde Park, New York: University Books, 1962), pp. 1-74.

Tamoanchan and Omeyocan are related as sites of "origin," original creation. (See León-Portilla's *Aztec Thought and Culture*, already cited, p. 110.) *Tamas*, of course, in classical Hinduism refers to a state of "liberation through nonaction" (Danielou, *Hindu Polytheism*, p. 26). The etymological connotation here seems to center around an idea and/or place of "peace," spiritual origin, strength.

MOTHER MOON and HYMN TO THE WORLD TREE
("Wanka") (Inca)—Peru/Bolivia

Pages 102-3

SOURCE: Lara's *Literatura de los Quechuas*, already cited, pp. 168 and 188-89.

Both these poems reflect the archaic juxtaposition of the Mother Goddess and Trees, Rain, Moon . . . in a word, World Fertility. As Eliade points out in his *Patterns in Comparative Religion*, already cited, "In the pre-Aryan civilization of the Indus Valley . . . the identification of the Great Goddess with vegetation is represented either by association— nude goddesses of the Yaksini type beside *ficus religiosa*—or by a plant emerging from the goddess's genital organs" (p. 280). The name of this goddess in historic Hinduism is Lakshmi Sri and she is Moon Goddess, Rain Goddess, Vegetation Goddess, Goddess of Childbirth, etc. In terms of Christian symbolism, Eve in the Garden *is* the Tree of Knowledge.

The use of "Wanka" here is much closer to that of the North American Great Plains—a sense of the sacred without a heavy overtone of punishment, negativity, evil.

LACADONE PRAYERS FROM CHIAPAS (Maya)—Mexico

Page 103

SOURCE: Demetrio Sodi M., *La Literatura de los Mayas* (Mexico: Editorial Joaquín Moritz, 1964), pp. 65-75.

The Lacadones are contemporary descendants of the Maya with some admixture of other "foreign" elements. (See J. Soustelle's *The Four Suns*, New York: Grossman Publishers, 1971.) These very specific prayers with their strong concentration on offering food and drink to Fire (a kind of "messenger" of the High God referred to as Father) can perhaps be best and most completely understood in the context of contemporary East Indian fire sacrifice. Mrs. Sinclair Stevenson's *The Rites of the Twice-Born* (New Delhi: Oriental Books Reprint Corporation, 1971) is an excellent insider's study of these rites, in which for the most part a sacrifice of liquid—clarified—butter takes the place of the sacrificial objects (pozole, beans, tamales, etc.) that we find used by the Lacadones; although, especially in East Indian Vishnu worship (see Stevenson, p. 402ff.), whole meals are still offered as sacrifice. Another very rewarding approach to the comparative study of these prayers is through the East Indian-Semitic tradition, which historically is another branch on the old Dravidian-Amerindian trunk. *Leviticus* in the Old Testament, for example, especially Chapter 1 (Holocausts or Burnt Offerings), Chapter 2 (Offerings of Flour and Fruit), and Chapter 3 (Burning of Animals for Sacrifice) are close parallels to Lacadone usages.

OFFERTORY PRAYERS FROM QUINTANA ROOS (Maya)— Mexico

Page 115

SOURCE: Sodi's *La Literatura de los Mayas,* already cited, pp. 53–60.

For background information on these prayers (and alternative translations into English) see Alfonso Villa Rojas' *The Maya of East Central Quintana Roo* (Publication 559 of the Carnegie Institution, Washington D.C., 1945, pp. 159–60) and the same author's (in collaboration with R. Redfield) *Chan Kom, A Maya Village* (Chicago: University of Chicago Press, 1934, Appendix C, beginning on p. 339).

These prayers, whose transcription dates from 1932–35, are highly syncretic. I've left out the "Dios Yumbil, Dios Mehenbil, Dios Espiritu Santo" (God the Father, Son, and Holy Ghost) formulas with which they usually begin, but the native gods are nicely mixed with the Christian Trinity and the saints to produce a whole new religion. Some of the old gods still survive intact, though, XKan Le Ox (Kanleox) is Mother of the Gods, creatrix of Lacadone women. The Chacs are the rain gods, the Hindu Dig-Gajas, the elephants of the four quarters. The Jaguars (Balams) aren't so much cosmic as municipal (the guardians of the city/farm), although here Balams and Chacs seem to have become almost interchangeable. The root meaning of *Balam* in both Maya and Sanskrit is connected with the idea of Guardian or Protector. (*Bal-a,* Sanskrit—Marital Strength; *Bal-am-il,* Maya—Guardian). See J. Eric S. Thompson's *Maya History and Religion* (Norman: University of Oklahoma Press, 1970) for more extensive information on the gods.

OFFERING TO THE EARTH SPIRIT (Chorti Maya)—Guatemala

Page 120

SOURCE: Fought's *Chorti (Mayan) Texts,* pp. 477–81.

This prayer is a good example of basic, essential worship of the Earth-Mother and is analagous to Dravidian worship of Machandri Puja

Dharti Mata, etc. (See W. Crooke's *The Popular Religion and Folklore of Northern India*, already cited, I, p. 31ff.) In both the Amerindian and Dravidian ceremonies, animals (usually fowl) and food are sacrificed. Chilate is made out of toasted corn, chili, and cocoa.

NAHUATL BIRTH-CEREMONY SONG (Aztec)—Mexico

Page 123

SOURCE: Codice Florentino, quoted in Miguel León-Portilla's *Aztec Thought and Culture* (Norman: University of Oklahoma Press, 1963), p. 88.

The apparent contradiction of calling Our Lord and Master "she of the jade skirt" is resolved in the Dravidian-Amerindian mind by the prehistoric Saivistic concept of Siva-Sakti (Danielou's *Hindu Polytheism*, already cited, pp. 254–55)—the Creative Divine Power—as bisexual. The image here in Nahuatl—as in classic Hinduism—is cosmic. Siva-Sakti represent the "form of the Immensity" (Danielou, p. 255).

NAMING CEREMONY (Cubeo)—Northwest Amazon

Page 124

SOURCE: I. Goldman, *The Cubeo*, already cited, pp. 172–73.

This Cubeo naming ceremony is a re-enactment of the ancient Dravidian-Mycenaean "myth" of the parenthood of Uranus (Uráhana) and Gaia (Hihédu). The sister in the myth is probably Rhea (the Cubeo Djurédo), and the child—unnamed—is Cronus. For details see Hesiod's *Theogony*, trans. R. Lattimore (Ann Arbor: University of Michigan Press, 1959), p. 130ff. The underlying motif here seems to be to re-enact Cronus' escape from being eaten by his father Uranus/Uráhana, and so with a kind of sympathetic "magic" assure the child's survival. Gaia/Hihédu, of course, is The Earth—as Hesiod describes her, "Gaia of the broad breast," an identification of Earth with maternity, which is also stressed in this Cubeo ceremony.

CURING (Chorti Maya)—Guatemala

Page 126

SOURCE: Fought's *Chorti (Mayan) Texts*, already cited, pp. 272–75.

Perhaps the best way to approach Amerindian curing rites is to compare them with Catholic exorcism. Disease comes from evil spirits; they must be named and then exorcised: "King Mountain . . . Lightning Aimer, Thunder Aimer carry you away." King Mountain/Lightning Aimer, of course, is the equivalent of Zeus. The "high" gods, the sky gods, drive out the "low" gods . . . the earth and under-earth spirits.

The blue and white rings seem to refer to the heavens through which the gods must pass on the way to earth to effect a cure/exorcism. (See Waddell's *Tibetan Buddhism*, already cited, p. 77ff.) The reference to the "rainbow of your appearance" ties in nicely with the identity of King Mountain/Lightning Aimer and Quetzalcoatl, the Plumed, the Rainbow Serpent. At the same time, it almost seems as if the "high" god coming to exorcise the sick person is also the tormentor; this is the same kind of dualistic, evil-good god-identification that is still common in contemporary Tibetan Buddhism. In a way, the demons to be exorcised are the same as the gods who drive them out.

EXORCISING THE XIXIMAI (Chorti Maya)—Guatemala

Page 129

SOURCE: Fought's *Chorti (Mayan) Texts*, pp. 503–5.

The exorcism here is concerned with the malevolent death, the *xiximai*. *Xib* in colonial Yucateca Maya refers to something that spreads like smoke or fog, an obvious reference to the spirits of the dead, and Xibalba in the classic Maya work *Popol Vuh* is the Underworld. It is very enlightening to contrast this Guatemala exorcism of the dead with that in contemporary India. Details correspond even down to the particular concentration on the hearth with which the Maya piece concludes. (See W. Crooke's *The Popular Religion and Folklore of Northern India*, already cited, I, especially 290ff.)

EXORCISING DISEASE (Chorti Maya)—Guatemala

Page 130

SOURCE: Fought's *Chorti (Mayan) Texts*, pp. 331–33.

This account is classic in its simplicity. A were-animal (Nagual—probably derived ultimately from Naga, someone of the Snake Clan in ancient India) serves as an intermediary between the diseased person and the Devil. The underground river of hell in Greek myth is the Styx, and in classic Hindu myth is Patala Ganga, the Underworld Ganges. The five hundred hells mentioned here are probably derived from the ancient Dravidian story that has survived in Lamaism as the story of the Yakshini (Female Fiend), Hariti, and her five hundred sons in hell. (See Waddell's *Tibetan Buddhism*, already cited, p. 99.)

OTOMI VISION-QUEST HYMN (Nahuatl)—Mexico

Page 133

SOURCE: *Ancient Nahuatl Poetry*, trans. by D. G. Brinton, New York: AMS Press, 1969) p. 75.

Brinton's translation of "Tlaocolcuica Otomitl" as "An Otomi Song of Sadness" is more *accurate* than my "Vision-Quest Hymn," but what I wanted to do was underline the extreme otherworldliness of the Nahuatl mind, which served as the starting point for their asceticism and ultimately their mysticism. The Spanish *padres* were very impressed by Aztec religious austerities, and this Otomi song or hymn must be properly placed in a context of transcendental movement away from this world into the divine, the Power World. (See, for example, Fray Diego Durán's *Book of the Gods and Rites,* already cited, p. 111ff.) Meditation, fasting, penance, a launching into vision has only recently been actually confronted in terms of a larger Semitic-Dravidian-Yogic tradition of Vision Quest.

POEM ON THE VALUE OF DEATH IN BATTLE (Nahuatl)— *Mexico*

Page 134

SOURCE: Angel M. Garibay K.'s *La Literatura de los Aztecas* (Mexico: Editorial Joaquín Moritz, 1964), p. 73.

The emeralds and turquoise feathers of the Giver of Life here echo Durán's description of the statue of Huitzilopochtli in his *Book of the Gods and Rites* (pp. 72–73). Huitzilopochtli is a Zeus-like sun god. The same kind of turquoise-sun link occurs in much of Amerindia. (See, for example, G. A. Reichard's *Navaho Religion* (New York: Pantheon Books, 1950), I, pp. 114 and 123–29; II, p. 495ff.) Obsidian has ritual-sacrifice as well as battle connotations. The Aztecs, more than any other Amerindian tribe, embodied the battle mystique of their remote Dravidian ancestors. As Alfonso Caso points out in his *El Pueblo del Sol* (Mexico, 1962), warriors who die in battle go to a special "House of the Sun" called Tonatiuhichan (p. 78). This House of the Sun, of Zeus the Thunderer, unmistakably shows its Greek or pre-Greek origin. Our English word "thunder" goes back to the Latin *tonare,* which in turn is derived from the Greek Bporth.

THE SONG OF THE COLIBRÍ THUNDERBIRD (Chiripá-Guaraní) —Paraguay

Page 134

SOURCE: *La Literatura de los Guaranies,* ed. by L. Cadogan (already cited).

In Guarani, the Colibrí is the mythical Bird Messenger of the Gods. He is always accompanied by lightning and gets drunk on nectar—the chicha (corn liquor) used during rituals. The classical Hindu equivalent of Colibrí is Garuda, whose name comes from the Sanskrit root *gr*—to speak. The equivalent contemporary Dravidian word-meaning grouping centers around a series KEL-words. (See Danielou, already cited, p. 160ff. and *A Dravidian Etymological Dictionary,* already cited, paragraph 1,677.) In classical Hinduism the Garuda bird is associated with

Soma, the ambrosia of the gods, the equivalent of the Guarani chicha. Hermes, in Greek mythology, although not a bird, still retains his winged snake staff and winged feet and serves the same function as messenger of the gods.

RITUAL SONG OF GOD THE GRANDFATHER (Paí-Kaiová-Guaraní)—Paraguay

Page 135

SOURCE: Same as the preceding, pp. 149–53.

Here we witness the creation of the world by means of ritual vestments and instruments, the *jasuká* (ritual adornment), the *jeguaká* (ritual cap), the *mba'ekuaa* (rattle), *nanduá* (adornment) and *kurusú* (cross). The thundering, flame-surrounded, law-giving god-portrait that emerges at the end is very much Zeus, our God the Father/Jaweh, and nowhere else do we see much importance given to the details of ritual; to re-enact the creation here, as among the Hopi, is to maintain it intact. There is an underlying uneasiness throughout the Amerindian-Dravidian mystique that if the proper rituals don't continue to be performed, the world will spiral down into dissolution.

RITUAL SONG OF TACUARA (Paí-Kaiová-Guaraní)—Paraguay

Page 137

SOURCE: Same as the preceding, pp. 153–54.

Essentially, what we have here is the ancient myth of the Sun (Zeus—Papa Rei) getting someone else's wife pregnant. There is a whole Mediterranean tradition of Zeus and his paramours. In the New World, Zeus is always the Sun, and the offspring are always the Twins. This is all the second part of the selection. The first part of the selection deals rather enigmatically with initial creation, climaxing with the creation of Our Grandmother (Spider Grandmother among the Hopi—in terms of a larger tradition of the First Woman) by Our Grandfather pulling on the center of his ritual cap. There is an analogy between this story and Eve being created out of Adam's rib that probably derives from a common pre-Semitic source.

RITUAL SONG WITH WHICH OUR GRANDMOTHER THRUST ASIDE THE WINDS OF THE HURRICANE (Paí-Kaiová-Guaraní)—Paraguay

Page 139

SOURCE: Same as the preceding, p. 155.

In this song, the true nature of "Our Grandfather" becomes a bit clearer. What we seem to have here is an echo of this ancient tradition that identifies what we might call the Snake Father (the snake in the Garden of Eden, Quetzalcoatl, Kanati in Cherokee Myth, Siva, etc.) with game, mineral wealth . . . and wind. Fernando Ortiz has a fascinating study on the motif called *El Huracan: Su Mitologia y sus Symbolos* (Mexico: Fondo De Cultura Edonomica, 1947). The Babylonian-Assyrian Epic of Creation, *Enuma Elish*, in which there is a battle between Marduk and the Chaos Dragon, Tiamat, is another version of this same conflict. See S. H. Hooke, *Babylonian and Assyrian Religion* (Norman: University of Oklahoma Press, 1963), pp. 53, 60ff. See also the "Adventures of the Sun God" (Guaraní-Mbyá) earlier in this volume for the identity of Paí.

SOLSTICES AND ECLIPSES (Maya)—Yucatan

Page 140

SOURCE: *The Book of Chilam Balam of Chumayel*, ed. Ralph L. Roys (Norman: University of Oklahoma Press, 1967), pp. 86–88.

Perhaps *the* central concern of the ancient peoples of the Great Tradition was the "Year-Round," the yearly cycle of solstices and equinoxes. The Egyptian pyramids, Stonehenge (and Maya temples) were all built around these points in the year's turning. (See Gerald S. Hawkins' *Beyond Stonehenge*, New York: Harper & Row, 1973, p. 183.) Here in *The Book of Chilam Balam of Chumayel* we can see some written record of these ancient concerns coming down to colonial times.

Oro means gold in Spanish. Here, it seems to mean "aura"/sunlight.

The diagram attesting to the fact that the sun and moon are not eaten during eclipses is an attempt to counter the popular belief that they are.

ASTRONOMY (Chorti Maya)—Guatemala

Page 140

SOURCE: Fought's *Chorti (Maya) Texts*, pp. 427–29.

To get some idea of the importance of stars in Amerindian ritual, see Frank Waters' *Book of the Hopi*, p. 183, where most of the stars mentioned in the Maya selection are linked to the Hopi Wúwuchim (Creation) ceremonies. I also suspect that individual stars were connected with the Olympians and Titans (the god-kings) so that stellar movements often coincide or duplicate actual historical events that have become elevated to the level of myth. The obvious tension here between Venus (Quetzalcoatl-Prometheus) and the Sun (Zeus) may be an echo, however remote, of the actual War of the Titans and Olympians.

BIRTH OF THE SUN (Chorti Maya)—Guatemala

Page 142

SOURCE: Same as the preceding, pp. 485–86.

The feast here described is the same as the Aztec sun feast on the seventeenth of March. (See Durán's *The Book of the Gods and Rites and the Ancient Calendar*, already cited, p. 414.) In the Amerindian-Dravidian calendar, our March–April is the beginning of the year. This was true not only among the Mayas and Aztecs and other New World tribes, but still holds true for Dravidians in southern India today (see S. Stevenson's *The Rites of the Twice-Born*, already cited, p. 287). Christ as Sun God is here made explicit as are the various sun-god avatars of forms, here syncretically using adopted saint names. The way that Christ and the Virgin are transformed into Sun and Moon is not in any way a contradiction to Christianity, but merely makes explicit that symbolism already contained in the Christ-Virgin iconography from the start. In a sense, what we have here are two expressions of the same ancient Semitic tradition. In contemporary India, the birth of Christ the Sun is the birth of the god Rama, the seventh incarnation of Vishnu, accompanied by the same kind of noise, incense and offerings (see *Rites of the Twice-Born*, p. 289).

ESQUIPULAS—BEGINNING OF THE YEAR (Chorti Maya)—Guatemala

Page 143

SOURCE: Same as the preceding, pp. 451–61.

Although there is a great deal of Christian overlay in the description of this feast (including the use of January as the beginning of the year), it is one of the most graphic examples possible of the conflict between the old snake-centered religion (Naga-worship) and the new Christianity. At the same time, the tension or conflict between Siva/Prometheus and Christ/God the Father fits very nicely in the older mythic pattern that was already part of Amerindian tradition—the war between Zeus (Christ/God the Father) and the Titans (the rebellious Snake-People) —so that you have layers of myth structures reaching back all the way to pre-Christianity that fit (are congruent with) the later Christian structures.

The description of people disappearing behind the altar of El Milagroso suggests human sacrifice.

I might also note that the Snake God is also Snake Goddess. We have here the old East Indian idea of a bisexual serpent deity.

BLESSING OF THE FIRST FRUITS (Paí-Kaiová)—Guarani Tribe, Paraguay

Page 151

SOURCE: *La Literatura de los Guaranies*, already cited, p. 158.

What we have here essentially is the Amerindian-Dravidian spring festival called by contemporary Hindu Holi (the basis for our word Holy, the equivalent of our Easter). Among the Dravidian hill tribes, a rag tree (Chir) is still erected during the spring ceremonies, and it is this rag tree that probably is the etymological remote cousin of Chiru in this selection. Certainly, the idea of "exchanging" adornments is common to both East Indian and Amerindian rites. In this blessing, Mburuvicha is probably a reference to MBIR (also called Miracucha), the giant-worm creator—an idea which has its origins in Siva (Lord-Snake) as creator. See Alfred Métraux, "Tribes of Eastern Bolivia and the Madeira Head-waters," in *Handbook of South American Indians* (Washington: U. S. Government Printing Office, 1948), III, p. 437. This is part of the Smithsonian Institution's Bulletin Series, Bulletin 143. See also William Crooke's *Folklore of Northern India*, already cited, p. 319.

SACRIFICIAL HARVEST CEREMONY AND PRAYERS (Mapuche-Araucanian)—Chile

Page 151

SOURCES: 1. Harvest Ceremony—*Huenun Namku—An Araucanian Indian of the Andes Remembers the Past* (Norman: University of Oklahoma Press, 1966), p. 76–81.
2. Prayers—*Estudio de Nillatun y la Religion Araucana* by Rodolfo M. Casamiquela (Bahia Blanca, Chile: Instituto de Humanidades, Universidad Nacional Del Sur, 1964), pp. 155–57.

These harvest sacrifices from Chile closely parallel their equivalents in India. (See W. Crooke and R. E. Enthoven, *Religion and Folklore of Northern India*, p. 264ff.) There is a general sense of relief, thanksgiving, a feeling that blood must be spilled to assure a continued pact with the Earth. I suspect the prayers to "Chau" here are etymologically related both to *Chacs* (the Maya rain gods) and *Chan/Kan* (the serpent). Thanksgiving is given here to Father Snake, the Lord of Animals, Rain, Fertility.

Some words that need explaining:
Kultrugn—Drum.
Gnillatun—The name of the ceremony itself.
Machi—A priest, an interesting inversion of the Maya Chilam.
Trutruka—A kind of "trumpet" made out of a hollow piece of wood tipped with a piece of corn horn.
Konchatun—Friendship, friendship ceremony.
Pifulkas—A whistle.
Mudai—Alcoholic drink of fermented grain or corn.

HARVEST SONGS OF ANGASMAYO (Quechua)—Peruvian-Bolivian Highlands

Page 158

428

SOURCE: *The Singing Mountaineers—Songs and Tales of the Quechua People*, collected by J. M. Arguedas, ed. by R. Stephan (Austin: University of Texas Press, 1957), pp. 75–90.

In the Amerindian-Dravidian world, the center of religious attention at harvest time is the Earth Mother, called in the Punjab in India Shaod Mata. (See Crooke's *Folklore of Northern India*, II, p. 309.) This same spirit of fertility—which in the Western world means smut, lasciviousness—is really the core of these Quechua harvest songs. "Guavas, guavas, guavas,/unmarried girl would you like,/guavas, guavas, guavas . . ." (song 2) is a slightly concealed invitation to sex. Nor is it a soft, pacific kind of sex. It is violent: "like an earthquake we will shake, like a thunderbolt we will sound."

Song 4 reflects the Amerindian-Dravidian preoccupation with rain/rain-dragons/thunderbirds. The little S referred to is the drawing of a snake. The "bagre" (song 5) is probably ultimately traceable back to Naga—the mythic snake people connected with fertility and rain.

HOLY WEEK (*Chorti Maya*)—*Guatemala*

Page 167

SOURCE: Fought's *Chorti (Maya) Texts*, already cited, pp. 496–99.

Here again, we encounter a tension between the old gods (the Nagas—the Christian Satan) and the new gods (Christ). Christ becomes identified with the old Maya corn god—as in all Christianity the serpent component of the Corn God disappears and he is put in opposition to his own old serpent-self. The idea of vegetation coming from blood (the sacrificial victim) is another basic element that is common both to the Dravidian-Amerindian mind and the Semitic-Christian mind that develops from it. So, Christianity and Dravidianism agree on the symbolic value of Christ as sacrificial victim essentially "causing" spring. See Mircea Eliade's *Patterns in Comparative Religion*, already cited, p. 303, Thompson's *Maya History and Religion*, already cited, p. 222ff., and Durán's *Book of the Gods and Rites and the Ancient Calendar*, p. 436ff.

THE HORNED SERPENT (*Chorti Maya*)—*Guatemala*

Page 170

SOURCE: Fought's *Chorti (Maya) Texts*, pp. 83–85.

This selection is one of the richest sources of pre-Columbian information in this volume. The Great Snake, referred to here as Sesekmil, is known in Hindu theology as Sesa. In classical Hinduism he is known as a Naga king: "Sesa . . . is the giant serpent which lies under the earth and supports its weight." (Danielou, *Hindu Polytheism*, already cited, p. 308). Atlas is his equivalent in Greek myth. The idea of the serpent being smitten by the gods refers to what is known in Greek myth as the War Against the Titans—the war between the Olympians (Zeus and his cohorts) and the earlier gods, the Titans (originally serpents). In India, its equivalent is the war between the Gods (read Aryans) and Anti-Gods (Asuras, Nagas, and other Dravidian tribes).

The association of wealth with the serpent turns up in the Western world as the Leprechaun's pot of gold. The horns refer to kingship. Sesa was a Dravidian Naga (snake)-tribe *king*.

TRUTH FROM THE SERPENT *(Maya)—Yucatan*

Page 172

SOURCE: Maud Worcester Makemson, *The Book of the Jaguar Priest*, (New York: Henry Schuman, 1951), pp. 41–66 (excerpted).

At the heart of Dravidian-Amerindian ritual is a powerful calendrical sense of the prophetic unfolding and evolving of time. We see a remnant of this in the Judeo-Christian liturgical year, but we have all but lost the archaic sense of "period"-unfolding, the Maya sense of "*katun*-prophecy."

A tun is a 360-day year, and a katun is twenty tuns—in other words, twenty years. I've taken most of the dating details out of the section here excerpted, but suggest that for further study you look at J. Eric S. Thompson's *Maya Hieroglyphic Writing* (Norman: University of Oklahoma Press, 1960), p. 145ff. What I've left is the Maya lament for the passage of the old ways, the invasion of the Spaniards, the replacing of the Truth of the Serpent by Christianity. Certainly, the Naga origin of the Mayas comes through very clearly: "Once there was truth, which we drew from the Serpent in ancient times . . ."

The Bacabs are the sky supporters, the equivalent of the classical Hindu Regents of the Four Quarters. (See Danielou, already cited, p. 131.) The Imix tree is the classical Hindu world-tree.

The men going around with trumpets, mentioned in the selection, may refer to tax collectors. When the author speaks of "the welfare of Pop and Zam," what he essentially means is "setting the calendar in order." Pop is the first month in the Maya calendar; Zam is a calendar god.

Some other words that need explanation:

Citbolon—God of Medicine.

Katun 10 Ahau—The time period 1673–93.

Sip—God who protects deer from hunters. Probably related to Xipe, the Mexican "flayed god."

The Book of the Jaguar Priest, a translation of the Book of Chilam Balam of Tizimin, was an attempt by native priests to preserve what they could of the ancient Maya lore. Their books had been burned, their priests killed, and any transmission of hieroglyphic writing (or decipherment) was forbidden. These Jaguar Priest books (written in Maya in Roman script) preserve at least some remnants of the pre-Columbian world.

LANDSLIDE (Chorti Maya)—Guatemala

Page 184

SOURCE: Fought's *Chorti (Maya) Myths*, pp. 96–99.

Another version of the Sesa myth. Again, there is the deep-rooted association between the Great Snake and money.

SNAKE-WOMAN/WOMAN-SNAKE (Chorti Maya)—Guatemala

Page 186

SOURCE: Fought's *Chorti (Maya) Myths*, pp. 110–13.

What we seem to have here is a variation of the very old (c. 7500 B.C.) tale of the Serpent and the Maiden—but with a very interesting twist to it . . . the fact that the Maiden is also a snake. (See Joseph Campbell's *The Masks of God: Primitive Mythology*, New York: Viking Press, 1970, p. 384ff.) In Hindu myth, of course, both Siva and Kali are "Snake People"—i.e., members of the Dravidian snake *clan*. In this myth, we walk into the middle of the Dravidian-Amerindian snake-god/snake-clan mystique. There is another very important point here, too: the snakes are both associated with the sea. We're not merely talking about snakes, but Naga-people rafts/boats. On one level, the breaking of the male snake's horn refers to the crippling of a boat; on the level of shamanism/mysticism, it refers to the anti-ascetic dangers of sex, which is a constant theme through Saivism in India.

THE UNDERWATER WORLD OF THE NABARAOS (Guarao)—Venezuela

Page 188

SOURCE: *Guarao Guarata—Lo que Cuentan los Indios Guaraos* (Barral), already cited, pp. 115–16.

The ultimate origin of the Nabaraos, like the Nahuatls (Mexico) or the Nazca culture (Peru) is the Nagas, the Snake Tribes from India. Here they take on a supernatural aquatic nature—probably because they are seen as "invaders" by tribes of Indians already established in Venezuela before the "invasion" from India begins. We have to keep in mind that the New World was inhabited (since at least 20,000 B.C.) by peoples who probably came into the New World across the Bering Straits. The Naga "wave," like the later Phoenicians, Vikings, Spaniards, etc., encounters, interacts with these earlier peoples.

THE SNAKE'S SWEETHEART (Quechua)—Peru-Bolivia

Page 189

SOURCE: Arguedas' *The Singing Mountaineers*, already cited, pp. 147–55.

It is rather interesting that when you actually study the myths of a Naga tribe, like the Tewa in Arizona, this story of supernatural impregnation becomes very different. It's not a snake that gets the virgin pregnant, but the sun. See Elsie Clews Parsons' *Tewa Tales, Memoirs of the American Folklore Society*, Vol. XIX (New York: American Folklore Society, 1926), p. 104ff. The Hopi version of this myth is practically the same. Presumably, what this Quechua version implies is that to the Quechuas the Naga tribes are perceived as outsiders. Nazea on the Peruvian Coast *is* Naga-based and the contact the Quechua peoples had was probably via these coastal snake tribes. In Greek myth, Zeus is sun, but also snake—an interesting blending (if not blurring) of tribal distinctions. There are a number of stories practically identical to "The Snake's Sweetheart" still circulating in India:

> There was an old woman and her daughter. One day, the girl went down to a stream and, removing her clothes, went into the water to bathe. Now, the King of Snakes was living in the stream and when he saw the girl he was very pleased and said to himself, "If I could get this girl as my wife, it would be wonderful . . . ," etc. (from Verrier Elwin's *Myths of the North-East Frontier of India*, already cited, p. 357)

All these stories may ultimately be derived from the encounter of Dravidian Naga Lord and Aryan princesses during the Aryan invasion of India. The prototype in classical Hinduism comes down to us as the marriage of Siva, Lord Naga, and the daughter of King Himalaya, Parvati.

THE MAN WHO BECAME A SNAKE (Kayapo)—Brazil

Page 196

SOURCE: *Mythos und Leben der Kayapo* by Anton Lukesch, Number 12 of the *Acta Ethnologica et Linguistica* series (Wien: Acta Ethnologica Et Linguistica, No. 12, 1968), p. 259.

Here, we have a mythic retelling of the history of the Brazilian invasion of the Naga tribes from India. The Nagas' cannibalism emerges, their alienation from the rest of the Indians. The whole mechanism of intertribal (exogamic) marriage emerges very nicely in a tale still told in Northeast India. One episode is practically a duplicate of the Brazilian tale:

> Tani went on his way and met a snake. He married her, and she bore him many children, but they were all like snakes and not human

beings. This upset Tani who said, "Your children are like you, but not like me; I'm not going to keep you any longer." He put the children in a basket and threw them away in the jungle and sent his wife after them. He thought that the snakes would die, but they lived on and became the parents of every kind of snake that is in the world today. (from Verrier Elwin's *Myths of the North-East Frontier of India*, already cited, p. 163)

This East Indian story is very helpful because it so emphatically underlines the basic problem confronted here—marrying outside your group, clan. The hero marries a bear, a deer, the snake . . . a whole series of animals (people from other clans), and the marriage always ends in disaster.

THE STORY OF THE DEVIL FROG (Tukano)—Colombia

Page 198

SOURCE: Alfonso Torres Laborde's *Mito y Cultura entre los Barasana*, already cited, pp. 50–52.

By a very curious transference, the Polynesian version of this myth, instead of calling the lover Híno, used Hina for the name of the wife. In the Polynesian version, Devil-Frog is called Monster Eel, Te Tuna— which also means The Penis. Essentially, the story revolves around the idea of ritual murder for the sake of agricultural fertility. Monster Eel dies, his head (the glans) is buried, and out of it sprouts the coconut palm. In this version, with Devil-Frog escaping, the main thrust of the myth is lost. See Joseph Campbell's *The Masks of God—Primitive Mythology* (New York: Viking Press, 1970), p. 190ff. for the original structure of the myth.

THE HEROIC MARIA-GUARI and THE VENGEANCE OF MARIA-GUARI (Guarao)—Venezuela

Page 200–2

SOURCE: *Lo que Cuentan los Indios Guaraos* (Barral), already cited, pp. 131–36.

These two stories are especially rich in echoes, traces, memories of the major proto-historical events that over the millennia became Amerindian.

Take the theme of the girl inexplicably becoming pregnant in "The Heroic Maria-Guari." In Greek myth (as well as Hopi myth—perhaps the most clear-cut of all North American myth collections), the father is always the Sun (Zeus-Hyperion), the offspring always the Twins/ Dioscuri. Here, the father doesn't descend from the sky as sunlight or a shower of gold, he seems to be a water-snake/water-monster, a Nabarao, which is a word probably ultimately derived from Naga. As I

433

point out in *Sun-World Across Ocean,* the historical father-figure behind these pregnancy myths is probably the figure known in Greek myth as Hyperion, in Hindu myth as Vishnu. He is a Titan in Greek myth—ultimately, I suppose, the best way to describe him symbolically is as a Sun Snake. The girl here comes down to us mythologically under various guises: Lakshmi (the Hindu goddess of fortune), Circe, Pandora, Aphrodite, Eve. What is extremely unusual here is the brother, Maria-Guari.[1]

"The Vengeance of Maria-Guari" is another mythologically rich story. The Witchbird and the wasps probably relate to the King of Tiahuanaco (King Vulture)/Vishnu/Hyperion—which would make the Caribs, who are destroyed in this episode, his allies. The conflict between Maria-Guari, the Nabaraos, and the Caribs, I would think, is a retelling of the war of the Gods and Anti-Gods and ultimately would reflect on interfamilial conflicts between those Dravidians who settled in Bolivia and those who settled in Ecuador, Colombia, and the Amazon Basin.

I would recommend to the interested reader that he study Chapter III of *Sun-World Across Ocean* and then reread these two myths.

FOX TAKES A WIFE, FOX TRICKS HIS PARENTS-IN-LAW, FOX BECOMES A GOOD-LOOKING YOUNG MAN AND IS ABOUT TO MARRY . . . *(Toba-Pilagá)—Chaco, Argentina*

Pages 203–5

SOURCE: *Myths of the Toba and Pilagá Indians of the Gran Chaco* by Alfred Métraux (Philadelphia: American Folklore Society, 1946). This is Volume 40 of the *Memoirs of the American Folklore Society*, pp. 122–23, 134.

Carancho is the equivalent of Prometheus in Greek myth, and Fox seems to be Epimetheus, Prometheus' brother. The Old World stories about the Titans don't help us much in identifying their antics in the New World, because the New World sources are much fuller than anything that comes down to us via the Greeks—probably because most of the events that historically happened (and are "mythically" described) to the Tricksters (read Titans) occurred in the New World. This "twin" or "brother" motif, though, is common throughout Amerindian Trickster stories. In the Assinbone Trickster myths we have Inktonmi and Sitconski, in the Aztec myths we have Quetzalcoatl and Tezcatlipoca, etc. See Paul Radin's *The Trickster—A Study in American Indian Mythology* (New York: Schocken Books, 1972). The ultimate source for all these Trickster tales seems to be in a Siva-like character

[1] If we look at the Rama avatar of Vishnu, then Rama's brother, Lakshmana, is probably an analogue for Maria-Guari. (See Danielou, *Hindu Polytheism,* p. 173.) Rama is the *solar* incarnation of Vishnu.

or characters who emigrated from India to the New World before 3000 B.C. Siva, as he emerges in, say the *Siva-Purana*, always changing forms, using his power of illusion (Maya) to assume different forms, fits the Trickster model very closely.

THE VULTURE KING'S DAUGHTER and THE FROG AND FIRE (Guarao)—Venezuela

Pages 206–9

SOURCE: *Lo que Cuentan los Indios Guaraos*, already cited, pp. 76–78, 101–2.

"The Vulture King's Daughter" almost exactly duplicates the events in the ancient Indian *Siva-Purana*. A king (King Himalaya in the *Siva-Purana*), a daughter (Parvati in India), and an unwilling son-in-law (Siva). Did the events described happen in the New World, or were they transferred from the Old World *as* myth and merely been handed down? The answer is further complicated by the fact that, as I point out in *Sun-World Across Ocean*, King Vulture certainly seems to be a reference to the King of Tiahuanaco, Bolivia. Now, Tiahuanaco is a huge, impressive ruin, but in 3,000 B.C. it was a highly developed, densely populated complex of palaces and temples. It may just be that the events described in the *Siva-Purana* did take place in the New World and that what we have here is a description of historical events that were—as story—later transferred to India and made their way into the *Siva-Purana*. At any rate, "The Vulture King's Daughter" is a description of Yogic Siva and King Himalaya's (King Vulture's) daughter.

"The Frog and Fire" is another Siva-Prometheus story. Instead of a Naga (snake), a frog is substituted—a common kind of substitution throughout Dravidian-Amerindian myth.

THE STORY OF THE PUMA AND THE FOX, THE NIGHT BUTTERFLY, THE MURDERER AND THE SHEPHERD and THE CONDOR AND THE FOX (Quechua)—Peru-Bolivia

Pages 210–12

SOURCE: Adolfo Vienrich's *Fabulous Quechuas* (Lima: Ediciones Lux, 1961), pp. 33, 41, 45, 74–76.

The stories here have almost lost their historicity and become just stories. Some trace of historicity, though, still hangs on.

"The Night Butterfly," for example, is a retelling of the classical Greek story of Amor and Psyche, which in turn plugs us into a whole series of Greek-Amerindian myths revolving around Persephone and the Underworld—probably "historically" based on the marriage of a Dravidian princess to a Snake-Clan priest/warrior exiled in the underground cavern world of Ecuador.[1] For the Greek version of the story with an extended commentary, see Erich Neumann's *Amor and Psyche*, trans. Ralph Manheim (Princeton: Princeton University Press, 1971).

The Fox-Condor and the Fox-Puma stories ultimately are traceable back to the conflict between the Gods (Condor-Puma) and the Titans (Fox). As a matter of fact, the Sun Gate at Tiahuanaco in Bolivia has as its main motif both condors and pumas, and it was in the area around Tiahuanaco that the Sun God (in Amerindian myth simply Sun, in Hindu myth Vishnu, in Greek myth Hyperion) actually lived. Through the millennia, the historical conflict between the King of Tiahuanaco and the other Dravidian princes has been watered down to these simple animal fables.

THE STORY OF YEBÁ (Barasana)—Northeast of Amazon Basin

Page 213

SOURCE: *Mito y Cultura entre los Barasana* by Alfonso Torres Laborde (Bogatá: University of the Andes, 1969), already cited, pp. 45–50.

Here, we are in the middle of the hallucinogenic Yagé world of the Barasana, where all myth takes on the coloration of hallucination. Claude Lévi-Strauss's *From Honey to Ashes* (New York: Harper and Row, 1973) is very helpful here. His structuralist technique is to isolate the bones of a basic "structure" under a number of myth-variants and then from knowns fill in "blanks"—unknowns. Yebá here is the culture hero who brings good tobacco into the world. Lévi-Strauss reasons that "a myth about the origin of tobacco . . . reflects myths about the origin of fire" (p. 61)—which makes Yebá a kind of Prometheus/Epimetheus, and his wife, Pandora. As I point out in *Sun-World Across Ocean*, Pandora in Greek myth is practically interchangeable with Circe, Aphrodite (which essentially means that Circe, Aphrodite and Pandora all arise from a common prototype), and it is under the guise of Aphrodite that we can relate this Amazon myth to its ancient Greek counterparts. In this context, Yebá becomes a god, interchangeable with Prometheus/Epimetheus—Hephaistos—and the story becomes that of Aphrodite's adulterous relation with Ares. See T. D. Seymour's *Life in the Homeric Age* (New York: Biblo and Tannen, 1963), pp. 433–34.

This kind of structuralist juggling, then, transforms what may at first look like nonsense into recognizable myth which, in turn, looks back to actual "history." The symbolic or etiological content of the myth, of course, now begins to make a lot more sense. The Titans (who ultimately seem to include Hephaistos) are the "Founding Fathers" of the

[1] See my *Sun-World Across Ocean*, Chapter IV, "Toward a Geography of Heaven and Hell." Von Daniken describes these caverns at some length in *The Gold of the Gods*.

South American tribes, their culture heros, "creators," the source of their entire way of life and material well-being.

THE GIRL AND THE "ACHACHILA," THE ORIGIN OF THE CHINCHILLA and THE ORIGIN OF COCA (Aymara)—Bolivia

Pages 219–21

SOURCE: La Piedra Mágica—*Vida y Costumbres de los Indios Calla-huayas de Bolivia* by Gustavo Adolfo Otero (Mexico: Instituto Indigonista Interamericano, 1951), pp. 226–28, 230–32.

"The Girl and the 'Achachila'" is a leprechaun story you'll never hear in Ireland. The closest North American counterparts to this story are the Cherokee myths about the Uktenas, Uksuhis, and Ustutlis—various kinds of giant serpents who inhabit out-of-the-way places and do various menacing things. (See James Mooney, "Myths of the Cherokee," *Nineteenth Annual Report of the U. S. Bureau of Ethnology*, already cited, pp. 294–30.) The originals, of course, are the Nagas in India, and this whole story reflects somewhat the fear that the Naga tribes in both India and the New World inspired in the rest of the tribes. For a number of East Indian equivalents, see Verrier Elwin's *Myths of the North-East Frontier of India*, already cited, p. 157ff.

"The Origin of the Chinchilla" is a variation on the Medea-Jason story in Apollonius Rhodius' *Argonautica*, which in turn is a variation of Homer's *Odyssey*. The parallel in the *Odyssey* is probably Books X and XII, the episodes involving Circe. In terms of the notes on "The Story of Yebá," the woman is Pandora, the young condor is Hephaistos, and the old condor is the Sun-King Aeëtes. In biblical terms, the condor-daughter is Eve, the old condor God the Father, and the young condor is the snake, Satan. Behind all these legends seems to lurk either "historical" adultery and/or incest. The daughter seems to sometimes be a wife—the constant is her running off with the son of an "enemy." Certainly, the banishment to the Underworld has strong overtones of Prometheus being tied to a rock—which would somehow lump Prometheus, Epimetheus, and Hephaistos together as one character, and Medea, Circe, and Pandora as another.

"The Origin of Coca" is another variation on the Medea-Circe-Pandora-Eve-Earth Mother theme, a variation in which I suspect a paleolithic motif (Death of Earth Mother-Birth of Plants) is attached to later historical happenings.

THE BAISANO: THE JAGUAR GHOST (Guarao)—Venezuela

Page 222

SOURCE: *Guarao Guarata—Lo que Cuentan los Indios Guaraos*, already cited, pp. 242–43.

Is this a variation of the Eve-Satan story that constantly recurred in the previous section? I suspect that again an archaic motif (here the man-tiger, a constant in both Amerindian and Dravidian myth) is being applied to a specific story: Hephaistos-Prometheus-Epimetheus seducing either the Sun-King's (i.e., Aeëtus in the *Argonautica*) daughter or his wife. As I point out in *Sun-World Across Ocean*, this kind of identification can be bolstered up by the fact that Quetzalcoatl (the Mexican Titan figure) often appears as a Tiger.

TALKING TO THE SPIRITS (Carib)—Surinam

Page 223

SOURCE: "Becoming a Piyei: Variability and Similarity in Carib Sha-
manism," *Antropologica* (Caracas: Instituto Caribe de An-
tropologia y Sociologia, Number 24, December 1968), p. 14.

Three informants were used here: *Alemunwa:le, Kuma:nda* and *Ka-bula:i*. To the Amerindian-Dravidian mind, the material, physical world was only an inferior extension of the spirit world. The world was in-habited by spirit. The point of life was—as in Yogic Buddhism and Hinduism—to leave body behind and enter into "spirit." Here is a North American description that parallels those from Surinam:

> The first step in the course of training is to teach the boy to make his mind stronger than his physical side—to make his mind master of his body, as it were. This is accomplished by making him go without food for many days at a time and undergo voluntary physical torture without flinching . . .
> [Then] he must go through a long, strenuous course in "medicine." This "medical" training consists of learning the art of conjuring, of learning the healing power of the various herbs, of learning to see into the future and of developing the "power to get in touch with the spirits" . . . Chief Buffalo Child Long Lance, *Long Lance*, London: Faber and Faber, 1956, pp. 54–55.

ITSEKES, MALIGNANT SPIRITS (Kalapalo)—Central Brazil

Page 224

SOURCE: Ellen B. Basso, *The Kalapalo Indians of Central Brazil* (New York: Holt, Rinehart and Winston, 1973), p. 22.

There are a number of ways to approach this myth: historically; in terms of comparative myth; in terms of actual tribal "theology." The three ways are not contradictory, but complementary. In terms of com-parative myth, we seem to have here a story relating to Lakshmi-Sri/Aphrodite/Circe/Pandora (Moon) and one of the Titans (Naki-Naga). In terms of tribal "theology," the malignant spirit here taking the shape of Moon is merely an Itsekes, but historically we are touching on the same conflict that gave rise to "The Story of Yebá," "The Vulture King's Daughter," and other stories we've already discussed. At the core of all these stories is a case of adultery of a snake-tribesman (Naga) with the daughter of King Tiahuanaco/Sun/The Vulture-King, etc.

A "GHOST" STORY (Mapuche/Araucanian)—Chile

Page 225

SOURCE: L. C. Faron, *Hawks of the Sun*, already cited, pp. 72–73.

At times, it is difficult to distinguish between pre-Columbian and post-Columbian folklore elements because at times the Spaniards brought elements with them that date all the way back to Mediterranean prehistory. In other words, a given element may have been brought to the New World in 3000 B.C. or in the sixteenth century A.D. and be more or less the same. This is the case here. Is the *witranalwe* indigenous or "imported"? Certainly, there are stories like this still current in contemporary Spanish folklore. See, for example, Julio Caro Baroja's *Algunos Mitos Espanoles* (Madrid: Editor Nacional, 1941), p. 100ff. One small detail here, though, does link this story to the ancient Nagas. The bowl of blood offering is called *nachi* in Araucanian.

THE STORY OF MAYAKOTO (Guarao)—Venezuela

Page 226

SOURCE: *Guarao Guarata—Lo que Cuentan los Indios Guaraos*, already cited, pp. 41–51.

What we have here is an almost surrealistic variation of the basic Twin-Spider Grandmother-Sun-Adultery story that keeps running through perhaps the majority of myths in this collection. I think the important thing to realize in reading this myth is that the characters and incidents are identifiable. The major differences that I find between this version and, say, the Hopi are:
1. The Spider Grandmother here, instead of helping the twins find their father, tries to actually kidnap them;
2. The mother of the Twins usually hardly appears at all, or plays a very minor role;
3. The Sun (the Twins' father) usually plays a much more important role; and
4. The Mayakoto-Jajuba incident, the high-born woman running off with a "commoner," is usually a separate incident.

The reader may want to compare this Venezuelan version with Stephen's *Hopi Tales*, already cited, pp. 10–21, and the Mayan *Popol Vuh*. The Duende, Jajuba, of course, is the classic Trickster, a place occupied in Greek myth by Prometheus. In terms of Amerindian-Dravidian myth, he is always a serpent, water monster, some type of

439

aquatic monster. The children are the Dioscuri/Twins, Spider-Grand-mother is a strange Great Mother figure who seems identifiable with a great number of Greek and Hindu mythic characters: Lakshmi, Aphro-dite, Circe, etc. Her fundamental symbolism wavers between being Mother of the Gods and Seductress. Often it is difficult to tell her apart from the mother of the Twins.

THE GREAT GOD, THE DEAD, GOOD AND BAD SMALL GODS (Aymara)—Bolivia

Page 233

SOURCE: Otero's *La Piedra Mágica*, already cited, pp. 108–9. Somewhat condensed and modified.

Viracocha is said to be not merely "God," but also the founder of the Inca Empire. As I point out in *The Gods of the Cataclysm*, the word *Vira* is Sanskrit for "man"—you can see the root in words like VIR-ility —and Cocha is probably related to the ancient Colchians mentioned in the *Argonautica*—the sea people. *Colcha* still means "river" in contem-porary Quechua. Viracocha, then, ultimately is probably equatable with the King of Tiahuanaco in ancient times: Son/Hyperion/Vishnu. Another easily identifiable god is the Thunder god Khon. Maya for Snake and Sky is KAN, and there is a Cherokee.myth in which KANATI (a Serpent-in-the-Garden of Eden figure) is married to Selu (probably related to Selene, the Moon). Kan, then, in terms of the overall Dravidian myth structure is Father Snake—in North America he develops into the Thunder Bird, the Flying Plumed Rain Snake.

Although the Achachilas in an early story seem to come out as practi-cally "demonic," here they are portrayed as guardian angels. How do you resolve this seeming contradiction? In the war between the Titans and Olympians the Achachilas are the Titans/Asuras/Nagas. Although they—like their "chief," Prometheus the Fire-Bringer—are supposed to be the helpers of mankind, one thing that is constant in their portrayals in, say, North American trickster cycles, is their double nature. They are never "angels" in the Christian sense, but always both evil and good simultaneously. It's the same kind of reconciliation of opposites you find in Hindu deities like Siva and Kali.

WHEN ALL THE DEAD COME DOWN (Maya)—Guatemala

Page 235

SOURCE: Fought's *Chorti (Maya) Texts*, already cited, pp. 291–94.

Here, the Catholic All Souls' Day and the pre-Columbian Feast of the Dead blend and merge so that they become practically indistinguishable from each other. You can get some idea of what is specifically "Indian" by comparing this account with Frank Waters' *Book of the Hopi*, already cited, p. 175ff. The Hopi equivalent feast is called Wúwuchim. Both Amerindian and Catholic feasts, of course, go back to ancient proto-Indo-Mediterranean times. Wúwuchim and All Souls' Day are just two variations of the same essential feast.

I suspect some sort of etymological link between the Kalapalo "it-sekes" (evil spirits) and the Maya "Tsikin" (Day of the Dead). In different cultures, the nature of the dead varies—from good, beneficent, helpful, to baleful, malevolent, punishing, demanding propitiation.

THE VILLAGE OF THE DEAD (Kalapalo)—Brazil

Page 238

SOURCE: Basso's *The Kalapalo Indians of Central Brazil*, already cited, p. 58.

There are a number of details in this account that are highly suggestive of East Indian origins. The female one-breasted god, for example, sounds very much like Siva in hermaphroditic form—male on one side, female on the other. Even the name SAKUfenu is reminiscent of the Hindu name for Siva's female self, SAKTI. I even suspect some etymological link between KWA-tini and Coatl (Snake) as in Quetzalcoatl.

At any rate, the village of the dead here described seems to be another variation on the voyage to Titicaca. The Land of the Dead is association with Sun, Sun is King Tiahuanaco/Vishnu/Hyperion. What seems to have filtered into "folk-memory" as the Land of the Dead is the head of King Tiahuanaco's empire at Lake Titicaca. Did ancient gurus go there for initiation purposes? Is some such death-rebirth ceremony the basis for this legend of the Land of the Dead?

ARAVUTARÁ: THE FATE OF THE DEAD (Xingu)—Brazil

Page 239

SOURCE: O. and C. Villas-Boas, *Xingu: The Indians, Their Myths* (New York: Farrar, Straus and Giroux, 1974), pp. 127–34.

In Greek legend, of course, this is the story of Orpheus and Eurydice. Eurydice dies; Orpheus, the Magic Musician, follows her into the Underworld and calms the Furies with his magic. (See E. E. Barthell, Jr., *Gods and Goddesses of Ancient Greece*, Coral Gables, Florida: University of Miami Press, 1971, p. 157.) But there's a lot more to the "myth" than a mere Orpheus story. One point opens the story up: the dead are snakes . . . and the dead are preyed upon by birds in the service of a cannibal eagle.

The bird-snake image is fundamental here. The birds represent Garuda (or in Greek myth Zeus's eagle), the cannibal eagle represents King Tiahuanaco/Vishnu/Zeus-Hyperion, and the conflict described probably refers to a forced labor in ancient Peru-Bolivia-Ecuador-Brazil run by King Tiahuanaco. The dead aren't really "dead," but conscripted into King Tiahuanaco's penal colony. The purpose of the colony? Most probably the prisoners were used to mine gold and/or tin.

The thing to remember here is that everything is in "code," on various levels (a real, historical level, a symbolic level, and emblematic level) and that there is a fundamental dichotomy that runs through the myth on all levels between Eagle Clan and Snake (Naga) Clan. More than anything else, this is the fundamental opposition in the symbol system of the ancient Dravidian-Amerindian world.

THE IAMURICUMÁ WOMEN AND THE JAKUÍ (Xingu)—Brazil
Page 247

SOURCE: Same as preceding, pp. 119–21.

There is a fundamental historical change embodied in this myth—the change from the matriarchal pre-Greek, Minoan-Mycenaean Indus Valley world to the world of the patriarchal Greeks. The earliest sociological structures seem inevitably to be matriarchal, and here in this Brazilian Indian myth we see a change illustrated that was taking place perhaps as early as 3000 B.C. in the Old World. As I point out in *The Gods of the Cataclysm*, "Amazons," female-warriors, weren't strange at all in the archaic matriarchal world, although they certainly were strange in a Greek world where women were treated almost like Arabs: secluded, cut off, kept out of "public" affairs.

There is a great deal of evidence dating back to Raleigh's *The Discovery of the Large, Rich and Beautiful Empire of Guina.* . . . up to the recent study of E. B. Prado, *The Lure of the Amazon* (London, Souvenir Press, 1959) to support the fact that there were (in fact *are*) Amazons in the Amazon jungles. The strangeness of the idea disappears, though, the moment you say "The Americas and the Old World were two provinces of the same ancient empire." In Greek myth, among the labors of Heracles are: (1) Stealing the Golden Apples, and (2) Sailing to the Thermodon River and fighting the Amazons, capturing the girdle of the Amazon Queen, Queen Hippolyte. The golden apples are symbolically equivalent to the golden fleece (the word for apples and fleece is the same in ancient Greek), and the fleece/apples actually were in present-day Bolivia—they belonged to King Aeëtes, the grandson of Hyperion the Sun God. The river Thermodon=the Amazon River.

This all seems very fanciful until you read about the Old World Amazons, that "of the children to whom they gave birth they reared only the females, and cut off their right breasts so as not to interfere with proper handling of the bow" (*Gods and Goddesses of Ancient Greece* by E. E. Barthell, already cited, p. 188), and then read the next selection in this anthology, which states that the Iamuricumá women *cut off their right breasts.* Greek myth and Amazonian Basin myth converge back to a common point in actual history.

THE IAMURICUMÁ WOMEN: THE WOMEN WITHOUT A RIGHT BREAST (Xingu)—Brazil

Page 249

SOURCE: Same as preceding, pp. 123–25.

See notes on previous selection. I might also add a note regarding the transformation of men into animals. The Greek equivalent centers around Odysseus and Circe. Transculturally, Circe is an Earth-Mother figure who in this selection emerges as an Amazon; her equivalent in Hindu myth is the cannibal goddess Kali (in Aztec Coatlicue); in the next selection from the Toba-Pilagá this other aspect of her nature emerges more prominently.

E. J. Harrison, in her *Prolegomena to the Study of Greek Religion* (Cambridge: Cambridge University Press, 1903, p. 283ff.), relates the "degraded" image of Earth-Mother as Pandora, the source of all the world's ills, to the shift from matriarchy to patriarchy in the ancient world.

CANNIBAL WOMAN (Toba-Pilagá)—Gran Chaco, Argentina

Page 251

SOURCE: Métraux's *Myths of the Toba and Pilagá*, already cited, pp. 62–64.

In Hindu myth, Kali, Siva's mythic consort, is always portrayed as a cannibal. She is usually portrayed, in fact, squatting over a corpse eating the entrails. In Hindu myth, somewhere behind Pandora-Circe-Lakshmi-Medea, there is also a cannibal goddess. I suspect that she is another version of the same historical personage who appears in the Aymara "The Origin of the Chinchilla." In other words, she is King Aeëtes' daughter —Medea. The Jaguar identification is important because it links her to the Titans/Quetzalcoatl. She doesn't start out as a Jaguar, but *becomes* a Jaguar; she shifts identities as she shifts alliances and clans. I would think that Cannibal Woman, like Kali, is a survival of the time when ritual cannibalistic rites were carried out by priestesses, not priests.

THE KUPE-NDÍYA, ALIEN WOMEN'S TRIBE (Apinaye)—Brazil

Page 253

SOURCE: *The Apinayé* by Curt Nimuendajú, already cited, pp. 177–79.

This myth casts the old triangle story we've seen so many times in this volume in a slightly different mold. We already know that the girl in the story is the Sun King's or Vulture King's (God the Father's) daughter and that she marries a "Naga"–here a crocodile. But the linking up of the Amazons with Circe-Pandora-Lakshmi-Aphrodite ties together two elements hitherto separate: the Earth-Mother and Warrior Women. We are being told that the South American Amazons are descended from a group of women who originally lived at Tiahuanaco.

THE LEGEND OF THE SUNS (Aztec)—Mexico

Page 255

SOURCE: Walter Lehmann, Die Geschichts der Konigreiche von Colhuacan und Mexico (Stuttgart–Berlin: Verlag von W. Kohlhammer, 1938), pp. 322–27.

It's very helpful to compare the four Aztec ages with their Greek, Jewish, and Hindu equivalents. The Greek, Hindu and Aztec are the most explicit:

GREEK	HINDU	AZTEC
Gold	Krita	4-Tiger
Silver	Treta	4-Wind
Brass	Dvapara	4-Rain
Iron	Kali	4-Water
		and the fifth (present) sun: 4-Movement[1]

It is impossible to do justice to the importance of these records of the ancient world in these notes, but I would like to point out that although the idea of an Iron Age following a Gold Age does indicate some sort of degradation, only in the Hindu Kali Yuga and the Aztec Sun of 4-Movement, do you find real desperation, hysteria, a fear of imminent destruction. The dating of the Maya and Hindu present ages are very close (sometime around 3000 B.C.), and I take this date to be not "mythic" but the actual historical date of the war of the gods and antigods, which may somewhat coincide with an actual cosmic catastrophe recorded in Jewish records as The Flood. I also believe the proto-Aztecs are linked to the Peruvian-Bolivian sun kingdom of Lake Titicaca and postulate that the blood sacrifices practiced by the historical Aztecs in order to maintain cosmic equilibrium reflect the actual state of affairs in the ancient Tiahuanacan kingdom where King Tiahuanaco ruled—as a cannibal similar to contemporary Jívaros in Ecuador—over most of

[1] For further study, see Heinrich Zimmer's Myths and Symbols in Indian Art and Civilization, ed. Joseph Campbell (Washington, D.C.: Bollingen Foundation), p. 13ff.; Jay Macpherson's Four Ages of Man (New York: St. Martin's Press, 1962); and Miguel León-Portilla's Aztec Thought and Culture (Norman: University of Oklahoma Press, 1963), p. 38ff.

South America. In other words, Aztec cannibalism and human sacrifice was but a pale reflection of previous cannibalism and human sacrifice in the Aztec homeland, the homeland of all American Indians—Ecuador-Peru-Brazil. The Aztecs of the *Conquista*, who had turned their entire national purpose to the procuring and slaughtering of captives to the Sun, were acting out a similar drama that had been previously acted out in South America sometime around 3000 B.C.

THE SONG OF QUETZALCOATL (Aztec)—Mexico

Page 257

SOURCES: *The Song of Quetzalcoatl* trans. by John Hubert Cornyn (Yellow Springs, Ohio: The Antioch Press, 1931) and the original Aztec (with gloss) published as Book III ("The Origin of the Gods") of Fray Bernardino de Sahagún's *General History of the Things of New Spain*, The Florentine Codex (Santa Fe, New Mexico: The School of American Research, 1952).

What I've tried to do here is greatly abbreviate, condense, and modernize the original—which, in true epic style, tends to be humdrum and repetitious.

A great deal has been written about Quetzalcoatl, most of it meaningless. Perhaps the most grievous of the errors about Quetzalcoatl is to treat him as someone who only lived in Mexico. Where else do we find this myth repeated? In the ancient *Siva-Purana* Siva's army is described as an army of cripples and dwarfs. In Hindu myth Siva is the shameless phallic god. There are whole temples dedicated to a huge stone phallus. In the *Siva-Purana* Parvati, the daughter of King Himalaya, is described as falling wildly in love with Siva. She marries him, and in the war that follows Siva sides with the Aryans (his wife's people) against his own people—the Dravidians. The Aryans win, Siva becomes a hero.

In the *Anales de Quauhtitlan* there is a variant version of the end of Quetzalcoatl: "he went to the east to die and burned himself; his heart survived, arose to the heavens and became the morning star" (Sahagún, cited above, note 7 on page 36). Who, in Hindu myth, is burned Phoenix-like and then reborn? Kama—the god of love, Siva's son, also Siva's enemy.

In North and South American myth, Siva is represented as the phallic, game-playing, profane Trickster. His equivalent in Greek myth (although the humorous side of his character is never fully developed) is Prometheus/Hermes.

I submit that the Quetzalcoatl story is a variation of the Dravidian-Amerindian-Greek Trickster stories and that if there was a real Quetzalcoatl in Mexico, he belonged to some sort of priesthood that ultimately had its origin in the historical reality behind titanic myth.

VITI-VITÍ, THE ORIGIN OF THE DITCHES (Xingu)—Brazil

Page 262

SOURCE: *Xingu: The Indians, Their Myths*, already cited, pp. 163–65.

Viti-Vití, the cripple, the man with the sharpened leg, is actually a very common figure in Greek myth: in *The Argonautica* he is pictured as a member of the household of King Aeëtes/King Tiahuanaco. He is the metallurgist of the Gods, and is one of a legion of metallurgist figures that walk through the world of Amerindian myth. The ditches, I imagine, are a reference to gold mining, and the fact that they are always close to water suggests placer mining; the water is used to separate out the gold. See my *Sun-World Across Ocean* for a much more extensive discussion of Hephaistos figures and their symbolism. Leonard Clark, in his *The Rivers Ran East* (New York: Funk & Wagnalls, 1953), claims that the Seven Cities of Cibola were originally Inca placer mines in Ecuador-Peru and locates six out of the seven mines from an old map. My guess is that the Inca mines—like everything else Inca—were based on earlier pre-Inca/Tiahuanacan sites.

The crippled/"sharpened" leg, incidentally, suggests ritual mutilation connected with metallurgical secret societies/guilds.

THE CONQUEST OF FIRE (Xingu)—Brazil

Page 264

SOURCE: *Xingu: The Indians, Their Myths*, already cited, pp. 105–10.

In Greek myth, the characters involved with the "stealing" of fire are: (1) The Fire-Stealer, Prometheus, and (2) Zeus, the Owner of Fire.[1] Essentially, the drama here is the same, but there seems to be quite a bit more behind this myth than merely a fairy story about Prometheus' heroically carrying fire to mankind. There are innumerable clues that indicate that the Titans who left the Old World and settled in the New were a clan/cast/brotherhood of mystic smiths like their Old World counterparts, the Asuras, in India. The importance of fire ceremonies, fire-walking, the rite of the new fire, the portrayal of Quetzalcoatl as fire-bringer, etc. all point to a conflict *concerning the knowledge of metallurgical processes.* Prometheus seems not to have merely stolen "fire" (which ultimately seems rather absurd, given the amount of fire there is in nature) but the *secret of smelting.* The Zeus people seem to have originally possessed this secret and somehow equated it with their divine-right rule; Prometheus *does* emerge as a kind of "democratic" figure in his role of breaking down the mysticism that was associated with this divine-right rule by simply distributing the knowledge of the smelting processes that invested this rule with an aura of magic. A read-

[1] See C. Kerenyi's *Prometheus*, already cited, p. 41ff.

ing of Mircea Eliade's *The Forge and the Crucible* (New York: Harper and Brothers, 1962) will prove a revelation at this point.

HOW PEOPLE WHO WANTED TO KILL RAINBOW WERE CAPTURED AND CHANGED INTO ANIMALS *(Toba-Pilagá)— Gran Chaco, Argentina*

Page 268

SOURCE: *Myths of the Toba and Pilagá Indians of the Gran Chaco,* already cited, pp. 38–39.

In Greek myth Circe changes men into animals. And in the pre-Homeric folklore that Homer drew on for *The Odyssey,* it seems likely that Circe and Aeolus (in Cherokee myth Selu and Kanati)[1] are the primordial couple Mother Earth and Father Snake, the Master of Animals. This is very important to understanding this Chaco myth because the moment we recognize Rainbow's powers as those of his wife's and see him as an Earth Snake, a Yaksa, a Leprechaun, then the whole myth makes a great deal of sense. The excrement talked about is, of course, the Pot at the End of the Rainbow in Celtic myth! What is behind this myth, then, is a leprechaun-like prototype, a rain-controlling, treasure-carrying serpent who has the power to transform men into animals and who lives underground.

For East Indian equivalents of these Amerindian myths, see Verrier Elwin's *Myths of the North-East Frontier of India,* already cited, p. 72ff.

STAR WOMAN *(Toba-Pilagá)—Gran Chaco, Argentina*

Page 271

SOURCE: Same as preceding, pp. 40–42.

It may seem rather odd that Earth-Mother (the real identity of Star Woman) should come from the sky. What I suspect is that behind this identity is a social-class difference between the patrician wife and her plebeian husband. Could we be facing the marriage of Parvati (King Himalaya's daughter in Hindu myth) with Siva (the "casteless," "classless" Dravidian Naga chief)? Certainly, there is a great deal of parallelism between the Star Woman tale and the East Indian *Siva-Purana.* Behind the myths of the Sun Father-in-law, the Woman who Fell from the Sky, etc., some sort of social snobbery seems to be implied.[2]

[1] See "Kanati and Selu: The Origin of Game and Corn," in *Myths of the Cherokee* by James Mooney, *Nineteenth Annual Report of the Bureau of American Ethnology,* already cited, pp. 242–49.
[2] For a fuller look at stories of this sort, see Sith Thompson's *Tales of the North American Indians,* already cited, notes 27, 37a, 123.

The "fire" here is a fire that's not a fire, a fire certainly not for warming. Perhaps a story from the Siang frontier in India can help us here:

> Now in those days, when gods and men lived together, a quarrel arose for the possession of the rich plain country. The gods said it belonged to them, but this the men disputed. At last, it was agreed that the decision should rest on the proof of a sign; the rich country should belong to whoever could cook a stone. So mortals and immortals took stones and earth in their hands. First of all, the gods tried to cook the stones, but fierce though they made the fire, the stones remained stones still. But the men cheated the gods and obtained the sign by a trick, for they hid an egg amidst the earth and stones; and this they roasted and showed to the gods . . . (Elwin's *Myths of the North-East Frontier*, already cited, p. 267)

The fire that isn't for warming just might be the fire for *smelting*. Isn't that what's behind this whole idea of trying to "cook stones"?

STAR WOMAN (Apinaye)—Brazil

Page 274

SOURCE: Nimuendajú's *Apinayé*, already cited, pp. 165–67.

See notes for previous tale, also notes on *Popol Vuh* regarding miraculous deaths and rebirths, aging and rejuvenation.

CARANCHO TEACHES MEN HOW TO MAKE FIRE (Toba-Pilagá)—Gran Chaco, Argentina

Page 276

SOURCE: Métraux's *Toba and Pilagá Myths*, already cited, pp. 54–56.

The sense of being trapped by water, the feathers in the wax wings of Fox, all reveal this Argentinian tale as a variant of the Greek Icarus story.[1] It's rather interesting to see the Prometheus legend intermingled this way with the Icarus legend, a common occurrence in folklore.[2] The telescoping of these two incidents together, though, may not be all that fortuitous. They have two figures in common: a tyrant (Zeus in the case of Prometheus, Minos in the case of Icarus-Daedalus) and a "democrat." (Fire here is structurally linked with beer, which I take to mean that "fire" hides not only metallurgical, but also drug-induced *mystical* know-how. What we seem to be getting here are echoes of the

[1] See E. E. Barthell, Jr.'s *Gods and Goddesses of Ancient Greece*, already cited, pp. 243–44.

[2] See, for example, Kaarle Krohn's *Folklore Methodology* (Austin–London: University of Texas Press, 1971), pp. 78–134 for an excellent discussion of basic forms and variants.

ancient Aryan (and Dravidian?) use of soma—the hallucinogenic base for all proto-Indo-Mediterranean-Amerindian religion. The emergence of Prometheus (here Carancho) into classical Greece as an egalitarian "leveler" seems to have a proto-historical base in the class struggle between the Aryans and Dravidians in India c. 5000 B.C.

HOW MANKIND RECEIVED FIRE (Taulipang)—Guianas

Page 278

SOURCE: *Geister am Roroima* by Dr. Theodore Koch-Grunberg (Kassel: Erich Röth-Verlag), pp. 95–96.

Usually the Fire-Bringer is Prometheus, but here Mother Earth is turned into a Toad—often Prometheus is portrayed as serpent, frog, etc. —and given the fire-bringing function. Such a transference of function is not particularly unexpected, though, seeing that Eve (Mother Earth) and the Serpent (Father Snake/Prometheus) are the primordial mythic pair.

J. G. Frazer, in what amounts to practically an "anthology" of fire-origin myths, not only discusses this particular myth, but similar myths coming from the same general area. See his *Myths of the Origin of Fire* (London: Macmillan and Co., 1930), p. 131ff.

THE UNDERWORLD (Apinaye)—Brazil

Page 279

SOURCE: Nimuendajú's *The Apinayé*, already cited, p. 175.

In ancient cosmogony, South becomes transformed into Heaven/the Underworld/Isles of the Blessed, etc. What seems to have happened in this Apinaye myth is a kind of double transposition: South not only becomes the Afterworld; it is also placed *under* this world. So, ironically, Lake Titicaca (heaven) retains its *altiplano* geography while at the same time being relegated to the Underworld. The placement of Parvati/Eve/Aphrodite in heaven where she would belong as daughter of King Himalaya (in terms of puranic lore) emerges most prominently in Iroquois lore, although this idea of a vertical cosmological order paralleling an analagous social order is a given throughout Amerindia. See Thompson's *Tales of the North American Indians*, note 27, p. 278, for further examples of this kind of structuring.

THE VISIT TO THE SKY (Apinaye)—Brazil

Page 279

SOURCE: Same as previous tale, pp. 184–86.

It's very instructive to compare details in this tale with those in the ancient Greek poem *The Argonautica*:

449

ARGONAUTICA	APINAYE
. . . the Harpies poured forth over all a loathsome stench and no one dared not merely to carry food to his mouth but even to stand at a distance; so foully reeked the remnants of the meal. (II: 185-95)	The vultures vomited carrion and served it to the man for manioc gruel . . .

In the much-neglected but brilliant book *The God-Kings and the Titans* (New York: St. Martin's Press, 1973), James Bailey claims that the Harpies in *The Argonautica* are the Hoatzin birds of the West Indies and the northern coast of South America (p. 301). I, too, think they are, and I also agree with Bailey that the trip discussed in *The Argonautica* is a trip to Lake Titicaca, Bolivia. This Apinaye story out of Brazil I take to be a "folklore memory" of the actual voyages up the Amazon to Bolivia. The unfaithful woman, her lover, and her husband probably are Aphrodite, Hephaistos (husband), and Ares (lover).

THE KUPE-KIKAMBLEG and THE KUPE-DYEB (Apinaye)— Brazil

Page 281

SOURCE: Same as preceding, pp. 179-81.

These two tales most probably are based on proto-historical remembrances of Dravidian tribes who one time lived in the Amazon Basin. The antagonism between the redheads and the Sun is a giveaway. We already know who is always fighting the Sun (Vishnu/Zeus/King Tiahuanaco): Prometheus, the Nagas, the anti-gods. I am inclined to identify the Bat People with the Nagas; their cave is strongly reminiscent of Patala, the Ecuadorian cave world where the Nagas live. This identification of bats with Nagas (the Titans, the "Prometheus people") is borne out in contemporary Indian folklore where bats at times fill the structural slot of Trickster. See Elwin's *Myths of the North-East Frontier*, already cited, pp. 282-83.

THE WAY: FATHER TO SON and THE WAY: THE KING TO HIS SONS (Aztec)—Mexico

Pages 283-85

SOURCE: *La Literatura de los Aztecas* by Angel M. Garibay K., already cited, pp. 107-11, 116.

Along with the Sioux, the Aztec statements on religion and philosophy are the most eloquent that have come down to us from the pre-Columbian world. A volume of commentary could be written on just these few lines. Who, for example, is the God of Time, the "Ancient God of the Region of the Mists of Death"? Why should the fire ritual be the center of all ritual life? Why "with the ritual of fire" should the individual wear the "obsidian sandals/of the Father and Mother of the Gods"?

The Ancient God of Time? The male-female, bisexual Aztec version of Siva and his Sakti, his female other-self: Ometéotl. It's difficult to pair up gods with functions among the Aztecs, much more difficult than the popularizers would have us believe, but I'm drawing from Miguel León-Portilla's excellent *Aztec Thought and Culture*, already cited, and it seems that the idea being dealt with in this poem is not merely a death god, but a foundation-of-being god. Hence, Ometéotl, not just Mictlantecuhtli and Mictlancihuatl, the Lord and Lady of the Dead.

And the importance of fire ritual? It's another critical study in itself. Mainly because we're dealing with Titans—Quetzalcoatl and Tezcatlipoca are the Aztec equivalents of Prometheus and Epimetheus; and as Cook points out in his monumental study of Zeus, behind the dioscuric Prometheus-Epimetheus lie fire gods, smiths, metallurgists. Tezcatlipoca is the Lord of the Smoking Mirror. Why does the mirror smoke? It is a fire-making mirror.

I would recommend to the interested reader that he/she tackle the Aztecs by reading not just León-Portilla (although maybe he's a good place to start), but also the two fundamental primary source books on Aztec culture: Fray Diego Durán's *Book of the Gods and Rites and the Ancient Calendar* and Fray Bernadino de Sahagún's *General History of the Things of New Spain*. These are two priests who saw the Aztec world before it had crumbled, and Sahagún's book, based on cross-referenced accounts from various Aztec informants, is even today a model anthropological case study.

THE OLD RELIGION AND THE OLD TIMES (Maya)—Yucatan

Page 288

SOURCE: *The Book of Chilam Balam of Chumayel* (Roys), already cited, pp. 83–84.

An eloquent statement as to just how readily the Mayas embraced Spanish Catholicism.

THE CALLAHUAYAS' MORAL CODE and THE PUNISHMENT OF THE GREEDY CALLAHUAYA (Aymara)—Bolivia

Pages 289–91

SOURCE: Gustavo Adolfo Otero, *La Piedra Mágica*, already cited, pp. 233–34 and 228–29.

As you can see in the statement of their "moral code," the Callahuayas make a virtue out of stealthiness and dissimulation. I find it sadly ironic that the Spaniards never tired of accusing the Amerindian world of devil worship, whereas they split themselves down the middle—word-worshiped god and acted like devils. There is no such split in the Amerindian spirit; philosophy is completely consistent with practice; action and theory match up.

The mountain mentioned in "The Punishment of the Greedy Callahuaya"—Illampu—is in western Bolivia, close to Lake Titicaca. I identify it with the golden mountain in Hindu tradition called Mount Meru . . . the "home of the gods." The conflict between the Fox and the Condor in this tale is merely another variant of the often-encountered theme that runs through Amerindian folklore—the fight between King Tiahuanaco/Vishnu/Zeus-Aeëtes and the Trickster/Coyote/Fox/Sesa/Prometheus.

SONG AT THE BEGINNING, OTOMI SPRING SONG, and A FLOWER SONG (Nahuatl)—Mexico

Pages 293–96

SOURCE: *Ancient Nahuatl Poetry*, trans. by D. G. Brinton, already cited, pp. 55–57, 59–61, 99–105.

The biggest problem I had with these selections was to try to rephrase them in a "dead" language (English) so that the freshness, sincerity, and lyricism of the original Nahuatl come through. The Flower and Song philosophy of the Aztecs that Miguel León-Portilla so stresses (see note on "The Way") is essentially a New World variation on the ancient Dravidian philosophy of Maya—Illusion. The world is suffused with an underlying unreality, nonexistence. Under the world of *samsara* (change) there is nothing but emptiness, void. The most depressing thing about Aztec epistemology is its uncertainty even about *Nirvana*—the escape from, the elevation above the Void. Somehow, the void takes over and engulfs everything.

THE ROAD TO PERFECTION, TWO HEROES: KUARACHY ETE AND KARAI RU ETE MIRI (Guarani)—Paraguay

Page 300

SOURCE: *La Literatura de los Guaranies* (Cadogan–Lopez Austin), already cited, pp. 93–95.

When the definitive works on Amerindian Yoga are finally written (and they certainly haven't been yet), the theological vision of the Guaranis will occupy a central position. There is very little that has come down to us from the other tribes that preserves the Dravidian-Amerindian Yogic impulse the way this selection does. For a fuller grasp of the place of jaguar symbolism in Yogic initiation, see Mircea Eliade's

Shamanism—Archaic Techniques of Ecstasy, trans. by W. R. Trask (New York: Bollingen Books, 1964), p. 129. Also *Pre-Columbian American Religions* by W. Krickeberg, *et al* (London: Weidenfeld and Nicolson, 1968), pp. 11–13, 33–36, 270–72.

THE ADVENTURES OF HUN-CAMÉ AND VUCUB-CAMÉ WITH THE LORDS OF XIBALBA (*Maya*)—*Guatemala*

Page 302

SOURCE: *Popol Vuh: The Sacred Book of the Ancient Quiché Maya*, trans. by Delia Goetz and S. G. Morley from the Spanish translation of Maya by Adrián Recinos (Norman: University of Oklahoma Press, 1950), pp. 41–66.

In what might be called the primordial Amerindian Twin myth, the Twins/the Dioscuri, make a kind of "pilgrimage" to the House of the Sun, their father, where they then undergo a series of "tests" such as having to fight monsters (oftentimes the Sun's own "children"), survive roasting in an oven, etc. The Hopi myth cycle more or less follows this pattern.[1] In the Zuni cycle, however, there is a visit to the Underworld that parallels very closely the *Popol Vuh*. The visit to the Sun, of course, is the visit to the Land of the Colchians described in the Greek poem *The Argonautica;* in *The Odyssey* the equivalent episode is Ulysses' visit to the cave of the Cyclops. The original behind all these variations seems to be: (1) A cave world which I postulate is the cave world recently discovered in Ecuador, and (2) the city on the shores of Lake Titicaca, which is still there—in ruins . . . Tiahuanaco. So, there are two historical sites behind the two mythic sites, and what is interesting about the *Popol Vuh* is the fact that Tiahuanaco is almost entirely ignored in favor of the cave world in Ecuador. In a sense, the Ecuadorian cave world was a kind of "dependency" of Tiahuanaco, which can partially account for the merging of two sites into one, but I can't help but wonder whether the Mayas had some special historical link in their past with the Ecuadorian site.

Another point that should be noted is the parallelism between the trick the Twins play on the Lords of Xibalba by killing themselves and resurrecting, then getting the Lords to allow themselves to be killed with the hope of a resurrection that never comes. It's an old ploy in the North American Trickster cycles, which hints at an identification of the Twins with Trickster, which in turn at least points to some sort of identity link between the Twins and Prometheus/Epimetheus.

On a purely symbolic level, as you read along, try to keep in mind that the multiple deaths and resurrections of the Twins indicate their importance as Year Heroes whose deaths and resurrections represent the

[1] See "Hopi Myths" by Alexander Stephen, Vol. 42 of *The Journal of American Folklore*, already cited, especially, pp. 15–21.

[2] See *Zuni Folk Tales* by F. H. Cushing (New York–London: G. P. Putnam's Sons, 1901), pp. 398–410.

death (winter) and resurrection (spring) of the year. Sociologically speaking, the trials of the Twins are initiation rites, *rites du passage*—Xibalba in Maya relates to the Underworld and Devil, but *Xib* also means penis. The rites the Twins undergo are puberty rites!

I might suggest the following works to the reader unfamiliar with death-and-resurrection/initiation rites:

1. "The Great Royal Myth of Egypt: Osiris, Isis, Set, and Horus," in Joseph Kaster's *The Literature and Mythology of Ancient Egypt* (London: Allen Lane, 1970), pp. 76–80.

2. J. E. Harrison's *Prolegomena to the Study of Greek Religion* (already cited), especially Chapter X, pp. 479–572.

3. C. Kerenyi's *Eleusis—Archetypal Image of Mother and Daughter*, trans. by Ralph Manheim (New York: Bollingen Books, 1967), especially pp. 26–44.

4. "Death and Rebirth: The Kwakiutl of British Columbia," by Werner Muller, in *Pre-Columbian American Religions*, Walter Krickeberg, *et al* (already cited), pp. 209–20.

OLLANTAY (Inca)—Peru

Page 340

SOURCE: *Apu Ollantay*, trans. by Sir Clements Markham, published in Lima in 1964 by Ediciones Markham. This edition contains both Spanish and English texts.

The drama *Ollantay* or *Apu* (Lord) *Ollantay* is purported to be an Inca drama which survived and was acted in Peru up into the eighteenth century, when it was committed to writing. Whether it represents "pure" Quechua drama is debatable, and certainly the play emerges in Sir Clements Markham's English with a strong flavor of Elizabethan (or Edad de Oro) dramatic conventions. At times, it plays like a watered-down *Anthony and Cleopatra* or *Romeo and Juliet*.

My own impulse was to radically update Markham, but when I confronted the octosyllabic Quechua (with songs and major speeches in octosyllabic quatrains, with the first and last and second and third lines rhyming), I thought better of changing anything as courtly and mannered into democratic contemporary English. Before democratizing any Amerindian "form," one should keep in mind that the Egyptian, Mesopotamian, modern Hindu, and Amerindian sacred and secular art forms proceed from the same common thrust and impulse. The Dravidian-Amerindian world was theocratic, hierarchial, obsessed with liturgical and profane formalities/form, and certainly the pre-Columbian courts of the Incas and Aztecs equaled in formality their European equivalents, which inclines me to believe that perhaps this play is indeed what it purports to be—a survival of pre-Conquest Inca drama . . . with inevitable stylistic interjections *à la* Tirso de Molina and Lope de Vega.